IMPLEMENTING AI
YOUTH CRIMINAL JUSTICE ACT ACROSS CANADA

Edited by Marc Alain, Raymond R. Corrado, and Susan Reid

Since its implementation in 2003, the *Youth Criminal Justice Act* has been the subject of intense political and scholarly debate. Criticized for being more complicated than its predecessor, the *Young Offenders Act*, the YCJA has detailed provisions intended to encourage positive, non-punitive interventions for less serious offences while reserving heavier consequences and custodial sentences for violent crimes.

Implementing and Working with the Youth Criminal Justice Act *across Canada* provides the first comprehensive, province-by-province analysis of how each Canadian jurisdiction has implemented the YCJA in accordance with its own history, traditions, and institutional arrangements. The contributors draw on the latest research and in-depth interviews with probation officers, counsellors, educators, and social workers, among others, to offer vital information and a new analytical perspective to practitioners and policymakers concerned with the administration of youth justice in Canada.

MARC ALAIN is a professor in the Department of Psychoeducation at the Université du Québec à Trois-Rivières

RAYMOND R. CORRADO is a professor in the School of Criminology at Simon Fraser University.

SUSAN REID is a professor in the Department of Criminology and Criminal Justice at St. Thomas University.

Implementing and Working with the *Youth Criminal Justice Act* across Canada

Edited by Marc Alain, Raymond R. Corrado, and Susan Reid

UNIVERSITY OF TORONTO PRESS
Toronto Buffalo London

© University of Toronto Press 2016
Toronto Buffalo London
www.utppublishing.com
Printed in the U.S.A.

ISBN 978-1-4426-3009-8 (cloth)   ISBN 978-1-4426-3010-9 (paper)

♾ Printed on acid-free, 100% post-consumer recycled paper with vegetable-based inks.

Library and Archives Canada Cataloguing in Publication

Implementing and working with the Youth Criminal Justice Act across Canada/edited by Marc Alain, Raymond R. Corrado, and Susan Reid.

Includes bibliographical references.
ISBN 978-1-4426-3009-3 (cloth).   ISBN 978-1-4426-3010-9 (paper)

1. Canada. Youth Criminal Justice Act.   2. Juvenile justice, Administration of–Canada–Provinces.   I. Alain, Marc, 1961–, author, editor   II. Corrado, Raymond, author, editor   III. Reid, Susan, 1958–, author, editor

HV9108.I46 2016   364.360971   C2015-907373-1

This book has been published with the help of a grant from the Federation for the Humanities and Social Sciences, through the Awards to Scholarly Publications Program, using funds provided by the Social Sciences and Humanities Research Council of Canada.

University of Toronto Press acknowledges the financial assistance to its publishing program of the Canada Council for the Arts and the Ontario Arts Council, an agency of the Government of Ontario.

**Canada Council
for the Arts**

**Conseil des Arts
du Canada**

**ONTARIO ARTS COUNCIL
CONSEIL DES ARTS DE L'ONTARIO**
an Ontario government agency
un organisme du gouvernement de l'Ontario

Funded by the   Financé par le
Government   gouvernement
of Canada   du Canada

Canadä

Contents

Figures and Tables

Figures

Tables

Preface

This book originated very simply as a result of a verbal engagement with a group of youth workers I interviewed in a schoolroom at the Justice Institute in Burnaby, BC, in 2010. The main topic of this meeting was their experience with the *Youth Criminal Justice Act* (YCJA) (2003), especially compared to their experience with the *Young Offenders Act* (YOA) (1982). A second topic was how and to what extent had their respective ministries/agencies prepared them to implement the extremely complicated YCJA. Finally, the last topic was what they perceived was the impact of the YCJA in its first decade on youth and young offenders and on their families, friends, and communities. I clearly remember that several of these youth workers seemed rather perplexed to be going through a group classroom interview with a French-speaking university researcher from a Quebec university, when they would likely rather be doing something else. This situation was openly discussed at the end of the meeting when one of the youth workers asked me in a very direct fashion: why are we here and what is there to gain from our participation? I responded that I believed that other youth workers across Canada could benefit from them sharing their knowledge about this critical law that affects so many youth, their families, and the youth workers themselves. Based on my experiences and research on the YCJA in Quebec I was struck by the diversity of perceptions and opinions among academics, politicians, and policymakers but also among youth practitioners from diverse ministries, their agencies, and non-government agencies. In Quebec, in particular, there was deep opposition to the YCJA and scepticism about the positive impacts asserted by its proponents in Ottawa and in other provinces. For many of its opponents in Quebec, there was simply no need for this new legislation since the province already had pioneered a comprehensive, long-standing youth justice system, which incorporated Quebec's distinctive history and culture. Outside of Quebec, several researchers, including a co-editor of this book, Professor Raymond Corrado, expressed the deep-seated concern that the YCJA was far too complicated with its extensive sections and subsections and with its mixture of contradictory youth justice models and principles.

With this diversity of opinions on the YCJA in mind, I applied for and received a Social Science Humanities Research Canada (SSHRC) faculty research grant to conduct a study of how the YCJA has been adopted in Quebec and three other provinces (British Columbia, Alberta, and New Brunswick). Unlike that of several other studies of the YCJA, my main research methodology involved neither statistical data, e.g., changes in custody rates and violent youth crime, nor legal themes, e.g., the absence of a deterrence sentencing principle, but rather addressed how youth justice personnel and related professionals responded in practice to the challenges of administering this complex new law. I identified several key decision-makers in these provinces and conducted in-depth and semi-structured interviews with them to understand both the common and unique policies that were employed by youth justice officials to respond to sentenced youth and their families. There was little doubt that there would be different responses in the four provinces given their substantially different experiences with the implementation of the previous two laws, the *Young Offenders Act* (1982) and the *Juvenile Delinquent Act* (1908). During my research, I approached Ray Corrado and Susan Reid, who had written extensively on youth justice issues in their respective provinces and, more generally, across Canada, about their interest in pursuing the publication of a co-edited book on the general theme of my research. We explored several approaches and agreed on the format and specific scholars for the chapters on the remaining provinces and territories. Again, the main theme was how key provincial policymakers and practitioners approached the YCJA in terms of specific policies and programs, their perception of effective and ineffective results, and future challenges. No such research or publication existed at the time yet there was an obvious need for this information to be shared across Canada from several perspectives. For much of the YCJA's short history there was an increasingly intense political debate about reforming the YCJA. One key theme promoted by graphic media presentations of serious and violent young offenders, anti-crime/pro-victim interest groups, and crime control-oriented politicians has been that this law has failed to protect the public from violent young offenders and to hold them responsible for their crimes. In other words, since 2003, contentious opinions about the YCJA have been voiced by politicians, social activists, and, of course, social scientists from an array of disciplines, most visibly, criminology. Yet, my initial research suggested a much more complex, innovative, and far more positive perspective of the YCJA at the level of the provincial practitioners. Their perceptions, though, have not been presented from a Canada-wide provincial perspective even though it always is practitioners who deal with the everyday realities of youth justice. For these professionals, the YCJA is not a social, statistical, or political "topic"; it is the legal basis of their professional practice. And as such, their day-to-day experiences dealing with youths and with the tools, measures, opportunities, and legal limits imposed by the YCJA on their work make them the primary witnesses to its implementation since 2003. One of the main purposes of our work and this book, therefore, is to present the accounts of probation officers, counsellors, educators, and social workers as well as a select group of policymakers. From these accounts, we can better understand how the provinces have implemented the YCJA in different communities and contexts, which can vary greatly from one region to the next and even within a province. These accounts highlight programs, interventions, and ways of using available resources that are still unfamiliar in other provinces. Our second purpose is to provide vital policy and program information to practitioners and policymakers that can facilitate more effective provincial youth justice systems. We hope that fellow researchers, teachers, and students can benefit from a comparative Canadian perspective. We thank all the practitioners and policymakers for their generous cooperation in providing much of the empirical research in these chapters. Finally, all of the authors appreciate the encouragement of the University of Toronto Press in bringing this book to fruition.

Marc Alain, October 2015

Contributors

Marc Alain, PhD, is a criminologist who graduated from the University of Montreal in 1997. He has been teaching program evaluation at the Department of Psychoeducation at the University of Quebec in Trois-Rivières since 2005. He was Director of the research centre at the Quebec School of Police between 2000 and 2005. His areas of research cover topics such as police ethics and police relationships with the public, program evaluation methodology and, of course, youth justice in Canada and in Europe.

Sandra Bell, PhD, is a retired professor with an adjunct appointment in the Department of Sociology and Criminology at Saint Mary's University. Her research interests and publications include young offenders, juvenile justice, law reform, and girls in the youth justice system. Her most recent work involves a historical comparative analysis of youth justice law reform in Scotland and Canada.

Kathryn M. Campbell, PhD, is an associate professor of criminology at the University of Ottawa. The bulk of her research in the previous decade has focused on areas related to miscarriages of justice, including research examining the limits of expert testimony in criminal trials, a comparative study regarding the impact of preventive detention strategies on wrongful conviction, an examination of schemes of exoneration and compensation for the wrongly convicted, as well as a study of questions around the admissibility of problematic evidence. For over the past decade, Professor Campbell has taught a third-year criminology course on youth justice as well as being involved in youth justice research on an international level mainly focusing on a comparative study on youth diversion in Canada, Kenya, Nicaragua, and El Salvador. Her other research interests include Indigenous justice and animal law.

Raymond R. Corrado, PhD, is a professor in the School of Criminology at Simon Fraser University and a visiting fellow at Clare Hall College and the Institute of Criminology, University of Cambridge, and visiting fellow at the Faculty of Law, University of Bergen. He is a founding member of the Mental Health, Law, and Policy Institute at SFU. He has published six co-edited books and over 200 articles, book chapters, and reports.

Julie Desrosiers, PhD, LLB, holds a doctorate in law from McGill University and teaches criminal law and fundamental rights at Laval University. She has written several articles on youth rights, and a book on disciplinary measures in youth rehabilitation centres (*Isolement et mesures disciplinaires dans les centres de réadaptation pour jeunes*). She is the author of *L'agression sexuelle en droit canadien* and coauthor of the *Traité de droit criminel: La peine*.

Murray Dyck, MA, received his BA in criminology and MA in sociology from the University of Manitoba and has worked as a police officer with the RCMP in rural and remote communities in Alberta and Manitoba.

Malin Enström, MSc, is a crime and intelligence analyst with the Royal Newfoundland Constabulary. She is also presently finishing her PhD in sociology (criminology), at Memorial University, with a focus on honour-related violence and homicide in Canada. She has presented at conferences and lectures on domestic violence and honour-related violence in Canada. A native of Stockholm, Sweden, she has lived and worked in Europe, Africa, and North America.

Karla Gronsdahl, PhD, has worked in the youth justice field for twenty-seven years. She began her career as a probation officer in British Columbia. She served as a program director at the Justice Institute of BC, where she managed youth justice dean with the Faculty of Child, Family and Community Studies at Douglas College.

Sylvie Hamel, PhD, holds a doctorate in psychology from the University of Quebec in Montreal and has completed her post-doctoral studies at

Laval University. She teaches at the Department of Psychoeducation of the University of Quebec in Trois-Rivieres and is a researcher in the International Center of Compared Criminology – UQTR unit. Her fields of interest cover the gang phenomenon and associated problems, criminality prevention, and community social development.

Crystal Hincks, MSc, completed a master's degree in sociology in 2014 at the University of Calgary with a focus on mental health programming. In addition to seven years of frontline experience in forensic mental health, Crystal also has over seven years of research consulting experience and now specializes in evaluation research with social return on investment (SROI) components in the areas of crime prevention, social development, and mental health.

Anne Kimmitt, LLB, has worked in youth justice for three decades as a probation officer, program analyst, and youth justice consultant. She was a project manager for implementation of the *Youth Criminal Justice Act*, and has provided support, expertise, and training on youth justice legislation and services. She represents the BC government on national committees, has provided expert testimony on the YCJA and related legislation, policies, and programs, and led a national project to update the YCJA sentence calculation rules.

Jodi Koffman, LLB, completed her law degree at the University of Manitoba. She has previously worked as a criminal defence counsel. She is currently employed by Manitoba Justice as a crown attorney.

Corey La Berge, LLB, completed his law degree at the University of Manitoba and has worked as a youth advocate and criminal defence counsel.

Frank T. Lavandier, MSc, a PhD candidate in the Department of Sociology, University of New Brunswick, was employed for 30 years with Department of Justice in Prince Edward Island, including two years as the provincial *Youth Criminal Justice Act* sessional instructor in the Department of Sociology and Anthropology, University of Prince Edward Island.

Alan Markwart, BA, BEd, MA, was the assistant deputy minister responsible for youth justice services in British Columbia for many years. He has more than forty years' experience in youth justice, including leading the implementation of *Youth Criminal Justice Act* in 2003 and extensive involvement in federal-provincial–territorial matters relating to youth justice. He is currently a consultant, an adjunct professor at Simon Fraser University, and a member of the BC Review Board.

Anne Morris, PhD, retired from Memorial University after teaching courses in sociology and police studies for 22 years. Anne served as the coordinator for the Royal Newfoundland Constabulary/MUN Police Studies Diploma Program, a partnership to train police cadets. Her interests include issues related to policing, youth justice, and corporate crime. She is a member of the Premier's Advisory Council on Crime and Community Safety, the Canadian Association of Police Educators, and other community volunteer committees.

Susan Reid, PhD, is a professor of criminology and criminal justice at St Thomas University. She has written a number of publications on youth justice since the implementation of the *Young Offenders Act* in 1984. She has recently published an entry-level textbook with Rebecca Bromwich and Sarah Gilliss entitled *Youth and the Law: New Approaches to Criminal Justice and Child Protection*. In 2014 she was inducted into the New Brunswick Crime Prevention Hall of Fame for her community outreach and service.

Josephine L. Savarese, BA, LLB, was a long-time resident of Saskatchewan. She is currently living in Fredericton, New Brunswick. She has degrees in law and sociology from the University of Saskatchewan. She is a former board member of Common Weal Community Arts, Inc., a Saskatchewan-based organization that addresses themes in cultural criminology and that advances social justice through arts based projects with marginalized youth including graffiti artists, hip-hop artists, and former gang-involved youth.

Russell Smandych, PhD, is a professor of sociology and criminology at the University of Manitoba, where he teaches and does research in the fields of British colonial legal history, global criminology and criminal justice, and Canadian and comparative youth justice.

Tim Stuempel, MSc, moved to Nunavut at the age of three, and spent much of his youth in Iqaluit, where he has worked in the correctional system as both a youth officer and an adult correctional officer in secure custody facilities. Tim has taught courses on Aboriginal peoples and justice at the University of Ottawa, where he holds a master's degree in applied criminology with a focus on Inuit Qaujimajatuqangit and criminal justice. He is a member and past president of the board of directors of a community residential facility in Ottawa for federally sentenced offenders, a member and past chair of the Canadian Criminal Justice Association's Policy Review Committee, and has provided testimony on justice-related legislation, especially as it relates to Aboriginal peoples in Canada.

John Winterdyk, PhD, is a professor of justice studies in the Department of Economics, Justice and Policy Studies of Mount Royal University. He has published extensively in the areas of youth justice, human trafficking, international criminal justice, and criminological issues, and has authored or edited more than 28 academic books and several dozen peer-reviewed articles. He is the former and founding director of the Centre for Criminology and Justice Research.

IMPLEMENTING AND WORKING WITH THE
YOUTH CRIMINAL JUSTICE ACT ACROSS CANADA

Introduction: Successes and Challenges in Implementing the YCJA: A Decade Later

RAYMOND R. CORRADO AND ALAN MARKWART

As explained in the forward, the genesis of this edited volume on the *Youth Criminal Justice Act* (YCJA) (2003) involved Professor Marc Alain's research project on the differences in how the provinces implemented this highly controversial law. As could be expected, the most intense initial opposition to the YCJA emanated from academics and senior youth justice officials in Quebec (Trépanier, 2004). Their primary concerns were the perceived attempt by the federal government to impose a culturally and historically unacceptable youth justice philosophy and related youth justice system on the province. The political and constitutional issue revolved around the federal government's sole prerogative to enact criminal justice legislation, and the responsibility of provincial governments to implement and administer that federal legislation. Of course, there were larger political issues involving the strength of federal and provincial Quebec separatist political parties, and their inherent opposition to any federal initiatives that were perceived to threaten their distinctive cultural and political vision of Quebec.

Beyond the Quebec nationalist vision, there was a far more general political opposition in Quebec to changing its distinctive youth justice system – a system that emphasized a non-judicial, administrative process designed to assess and address the needs of the youth who allegedly committed a criminal act, instead of a formalized criminal/judicial process that emphasized procedural safeguards, the determination of legal guilt/responsibility, and proportional sentencing.

Some academics from other provinces also expressed concerns that the YCJA was based on the largely misguided crime control principles of the two main national political parties, the Liberals and the Conservatives

(Corrado, Gronsdahl, & MacAlister, 2007), albeit the then-Liberal government approach was arguably somewhat tempered and targeted to only the most serious violent young offenders. These political parties were seen as reacting to the "moral panic" created by sensationalized media representations of rare but brutal youth murderers who received relatively short custody sentences under the *Young Offenders Act* (YOA) (1984) (Schissel, 2001).

On the other hand, proponents of the YCJA argued that the YOA had fundamental flaws that resulted in punitively high custody rates; disproportionate involvement of Aboriginal youth in the youth criminal justice system, especially in custody; overuse of formal court processing and under-use of diversion including restorative justice approaches for minor offences; and inappropriate use of custody sentences for less serious young offenders in order to facilitate treatment and protection of highly vulnerable youth, such as girls involved in the sex trade and youth with serious addictions or mental health disorders (Barnhorst, 2004; Carrington & Schulenberg, 2004; Corrado & Markwart, 1994).

Despite these compelling critiques of the YOA, some critics argued that some of its fundamental flaws would be unresolved by the YCJA. Most importantly, the former law did not prioritize potentially conflicting principles – drawn from various youth justice models – that explained the need for Supreme Court of Canada decisions to clarify sentencing principles and guidelines (see Bala & Anand, 2004; Bala, Carrington, & Roberts, 2009; Corrado, Gronsdahl, MacAlister, & Cohen, 2006), arguably unsuccessfully, because wide and seemingly unfair disparities in how young offenders were processed and sentenced across provinces/territories continued throughout the YOA regime. The parallel concern with the YCJA was that it introduced a very complex set of principles, criteria, and procedures – again, based on several models of youth justice – that potentially would be difficult to implement consistently across the country.

Another concern was that, like the YOA, the YCJA still did not address the fundamental need for provinces to mandate the coordination of their numerous government ministries and agencies that deliver health, mental health, child welfare, educational, and housing services to multi-problem young offenders, which were too often administered in a separate and uncoordinated manner. As well, the disparities under the YOA were partly related to the variability in the availability of intervention and support programs for young offenders across provinces/territories, which was the result of insufficient and/or inconsistent funding (Bala et al., 2009). Without supplementary federal financing, inadequate funding would still inhibit the availability and effectiveness of programs (Kuehn & Corrado, 2011).

Professor Alain's initial research explored how several provinces prepared for and implemented the YCJA, and whether these initiatives affected the impact of this controversial law in their jurisdictions. As discussed in his forward, he was enormously impressed with the professional dedication of so many line-level staff, including police officers, youth care workers, youth probation officers, Crown prosecutors, as well policy analysts and senior government officials, in effectively implementing the YCJA.

There is no doubt that a theme of this volume is that the YCJA has, generally speaking, been "successful" in many provinces/territories, since most of its key legal philosophical and related policy objectives have been met (Bala et al., 2009; Carrington & Schulenberg, 2005). Nonetheless, while the successes will be evident upon reading the following chapters on each province and the Nunavut territory, there are other fundamental policy issues that remain unresolved. The key issues will be identified and briefly discussed in the next section, but not in any theoretical or policy priority basis because the policy salience of many of the issues vary by province and territory. Again, it is important to identify common themes across the individual province and territory chapters, partly because these themes were brought about by the YCJA controversies stated above, as well as the broader research and theoretical literature on the impact of similar laws in other countries (Corrado, Bala, Linden, & LeBlanc,1992; Solomon & Allen, 2009). Still, the distinctiveness of each province and Nunavut in implementing the YCJA, and its resulting impacts, will also be evident from the in-depth research presented in each chapter.

Custody Trends and Policy Themes

The purported high rates of custody that ostensibly ranked Canada as one of the most punitive youth justice systems among Westernized countries actually began to decline before the YCJA implementation, yet there is a consensus that this law, at a minimum, accelerated this downward trend directly or at least, indirectly (Bala et al., 2009; Doob & Sprott, 2005). For example, British Columbia responded to the YOA-related increased use of custody by initiating provincial policies and programs in the mid-1990s that contributed to substantive decreases in the use of custody. As well, by the advent of the new millennium, other provinces anticipated the inevitable passage of the YCJA, and several put in place new policies and programs that appear to have contributed to declining custody rates.

These provincial initiatives were no doubt considerably helped along by the federal Youth Justice Renewal strategy that began in 1998, well before the implementation of the YCJA in 2003. This renewal strategy included the infusion of substantive increases in federal funding to provinces and territories for young offender services, effectively restoring and enhancing funding that had been previously capped and then cut by earlier Liberal and Conservative federal governments. This new federal funding, established under restructured cost-sharing arrangements, were aligned with the eventual objectives of the YCJA by targeting enhanced diversion, community-based alternatives to custody and rehabilitative services for young offenders, along with additional federal funding for demonstration projects, training, and research.

It is also important to acknowledge that during the period leading up to and following the introduction of the YCJA in Parliament, the federal government consulted extensively across jurisdictions including, for example, in meetings with an array of public and professional interest groups involved with youth justice services and issues such as police, Crown counsel, defence counsel, youth corrections, non-governmental agencies and advocacy groups, First Nations/Aboriginal organizations, and academics. Despite the expressed concern by some critics that the YCJA overemphasized the crime control principles of protecting the public from serious and violent young offenders by establishing a presumption of adult sentencing in a narrowly defined range of cases, it was abundantly clear that diversion and non-custodial sentences were intended to be used far more than under the YOA (Corrado, Bala, Linden, & LeBlanc, 1992; Markwart, 2010, as cited in Prevost, 2011). In other words, there was no doubt that the provinces/territories and their key leaders in administering the system were well aware of these expected changes.

Several custody themes emerged from the provincial and territorial data presented in the chapters in this volume. First, with a few important exceptions, custody rates continued to decline to such low levels that a consensus has emerged among academics that the YCJA has succeeded even beyond original expectations (Bala et al., 2009). On the face of it, the Bill C-10 amendments to the YCJA enacted by the Conservative government in 2012 might appear to threaten these successes by, for example, including specific deterrence and denunciation as principles of sentencing, expanding the number of youth eligible for custody by expanding the definition of violent offences, and completely reworking the provisions for pretrial detention. It is more likely, however, that these legislative changes, which are hardly draconian, will only have a modest impact, if any, on custody rates that have already declined dramatically.

Second, an unintended consequence of decreasing youth incarceration rates has been a greater concentration and centralization in major urban centres of youth custody services due to the closure of smaller youth custody centres in small communities in several provinces such as Alberta, British Columbia, and Ontario. This has resulted in significant policy and program concerns about these incarcerated young offenders regarding, for example, access to their family and local community service providers who live far from these large urban centres, and the potentially negative effects this lack of access could have on treatment interventions and transitions back to the community. This will be discussed further below.

Third, the exceptions to the otherwise substantive declines in custody rates included Quebec, Manitoba, Saskatchewan, and Nunavut (Munch, 2012). The latter three jurisdictions have a relatively larger proportion of Aboriginal youth in their general populations and related serious Aboriginal young offender risk profiles which, in combination with the disproportionately high rates of incarceration of Aboriginal youth – unfortunately common across all jurisdictions – have produced very high rates of pretrial detention and custody of Aboriginal youth in these jurisdictions. The authors of each of these chapters provide insightful explanations for these anomalies to the national custody trend based on broader, enormously complex, and challenging policy issues involving historical federal colonial policies directed towards Aboriginal peoples.

Fourth, pretrial detention rates in many jurisdictions have been unexpectedly high, and have not declined to nearly the same degree as sentenced custody. Ironically, the most controversial event that emerged in relation to this issue involved a youth in Nova Scotia in 2005 who was not detained in custody. In that case, the youth, who had previously been involved in several alleged offences, was released from detention, stole a car and while driving recklessly at high speed caused a fatal accident involving a young mother (Nunn, 2006). This case is discussed in considerable detail in the Nova Scotia chapter. The incident and the subsequent public outcry over the death of the accident victim, Theresa

McEvoy, resulted in the Nova Scotia Nunn Commission recommending key changes to the YCJA sections dealing with the definition of violent offenders and the legal criteria for pretrial detention which, it was argued, would better protect the public.[1] The highly publicized Nunn Commission provided the Harper Conservative government, recently re-elected with a majority, with the additional political impetus to enact the highly controversial and much opposed Bill C-10 to amend the YCJA, which included a complete reworking of the YCJA provisions for pretrial detention. Whether these legally complex changes will, in fact, result in an appreciable increase in pretrial detention rates remains to be seen. At the least, it seems doubtful that the stubbornly higher rates of pretrial detention in many jurisdictions will be mitigated by these legislative changes.

Another policy theme related to pretrial detention is that police officers' decisions to detain youth are sometimes based on the arresting officer having incomplete risk profile information (Moyer & Basic, 2004; Nunn, 2006). This lack of shared information was central to the court decision in the McEvoy tragedy. These concerns point to the larger policy theme that, all too commonly, there appears to be a lack of coordinated, routine communication about higher risk young offenders among key youth justice decision-makers and related government ministries/ agencies providing services to youth.

Fifth, paradoxically, while relatively short custodial sentence lengths are common across all the provincial and territorial youth justice systems (Calverley, Cotter, & Halla, 2010; Munch, 2012), these short periods of incarceration do not afford sufficient time for full assessment of treatment needs and participation in related custody-based treatment programs (Penner, Roesch, & Viljoen, 2011). As well, the reduction in the use of custody has resulted in youth custody centres holding a smaller, more distilled population of the most serious and violent young offenders with extensive high risk profiles that are associated with longer term criminal trajectories (Department of Justice Canada, 2011). Further, as discussed below, these profiles often include major mental disorders (e.g., Smith, Cox, Poon, Stewart, & McCreary Centre Society, 2013). Theoretically, these factors may increase the likelihood that serious recidivism will occur following release from a short custodial period, thereby leading to a cycle of additional short custodial sentences.

Sixth, once released into their communities, many of these serious young offenders did not abide by their community supervision conditions, were charged with administrative offences, and again sentenced to custody (Brennan, 2012; Department of Justice, 2013b). In effect, it seems possible that the limited ability to attend to young offenders' social/psychological needs while in short-term sentenced custody may have increased the likelihood that these young offenders would either not attend or not comply with community-based programs.

Seventh, while, the number of Aboriginal young offenders committed to custody has generally been reduced, they have not reduced to the same degree as non-Aboriginal offenders, which means that Aboriginal youth comprise an increasingly larger share of the total youth custody population (Kong, 2009; Munch, 2012). So, despite smaller absolute numbers, the disproportionate over-representation of Aboriginal youth in custody has been aggravated. This phenomenon raises policy, program, and research issues about whether distinctive intervention programs are needed for Aboriginal young offenders, because their risk/protective profiles are fundamentally different from non-Aboriginal young offenders. The over-representation of Aboriginal youth appears to be evident in all provinces, and in Nunavut; however, the issue is most salient in the provinces with the highest ratios of Aboriginal young offenders to non-Aboriginal young offenders, that is, the Western provinces and the territories.

Finally, in terms of broad outcomes, the changes in youth custody rates appear to have had mixed outcomes. As discussed earlier, the YCJA was intended to address two different populations of young offenders: first, the less serious and non-violent young offenders who were being over-processed in courts and over-incarcerated under the YOA and, second, the small number of serious violent young offenders who were arguably being inadequately addressed by the YOA. With respect to the first group, it is clear that the general decarceration of young offenders has not resulted in an increase in general youth crime rates during the YCJA period, at least at the national level. In fact, an examination of Statistics Canada data indicates that during the period from 2002 to 2012, both the police-reported per capita youth crime rate and the youth Crime Severity Index for Canada declined appreciably (−26% and −25%, respectively), recognizing that there were some differences in individual jurisdictions.[2] From this perspective, the YCJA can be considered a success.

There is a somewhat different picture in relation to violent youth crime. In this regard, the YCJA was presumably intended to constrain serious violent offenders through the incapacitation and deterrence arising from presumptive sentencing (at least until struck down by the Supreme Court of Canada), while serious violent offenders who remained in the youth system would benefit from the specialized individualized funding available to those who received an intensive rehabilitative custody and supervision (IRCS) sentence. Yet, an examination of Statistics Canada data indicates that there has not been a stable pattern of decreases in the police-reported per capita youth violent crime rate, the youth violent crime severity index, or the youth homicide rate in the YCJA period between 2002 and 2012.[3] Again, there are, however, sharp differences in individual jurisdictions. For example, the youth violent crime severity index declined sharply in British Columbia, yet increased substantially in Manitoba. Such sharp differences point, again, to the need to examine the ostensible impact of legislation nationally but also the distinctive contexts and dynamics at play within individual provinces and territories, as outlined in the forthcoming chapters.

Historically, serious violent young offenders have been the most challenging from a policy (and political) perspective, and that will likely always be the case given the media sensationalism often accompanying these small number of high profile cases. As will be discussed under the Treatment/Intervention Trends and Policy Themes subsection of this chapter, most provinces have specialized programs for these multi-problem high risk young offenders, including gang prevention and desistence programs (Caputo & Vallée, 2010). These programs, however, have often encountered significant impediments, such as stable and adequate funding, information sharing, access and coordination of multi-ministerial resources, and effective engagement of youth, families, and communities.

It seems doubtful that the changes arising from Bill C-10 will appreciably impact the treatment of serious violent young offenders under the YCJA. In this regard, the Bill C-10 changes to adult sentencing merely reflect changes to the law that were already made by the Supreme Court of Canada, which threw out presumptive adult sentencing of serious violent young offenders and entrenched the principle that youth are to be afforded a presumption of diminished moral blameworthiness. One notable exception involves a new Bill C-10 provision permitting the publication of the identities of youth found guilty of violent offences; however, these provisions appear to have been widely ignored to date, perhaps because they are limited by a difficult legal test.

At the other end of the offence seriousness spectrum (i.e., minor offences), the YCJA has had impressive diversion policy outcomes in most provinces/territories but, again, with new policy concerns. As with custody policies, there were both common themes across the jurisdictions and distinctive themes within each.

Diversion Trends and Policy Themes

Under the YCJA, Quebec was the only province not expected to alter its rate of diverting youth who admitted to an alleged minor offence (Trépanier, 2004). From its 1977 *Youth Protection Act* forward, the Quebec youth justice system has had a formal diversion process to respond to all but the most serious offences, and when a youth denies responsibility for the alleged offence(s). Even cases that proceeded through the youth court could involve the young offender being subsequently processed through the administratively focused youth bureau rather than the judge-directed youth corrections system. Nonetheless, Professor Alain identified substantial changes in the degree of formality of how youth are processed under the new law in Quebec, though not necessarily with more effective outcomes. The two YCJA diversion options involved extrajudicial measures (EJM) or, more simply, informal police diversion and more formal extrajudicial sanctions (EJS), following a report or charge by the police (Bala et al., 2009; Barnhorst, 2004; Department of Justice, 2013a). With the exception of Quebec, these measures generally resulted in substantial increased use of diversion by the police and Crown prosecutors nearly commensurate with a drop in the number of court cases processed in most provinces. In Alberta, for example, there was a substantial reliance on volunteer youth justice committees for EJS, but a decline in the use of these committees in Manitoba and greater reliance on formal diversion (see Hann & Associates, 2003).

Along with the general acknowledgement that the police have diverted substantial and increasing numbers of youth in most provinces, several challenging policy themes emerged. These included insufficient community program resources, strains on police time and resources, documentation processing, training, and coordination with other agencies. Again, these issues varied across provinces and territories as well as within them. Similarly, restorative justice programs for EJM and EJS were not widely used outside of certain jurisdictions, particularly several smaller cities in British Columbia (Canadian Resource Centre for Victims of Crime, 2011). As well, youth justice officials involved in these

diversion programs wanted more training and feedback about the effectiveness of such programs. Even in Nunavut, unequally distributed
community resources across numerous small communities spanning
enormous geographic distances resulted in highly variable use of diversion programs (Scott Clark Consulting, 2004).

A common theme, though, was the challenge of coordinating and integrating formal youth justice officials, mainly police officers and youth
probation officers, with community and volunteer resources in highly
disparate and geographically distributed communities. The enormous
differences in population sizes and program resources for the larger provinces and Nunavut were also a concern. While this challenge of adequate-
ly and fairly resourcing diversion programs in small rural communities
is common to most provinces and Nunavut, as mentioned above, finding
adequate resources for young offenders who have committed more serious offences and who are not subject to diversion is also a challenge.

Treatment/Intervention Trends and Policy Themes

Historically, as Alain and Desrosiers describe in detail in their chapter on
the evolution of juvenile youth justice laws in Canada, a central philosophical and legal theme has been the justification for the need to have a
separate or distinctive legal system for youth, which is based on the rationale that youth under a certain age are fundamentally different from
adults in their mental and emotional maturation (Doob & Cesaroni,
2004). When this premise was accepted, then laws such as the *Juvenile
Delinquents Act* (JDA) (1908) and Quebec's *Youth Protection Act* (1977)
incorporated the welfare or treatment of youth needs as the paramount
policy objective. Corrado (1992) has described elsewhere the Welfare
Model of youth justice and other models to highlight the underlying
theories, legal principles, and policy goals for the JDA, YOA, and YCJA.
The essence of this model is the assessment of the range of needs for
youth who have engaged in serious delinquencies/criminal offences,
and the provision of program resources to meet these needs. For proponents of the Welfare Model of youth justice (which still predominates
in most European Union countries), the distinct advantage of this approach is that it facilitates a highly individualized case management response that requires multiple ministries/agencies to better coordinate
their program services, in part, because youth court judges mandate
this cooperation (Corrado et al., 2007). This is one apparent advantage
of the Corporatist Model approach evident in the Quebec youth justice

system. Even though there has been considerable diversity in how all three youth justice laws were implemented in the provinces/territories, a common policy theme has been the inherent difficulties in ensuring the consistent cooperation and integration of clinical assessment and program services from the broad array of ministries and agencies that provide those services. Nonetheless, most provinces have introduced some form of coordination and integration for case management and service delivery, albeit in varying degrees. Beyond the Quebec approach, British Columbia created an integrated multi-service children's ministry, including youth justice and youth forensic psychiatric services, in 1997, while Ontario and other provinces have introduced "collaborative case management" approaches.

Despite these innovative approaches – many of which were begun under the JDA or YOA – fundamental policy issues remain for all provinces and Nunavut. These issues have been mentioned: the long-standing difficulties in providing adequate program funding and services, especially across small and geographically dispersed communities, which is especially acute for high-risk vulnerable young offender groups such as girls, polydrug addicts, children-in-care, gang-involved youth, and those with major mental health disorders. Among incarcerated serious and violent young offenders, for example, it has not been uncommon for this group to have a very high prevalence of youth with several of these risk factors and related treatment needs (e.g., Smith et al., 2013).

While all these risk factors and treatment needs obviously and incontestably are important policy themes for all the provinces and Nunavut under the YCJA, the subset of mental health disorders is among the most challenging, as discussed below.

Mental Health Treatment Trends and Policy Themes

With few exceptions, the mental health of a substantial minority of youth who enter the youth justice system, even at the diversion stages, has remained a major policy concern under the YCJA (Odgers, Burnette, Chauhan, Moretti, & Reppucci, 2005). For some provinces such as Manitoba and Saskatchewan, this has been an acute issue because of the high prevalence of Aboriginal young offenders in their youth justice systems, and the similarly high prevalence of Aboriginal youth and families who have experienced intergenerational poverty and related inadequate housing and high unemployment (Hogeveen, 2005; Totten, 2009). While these economic and social risk factors are evident for many non-Aboriginal young offenders as well (e.g., Smith et al., 2013), the high prevalence of youth and families from this historically unique and disadvantaged ethnic group and their high population concentration levels in the Prairie provinces pose especially great challenges. Major Aboriginal gangs and organized crime organizations, for example, started in Winnipeg and have expanded their presence to Saskatoon, Regina, Edmonton, and, more recently, Vancouver, as well as to smaller towns in the Western provinces and northern Ontario (Grekul & LaBoucane-Benson, 2008).

The mental health needs of a substantial number of youth across all ethnic and racial groups has remained challenging for four primary reasons: inadequate/inconsistent funding of programs; unequal and inadequate distribution of services to geographically disparate small communities; difficulties in using appropriate assessment and diagnostic instruments; and, often, insufficient or inadequate research that would help justify costly treatment programs (e.g., Penner et al., 2011). The latter policy concern has been a significant political issue since the implementation of the YCJA. Since 2008, Canada, like all advanced industrial economies, has experienced a major financial crisis that resulted in funding reductions in certain provinces for many programs important to the treatment needs of vulnerable youth and their families. These program needs are most obvious for serious and violent young offenders sentenced to custody, however, much research has strongly suggested that early intervention programs for children who exhibit a wide range of antisocial behaviours reduce the likelihood of long-term, serious and violent criminal trajectories.

The most recent research – much of it Canadian – on mental health risk factors and treatment responses has identified that serious antisocial behaviours, including violent assaults and fire setting, often emerge in middle childhood (8–11 years old), though they are always few in number (Loeber & Hay, 1997; Lussier, Tzoumakis, Corrado, Reebye, & Healey, 2011; Tremblay et al., 1999). The explanation for these unusual childhood antisocial acts typically involved developmental disorders, such as fetal alcohol spectrum disorders (FASD) and autism spectrum disorders (ASD), or the major childhood disorders, including oppositional defiant disorder (ODD) and conduct disorder (CD) (Corrado & Freedman, 2011).

Connected to these research findings, there has been an ongoing controversy under both the YOA and YCJA about how provinces have responded to serious and/or chronic offences by children under the age of 12 since the jurisdiction of the YCJA is limited to children who are 12 years or older. The most recent incident involved a 10-year-old youth who allegedly murdered a 6-year-old child in Saskatchewan. Purportedly, the older child had an extensive history of antisocial behaviour for which there had been very limited intervention. Other than removing children from their family and providing a child welfare placement, there were few options available to assist a child, especially since no coercive/restrictive interventions can be imposed by judges due to the lack of jurisdiction of the criminal law (Pringle, 2014). In responding to this issue, Professor Nicholas Bala, Canada's leading legal scholar on youth justice legislation, has previously argued that the YCJA minimum age should be lowered to 10 years old as it is in England and Wales (House of Commons, 2000). He has argued that for the exceptional and few cases of very serious violent children, there needs to be a youth justice response to both assist the child offender with more enforceable treatment programs and to protect the public from potential future serious violent offences. Other experts, however, have responded to Bala's arguments by strenuously asserting that criminalizing even the most extreme violent acts by children under the age of 12 would be ineffective and, possibly, even counterproductive (Augimeri, as cited in Cryderman & Mahoney, 2013; Peterson-Badali, as cited in Cryderman & Mahoney, 2013). Instead, they argue that there are appropriate and effective non-youth-justice-based treatment interventions for these children.

Independent of this debate over the YCJA's minimum age of jurisdiction, there is a near consensus, theoretically, that programs that address the child's psychological/emotional needs and his or her family risk/protective needs, are most likely to effectively assist many children who engage in an early onset pattern of serious antisocial behaviours. Several provinces have introduced such programs. For example, many jurisdictions in Ontario have incorporated the Stop Now And Plan (SNAP) program for 8- to 11-year-old children who have engaged in serious antisocial acts (Augimeri, Farrington, Koegl, & Day, 2007). This program activates a diagnostic assessment of the youth and family needs, and then develops and implements a coordinated multi-program case plan. Quebec, too, has long adopted early intervention approaches. As well, many provinces have adopted programs directed at children (and, primarily, young adolescents) seen as at risk for gang involvement, as well as those already involved.

As is discussed in each forthcoming chapter, virtually all the provinces and Nunavut have recognized the importance of mental health risk factors in youth justice decision-making under the YCJA, however, consistent and universal approaches have not been evident. At the youth court stage, for example, Ontario introduced the Youth Mental Health Court. In New Brunswick, a youth treatment program (with a clinician being a key resource) was added to address the highly specialized mental health needs not being directly and routinely met by its larger Therapeutic Community program. In contrast, British Columbia, like Quebec, has had long-standing diagnostic service and treatment programs for serious mental health needs. In BC, for example, psychiatrists and clinical psychologists at the Youth Forensic Psychiatric Services clinics throughout the province, and mental health specialists at the Maples Adolescent Treatment Centre – both under the Ministry of Children and Family Development – have provided key program services for youth justice clients and mentally disordered young offenders. As well, the federal National Crime Prevention Centre has funded numerous research and model experimental programs across provinces and territories to address this complex and often perplexing social problem. Despite these innovative programs, fundamental social policy and program issues remained unresolved under the YCJA, including several mentioned above.

To reiterate, certain challenges remain somewhat more intractable than others. For example, major advances have been made in diagnosing mental health needs and responding with various related therapies, including both cognitive behavioural and drug treatments (e.g., American Psychiatric Association, 2013; Kazdin, 2011; Lipsey, Tanner-Smith, & Wilson, 2010). In contrast, long-term budget restraints mentioned above have added to the inherent difficulties in providing costly mental health program services in geographically dispersed small and rural communities (e.g., Canadian Mental Health Association, 2009; Pong et al., 1999). Also, while treatment programs directed towards youth with special education needs have been widely available, programs for diagnosing FASD and its treatment programs have not (Clarren & Lutke, 2008; Werk, Cui, & Tough, 2013). Of course, this developmental disorder requires extensive and costly diagnostic resources, as well as long-term support resources for the youth and their families/caregivers. Yet, there is an expanding consensus that FASD is a high risk factor for serious and violent offending, which also has been disproportionately prevalent among Aboriginal youth, though widely undiagnosed and untreated.

Conclusion

The editors of this volume asked the authors of each of the chapters to research the key policy themes that the lead author uncovered in his original research project, which focused on how the YCJA was implemented in their respective provinces. The methodological focus of the research also involved individuals working in youth justice, both at the policy level and field level. As Professor Alain explained in his forward, this methodology allowed for an understanding of the YCJA that is unique; it was these individuals alone who lived through the initial implementation stages and ensuing period. Their experiences and insights, therefore, have been central to each chapter since they allowed the authors to contextualize the additional aggregate and case study information they integrated into their chapters' descriptions and policy narratives.

The final theme of this necessarily short introductory chapter is the considerable complexity of the numerous policies that officials in each province and Nunavut had to address. This difficulty included not only the intricate inter-relatedness of all of the above-noted broad policy and program issues, but also the even more challenging connectedness of these issues and challenges to provincial and federal politics and economics. It could have been expected that the extraordinarily complex YCJA, which has integrated key theoretical ideas from disparate youth justice models and related criminological theories, would be daunting to implement. It has been somewhat surprising, though, that the overwhelming impression reported in each chapter was how well prepared officials were in their respective provinces and in Nunavut despite the distinctiveness of the challenges in each jurisdiction. In addition, despite the above-noted ongoing challenging policy issues, it appears that most authors depict a very favourable view of the YCJA, especially regarding custody and diversion trends.

NOTES

1 See Nunn, D. M. (2006). *Spiralling out of control: Lessons learned from a boy in trouble: Report of the Nunn Commission of Inquiry*. Halifax, NS: Government of Nova Scotia.
2 See, Statistics Canada CANSIM (Crime and Justice) tables at http://www5.statcan.gc.ca/cansim/a01?lang=en.
3 *Ibid.*

REFERENCES

American Psychiatric Association. (2013). *Diagnostic and statistical manual of mental disorders (5th ed.)*. Arlington, VA: American Psychiatric Publishing.

Augimeri, L. K., Farrington, D. P., Koegl, C. J., & Day, D. M. (2007). The SNAP™ Under 12 Outreach Project: Effects of a community based program for children with conduct problems. *Journal of Child and Family Studies, 16*(6), 799–807.

Bala, N., & Anand, S. (2004). The first months under the Youth Criminal Justice Act: A survey and analysis of case law. *Canadian Journal of Criminology and Criminal Justice, 46*, 251–271.

Bala, N., Carrington, P. J., & Roberts, J. V. (2009). Evaluating the *Youth Criminal Justice Act* after five years: A qualified success. *Canadian Journal of Criminology and Criminal Justice, 51*, 131–167.

Barnhorst, R. (2004). The Youth Criminal Justice Act: New directions and implementation issues. *Canadian Journal of Criminology and Criminal Justice, 46*, 231–250.

Brennan, S. (2012). Police-reported crime statistics in Canada, 2011. *Juristat* [Catalogue no. 85–002-X]. Ottawa, ON: Statistics Canada.

Calverley, D., Cotter, A., & Halla, E. (2010). Youth custody and community services in Canada, 2008/2009. *Juristat, 30*(1) [Catalogue no. 85–002-X]. Ottawa, ON: Statistics Canada.

Canadian Mental Health Association. (2009). *Rural and northern community issues in mental health*. Toronto, ON: Canadian Mental Health Association, Ontario.

Canadian Resource Centre for Victims of Crime. (2011). *Restorative justice in Canada: What victims should know*. Ottawa, ON: Author. Retrieved from http://www.rjlillooet.ca/documents/restjust.pdf

Caputo, T., & Vallée, M. (2010). *Review of the Roots of Youth Violence: Research papers (vol. 4): A comparative analysis of youth justice approaches*. Ottawa, ON: Centre for Initiatives on Children, Youth and Community, Carleton University. Retrieved from http://www.children.gov.on.ca/htdocs/English/topics/youthandthelaw/roots/volume4/comparative_analysis.aspx

Carrington, P. J., & Schulenberg, J. L. (2004). The Youth Criminal Justice Act: A new era in Canadian juvenile justice. *Canadian Journal of Criminology and Criminal Justice, 46*(3), 219–223.

Carrington, P. J., & Schulenberg, J. L. (2005). *The impact of the Youth Criminal Justice Act on police charging practices with young persons: A preliminary statistical assessment*. Ottawa, ON: Youth Justice Policy Branch, Department of

Justice Canada. Retrieved from http://www.justice.gc.ca/eng/rp-pr/cj-jp/yj-jj/pdf/prelimin.pdf

Clarren, S. K., & Lutke, J. (2008). Building clinical capacity for Fetal Alcohol Spectrum Disorder diagnoses in Western and Northern Canada. *Canadian Journal of Clinical Pharmacology, 15,* e223–e237.

Corrado, R. R. (1992). Introduction. In R. R. Corrado, N. Bala, R. Linden, & M. LeBlanc (Eds.), *Juvenile justice in Canada: A theoretical and analytical assessment* (pp. 1–20). Toronto, ON: Butterworths.

Corrado, R. R., Bala, N., Linden, R., & LeBlanc, M. (Eds.). (1992). *Juvenile justice in Canada: A theoretical and analytical assessment.* Toronto, ON: Butterworths.

Corrado, R. R., & Freedman, L. (2011). Risk profiles, trajectories and intervention points for serious and chronic young offenders. *International Journal of Child, Youth & Family Studies, 2,* 197–232.

Corrado, R. R., Gronsdahl, K., & MacAlister, D. (2007). The Youth Criminal Justice Act: Can the Supreme Court of Canada balance the competing and conflicting models of youth justice? *Criminal Law Quarterly, 53,* 14–66.

Corrado, R. R., Gronsdahl, K., MacAlister, D., & Cohen, I. (2006). Should deterrence be a sentencing principle under the YCJA? *The Canadian Bar Review, 85,* 539–568.

Corrado, R. R., & Markwart, A. (1994). The need to reform the YOA in response to violent young offenders: Confusion, reality or myth? *Canadian Journal of Criminology, 36*(3), 343–378.

Cryderman, K., & Mahoney, J. (2013, September 6). In Saskatchewan, native community grapples with brutal child slaying. *The Globe and Mail.*

Department of Justice Canada. (2013). *The Youth Criminal Justice Act: Summary and background.* Ottawa, ON: Author. Retrieved from http://www.justice.gc.ca/eng/cj-jp/tools-outils/back-hist.html

Department of Justice Canada. (2013a). *Extrajudicial measures.* Ottawa, ON: Author. Retrieved from http://www.justice.gc.ca/eng/cj-jp/yj-jj/tools-outils/sheets feuillets/measu-mesur.html.

Department of Justice Canada. (2013b). *The Youth Criminal Justice Act: Summary and background.* Ottawa, Ontario: Author. Retrieved from http://www.justice.gc.ca/eng/cj-jp/yj-jj/tools-outils/back-hist.html

Doob, A. N., & Cesaroni, C. (2004). *Responding to youth crime in Canada.* Toronto, ON: University of Toronto Press Inc.

Doob, A. N., & Sprott, J. (2005). *The use of custody under the Youth Criminal Justice Act.* Youth Justice Policy, Department of Justice Canada. Retrieved from http://www.justice.gc.ca/eng/rp-pr/cj-jp/yj-jj/pdf/doob-sprott.pdf

Fowlie, J. (2012, January 19). B.C. closing two detention centres for girls, consolidating in Burnaby. *Vancouver Sun.* Retrieved July 31, 2014, from http://

www.canada.com/vancouversun/news/westcoastnews/story.html?id=
784ea397-4b82-4911-8f2b-9de6ae6264ef

Grekul, J., & LaBoucane-Benson, P. (2008). Aboriginal gangs and their (dis)
placement: Contextualizing recruitment, membership, and status. *Canadian
Journal of Criminology and Criminal Justice, 50*, 59–82. doi:10.1353/ccj.0.0000

Hann & Associates. (2003). *A national survey of youth justice committees in
Canada*. Ottawa, ON: Department of Justice Canada, Youth Justice Research.
Retrieved from http://www.justice.gc.ca/eng/rp-pr/cj-jp/yj-jj/rr03_yj7-
rr03_jj7/rr03_yj7.pdf

Hogeveen, B. R. (2005). Toward "safer" and "better" communities?: Canada's
Youth Criminal Justice Act, Aboriginal youth and the processes of exclusion. *Critical Criminology, 13*(3), 287–305.

House of Commons (2000). Proceedings of the Justice and Human Rights
Committee, February 16, 2000.

Kazdin, A. E. (2011). Evidence-based treatment research: Advances, limitations, and next steps. *The American Psychologist, 66*, 685–698.

Kong, R. (2009). Youth custody and community services in Canada, 2007/2008.
Juristat [Catalogue no. 85–002-X]. Ottawa, ON: Statistics Canada.

Kuehn, S., & Corrado, R. R. (2011). Youth probation officers' interpretation and
implementation of the Youth Criminal Justice Act: A case study of youth
justice in Canada. *International Journal of Comparative and Applied Criminal
Justice, 35*(3), 221–241.

Lipsey, M. W., Tanner-Smith, E. E., & Wilson, S. J. (2010). *Comparative effectiveness of adolescent substance abuse treatment: Three meta-analyses with implications for practice*. Nashville, TN: Peabody Research Institute, Vanderbilt
University.

Loeber, R., & Hay, D. (1997). Key issues in the development of aggression and
violence from childhood to early adulthood. *Annual Review of Psychology,
48*, 371–410.

Lussier, P., Tzoumakis, S., Corrado, R., Reebye, P., & Healey, J. (2011). Pre/
perinatal adversities and behavioural outcomes in early childhood:
Preliminary findings from the Vancouver Longitudinal Study. *International
Journal of Child, Youth and Family Studies, 2*, 36–64.

Ministry of Children and Family Development, Government of British
Columbia. (2014). *Information bulletin: Update on Victoria youth custody centre
closure*. Retrieved from http://www2.news.gov.bc.ca/news_releases_2013-
2017/2014CFD0018-000771.htm

Moyer, S., & Basic, M. (2004). *Pre-trial detention under the Young Offenders Act:
A study of urban courts*. Ottawa, ON: Department of Justice Canada, Youth

Justice Research. Retrieved from http://www.justice.gc.ca/eng/rp-pr/
cj-jp/yj-jj/rr04_yj1-rr04_jj1/rr04_yj1.pdf

Munch, C. (2012). Youth correctional statistics in Canada, 2010/2011. *Juristat*
(Catalogue no. 85–002-X). Ottawa, ON: Statistics Canada.

Nunn, D. M. (2006). *Spiralling out of control: Lessons learned from a boy in trouble:
Report of the Nunn Commission of Inquiry*. Halifax, NS: Government of Nova
Scotia. Retrieved from www.novascotia.ca/just/nunn_commission/_docs/
Report_Nunn_Final.pdf

Odgers, C. L., Burnette, M. L., Chauhan, P., Moretti, M. M., & Reppucci, N. D.
(2005). Misdiagnosing the problem: Mental health profiles of incarcerated
juveniles. *The Canadian Child Adolescent Psychiatry Review, 14*(1), 26–29.

Penner, E., Roesch, R., & Viljoen, J. (2011). Juvenile offenders: An international comparison of mental health assessment and treatment practices.
International Journal of Forensic Mental Health Services, 10, 215–232.

Pong, R. W., Atkinson, A. M., Irvine, A., MacLeod, M., Minore, B., Pegoraro,
A., Pitblado, J. R., Stones, M., & Tesson, G. (1999). *Rural health re-
search in the Canadian Institutes of Health Research*. Thunder Bay, ON:
Centre for Rural and Northern Health Research (CRaNHR), Lakehead
University. Retrieved from http://ruralontarioinstitute.ca/file.
aspx?id=79b0a603-71c7-40c2-afcc-35afe37c9f84

Prevost, A. (2011). *Empirical exploration of the importation, deprivation and integrated models concerning types of aggression in youth custody* (Doctoral
dissertation). Retrieved from SFU Summit. (etd6571)

Pringle, B. (2014). *Two tragedies: Holding systems accountable*. Saskatoon, SK:
Advocate for Children and Youth. Retrieved from http://www.saskadvocate.
ca/sites/default/files//u3/Two_Tragedies_Holding_Systems_Accountable_
Advocate_%20Childre_%20Youth_May_2014.pdf

Schissel, B. (2001). Youth crime, moral panics, and the news: The conspiracy
against the marginalized in Canada. In R. C. Smandych (Ed.), *Youth justice:
History, legislation, and reform* (pp. 84–103). Toronto, ON: Harcourt Canada.

Scott Clark Consulting (2004). *Review of Nunavut community justice program:
Final report*. Ottawa, ON: Department of Justice, Research and Statistics
Division. Retrieved from http://www.justice.gc.ca/eng/rp-pr/aj-ja/
rr05_7/rr05_7.pdf

Smith, A., Cox, K., Poon, C., Stewart, D., & McCreary Centre Society (2013).
Time Out III: A profile of BC youth in custody. Vancouver, BC: McCreary
Centre Society.

Solomon, E., & Allen, R. (2009). *Out of trouble: Reducing child imprisonment in
England and Wales: Lessons from abroad*. London, UK: Prison Reform Trust.

Totten, M. (2009). Aboriginal youth and violent gang involvement in Canada: Quality prevention strategies. *Information and Privacy Commissioner Review, 3*, 135–156.

Tremblay, R. E., Japel, C., Pérusse, D., McDuff, P., Boivin, M., Zoccolillo, M., & Montplaisir, J. (1999). The search for the age of "onset" of physical aggression: Rousseau and Bandura revisited. *Criminal Behaviour and Mental Health, 9*, 8–23.

Trépanier, J. (2004). What Did Quebec not want? Opposition to the adoption of the YCJA in Quebec. *Canadian Journal of Criminology and Criminal Justice, 46*, 273–299.

Werk, C. M., Cui, X., & Tough, S. (2013). Fetal Alcohol Spectrum Disorder among Aboriginal children under six years of age and living off reserve. *First Peoples Child & Family Review, 8*, 7–16.

1 A Fairly Short History of Youth Criminal Justice in Canada

MARC ALAIN AND JULIE DESROSIERS

Introduction

Looking at legislators' intentions in creating laws to attempt to control crime and delinquency among youth in Canada reveals a common trait: these laws, and modifications to them, seem to oscillate between trying to establish systems that provide fair punishments and ways of protecting society on one hand and, on the other, trying to find ways to help youth rebuild social skills and improve their social networks. Not surprisingly, anyone who looks quickly at Canadian legal history in this area might think that these two sets of objectives are antithetical. A quick tour through the texts of the laws, however, shows that they are actually much more nuanced. And none of them, of course, was ever intended to deal with only one of these sets of objectives without taking the other into account. The attempt to deal with these two goals provides the main frame of reference for the historical, political, and legal analysis of the evolution of Canadian measures intended to deal with youth delinquency and the criminality that follows.

The first, fairly short, part of this chapter is devoted to outlining how youth crime and delinquency were treated during the French Regime, a harsh time when stages of development such as infancy and adolescence were seen as, to say the least, more theory than reality when the time came to punish a youngster who had been found guilty of a criminal offence. We then describe the period between the start of the English Regime in 1760 to the onset of the first legislations specifically intended to deal with youth criminality, which occurred in 1857. By looking at this period we start to better understand the way in which the treatment of younger criminals began to change in both the French- and English-speaking parts of Canada. The third part of the chapter covers discussions surrounding the 1908 enactment of the first act concerning juvenile criminals up to the reforms that gave birth to the second piece of legislation intended to deal with youth delinquency and crime, the 1984 *Young Offenders Act*. It will be obvious that over this rather long period of time the treatment of delinquents changed across Canada, as clearly documented in the federal government's 1965 report *Juvenile Delinquency in Canada*. The fourth and final part of the chapter is devoted to the reforms that led to the 2003 *Youth Criminal Justice Act*, and the enactment of the new law.

The Period before 1908

The idea of a period know as childhood, during which children should be treated differently from adults, did not fully develop before the 19th century. Throughout the 17th and 18th centuries, the harsh living conditions in North America required strict adherence to social rules and conduct for children and adults alike. From the end of the French Regime to the establishment of the Canadian Dominion in 1867, there was no distinction between the way juveniles and adults accused or convicted of crimes were treated, with the notable exception of the *doli incapax* (Latin for "incapacity to do wrong") defence as the way of acquittal for youth aged between 7 and 13.[1] According to this principle, children under 7 were thought to be incapable of distinguishing between good and evil and were therefore not held responsible for their actions. The same presumption of incapacity was extended to children aged between 7 and 13, but it could be rebutted by establishing that the child was sufficiently mature to appreciate that his or her conduct was wrong. Children between these ages who were deemed capable of understanding the nature and consequences of their actions – which was apparently quite often the case (Normand, 1999, p. 25) – were sentenced as adults, which could mean imprisonment, physical punishment, or death. Adults and children were imprisoned in the same facilities. Thus, the *doli incapax* defence was not applied in every case, and its use varied greatly from case to case throughout what constituted Canada in that period, demonstrating a mix of rigidity and harsh punishment as well as, occasionally, some compassion, especially for younger children.

The reform movement of the 19th century emerged in Canada, as elsewhere, as a continuation of the Enlightenment. Enlightenment thinkers called for reforms in a great number of domains, ranging from economics to religion. Some called for the abolition of slavery, and others for the end of corporal punishments and cruel practices that characterized the penal system throughout the world. The intellectual revolution engaged by thinkers such as Rousseau, Diderot, Bentham, Hume, and Beccaria, to name a few, continued throughout the 19th century and gave rise to social reforms movements aimed at improving the lives of children, whether by prohibiting child labour in mines and factory or by promoting publicly funded education. With the development of criminology, the idea emerged that delinquency was the result of a bad environment and did not lay in the individual's character. Consequently, young delinquents were not to be punished, but treated, as appropriate social interventions could "save" them from crime (Bala & Anand, 2012, p. 8 ; Department of Justice Canada, 2004, pp. 6–10).

But reformist ideas did not go unchallenged. Many still believed that criminals, including children, should be severely punished. By the end of the 19th century, two trends started to emerge among the public, the first advocating still tougher sentences, while the other pleaded for more lenient measures for children and juveniles found guilty of crimes. Among supporters of the first trend, physical punishment for both children and adults was considered to be not only more effective than imprisonment in preventing recidivism but also more economical, since it eliminated the need for expenses for meals, shelter, and sanitary facilities. As for the trend towards leniency, it was supported by a strong humanist reform movement that argued for a clear distinction between adults and juveniles, as well as an end to cruel physical punishment for the youngest convicts.

1857 to 2003: Four Periods in the Treatment of Juvenile Delinquency in Canada

There were four key periods in the treatment of juvenile delinquency from the end of the 19th century to the first years of the 21st century. We have already seen that by 1857 the *doli incapax* defence that was developed under English common law had been introduced in Canada and could sometimes provide immunity from prosecution. New trends in criminality, as well as new forms of sentences, led gradually to the first youth justice legislations in 1857 and to the adoption of the first Canadian *Criminal Code* in 1892, which mark the beginning of the first of these four periods. The second period starts with the *Juvenile Delinquents Act* of 1908, a law that remained in force until the start of the third period, in 1984, with the enactment of the *Young Offenders Act*.

The fourth period began with the discussions at the end of the 1990s that finally led to the enactment of the *Youth Criminal Justice Act* in 2003.

The first prisons intended specifically for juveniles opened their doors in the second part of the 19th century. It was quickly apparent, however, that they were completely ineffective at preventing recidivism. What was already well documented for adult prisons – that they were crime schools and incubators for criminal networks – was evident for institutions intended at juveniles as well. As was the case in the adult system, juvenile detention centres seemed to be far more efficient at training future gang members than at re-educating their clients to become law-abiding citizens. It is during this era that, closely following a system initiated by the Massachusetts legislature in 1876, the first probation sentences were introduced in Canada. Probation was seen as a middle-of-the-road punishment for first-time offenders, who were informed by the court that the probation officer assigned to their case could send them to prison at any time, without notice or warning.

During this time, industrialization and a significant movement of immigrants towards the cities were accompanied by an important rise in crime rates. Reformers and conservatives alike demanded new laws and measures to deal with crime, which eventually led to the adoption of the 1892 Canadian *Criminal Code*. The reform introduced specific measures related to the treatment of juvenile delinquents. For example, minor offences and misdemeanours committed by individuals under the age of 16 were to be handled in a separate and distinct trial procedure. Children under the age of 7 could never be found guilty of a criminal offence, and trials of juveniles were not to be subject to public discussions. Both the right and the left wings of the political spectrum regarded this reform as far too timid, arguing for more vigorous changes towards either tougher measures or increased leniency.

In their analysis of press coverage in Montreal and Toronto between April 1907 and July 1908 related to discussion of a new law dealing with crime, Dubois and Trépanier (1999) show that press columnists of the two main Canadian cities of that time shared the general fear that crime rates[2] among youth were increasing. In fact, as the editorials reviewed by the two researchers show, the new law was essentially designed for these two cities in terms of institutions and state apparatus. The ways in which these institutions were to be used, however, varied: Toronto's public opinion makers argued for increased disciplinary measures and punitive actions against delinquents, while Montreal's columnists pleaded that youths should be seen as suffering from family neglect and therefore should be treated more leniently.[3]

With the enactment of the *Juvenile Delinquents Act* (JDA) in 1908, it seemed that the liberal reformers had succeeded. The JDA included measures and sentencing processes that seemed to rest more on the premises of social work than on punitive objectives. Instead of punishing a youth who was found guilty, the key legal construct was the determination that the youth was "in a state of delinquency." The new law paid very little attention to the criminal act itself, focusing instead on the social, familial, and personal deficiencies that were thought to be the main causes of delinquent behaviour. The delinquent was to be seen as a child who had suffered from a lack of effective parental and social supervision and, accordingly, the state would have to assume this role, a principle articulated in the *parens patriae* doctrine (Latin for parent of the country), which refers to the inherent jurisdiction of the courts to make decisions concerning people who are not able to take care of themselves. Probation dispositions were seen as the best way for state-sponsored justice representatives to achieve the goal of assisting parents in educating youths about the best social conduct to adopt. The law went further with measures intended at replacing parents by removing youths from their family and making them temporary wards of the juvenile court under the delegated supervision of a probation officer. Longer or permanent placements as wards of the superintendent of child welfare would be under the temporary supervision of a social worker or a foster family, with the possibility of permanent placement with the latter. The notion of proportionality between the seriousness of the alleged criminal conduct and the severity of punishment was more or less abandoned in favour of considering the delinquent as suffering from various deficiencies that the system would have to work on until the youth could be considered "cured" and fit to live freely in society.

When the JDA was implemented in the new provinces of Canada, there were major differences in the way it was applied. Partly because of the sentencing flexibility that was allowed by provincial youth correctional systems, these provincial systems derived policies tailored to local public opinion. Thus in some Canadian provinces probation sentences did not require a time limit and could be enforced until the youth reached age 21. Probation dispositions varied so much provincially that a delinquent in one province could have their probation order last 10 times longer than the same probation order in another province. These provincial disparities were so substantial that in some cases adult sentences were considered a fairer outcome. The disparities prevailed in varying degrees until the *Juvenile Delinquency in Canada* report was published in 1965.

Based on the century-old legal principle that federal statutes, especially criminal laws, should be applied as uniformly as possible in all provinces, the *Juvenile Delinquency in Canada* report was extremely critical of the enormous variability in how juvenile delinquents were processed dispositionally:

> Thus an adult sent to a federal prison in one part of Canada receives the same treatment as a similar adult sent to another penitentiary in a different part of the country … At the present time children are treated differently. The treatment and services accorded to children adjudged delinquent under the federal statute are provided entirely by provincial authorities. The degree of prosperity and social conscience of the province in which they live usually determine the adequacy of the treatment they receive. (p. 26)

The 1965 report revealed yet another important inequity involving the blurred policy lines between the federal JDA and provincial child protection statutes generally, and by province. For example, vagrancy could be treated either as a social problem dealt with by the child protection services in one province or as a delinquent act in another, which then involved the juvenile court:

> The distinction between a "neglected" and a "delinquent" child is in some respects an artificial one. Viewed in terms of his behavioural problem, the delinquent child is usually one who has suffered some form of deprivation – a deprivation in many cases of a nature sufficient to justify proceedings for neglect under child welfare legislation. In some provinces a child coming from a certain home environment will be charged and adjudged as a delinquent in proceedings before the juvenile court. In another province, coming from the same kind of home environment, he will be dealt with as a so-called "protection" or "neglect" case, against whom no charge is laid and no adjudication is made. In the first case, having been labelled a delinquent, the child is likely to be scorned by the public as a young malefactor. In the second case, because he is found to be a neglected child, and needing protection, he is the object of public sympathy and understanding. Yet in both cases the act or error or omission that brings the child to the attention of the authorities is the same. (p. 43)

In comments that reflected the beginning of Labelling theory, the authors of the 1965 report even identified the potential dangers of the use of the essential JDA legal construct, "delinquent":

Most of those who have addressed themselves to the question of terminology have been concerned with the problem of stigma. What is in issue are the possible effects of what is called "labelling." "To a child and his family," the Ontario Probation Officers Association suggests, "there is a vast difference between telling him that he has committed a delinquency and telling him that he is a juvenile delinquent."... Not infrequently, we have been informed, lesser offences committed by juveniles are not prosecuted at all because there is a reluctance on the part of the police, the courts and other authorities to have to charge and brand a child as a juvenile delinquent in order to enforce the law." (p. 36)

Regarding the growing political concern about the perceived increase in adult serious crime and actual custody rates, the 1965 report pointed out that the JDA provincial systems had had no measurable effect on adult recidivism rates across Canada. Researchers consulted by the commissioners also reported that the JDA seemed to have had no measurable impact on criminal rates for youth in Canada. Part of the explanation for these outcomes, or lack of effectiveness, was attributed to the above provincial sentence discrepancies and, more generally, the little or no relationship between the severity of the sentence and the severity, that is, harm of the alleged delinquent act. Again, another critical concern in this report was that probation orders affected not only adjudicated delinquents, but also, unfairly, their parents. Too often the latter were labelled or considered by the youth court and public opinion as both incompetent parents and primarily responsible for their child's delinquency. By the late 1960s, other common law jurisdictions, mainly manifested in landmark United States Supreme Court cases such as *Kent* (383 US 541 (1966)) and *In re Gault* (387 US 1 (1967)), proffered fundamental criticisms of laws such as the JDA because they provided neither rehabilitation nor fundamental procedural safeguards for youth adjudicated delinquents. There were three major legislative attempts to replace the JDA, but reform required 16 years and, arguably, the enactment of the Canadian Charter of Rights and Freedoms in 1982 for it to occur.

In 1981, the Liberal government proposed a "revolutionary" youth law, historically unprecedented in its scope. In contrast to the 1908 JDA legislative experience that involved only a few hours of discussion in the House of Commons before being quickly passed into law, the 1981 proposed *Young Offenders Act* (YOA) required three years of vigorous parliamentary debates among the political parties and interest groups ranging from the Canadian Bar Association (particularly, defence counsels) to police unions to the association of social workers. As mentioned above, the repatriation of the Canadian constitution from Great Britain in 1982 had a considerable effect on the YOA debate and how senior bureaucrats in the Ministry of the Solicitor General (responsible for drafting the YOA), and related provincial ministries, drafted key segments of the Act. Under the 1982 constitutional provisions, the Canadian Charter of Rights and Freedoms would have a higher precedence than all parliamentary laws. There was little doubt that some of the central legal principles of the 1908 JDA would had been declared unconstitutional had it remained in effect (Corrado, Bala et al., 1992).

The YOA was finally enacted and took effect in April 1984. The previous *parens patriae* doctrine that provided the juvenile court enormous latitude was replaced by a more balanced legal philosophy that combined the previous JDA welfare model principle of meeting the "special needs" of young person with ensuring full procedural safe- guards/rights, proportional sentencing, deterrence, and protecting society from the effects of recidivism. Once again, the provinces were required to pass parallel legislation to implement the YOA. Each province created policies, procedures, and programs to deal with youth offending based on its own political and cultural priorities, as occurred under the 1908 JDA.[4]

As mentioned above, there was considerable variation in how the provinces could implement the two main principles of the YOA: making youth more responsible for their actions and protecting society from recidivism, and the rights of young offenders to fair treatment and access to due process. Regarding the latter principle, the right to access to the appeal process was held to be equal to that guaranteed to any adult, as was the need to be represented by a defence attorney. This fair procedure principle resulted, in certain provinces, in a substantial increase in the number of court hearings and a decrease in treatment orders. In effect, the principle that youth courts should always take into consideration personal characteristics/needs and socio-economic background appeared diminished in several provinces, including Ontario and Manitoba (Corrado & Markwart, in Corrado, Bala et al., 1992).

This shift away from the welfare principle in these provinces accentuated the already existing sentencing discrepancies among provinces, especially in Quebec. In this province, particularly since the end of the 1970s, sentencing of young offenders to established treatment programs intended for youth in need of social protection has been the responsibility of one institution: the youth centres. Each one of the 13 administrative regions in Quebec had and still has its own centre, located frequently in historic buildings constructed and occupied by religious congregations. Roman Catholic, Protestant, and Jewish organizations had been responsible for providing social protection in the province for most of its history.

With the enactment of the YOA in 1984, certain senior officials responsible for the administration of youth centres chose to diminish the traditional emphasis on community networks and private charities in favour of highly institutionalized or government-based programs. As discussed in more detail in Chapter 11, this major bureaucratic shift in administering youth protection in Quebec gradually led to blurring in the processing and the delivery of programs for youth in need of social protection and youth sentenced as young offenders. While this change to increased bureaucracy and emphasis on government institutions for young offenders occurred first in Quebec, the trend appeared eventually in other provinces in the unexpected and unintended rise in young offender incarceration rates, which, at the national level, increased steadily until at least 1993 (Doob & Sprott, 2007). Several renowned academics asserted that Canada had the dubious distinction of having one of the highest youth incarceration rates among westernized countries (Bala, Carrington, & Roberts, 2009), even surpassing the United States (Hogeveen, 2005). This incarceration trend led to intense debates among academics about whether the YOA was too punitive or crime control focused (see, for instance, Doob & Sprott, 2004, 2005, and 2006; Hogeveen, 2006).[5]

In addition, general population surveys in the 1990s showed increasing public demand for even tougher measures against youth crime. This public reaction was significant because, for the first time in Canadian history, youth justice became an important national political issue. Even though the Liberals won a majority of seats for the third time in a row in the 2000 Canadian elections, a recently created political party, the Reform Party based in Alberta, had emerged with increased numbers of Members of Parliament based on public safety and security, low taxes, and anti-"big government" issues. The political push for a more "crime control" youth justice law became the impetus for another major reform of the relatively recently enacted YOA, even though there were definitive and substantial downward trends or declines in youth crime across all Canadian provinces/territories (Taylor-Butts & Bressan, 2008).

The 2000s and the Discussions around Reform of the Law

While the Liberal governments had previously initiated major reviews and attempts to reform the YOA, especially regarding amendments for increased sentencing lengths for the serious violent offences (Corrado &

Markwart, 1996), discussions around a new law began in earnest during the initial months of 2000. An essential part of the process of drafting the new law involved seconding several of Canada's leading academic researchers, including Professor Nicholas Bala from Queen's University Faculty of Law and Professor Anthony Doob from the University of Toronto Centre for Criminology & Sociolegal Studies. In addition, various meetings were held across Canada where the federal Ministry of Justice responsible for drafting the new law, sought critical feedback from other academics, but, even more importantly, from key senior policy officials and ministers from each province and territory. Importantly, then, the federal government appeared to have considered the inclusion of a wide range of input into the construction of the proposed YCJA, and, not surprisingly, this act emerged as one of the most extensive and complicated pieces of criminal justice legislation in Canadian history. In this regards, the YCJA is not different from other modern legislations in the criminal field, which are generally growing in length. As such, the YCJA has an enormous number of sections and subsections designed to provide exact details to guide youth justice officials in implementing its vast range of philosophical principles.

The proposed reform reaffirmed the objective of re-socializing youth, while protecting society from potentially violent acts committed by them. The idea of re-socialization was accompanied by new sentencing principles that were intended to recognize the importance of proportionality between the seriousness of the offence and the severity of the sentence. Under the YOA, the courts had recognized that the principle of proportionality could play a role in youth sentencing, but it was not formally recognized in the legislation and its importance was not clearly affirmed, as it is in the YCJA.

The new sentencing principles emphasize that a youth sentence must not be more severe than what an adult would receive for the same offence, be similar to youth sentences in similar cases, and be proportionate to the seriousness of the offence and the degree of responsibility of the adolescent. The principles also state that "all available sanctions other than custody that are reasonable in the circumstances should be considered for all young persons, with particular attention to the circumstances of aboriginal young persons" (YCJA, 2003). Custody sentences are to be reserved primarily for violent offenders and serious repeat offenders. As can be seen, the YCJA tends to restrict the use of custody. At the same time, probably in order to respond to public demands for tougher measures, the new Act provided that for severe offences, offenders over 14 years could be given adult sentences. This provision created significant turmoil in the more progressive parts of the country, especially among those involved with Quebec's youth intervention system.[6] To some extent, debate over this issue seems to have overshadowed review of the more lenient aspects of the proposed reform, which were seldom discussed.

Regarding these more lenient measures, the bill proposed redefining police discretionary powers in order to increase police discretion over pressing charges for youth who commit petty crimes and misdemeanours. The YCJA also improved sentencing options, notably by replacing the usual custody order with a custody and supervision order, though easing the reintegration of a young person into community after being released. The immediate family was to be integrated in the process, especially with regard to the conditions their son or daughter would have to fulfil while under supervision (imposed curfew, appropriate social behaviour and conduct, etc.).

Once again, as it has been the case on numerous occasions and for a wide range of different issues, the proposed reform seemed to place Quebec in opposition to the other provinces. The Quebec politicians and the state-supported youth intervention system were vigorously opposed to the reinstated proportionality principle. The youth system in particular considered proportionality to be at odds with the social intervention programs designed and administered by the 13 youth centres, as these programs saw juvenile delinquency as a social and personal problem that should be cured, rather than as something that should involve punishment. Quebec and its institutions considered the way they dealt with intervention to be more efficient and less punitive than what was happening in the rest of Canada. As this book tries to show, however, such an understanding of how youth delinquency treatment was and is conducted in the English-speaking provinces may rest on a Manichaean divide that does not actually exist. Youth delinquency and criminality in Canada has been dealt with in ways that are as diverse as the history, tradition, and social diversity of the different parts of the country. Recognizing the barriers of language and tradition that exist between Quebec and the rest of the country might help us to better understand why Quebec reacted as it did during discussions in Ottawa and the provincial capitals of what would come to be known as the *Youth Criminal Justice Act*. Regarding the law's content and the political discussions held in Ottawa during the early 2000s, in retrospect it appears that the federal government might have been trying to respond to public opinion from most provinces in Canada, including

Quebec, and therefore advocated that the new law include more punitive measures and sanctions. However, the social and financial costs of sentencing large numbers of adolescents to closed confinement had also become impossible to ignore, and legal changes had to take these costs into account by proposing alternatives to incarceration.

From 2003 and Beyond: Canada under the YCJA

The *Youth Criminal Justice Act* was passed in 2002 and came into force in April 2003. It contains a Declaration of Principle applicable to the entire Act. But contrary to the YOA, which relied upon its general Declaration of Principle to guide all provisions, the YJCA explicitly states the purpose, principles, and factors to be considered when sentencing young persons. Aiming at reducing custody and allowing for more use of community-based sentences, the YCJA adds new sentencing options: a reprimand, an intensive support and supervision program order, a program attendance order, a deferred custody and supervision order, and an intensive rehabilitative custody and supervision order. As was the case under the YOA, other sentencing options include absolute discharge, conditional discharge, fine, compensation or restitution order, community service order, prohibition order (e.g., weapons), probation, and open custody or secure custody. The YCJA also replaces transfers to adult court with a system of adult sentencing, permitting that some juveniles receive adult sentences in certain circumstances, but through the youth court justice system.

In retrospect, there is absolutely no doubt, regardless of the political discussions that occurred before the enactment of the YCJA (Hogeveen, 2005), that the new law did not call for more severe sentences for delinquent juveniles. Almost immediately after enactment of the YCJA, Statistics Canada documented these trends:

> The rate of youth admitted to the community under a deferred custody order has grown 15% since 2003/2004, according to nine jurisdictions that have reported data. ... The rate for youth aged 12 to 17 years entering custody declined 5% from the previous year and 30% from 2003/2004. Since 2003/2004, the number of youth admitted to sentenced custody for property offences has decreased by over half. As a result, the composition of youth entering custody has shifted whereby the largest proportion (39%) was admitted for violent offences. (Kong, 2009, p. 5)
>
> During the first year following the enactment of the YCJA, custody rates dropped by 38% (from 15 to 9 youth out of 10 000), the biggest drop in the

Figure 1.1 Youth accused of crime, by clearance status, Canada, 2001–2011

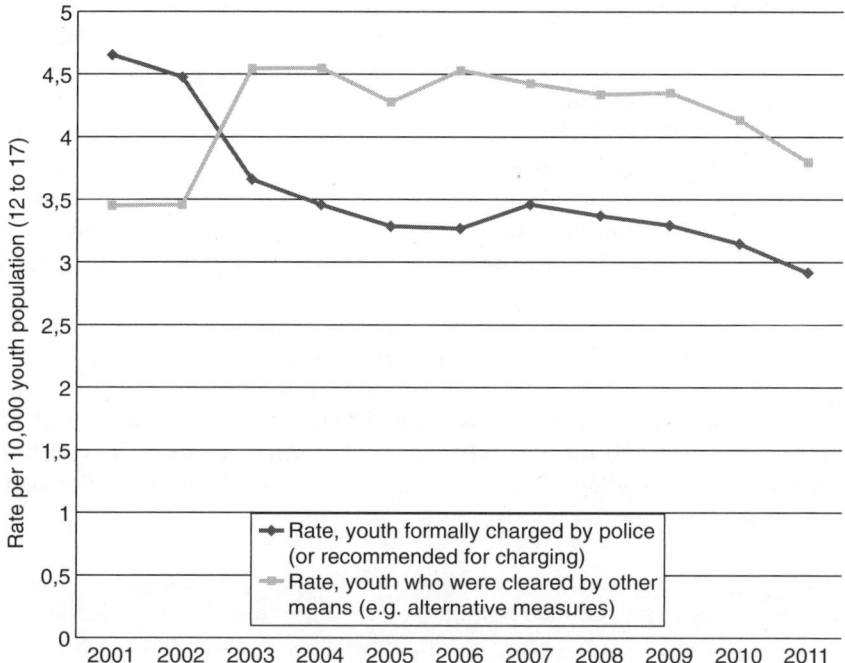

Source: Statistics Canada, Canadian Centre for Justice Statistics, Uniform Crime Reporting Survey.

last ten years. During 2004–2005, the custody rate remained stable and, in 2005–2006, it dropped to 8 youth out of 10 000. (Calverley, 2007, p. 6)

Perhaps, however, one of the most striking effects of the YCJA has been the increasing numbers of young offenders who are now treated outside the judicial apparatus through what is referred to in the law as alternative extrajudicial measures, as the above figure from Statistics Canada clearly shows.

Even among youths found guilty by the courts, the sentences clearly showed a tendency towards solutions other than custody, whether closed or open. Such a tendency was, however, not equally present in all provinces, as this excerpt from a 2007 Statistics Canada report clearly shows:

In the second year of the YCJA, admissions to provincial and territorial sentenced custody decreased 7% from 4,800 in 2003/2004 to 4,400 in 2004/2005. Admissions to secure custody declined 12%, while open custody admissions were relatively unchanged (−1%). Jurisdictions varied in the change in admissions to both open and secure custody. Between 2003/2004 and 2004/2005, the percent change in admissions to secure custody ranged from a 41% decline in Nova Scotia to increases of 19% in Manitoba and 33% in the Northwest Territories. There was also some variation in admissions to open custody among jurisdictions, ranging from a 40% decline in Nova Scotia to a 45% increase in the Northwest Territories. (Calverley, 2007, p. 4)

As Bala (2003) noted shortly before the enactment of the new law and restated five years later (Bala, Carrington, & Roberts, 2009), the measures and sentences proposed in the YCJA should be understood not as being increasingly punitive and correlated as much as possible with the seriousness of the alleged crime but as being tailored to the problems of youths and their social history:

This legislation states in its preamble that the youth justice system "reserves its most serious intervention for the most serious crimes." The new Act implements a larger array of extrajudicial measures and, when entering the formal system, encourages the use of a number of new community supervision options – including deferred custody, the community portion of a custody and supervision order, and an intensive support and supervision order. (Calverley, 2007, p. 2)

The federal legislation seems to have fostered provincial approaches similar to the one favoured in Quebec, that is, to make sentenced adolescents the responsibility of the ministries of Health and Social Services, and Family rather than the Ministry of Community Safety and Correctional Services. Generally speaking, under the YOA as well as under the JDA, the Canadian provinces had kept these two mandates under separate institutions, with the ministries of Social Services and Family Affairs responsible for youth social protection, while ministries of Public Safety and Correctional Services were responsible for youth sentencing. During the first few years of the YCJA, however, some of the provinces started to rearrange their youth justice systems to resemble what had been done in Quebec since the time of the French Regime.

Concluding Remarks

Anyone reading this chapter now, some 10 years after the enactment of the YCJA, is surely thinking: "And where are we now?" At least two aspects of the YCJA, discussed in the last few pages, have changed the way delinquent or criminal youth are treated: (a) since 2003, a growing number have avoided official judicial procedures because police officers or other agents have made use of the alternative extrajudicial measures now available to deal with first offenders and/or those who commit less serious offences; (b) even for those found guilty of more serious offences or of repeated offences, custody has gradually come to be seen as a last resort, one that should be used only after all other available means and resources have been tried, including supervision within the community or by more official institutions. It is also noteworthy that enactment of the YCJA and the gradual adaptation of its regulations were not accompanied by any significant shift in the statistics of crimes committed by adolescents in Canada. According to Taylor-Butts and Bressan, the reported youth crime rate in 2006 "was up 3% over the previous year, but remained 6% lower than the rate a decade earlier and 25% below the 1991 peak" (Taylor-Butts & Bressans, 2006: 1).

That being said, while it is reassuring to see that the changes introduced by the YCJA were not accompanied by a crime wave, it is important to recognize that the trend towards lower crime rates had begun much earlier than 2003. In other words, it remains to be proven that any change in the law, such as the passage from the YOA to the YCJA in Canada, can significantly affect the general crime statistics (Ferson, 1994 ; Clarke, 1992).

As for the general drop in the youth incarceration rate, which, without any doubt, is directly linked to the reform, it might be important to note that it was not uniform throughout Canada, with some provinces even experiencing a new rise:

> The largest drop in the youth incarceration rate was reported in Newfoundland and Labrador, down 58% between 2005/2006 and 2010/2011. In contrast, the rate in Manitoba rose 38% over the same period. (Calverley, 2007: 1)

Another troubling statistics reveals a difference in the way the measures in the YCJA seem to have affected different populations in Canada:

Aboriginal youth tend to be over-represented in correctional services. Among the reporting jurisdictions in 2010/2011, Aboriginal youth accounted for 26% of the youth admitted to the correctional system, yet represented 6% of the general youth population. (Calverley, 2007: 1)

The rest of this book is dedicated to discussing the sometimes widely different experiences and arrangements various Canadian provinces have implemented in their justice systems in order to comply with the *Youth Criminal Justice Act*, the third and most recent law dealing with youth, crime, and Canadian society.

NOTES

1 "A child under the age of seven was deemed incapable of committing a criminal act. This same immunity from prosecution was extended to children aged seven to thirteen inclusive, but the presumption of incapacity could be rebutted by establishing that the child had sufficient intelligence and experience to know the nature and consequences of the conduct and to appreciate that it was wrong. Thus, while the *doli incapax* defence afforded certain protections to children, it could not be applied in every case. As a final result, children who were convicted faced the same penalties as did adult offenders, including hanging and incarceration in prisons for adults." Retrieved October 2, 2014 from http://www.justice.gc.ca/eng/abt-apd/icg-gci/jj2-jm2/jj2-jm2.pdf.
2 Throughout this book, the expressions "youth crime rates" and "crime rates" are to be understood as "reported (youth) crime rates" or "recorded (youth) crime rates," unless specifically reported as "actual" rates.
3 Curiously enough, at that time, the language difference seemed not to be an issue: Montreal's English press agreed with its French counterpart in asking for more social intervention rather than more punitive measures.
4 As discussed in greater detail in chapter 11, Quebec seems to have treated delinquent youth differently than the other provinces. A closer analysis of the situation in Quebec, however, revealed that these differences were due largely to the substantial re-engineering of the social affairs apparatus that took place in the late 1970s and really began to show its true effects in the early 1980s.
5 Doob and Sprott (2004, 2005, and 2006) repeated that no available data support the claim made by some observers of the Canadian youth justice system

– Hogeveen (2005; 2006) for instance – that Canadian law might have been "tougher" than what was practised elsewhere in westernized countries. Sprott (2006), however, clearly demonstrated that Canada's use of custodial sentences for youth that failed to comply with conditions imposed under previous non-custodial sentences rose continually between 1991 and 2003.

6 This specific provision was contested in court by Quebec's authorities, a case eventually won in Appeal Court in 2004 and further confirmed by the Supreme Court in 2008 (*R. v. D. B.*, 2008 CSC 25).

REFERENCES

Bala, N. (2003). *Youth criminal justice law.* Toronto, ON: Irwin Law.

Bala, N., & Anand, S. (2012). *Youth criminal justice law*, 3rd ed. Toronto, ON: Irwin Law.

Bala, N., Carrington, P., & Roberts, J. (2009). Evaluating the Youth Criminal Justice Act after five years: A qualified success. *Canadian Journal of Criminology and Criminal Justice, 51*(1), 131–167.

Canada, Department of Justice. (2004). *The evolution of juvenile justice in Canada.* Ottawa, ON: The International Cooperation Group – Department of Justice Canada.

Clarke, R. V. (1992). *Situational crime prevention: Successful case studies.* Albany, NY: Harrow and Heston.

Calverley, D. (2007). Youth custody and community services in Canada, 2004/2005. *Juristat,* 27(2).

Corrado, R. R., Bala, N., & LeBlanc, M. (Eds.). (1992). *Juvenile justice in Canada: A theoretical and analytic assessment.* Toronto, ON: Butterworths.

Corrado, R. R., & Markwart, A. (1992). The evolution and implementation of a new era in juvenile justice in Canada. In R. R. Corrado, N. Bala, R. Linden & M. L. Blanc (Eds.), *Juvenile justice in Canada: A theoretical and analytical assessment.* Toronto, ON: Butterworths.

Corrado, R. R., & Markwart, A. (1996). The modified justice model experiment in Canada: Success or failure? In D. J. Shoemaker (Ed.), *International handbook on juvenile justice.* Westport, CT: Greenwood Press.

Doob, A. N., & Sprott, J. B. (2004). Changing models of youth justice in Canada. In M. Tonry & A. N. Doob (Eds.), *Crime and justice: A review of the research* (vol. 31). Chicago, IL: University of Chicago Press.

Doob, A. N., & Sprott, J. B. (2006a). Assessing punitiveness in Canadian youth justice. *Punishment & Society, 8*(4), 477–480.

Doob, A. N., & Sprott, J. B. (2006b). Punishing youth crime in Canada. The blind men and the elephant. *Punishment & Society, 8*(2), 223–233.

Doob, A. N., & Sprott, J. B. (2007). The sentencing of aboriginal and non-aboriginal youth: Understanding local variation. *Canadian Journal of Criminology and Criminal Justice,* 49(1), 109–123.

Dubois, P., & Trépanier, J. (1999). L'adoption de la Loi sur les jeunes déliquants de 1908: Étude comparée des quotidiens montréalais et torontois . *Revue d'histoire de l'Amérique française, 52,* 345–381.

Felson, M. (1994). *Crime and everyday life: Insights and implications for society.* Thousand Oaks, CA: Pine Forge Press.

Hogeveen, R. B. (2005). If we are tough on crime, if we punish crime, then people get the message. *Punishment & Society,* 7(1), 73–89.

Hogeveen, R. B. (2006). Memoir of a/the blind: A reply to Doob and Sprott. *Punishment & Society,* 10.1177/1462474506067568(8), 469–475. doi: 10.1177/1462474506067568

Kong, R. (2009). Youth custody and community services. *Juristat, 29*(2), 26.

Normand, S. (1999). De la difficulté de rendre une justice rapide et peu coûteuse: Une perspective historique (1840–1965). *Les Cahiers de droit, 40*(1), 13–31.

Sprott, J. B. (2006). The use of custody for failing to comply with a disposition cases under the Young Offenders Act. *Canadian Journal of Criminology and Criminal Justice, 48*(4), 609–622.

Taylor-Butts, A., & Bressan, A. (2008). La criminalité chez les jeunes au Canada, 2006. *Juristat, 28*(3), 1–17.

Youth Criminal Justice Act. (2003). Art. 38, s. 2, Ss. (d.).

2 The Youth Justice System: An Alberta Overview

CRYSTAL HINCKS AND JOHN WINTERDYK

About Alberta

Alberta is located in the western prairies of Canada, with British Columbia to its west, Saskatchewan to the east, the Northwest Territories along its northern border, and the American state of Montana along its southern border. With Calgary and Edmonton being the major cities, Alberta's population is just over 4 million (Statistics Canada, 2014). Alberta has a First Nations population of approximately 250,000 that makes up 45 First Nations in three treaty areas, and 140 reserves on approximately 812,000 hectares of reserve land (Government of Alberta, 2012). With an abundance of natural resources, such as land, energy, and forest resources, Alberta maintains a thriving economy, as well as a competitive business climate. In 2010, the province successfully recovered from the global recession and expanded by 3.3%, and over the past two decades has led all provinces in economic growth (Government of Alberta, 2012). Furthermore, Albertans pay low personal income taxes and do not pay provincial sales tax. Combined with a publicly administered health care system, lower than national average gasoline prices, and affordable housing costs and property taxes, Alberta is a province that is prone to emigration[1] from other provinces by individuals and families drawn to the highest employment rate in the country – the January 2014 unemployment rate was 4.7% – coupled with a comparatively low cost of living (Government of Alberta, 2014a).

The 2006 Canadian census indicated that in Alberta there were 224,810 youths between the ages of 10 and 14, and 489,285 youths between the ages of 15 and 24. Combined, these two age groups made-up nearly one-quarter (21.7%) of Alberta's 2006 population (Statistics

Canada, 2007). By law, children and youth in Alberta (and Canada at large) are required to attend school up to the age of 16. According to official provincial data, approximately 72% – or 76% including drop-out and returning rates – of youths in Alberta complete high school (Government of Alberta, 2006).

History of Youth Justice in Alberta

"There are no easy victories to be won in the war against crime"

(Wyman, 1977, p. 130)

Canada has seen several shifts over the last century with respect to the ways that young offenders are dealt with by the justice system (Carrigan, 1998). However, as Wyman (1997) points out: "Canada has always been a follower, never a leader, of the United States in the field of juvenile justice" (p. 20). As described in Chapter 1, prior to the introduction of the *Juvenile Delinquents Act* in 1908, young offenders were not differentiated from adults in the justice system. Children and adolescents who broke the law were subjected to the same arrest processes, trial procedures, prison sentences, and even hangings as their adult counterparts (Bala & Anand, 2004). By the turn of the 20th century, several reformist groups had become outraged at the uncivil and harsh punishments that children and youth were faced with, and demanded change. The result was a ju-venile court reform in which young criminals would be treated by civil process (Bala & Anand, 2004) (see Chapter 1 for a more detailed histori-cal overview of the youth justice system in Canada).

The maximum age at which a youth could be prosecuted under the JDA varied from province to province; in Alberta, it was set at 16 for boys and 18 for girls. Alberta was the only province that used the age differential to define a "child." While the age limits were determined in the province almost immediately after the JDA was enacted, a for-mal youth court was not actually established in major cities (specifically Calgary and Edmonton) until 1917 (Sutherland, 2000). In the interim, local police magistrates or probation officers in Alberta (from the then Department of Neglected and Dependent Children) held youth court proceedings in their offices. This, understandably, led to vastly differ-ent interpretations of the Act. Particularly, each province had its own set of legislative statutes, which directly affected the manner in which youth were dealt with. Alberta, for example, had 39 provincial statute enactments which, compared to the two that New Brunswick had, created significant differences in the numbers of youth being dealt with by the JDA (Sutherland, 2000).

As described by Winterdyk (forthcoming), the JDA was characterized as a "welfare model" that focuses on informality, relies on childcare experts as key personnel, has social workers serve as the key agencies of contact, and provides diagnosis and treatment. However, in practice, the Act was not nearly as protective of the welfare of young persons as it (see sections 3(2) and 38 of the JDA) seemed (Wyman, 1977). Nevertheless, despite the intentions of such facilities to rehabilitate young persons, punishment often replaced rehabilitation, and many of the incarcerated youths were subjected to physical, psychological, and sexual abuse (Bala & Anand, 2004).

The conditions for children and adolescents under the JDA in Alberta continued to deteriorate until the system was radically altered with the implementation of the controversial *Young Offenders Act* in 1984. In addition to the discriminatory matter of defining a child in Alberta, the legal age of juvenile delinquents (as they were referred to then) was also complicated by sections 74 and 75 of the *Child Welfare Act* of Alberta. Both sections essentially said that no child "apparently or actually under the age of 12" could be held criminally responsible under the JDA. The contradiction and legal inconsistency fuelled considerable controversy. It was perhaps best summarized in a report to the Alberta Board of Review authored by Max Wyman (1977) who lamented that after reflecting on "four years of study of the literature of juvenile delinquency" in Alberta, he concluded that "it is a philosophy whose validity I cannot accept" (p. i).

Under the JDA in Alberta, and in virtually every jurisdiction, the most common first point of contact with the juvenile justice system was/is the police. In Alberta, the police used their discretionary powers to release approximately 75% of all juveniles they came into contact with (Wyman, 1977). And while Edmonton and Calgary had similar outcomes, both cities used slightly different approaches to dealing with juvenile offenders. In 1973 there were about 400,000 young persons residing in Alberta. Of these, between 20,000 and 30,000 had some direct contact with the police. According to Wyman (1977, p. 28), in 1973 only 3,592 juveniles were convicted of delinquency and somewhere between 150 and 250 l trials were held. The most common offence was "breaking and entering" (N = 1,058), followed by theft (N = 907 cases). In terms of dispositions, the most common adjudications were probation, fine, or restitution, followed by "adjourned *sine die.*" The adjudication process clearly reflected a welfare approach and one where the system attempted to practise patience as the young person was growing up and/or to allow the probation officers and social workers to try and improve the family environment (see Box 2.1 below).

Box 2.1 Youth Crime and Justice in Alberta

In a report to the Parkland Institute in 2002 entitled *Youth Crime and Justice in Alberta: Rhetoric and Reality,* author Timothy Hartnagel offered the following example of how a single youth-perpetrated crime can spark controversy and debate about how Alberta deals with young offenders:

In the early hours on April 16th, 1994, Barb Danelesko was awakened by a noise in her home in Mill Woods, a suburban Edmonton neighbourhood. While her husband slept, Danelesko went to check on their children. In doing so, she surprised three young intruders who had broken into the home. Danelesko was fatally stabbed before her husband awoke. Two of the intruders, Sonny Head and David Larocque, both minors at the time, pleaded guilty part way through their trials in adult court. Head was convicted of second-degree murder and sentenced to life in prison without parole eligibility for at least seven years. Larocque was convicted of manslaughter and sentenced to four years without parole eligibility for at least two years. A third youth, who was not named, was convicted under the *Young Offenders Act* and was sentenced to three years, the maximum sentence available in youth court. The murder drew national attention, particularly that of the public, who made calls to change the Act. Demands from politicians and the public included the re-enactment of capital punishment, boot camps, reinstitution of the strap, and possibly most extreme, revoking the Charter of Rights and Freedoms. Then Alberta Premier Ralph Klein told attendees at the premier's dinner, "The outcry is overwhelming from people concerned with youth crime and the punishment it receives, or, more to the point, the punishment it appears not to receive" (Hartnagel, 2002, p. 8). When Sonny Head was granted day parole in 2002, public outrage resurfaced and brought with it new demands that youth justice be effectively dealt with. Fortunately, the government was already in the process of implementing the YCJA, which was to be the answer to the nation's youth crime debate.

Table 2.1 Percentage of cases with findings of guilt committed to custody and per cent change in use of custody in eight provinces for the fiscal years 1984/85 and 1989/90

Province	1984/85	1989/90	% Change
British Columbia	11.2	23.4	+109
Alberta	10.3	18.9	+83
Manitoba	13.9	25.2	+81
Nova Scotia	12.7	22.7	+79
Newfoundland	14.4	24.1	+67
New Brunswick	20.8	31.3	+50
Quebec	28.9	32.1	+11
Saskatchewan	25.2	25.7	+2

Source: Youth Court Survey, 1984/85 and 1989/90.

In Alberta, the crime trends and rates for youth under the YOA increased along with the rest of Canada. Because the YOA had established a uniform minimum age of 12 years and a maximum age of 17 years across the country, there was some consistency among the provinces with respect to the age at which a young offender would be processed through youth courts. There were, however, considerable differences in the use of sanctions between provinces. In Table 2.1 above, the percentage change in the use of custody for eight provinces between 1984/1985, when the YOA was implemented, and 1989/1990, five years later, is indicated. Alberta had the highest percentage increase (+ 83%), second only to British Columbia. It is important to note, however, that while the use of custodial sentences increased with the YOA, the length of the sentences actually decreased. In Alberta, for example, the median lengths of secure custody sentences decreased by two-thirds between 1984/1985 and 1989/90 (Markwart, 1992).

Following several amendments throughout its two decade-long life, the YOA was replaced by the *Youth Criminal Justice Act* (YCJA) in 2003 as a response to the continued dissatisfaction of justice professionals attempting to effectively utilize the YOA legislation (see Green, 2012 and Chapter 1 for further discussion).

In order to rectify the overuse of custodial sentences under the YOA, the Alberta government was considerably proactive before the YCJA was implemented. Jurisdiction in Alberta was split between the Ministry of Justice and Attorney General, which oversees Crown prosecutors, youth justice committees, and extrajudicial sanctions, and the Ministry of the

Table 2.2 Snapshot of the number of youth serving custodial and non-custodial sentences in Alberta on an average day

		2006	2007	2008	2009	2010
Number of youth by sentence	Total Sentenced Custody	112	87	80	74	70
	Sentenced Secure Custody	66	58	58	51	50
	Sentenced Open Custody	45	28	23	23	20
	Total	206	187	179	173	161

Source: Statistics Canada. Table 251-0008.Youth correctional services, average counts of young persons in provincial and territorial correctional services, annual (persons unless otherwise noted), CANSIM (database).

Solicitor General and Public Security, which is responsible for provincial policing and youth corrections (Caputo & Vallée, 2007). The province also introduced an Intensive Rehabilitative Custody and Supervision program and new attendance centres were opened in both Calgary and Edmonton. These were intended to meet the requirements of the new legislation (ibid).

Following a comprehensive review of the YCJA, the Alberta government then made the appropriate updates to provincial legislation before actively training all justice stakeholders. Initial changes to the provincial framework for young offenders included the formation of youth justice committees and the development of policies and procedures surrounding the new sentencing options under the YCJA (Caputo & Vallée, 2007). Since then, Alberta has continued to assertively address youth crime through preventative measures such as the establishment of diversion sanctions, crime prevention initiatives, community support networks, and mental health programming. Arguably, the Alberta government has successfully embraced the philosophy underlying the YCJA. As one probation officer stated during a focus group conducted by DeGusti (2008, p. 35): "There is a different level of accountability now. The philosophy around the Act that says that punishment isn't the answer, we need to address the underlying issues for the young person. There's more of a social work perspective."

Extrajudicial Sanctions

In 2003, coupled with the introduction of the YCJA, the YCJA Extrajudicial Sanctions Program (EJS) was authorized in Alberta by the Honourable David G. Hancock, Q.C., then Minister of Justice and Attorney General following consultation with the Honourable Heather Forsyth, then Solicitor

General for the province. Academics and justice professionals alike agreed that under the YOA, there was little guidance with respect to the use of police discretion (Bala et al., 2010). This program was designed to allow police to utilize their discretion with respect to extrajudicial sanctions based on an established set of criteria, in order to divert youth away from the justice system. While police traditionally had the discretion of using police extrajudicial measures, section 10(1) of the YCJA offers police officers specific sanctions, such as directly diverting a youth to a youth justice committee without first requiring Crown approval. These measures, however, may only be used in relation to the seriousness of the offence, the nature and number of previous offences committed by the young person, or any other aggravating circumstances (Government of Alberta, 2008).

Extrajudicial sanctions offered by a police officer under the YCJA require supervision of the youth to ensure compliance, which is important because if the young person fails to comply with the agreement negotiated, the Crown is unable to take action with respect to the alleged offence. This places considerable onus on the front-line police officers to ensure that both the program is used in only the most appropriate cases, and that there is suitable follow-up by the officer. In most cases, police opt to refer the youth to the Crown, which then refers the young person to the Extrajudicial Sanctions Program.

In addition, there are specific offences that are eligible for the Extrajudicial Sanctions Program (Government of Alberta, 2008):

Federal

- All *Criminal Code* of Canada offences except offences involving violence or the threat of violence, break and enter of a dwelling or house, perjury or contradictory evidence, and all driving-related offences.
- Simple possession offences, such as marijuana or its product contrary to the *Controlled Drugs and Substances Act*. All other drug offences are excluded.

Provincial

- Section 78 of the *Public Health Act* (glue and solvent sniffing)
- *Trespass to Premises Act*
- *Petty Trespass Act*

- *School Act*
- *Gaming and Liquor Act*

Each branch of the Alberta justice system plays a key role in the application of the Extrajudicial Sanctions Program. The police, when it is decided that a police extrajudicial measure is inappropriate, will refer the case to the local chief Crown prosecutor, or a designate, via a notification form, which includes an occurrence report (Government of Alberta, 2014b).

The Crown can exercise one of three initial options: decline to divert the young person, and instead request that a charge be laid in cases where it is believed that program participation is inappropriate; divert the young person through the Extrajudicial Sanctions Program by forwarding the appropriate paperwork to the Correctional Services Division of Alberta Justice and Solicitor General; or to issue a caution letter to the young person that outlines the appropriate behaviour expected of the youth in the future. A caution letter is not used in cases where the victim has suffered damages and the young person has not made full restitution (Government of Alberta, 2008).

The Correctional Services Division, Alberta Justice and Solicitor General, administers the Extrajudicial Sanctions Program either directly, or through the referral of cases received from the Crown to formally designated youth justice committees. Should the youth not comply with outcomes agreed upon through either a corrections-based program or a youth justice committee, the young person may be referred back to the Crown, at which point a charge may be laid (Government of Alberta, 2014a).

A Youth Justice Committee can utilize a maximum of three measures within the Extrajudicial Sanctions Program, which include:

- a personal or written apology to the victim(s);
- personal service to the victim(s);
- community service to a non-profit community or government agency;
- restitution/return of property to the victim(s);
- donation to a registered charity;
- participation in Aboriginal cultural/spiritual activities;
- completion of an essay or poster about the offence and its consequences;

Figure 2.1 Progression of available sanctions. Young offenders are ideally given extrajudicial measures for first and lesser offences. Extrajudicial sanctions are used as the next step in cases where the youth can be diverted from youth courts rather than being formally charged. Probation is often used for youth requiring closer supervision. Lastly, custody is used in more severe cases.

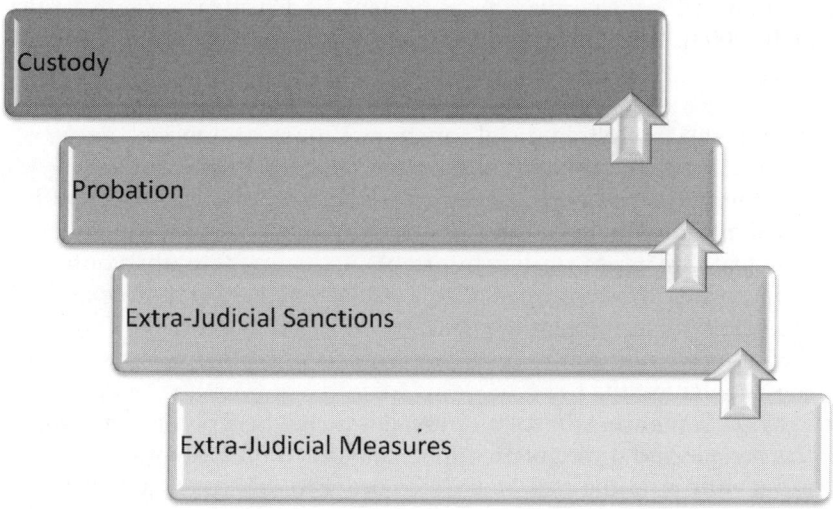

- attendance and participation in an available community counselling or intervention program (Addictions Services, Alberta Mental Health Services, Family and Community Support Services, etc.);
- supervision by a probation officer or other service provider until all conditions of the Extrajudicial Sanctions Program Agreement are completed; and
- participation in victim/offender reconciliation where the victim is available and consents.

The Extrajudicial Sanctions Program in Canada is administered through Youth Justice Committees (YJCs), which were formerly known as Alternative Measures Programs (AMPs) under the YOA. In Alberta, there are 131 YJCs with some 1,500 volunteers, which is the largest number in all of Canada, and the Alberta Justice and Solicitor General's office reports an 80 to 90% success rate (meaning youth who have successfully completed their EJS program requirements) for youth who are dealt with by Youth Justice Committees (Justice and Solicitor General: *Annual Report 2013–14*). Community volunteers on the YJCs work with local police, the court, community corrections, and other community agencies that provide legal services or community services. Professional justice agencies, such as lawyers' offices, Legal Aid, social workers, and probation officers also play an important part (Calgary Youth Justice Society, 2008). Within Alberta, YJCs are sanctioned to perform the following tasks:

- Administer the Extrajudicial Sanctions Program – Once a young person is referred to the program, the YJC will assess the case to determine if the referral was appropriate. In some cases, the youth may have already been through the program, committee members may feel threatened or uncomfortable in dealing with the youth or his or her family, or the youth's issues may be too complex for the program. In these cases, the file will be returned to the Crown through the community corrections office with cited reasons why the YJC denied the file.
- Provide Sentence Advisory – In some cases where a young person has been found guilty of an offence in youth court, a youth court judge may refer the case to a YJC in order to determine an appropriate sentence. While the YJC does not have the final say with respect to the sentence of the youth, committee suggestions are taken under consideration by the judge.
- Public Awareness and Crime Prevention – YJC members often volunteer in other areas of the youth justice field, such as in crime prevention, crime education, and youth mentoring program.

While the EJS Program is first and foremost intended to sanction the offending behaviour of young persons, YJCs often use the involvement of the youth in the program as an opportunity to offer additional and ongoing resources and services to the young person in order to encourage continued success. Based on "relationships, opportunities, and personal qualities that young people need to avoid risks and to thrive" the Developmental Assets list is made up of 40 common sense, positive experiences and qualities that can influence young people to help them make good choices in order to become responsible, successful adults (Search Institute, 2011). Some examples of *external assets* are family support; positive school climate; a caring neighbourhood; service to others; safety; family, school, and neighbourhood boundaries; positive peer influence; creative activities; and time at home. *Internal assets* include achievement motivation, school engagement, integrity, responsibility, planning and decision-making, cultural competence, self-esteem, and sense of power (Search Institute, 2011). YJCs in Alberta are all trained to implement the Search Institute's Developmental Assets framework by offering youth opportunities to build or reinforce new or existing positive assets, such as athletic ability, create pursuits (e.g., art or music), or to explore options such as one-to-one mentoring or counselling (Calgary Youth Justice Society, 2008).

Youth Court Trends in Alberta

In 2013, Statistics Canada released a *Juristat* report on Canadian youth court statistics highlighting the changes within the courts from 2002/2003 (the year prior to the enactment of the YCJA) until 2010/2011 (Brennan, 2013). Some key highlights as they relate to Alberta include:

- In 2002/2003 (during the last year of the YOA), there were 76,204 completed youth court cases in Canada, of which 10,446 (13.7%) were in Alberta.
- In 2010/2011 there were 52,904 completed cases in Canada, with 7,521 (14.2%) of those cases in Alberta.
- Overall, from 2002/2003 to 2010/2011, Canada experienced approximately a 32% reduction in cases, while Alberta experienced about an 18% reduction.
- Under the YOA, the use of the courts and custody had risen to the point that by the early 2000s, Canada had one of the highest incarceration rates in the world, along with one of the lowest rates of youth diversion (Bala et al., 2009).
- In 2002/2003 in Canada, 26.9% of guilty youth were sentenced to custody, while 19.3% of Alberta youth were sentenced to custody. By 2010/2011, the percentage of Canadian youth sentenced to custody had edged up to 16% after being at an all-time low of 15.4% in 2008/2009, and in Alberta only 12.5% of young persons were sentenced to custody (Brennan, 2013).[2]

After the first five years of the implementation of the YCJA, sentences in youth courts changed considerably from the overuse of custody to alternative measures (Bala et al., 2009). As mentioned above, custody use in Canada was reduced to 16% and 12.5% in Alberta, which was

Table 2.3 Sentences in youth courts, Canada, provinces, and territories, 2010–2011

	Custody & supervision	Conditional sentence	Deferred custody and supervision	Intensive support and supervision	Non-residential program attendance	Probation	Fine	Community service	Reprimand	Other
Canada	15.4	0.1	3.8	1.4	0.6	60.3	5.6	24.1	1.8	36.6
Newfoundland/ Labrador	15.6	...	1.8	...	...	70.9	3.8	30.6	1.6	30.4
Prince Edward Island	19.4	...	...	...	...	78.3	14	...	...	15.5
Nova Scotia	11	...	11.2	...	...	64.6	4.4	24.5	3.9	25.6
New Brunswick	12.2	...	11	...	...	47.6	3.7	4	...	18.9
Quebec	12	...	3	0.6	0.5	68.8	4.4	48.9	0.6	38.5
Ontario	20.3	0.2	4	0.1	0.3	68.5	2.6	22.6	3	50.6
Manitoba	6.2	0.1	1.5	...	...	57.3	4.3	13.4	1.1	10.8
Saskatchewan	16.3	...	...	...	...	43.1	5.7	21.8	...	5.3
Alberta	10.5	...	3.7	0.7	2.7	49.7	16.5	17.3	1.8	39.8
British Columbia	15.6	...	5.8	13.5	...	43.2	5.8	16.9	1.2	31.4
Yukon	41.2	...	3.9	...	...	51	3.9	11.8	...	27.5
Northwest Territories	17.3	...	...	...	...	60.3	7.1	...	...	26.3
Nunavut	14.6	...	3.1	...	...	86.2	4.6	...	...	18.5

the second lowest provincial rate (Manitoba had the lowest overall rate of custody sentences at 6.8%). As seen in Table 2.3 probation and other measures were the sentencing options used the most often in Alberta (49.7% and 39.8%, respectively), followed by community service and the payment of fines (17.3% and 16.5%, respectively) (Brennan, 2013).

Workload Changes among Justice Levels

All sectors of the justice system across Canada experienced considerable changes when the YCJA was implemented, including the policing, court, and correctional systems in Alberta. In a comprehensive report submitted to the Alberta Law Foundation by DeGusti (2008), several trends were found to be impacting each level of the judicial system within Alberta. A major overall finding was, as anticipated, a sharp decline in the flow of cases through the various levels of the justice system in Alberta, which was a clear indication that youth were successfully being diverted away from formal punitive measures. It was also found that several departments, including police and probation, experienced various changes to their policies and procedures that both positively and negatively affected their workloads.

Front-line police officers in Alberta noted significant changes in their workloads following the introduction of the YCJA; police-based community supervision programs, such as the Serious Habitual Offender Program (SHOP; see Box 2.2), reported an increase in workload due to the number of serious habitual offenders that were serving their sentences in the community (DeGusti, 2008). While a strategic direction of the YCJA legislation was to have young offenders serving more community-based sentences, DeGusti (2008) reported mixed feelings among front-line police officers with respect to the changes that they experienced under the new YCJA. While the decreasing number of youth being formally charged led to less charge-related paperwork required by officers, the workload to accommodate the extrajudicial measures had increased significantly, and "overall the frontline officers who participated in the study asserted that their workload had increased following the implementation of the YCJA" (p. 8).

Interestingly, DeGusti (2008) found that School Resource Officers (SROs) did not notice a significant change in their workloads, despite their almost exclusive interactions with youth. Major changes experienced by SROs included the necessity to conduct additional research into the background of the youth they were dealing with, the requirement of additional administrative paperwork, as well as staff shortages

Box 2.2 Serious Habitual Offender Program (SHOP)

The Serious Habitual Offender Program (SHOP) targets habitual offenders between the ages of 12 and 21 through community-based prevention and enforcement programming. The majority of youth crimes are committed by a small percentage of habitual offenders. As such, SHOP partners with several key community partners to develop a profile of referred and sentenced youth based on their criminal histories, family backgrounds, living conditions, psychological histories, and other relevant risk factors. The youth are then referred to appropriate programs with the goal of preventing them from offending further.

Partner agencies include:

- Calgary Young Offenders Centre
- Calgary Youth Attendance Centre
- Calgary and Area Child and Family Services
- City of Calgary, Youth Probation Services
- Calgary School Boards
- Calgary Police Service

Source: Calgary Police Service, 2014

---

throughout the province, mainly at junior high schools serving Grades 6 through 9. These challenges, however, are an indication of the challenges faced by police departments in Alberta, and not a result of the YCJA legislation itself. Unfortunately, there have been no reported updated studies of the program.

Regarding the use of extrajudicial measures among front-line police officers and SROs, it was reported that warnings were used more upon the induction of the YCJA. While warnings were previously commonly used by SROs, police officers began using them, coupled with referrals to diversion programs, as a means of dealing with youth committing non-violent crimes, and also for first-time offenders (DeGusti, 2008). Of concern to police officers was the inability to determine if the measures they were implementing were effective, because many extrajudicial measures do not require mandatory completion. However, given that the program has been in existence for a number of years, an updated evaluation is considered to be in order.

A consequence of the YCJA for youth or police officers, depending on how one perceives it, is the amount of discretion available to police officers with respect to charging a youth or simply offering a warning. Police officers in DeGusti's (2008) focus group noted that the new legislation makes it easy for officers to take advantage of their new found discretion by giving warnings simply to decrease their workload. While this frees up the officer to respond to other, potentially more important, calls, there may be instances where the youth has committed a crime that deserves a charge. In addition, officers noted that while they are supposed to report any warnings given, many do not because of the time it takes to complete the report. Instead they issue a verbal warning to the youth and "cut them loose," which results in a lack of accurate statistics about youth crime in Alberta, as well as a decrease in the ability to determine the needs of youth that come into contact with the law (see Box 2.3).

Probation officers in Alberta reported an increase in their workload following the implementation of the YCJA (DeGusti, 2008). It was noted that their caseloads had decreased, however, the nature of their procedures had changed, which resulted in them having to dedicate significantly more time to supervising youth with mental health and drug-related issues, as well as liaising with other members of the judicial system about youth who have committed more serious offences (DeGusti, 2008). Several respondents in DeGusti's (2008) study commented on the steep learning curve for a probation officer under the YCJA. While the number of cases for probation officers has decreased, the complexity of the cases has become such that the officers are often required to do their job with minimal formal training in the abovementioned areas.

In addition, new sentence orders under the YCJA led to an increase in the number of reports required from probation officers, and also the amount of time spent "conferencing, getting information from victims, and justifying recommendations for pre-sentence reports" (p. 10). Lastly, like front-line police officers, probation officers reported a shortage in staffing and resources brought about by having to operate under the new legislation.

Among both police and probation officers in Alberta, there was a general consensus that the YCJA was, and will continue to be, an effective framework for dealing with youth (DeGusti, 2008). Furthermore, both probation and police officers reported consistency under the YCJA, specifically related to the sentencing decisions across different jurisdictions, despite the efforts of the YCJA legislation to prevent such disparities. Police officers from Calgary reported that they felt "youth who violate the conditions of their probation and repeat offenders

Box 2.3 Recent High Profile Youth Crime Cases in Alberta

- In March 2012, while a 17-year-old male from Fort Macleod, who had been violently attacked in his home – which was then set on fire – was recovering in hospital, another Fort Macleod teen was charged with his attempted murder and four counts of arson with disregard for life.
- In January 2012, three Samson Cree reserve youth were charged with manslaughter after Ethan Yellowbird, the grandson of the reserve's chief, Marvin Yellowbird, was fatally shot. The five-year-old victim was sleeping in his bed when a stray bullet from a shooting outside of his bedroom struck him in the head. The shooting was another tragic consequence of the crime-troubled Hobbema community, in which gang violence is prominent.
- In November 2011, a 13-year-old and 14-year-old were each charged with sex-related charges in relation to the assault of a 21-year-old Calmar youth. The victim was lured to an apartment, forced to drink alcohol, and subsequently burned, physically assaulted, cut, and sexually assaulted. The two offenders were charged with assault causing bodily harm, sexual assault, sexual invitation, sexual interference, forcible confinement, and administering a noxious substance.
- In September 2010, a 17-year-old male was charged with second-degree murder after he killed his mother with an axe. The youth was not tried as an adult, despite a court-ordered assessment that indicated he was at a high risk to reoffend. The judge in the case called the murder "brutal, savage, senseless and unexplainable," but rather than moving the case to adult court, decided to sentence the youth to the maximum sentence under the intensive rehabilitative custody and supervision sentencing option of the YCJA.
- In April 2006, a 12-year-old girl and her 23-year-old boyfriend, Jeremy Steinke, murdered the girl's parents and 8-year-old brother because the girl's parents disapproved of her relationship with Steinke. The case attracted significant media attention because of the girl's age. Under the YCJA, 12 is the youngest possible age that a person can be charged with a crime, however, the Act does not allow for youth under 14 to be given more than a 10-year sentence. In what may be one of the most notorious crimes committed by an Alberta youth, the girl was found guilty of three counts of first-degree murder, and became the youngest person in Canada to ever be convicted of a multiple murder.

should be punished more harshly" (p. 10). Probation officers, on the other hand, applauded judges in Calgary for their "'rehabilitative social work approach' to young offenders" (p. 11). Despite the differences between the two groups, both police and probation officers agreed that the principles and philosophy of the YCJA are promising. Yet, in March 2014, Alberta Justice abruptly informed Native Counselling Services of Alberta (successfully operating since the mid-1990s) that it would not be renewing their $80,000 funding allocation to the program due to the decline in the number of Aboriginal youth on probation (Wittmeier, 2014). What the long-term implications will mean for the Aboriginal youth on probation is unclear, but it is perhaps suggestive of a changing sociopolitical climate in the province as well as suggestive of an ideological shift in how youth justice is administered in Alberta.

Programs and Facilities in Alberta

Once a custodial sentence has been determined by the youth court, the case is referred to the Provincial Placement Authority in order to determine where the young offender should be placed. There are several factors taken into account when a young offender is placed in a custodial facility, including the type of custody, age, security risk, custody history, the offence, degree of supervision required, program needs, and the proximity of the placement to family and community resources (Government of Alberta, 2014b). For custodial sentences given to young offenders in Alberta, the youth can be confined to any one of the available secure custody facilities, or can be referred to an open custody group home or work program. Administered by the Ministry of the Solicitor General and Public Safety, each form of custody offers young offenders the opportunity to participate in programs, access services, and prepare for eventual reintegration into society.

Two Alberta young offenders centres, located in Calgary and Edmonton, house youths serving secure custodial sentences. A third centre, located in Grande Prairie, was controversially closed in 2009 due to provincial government budget cuts. Of particular concern following the closure was the movement of youths at the Grande Prairie Young Offenders Centre (GPYOC) to the Edmonton Young Offenders Centre (EYOC). The GPYOC youths would be in a larger population of inmates in the EYOC, thus increasing their exposure to gangs and more serious offenders. In addition, because the GPYOC served the entire northwest corner of the province, families from northern communities had much farther to travel for visits, which led to a disruption of the support network that is instrumental in the efforts of the YCJA. Despite the efforts of affected communities to appeal to the government, the GPYOA was closed in April 2009, and the 10 young offenders housed there were moved to the EYOC (Given, 2009). Again, this may be suggestive of an ideological shift in the administration of youth justice in Alberta, and one that deserves closer study and evaluation.

The remaining two provincial custodial centres, the EYOC and the Calgary Young Offenders Centre (CYOC), "promote positive behaviour change in the young offender's custody, while preparing the young person for reintegration to the community" (Government of Alberta, 2012b, home page). Upon entering a young offenders centre (YOC), each youth is assigned a caseworker who identifies problem areas that the youth will need to work on before release. The caseworker then arranges the appropriate referral to any number of programs or services that are available while the youth is in custody, including:

Education Programs

Under section 3 (i.e., extrajudicial measures – meaning "outside the court") of the YCJA, the provision for educational programs are available to meet any academic and instructional needs that a youth might have. Because all young offenders in custody under the age of 16 are required to attend school, various programs from elementary to high school are available, with a focus on small classes and attention to the specific learning needs of the youth.

At the Calgary Young Offenders Centre (CYOC), the West View School was established to meet the education needs of youth in custody, including programming for addictions, learning disabilities, low literacy rates, low IQ, Fetal Alcohol Spectrum Disorder (FASD), and other emotional, social, psychiatric, and medical needs (Calgary Board of Education, 2014). In addition, West View School oversees a number of programs for youth who are transitioning from custody into the community but who require ongoing structure and support:

• The Calgary Youth Attendance Centre (CYAC) offers high school programming for youth who do not function well in traditional community high school settings and instead require more highly structured programming in an individual or small classroom setting.

- Enviros Wilderness Base Camp offers addiction treatment in a wilderness camp setting. Youth in this program often have severe addiction issues and attend on a voluntary basis.
- ExCEL works with youth with a variety of mental, emotional, social, addiction, and learning needs in a residential setting as they are transitioning back into the community (Calgary Board of Education, 2014).

Life Skills Programs

Life skills programs are available, which give youth basic tools and skills meant to facilitate their reintegration back into the community. Program topics include: stress management, relationship building, decision-making, family violence, budgeting/banking, nutrition, job/employability skills, cooking, health, and so on (Government of Alberta, 2014b).

Work Programs

Alberta youth are also able to participate in work programs, which allow for the development of practical employment skills. Placements may range from meal preparation to kitchen cleaning, or to engaging in community service work that is provided to other government departments, municipalities, and non-profit organizations (Government of Alberta, 2014b).

Recreational Programs

Young offenders are particularly encouraged to participate in comprehensive recreational programming, which promotes mental and physical health as well as fosters their interest in activities that can be pursued once they are released into the community. Activities can include: weight training, various sports, hobbies and handcrafts, Boy Scouts and Cadets, and are available in the evenings and weekends so as not to interfere with school or work programs.

Aboriginal Programs

In 2011 an estimated 13.7% of Alberta's population was comprised of Aboriginal youth between the ages of 15 and 24 (Statistics Canada, 2014b).

Many Aboriginal communities in Alberta face social and economic challenges that contribute to the over-representation of Aboriginal youth in the justice system. Specialized services, coordinated and carried out by Aboriginal elders, are available for young offenders in secure custody to provide spiritual guidance, cultural awareness, sweet grass ceremonies, and sweat lodges.

Medical and Mental Health Programs

All young offenders in secure custody have access to a variety of medical and mental health services, including nursing, dental, psychological, and psychiatric care. A variety of individual and group health programs that vary from centre to centre are available, which target such issues as sex offender treatment, addiction treatment, anger management, sexuality, distress, sexual and physical abuse, parenting, mental health programming, family counselling, trauma, etc.

Youth sentenced to community-based open custody serve their sentences in group homes that are located in Edmonton and Calgary. With staff supervision as the main security feature, young offenders are able to access numerous services in the community, such as education or treatment programs and employment opportunities. Group homes encourage young offenders to maintain contact with family and significant others, and access community resources in preparation for full release into the community (Government of Alberta, 2014b). In addition, group homes, such as Woods Homes and Hull Family Services in Calgary, or ELPIDA for Youth and Enviros ExCEL Group Home in Edmonton, typically not only offer services for the young offender, but for the offender's family as well. Through in-home and out-of-home programs, family breakdown that can occur before, during, or after a young person comes into conflict with the law can be addressed so that the young offender will have a higher chance of successful reintegration into the community. Although Alberta arguably has a diverse range of medical and mental health programs for its youth at risk, the programs are typically marginally funded and staffed (Kim, 2003).

Conclusion

Hylton (1994) astutely noted that society's response to crime has been predominantly and frequently characterized by controversy. The *Juvenile*

Delinquents Act (JDA) of 1908 was highly criticized for a number of reasons. The vague definition of delinquency and its non-adversarial welfare approach, lack of due process rights, disparities in sentencing due to the over-reliance of informality, and lack of uniform implementation across the country made the JDA an easy target of reformists. The new philosophy offered by the *Young Offenders Act* of 1984 appeared to be the response to the issue of youth crime.

It appears that the foremost criticism of the YCJA in Alberta is the lack of resources allowing justice professionals to effectively deal with youth under its legislation. Although policymakers do not have the ability to see around corners, the lack of forethought and planning for the considerable increase in the workloads of affected justice professionals has left both the government and non-government sectors unable to bear the weight of the resulting juvenile justice system. For example, in 2011 when Alison Redford became Alberta's 14th premier, the province's highly success and widely recognized crime prevention initiatives under the banner of the Safe Communities Initiative Fund was suddenly cut, and the province returned to more conventional crime control strategies not only for adults but also for young offenders. The promising principles of the YCJA, therefore, appear to be overshadowed by the frustrations of youth justice practitioners who struggle to offer effective youth measures and sanctions with small budgets and limited numbers of staff. Despite their struggles, efforts by such practitioners in Alberta seem to be having an effect, as evidenced by the falling youth crime rates and decreased utilization of custodial sentences.

NOTES

1 Despite Alberta's ability to attract interprovincial emigration because of its economy, interprovincial emigration has actually been steadily declining since 2006/2007 (during which 33,809 people emigrated to Alberta). In 2010/2011, just 13,660 people emigrated to Alberta. And perhaps most notable, in 2009/2010, there was an inverse total, after 3,271 more people left the province than entered it. See Statistics Canada, http://www.statcan.gc.ca/pub/91-215-x/2011000/t465-eng.htm.
2 A major change to the YOA is the YCJA's mandate that part of a youth's custodial change must be served in the community under supervision (Bryant, 2003).

REFERENCES

Bala, N., & Anand, S. (2004). The first months under the Youth Criminal Justice Act: A survey and analysis of case law. *Canadian Journal of Criminology and Criminal Justice, 46*(3), 251–271.

Bala, N., Carrington, P. J., & Roberts, J. V. (2010). Evaluating the success of the Youth Criminal Justice Act after five years: A qualified success. *Canadian Journal of Criminology and Criminal Justice, 51*(2), 131–167.

Baron, S. W., & Hartnagel, T. F. (1996). "Lock 'em up": Attitudes toward punishing juvenile offenders. *Canadian Journal of Criminology, 4*, 191–212.

Brennan, S. (2013). Youth court statistics 2010/2011. *Juristat* article. Retrieved from http://www.statcan.gc.ca/pub/85-002-x/2012001/article/11645-eng.htm.

Bryant, M. E. *Law Now.* Edmonton, AB: Oct/Nov 2003. Vol. 28, Issue 2.

Calgary Board of Education. (2014). Schools and areas – Unique Settings Section. http://www.cbe.ab.ca/schools/unique_settings.asp.

Calgary Police Service. (2014). Serious Habitual Offenders Program (SHOP). Retrieved from http://www.calgary.ca/cps/Pages/Youth-programs-and-resources/Serious-Habitual-Offenders-Program-SHOP/Serious-Habitual-Offender-Program.aspx.

Calgary Youth Justice Society. (2008). The youth criminal justice system in Alberta. Course training module. Retrieved from http://calgaryyouthjustice.ca/cms/wp-content/uploads/2012/04/course1.pdf.

Caputo, T., & Vallée, M. (2007). A comparative analysis of youth justice approaches: A report prepared for the *Review of the Roots of Youth Violence*, Volume 4. Ottawa, ON: Centre for Initiatives on Children, Youth and Community.

Carrigan, D. O. (1998). *Juvenile Delinquency in Canada: A History.* Concord, ON: Irwin Publishing.

DeGusti, B. (2008). *The impact of the youth criminal justice act on case flow in Alberta and system response in Calgary.* Report prepared by the Canadian Research Institute for Law and the Family.

Given, B. (2009). *Blog of Bill Given – Mayor of Grande Prairie.* Retrieved from http://bill-given.blogspot.ca/2009/04/young-offenders-centre-closure-who-to.html.

Government of Alberta. (2006). *Educational portrait of Canada, 2006 census.* Retrieved from www12.statcan.ca/census-recensement/2006/as-sa/97-560-XIE2006001.pdf

Government of Alberta. (2008). *Youth Criminal Justice Act* extrajudicial sanctions program. Retrieved December 8, 2011 from http://justice.alberta.ca/programs_services/ criminal_pros/crown_prosecutor/Pages/youth_extrajudicial_sanctions_program.aspx.

Government of Alberta. (2012). Economic growth – Economic fast facts section. Retrieved from http://www.albertacanada.com/about-alberta/economic-results.html.

Government of Alberta. (2014a). Economic Dashboard – Unemployment Rates. Retrieved from http://www.statcan.gc.ca/pub/91-002-x/2014001/t329-eng.htm.

Government of Alberta. (2014b). Justice and Solicitor General – Youth Programs. Retrieved from http://www.solgps.alberta.ca/programs_and_services/correctional_services/community_corrections/Pages/youth_programs.aspx.

Green. R. (2012). Explaining the Youth Criminal Justice Act. In J. Winterdyk & R. Smandych (Eds.), *Youth at risk and youth justice: A Canadian overview.* Don Mills, ON: Oxford University Press. 54–79.

Hylton, J. H. (1994). Get tough or get smart? Options for Canada's youth justice system in the twenty-first century. *Canadian Journal of Criminology, 36,* 229–246.

Justice and Solicitor General. (2014). *Annual Report 2013–14.* Edmonton, AB: Justice and Solicitor General Communications.

Kim, W. J. (2003). Child and adolescent psychiatry workforce: A critical shortage and national challenge. *Academic Psychiatry, 27*(4), 277–282.

Markwart, A. (1992). Custodial sanctions under the Young Offenders Act. In R. R. Corrado, N. Bala, R. Linden, & M. LeBlanc (Eds.), *Juvenile justice in Canada: A theoretical and analytical assessment* (pp. 229– 281). Toronto, ON: Butterworths.

Search Institute. (2012). *Developmental assets.* Retrieved from http://www.search-institute.org/research/developmental-assets.

Statistics Canada. (2010). Youth court statistics 2008/2009. *Juristat* article. Retrieved from http://www.statcan.gc.ca/pub/85-002-x/2010002/article/11294-eng.htm.

Statistics Canada. (2014). *Quarterly demographic estimates.* Retrieved from http://www.statcan.gc.ca/pub/91-002-x/2014001/t329-eng.htm.

Statistics Canada. (2014b). *Aboriginal peoples in Canada: First Nations Peoples, Métis, Inuit.* Retrieved from http://www12.statcan.gc.ca/nhs-enm/2011/as-sa/99-011-x/99-011-x2011001-eng.cfm

Sutherland, N. (2000). *Children in English-Canadian society: Framing the twentieth-century consensus.* Waterloo, ON: Wilfrid Laurier University Press.

Winterdyk, J. (Ed.). (forthcoming). *Juvenile justice: International perspectives, models, and trends.* Boca Raton, FL: CRC Press.

Wittmeier, B. (2014). Province axes Aboriginal youth probation officer position. *Edmonton Journal.* Retrieved from http://www.edmontonjournal.com/Province+axes+aboriginal+youth+probation+position/9633150/story.html.

3 The YCJA in British Columbia

RAYMOND R. CORRADO, ALAN MARKWART,
KARLA GRONSDAHL, AND ANNE KIMMITT[1]

Similar to the other provinces and territories, middle and senior officials from the then British Columbia (BC) Ministry of Attorney General, an integrated justice ministry which was also responsible for youth correctional services, participated in the 1984 implementation of the *Young Offenders Act* (YOA) (1982) and subsequently the ongoing and ultimately unsuccessful efforts to salvage this controversial law by way of three amendment bills in 1986, 1992, and 1995 before its eventual replacement by the *Youth Criminal Justice Act* (YCJA) (2003). From the perspective of key actors from the academic, executive, senior policy, and field practitioner levels, it will be argued that the difficulty in adjusting from the YOA to the YCJA has been fairly minimal since the inception of this federal law a decade ago because the related provincial law, programs, and policy – and youth justice system culture and philosophy – in BC was already largely congruent with both the strategic directions and substantive aspects of the YCJA.

The reasons for this smooth transition are many; however, four central themes will be discussed. First, as we asserted in our publications concerning the transition to the YOA from the *Juvenile Delinquents Act* (JDA),[2] BC senior policymakers and legislators initiated a policy trend as far back as the 1970s wherein many of the key policy thrusts of the YOA, and even of the YCJA, had already been put in place in the province. We described this BC provincial youth justice system as a Modified Justice Model.[3] The essence of this model is that only the most serious offences and the most serious young offenders are to be processed formally in the youth justice system, which also incorporates a complete range of legal and procedural safeguards for youth. Under this model, minor offenders are to be diverted from the formal justice system altogether, community-based alternatives to custody are to be promoted, and legislated and policy restrictions on the use of custody are imposed so that only the most violent offenders and serious repeat offenders are to be sentenced to custody, and for far shorter periods than adults for similar offence profiles.

Second, through the 1980s and 1990s, Alan Markwart was the senior youth justice policy lead for BC and a key player in federal/provincial/territorial efforts to reform the YOA, including as the co-chair and principal author of the 1996 *Report of the Federal-Provincial-Territorial Task Force on Youth Justice* in Canada,[4] which was referred to the House of Commons Standing Committee on Justice and Legal Affairs. This 649-page report comprehensively addressed the outstanding issues with the YOA, recommending many reforms that would eventually emerge under the YCJA.

Third, in 1996, BC underwent a major restructuring of the responsibilities of several provincial ministries, which resulted in unification of a wide range of programs and services for children, youth, and their families under the umbrella of the newly formed Ministry of Children and Family Development (MCFD).[5] This organizational shift and greater integration of service delivery for youth – including youth justice (correctional), child welfare, and mental health services – coincided with and contributed to the beginning of an enormous downward trend in the use of custody in BC, which has continued into 2014.

Fourth, several ministries and departments responsible for youth criminal justice in BC and the Justice Institute of British Columbia (JIBC), undertook an extensive and multifaceted education/instruction program for many of the key youth justice personnel to assist them in preparing to administer this very complex law in advance of the YCJA taking effect in 2003.

These four themes underlie the development of the youth justice system and culture in British Columbia during the last 35 years and explain why youth justice practitioners, with few exceptions, had relatively little difficulty implementing the new directions and complex provisions of the YCJA. These themes will be integrated into the following sections, beginning with a more detailed discussion of the fourth theme.

Integrated Multi-ministerial Education and Instruction Program for the YCJA

Even before the YCJA was given Royal Assent in 2002, "bridge funding" under the federal/provincial cost-sharing agreement, as well as grant funding under the federal Youth Justice Renewal fund, was provided to

BC and other jurisdictions between 1999 and 2003 to assist with the required program, policy, information systems, and training requirements associated with implementation of the new Act.[6] Specifically, these funds provided for curriculum development by the JIBC and for a youth justice policy consultant to be temporarily assigned to work primarily on the rewriting of the Youth Justice Policy and Program Support manuals for both youth community and custody. These manuals described in detail how the YCJA was to be administered in British Columbia by youth probation officers and youth custody workers. Equally important, additional staff time focused on the technical information systems, including the current CORNET and JUSTIN computer systems, which required substantial changes to adapt to the new requirements of the Act. Corrections Network System (CORNET) is a secure, adult and youth offender computerized case management system that enables correctional officers, probation officers, and youth justice workers to store and access sensitive client information across the province. Justice Information System (JUSTIN) is an integrated case management system used to manage and administer the criminal justice process. It allows youth and adult criminal cases to be processed and monitored from initial police arrest to Crown counsel assessment of charges through to court case tracking and judgements. JUSTIN is integrated with CORNET to provide electronic court documents and orders. These orders define the terms and conditions of adults and youth that are administered in community probation offices and custodial institutions across BC.

Because the Justice Institute of British Columbia has been the main training facility for justice services for the past 30 years, it had a central role. This training institute is responsible for the education and training of police officers from all the municipal police forces in BC as well as for all youth and adult probation officers, youth custody and adult correctional staff, sheriffs (responsible for transporting individuals from custody facilities to and from courts, and for court security), and first responders including fire, emergency, and paramedic/ambulance services. The Corrections and Community Justice Division at the JIBC received federal funding (from 2000 to 2003) to develop and deliver a training program. Specifically, a training team comprised of seconded staff from the MCFD, the Attorney General, and the Solicitor General developed and delivered extensive YCJA training materials (e.g., videos, training binders) for 650 staff from the three ministries who received this education and training during the three months prior to the YCJA coming into effect in 2003. This team also developed the training materials for the Government of the Northwest Territories. As well, MCFD Youth Justice policies and training materials were provided to several other provinces/territories to help them with their implementation. A national train-the-trainers curriculum program developed by the National Judicial Institute (assisted by Markwart) facilitated the training of Provincial Court and Supreme Court judges in BC (and other jurisdictions). Finally, MCFD youth justice staff were provided two days of update training a year later, which included a review of several key case law decisions from BC and across the country concerning how certain key sections of the YCJA had been interpreted by the courts.

Approximately a decade after the YCJA took effect in British Columbia, its impact is more completely assessed below by examining the roles of key youth justice players in the system.

Youth Justice Roles in BC under the YCJA

Police

Corrado and Markwart[7] have previously explained in several publications that even before the YOA took effect in 1984, and unlike other provinces and territories (except Quebec), Crown counsel (prosecutors) from the (now) Ministry of Justice have been the gatekeepers or key decision-makers who determine whether a young person will be subject to formal diversion – extrajudicial sanctions – or formally charged and subject to the full youth justice court process, that is, the police in BC do not have the authority to lay a criminal charge. Instead, the police file a "Report to Crown Counsel" which is then reviewed by the prosecutor to determine whether, first, there is a "substantial likelihood of conviction" and, if so, whether it is "in the public interest" to proceed with formal measures, including a Crown counsel caution letter, extrajudicial sanctions, or formal court proceedings. If a youth comes into contact with police for a less serious offence and does not have previous justice system involvement, the youth will almost certainly be dealt with through a police warning or referral, quite possibly more than once. Canadian Centre for Justice Statistics (Statistics Canada) data confirm that over two-thirds of youth cases cleared by police in BC do not result in a report to Crown counsel or formal charges. For repeat offenders or more serious offences, police may forward a report to Crown counsel, who will consider whether to refer the matter to extrajudicial sanctions, send a caution letter, or approve the matter to court.

If Crown counsel opts to consider extrajudicial sanctions, the youth matter may be referred to a youth probation officer for an extrajudicial sanctions inquiry, or, in some locations, Crown counsel may refer the matter directly to a community-based program. For those matters that proceed to court, with the exception of cases involving serious violence, or youth with significant histories of offending, a community-based sentence will be the most likely outcome.

Stated another way, the least level of intervention considered necessary to address the young person's offending behaviour will normally be used, with the more intrusive interventions (community-based and custody sentences) being reserved for offences involving violence or more serious and repeat property offences.

Notwithstanding their more limited role in respect of charging decisions than in most other jurisdictions, the police continued to engage in their traditional roles to investigate and then either divert, arrest, release on conditions, or begin the more formal justice system processes by holding accused youth in temporary custody prior to Crown counsel approval of charges and appearance before a judge or justice. As aforementioned, one of the major reforms of the YCJA involves the promotion of diversion from the formal court process through "extrajudicial measures" (Part 1, sections 4 to 12), especially through police diversion. Extrajudicial measures are "presumed to be adequate" if the youth has committed a non-violent offence and has not been previously found guilty of an offence, and these measures are not precluded from being used repeatedly or in cases where the youth has previously been found guilty of an offence (section 4, YCJA). In law, a police officer in fact "shall" consider taking no further action, a warning, a caution, or a voluntary referral to program or agency in the community instead of formal proceedings (section 6 YCJA).

Given this legislated emphasis on extrajudicial measures, one would expect there would be consequent marked increases in the use of police diversion and a decrease in the proportion and number of youth "charged" with criminal offences (or, since the police in BC do not charge, in police Reports to Crown Counsel). This pronounced trend of an increasing use of police diversion for youth in BC is affirmed in Figure 3.1, which describes the proportion of youth "charged" (Report to Crown Counsel) with criminal offences in BC between 1991 and 2013.

What is most notable about the trend in Figure 3.1, however, is that most of the changes occurred before implementation of the YCJA in 2003 – between 1991 and 2002 the proportion of youth diverted by the

Figure 3.1 Percentage of youth diverted by police in BC

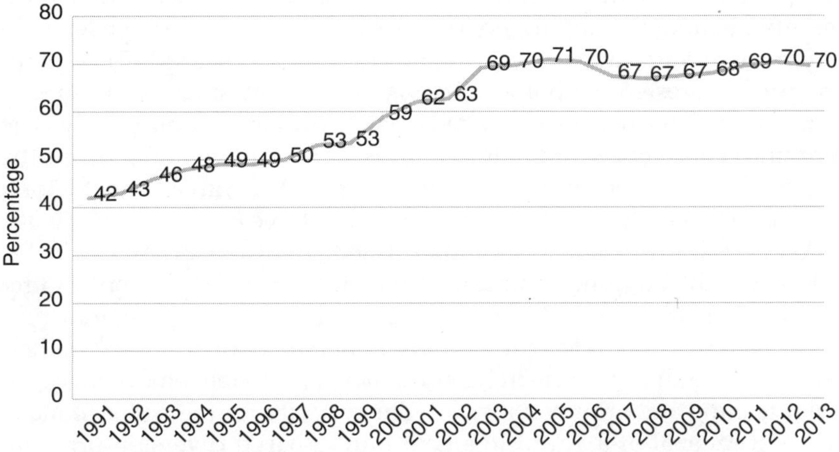

Source: Statistics Canada, Incident-based crime statistics by detailed violations,
Table 252-0051

police increased from 43% to 63% and after implementation of the YCJA
increased further to about 70%. This is a good example of how changes
that were consistent with the strategic directions and substantive provisions of the YCJA had already been implemented in BC through new
policies and programs, which consequently made the transition to the
YCJA relatively smooth.

In this regard, throughout the 1990s there were extensive efforts
by the Community Justice Services Division of the (then) Ministry
of Attorney General to promote and develop police-based diversion
programs for youth throughout the province, especially programs
with a restorative justice focus, which became generically known as
Community Accountability Programs.[8] These were largely volunteer-
based programs that were supported by the ministry through community development, volunteer recruitment, and training supports along
with minimal annual funding support for infrastructure services (e.g.,
training and supplies). They proliferated throughout the province,
employing a range of approaches such as victim offender mediation,
New Zealand- or Australian-style conferencing approaches and neighbourhood accountability panels.[9] This thrust aligned with the trends

towards the "softer" approaches of community policing and crime prevention at about the same time, and in particular with the RCMP promoting and developing police-led restorative justice diversion programs for youth known as Community Justice Forums.[10] This alignment of interests is important because the RCMP is the major police force in British Columbia – there is no BC provincial police force. The province contracts with the RCMP to play this role while most of the major municipalities outside of the cities of Vancouver and Victoria contract with the RCMP as municipal police forces.

While the growth in community-based diversion programs in BC aligned with emerging community policing, crime prevention, and restorative justice approaches of the 1990s, their increased use may also have been promoted by an undercurrent of police frustration with their incapacity to charge youth in BC since they have to rely on Crown counsel screening and approval instead. The capacity for the police to make a direct referral of a youth to a community-based diversion program is arguably empowering and appealing to the police in BC because it restores an element of direct decision-making and provides for a visible and relatively quick (compared to a court process) consequence for the youth.[11] Regardless, it is evident the extrajudicial measures goal of the YCJA had, in effect, already been administratively implemented in BC long before that legislation was brought into force or even drafted.

The extrajudicial measures provisions of the YCJA were the key change that most directly impacted policing.[12] Generally speaking, there appears to be less frustration among police officers under the YCJA than the YOA. As will be discussed later, there are far fewer youth committed to custody – a trend that began long before the YCJA – in BC, which already had a very low incarceration rate compared to other provinces. Yet there appears to be less police-generated public concern about young offenders than there was, for example, in the 1990s when police officers frequently expressed frustration about the perceived leniency of the YOA. In addition, there appears to be little police support of Bill C-10 changes to the YCJA, which involve court hearings to decide on the publication of the identities of young offenders who have committed a "violent" offence (section 75 YCJA, as amended), and the relaxed legal constraints on the use of pretrial detention and sentenced custody. This suggests that police officers may be encountering fewer serious and/or violent youth and, therefore, are less concerned about or have undergone a change in attitude towards young offenders – or perhaps it is a combination of both.

The police are certainly encountering fewer young offenders because per capita youth crime rates have dropped markedly in BC, and significantly more so than the national trend. Between 1998 and 2013 for example, the police-reported per capita youth crime rate in the province declined by 60% while the youth violent Crime Severity Index dropped by 43%.[13] Again, these are not YCJA-related as these trends began long before the YCJA.

Another possible explanation for the apparent change in police attitudes is that most municipal police departments and the RCMP require either some college/university courses or post-secondary degree credentials. Several universities and colleges in BC have undergraduate departments of criminology and/or criminal justice while Simon Fraser University and the University of the Fraser Valley have graduate programs. All these universities and colleges have basic and even advanced courses on youth justice and the YCJA. It is therefore very likely that many police officers and RCMP officers over the past 20 years have increasingly attended courses and programs that exposed them to the literature about the complexities of the antecedents to the YCJA, and the effectiveness of different approaches to youthful offending.

In contrast to the apparent muted police concerns about the YCJA in BC, there is far more concern about the few young offenders who belong in some capacity, usually minor, to adult criminal gangs/organizations. Several of these youths have been targeted by adults from rival gangs for brutal and senseless assassinations to intimidate other youths who typically engage in drug trafficking around schools and other youth hangouts. A related concern has been the emergence of Aboriginal adult/youth gangs in Vancouver, as well as interior cities and nearby reserves. Several detachments and municipal departments, such as in Vancouver and Abbotsford, have created specialized anti-gang recruitment programs and squads[14] to discourage youth from joining these gangs or to quit them. The key police message is not the threat of arrest and long custody sentences, but rather the need to provide programs for youth to avoid gang involvement and, most importantly, the inevitability of being murdered or seriously injured.

Crown Counsel

As mentioned above, Crown counsel continues to have a key function in BC youth justice under the YCJA just as they did under the YOA. The key areas of change – or at least potential for change – under the YCJA were in relation to adult sentencing and extrajudicial measures.

The YCJA post-adjudication adult sentencing process that replaced the YOA's transfer to adult court process along with the mandatory adult sentencing hearings for presumptive serious violent offences such as murder – since struck down by the Supreme Court of Canada – did involve significant changes in court procedure for Crown counsel (e.g., preliminary hearings, Supreme Court jury trials), but only in a small number of cases. Adult sentences for youth have typically only been sought by Crown counsel in British Columbia – under both the YOA and YCJA – in murder cases or especially heinous violent crimes involving very high risk youth, and are quite uncommon.

Although the political rhetoric associated with the YCJA tended to focus on "getting tough" on violent offences and presumptive adult sentencing for a narrowly defined range of offences, a close analysis of the principles and substantive provisions of the new legislation suggested from the outset that the rhetoric was considerably overblown and that the changes would be very unlikely to result in widespread use of draconian American-style adult sentences for youth. Indeed this has proven to be the case as adult sentences for youth continued to be very uncommon in BC under the YCJA – as they were under the YOA – even before presumptive adult sentencing provisions were found to be constitutionally invalid by the Supreme Court of Canada. There is no evidence the enhanced crime control model found in the YCJA was translated into more crime control prosecutorial or other related criminal justice policies under the YCJA, even with the political change from the left wing New Democratic Party to a right-of-centre Liberal provincial government in 2001, which stayed in power throughout the YCJA. In effect, regardless of the YCJA and the provincial government's political shift to the right, a punitive crime control approach was avoided and there were virtually no differences in the type of youth justice model policies before and after the YCJA. This consistency was abetted by the continuity of several senior civil servants in key ministries during the transition from the YOA to the YCJA and thereafter.

Other areas where the YCJA might have impacted Crown counsel were cautions and pre-charge screening, the latter of which was described earlier and is a system that facilitates and encourages the screening and diversion of cases from the courts by Crown counsel. The YCJA enacted "new" provisions that permitted jurisdictions to establish a Crown counsel pre-charge screening program (section 23 YCJA) and a program of Crown counsel cautions (section 7 YCJA), even though the pre-charge screening process had been implemented province-wide in British Columbia for more than 30 years before this Act and a system similar to a Crown counsel letter of caution process had been in place for more than 20 years. While these new provisions were not mandatory, they were intended to promote and facilitate the establishment of such approaches among the provinces. Obviously these "new" provisions had no impact at all in BC precisely because they had been universally practiced across the province, literally for decades. Again, these are examples of how BC had administratively put in place congruent youth justice policies well in advance of the YCJA.

Defence Counsel

There has been no substantive change in the role of defence counsel in British Columbia under the YCJA, making the transition from the YOA fairly uncomplicated, with a general exception noted below.

The legally guaranteed right to state-funded counsel at all formal stages of proceedings continued under both laws. The BC Legal Services Society, which administers legal aid and is largely funded by the BC Ministry of Justice, continues to provide defence counsel for youths who exercise their YCJA (and YOA) rights to consult counsel during the police investigation stage and upon police arrest and detention, and provides legal representation at bail and subsequent proceedings including trials, sentencing, and appeals.

As with Crown counsel, the considerable changes to the adult sentencing process involved significant and complex procedural change, yet these types of hearings are uncommon and most defence counsel would not have experienced even one case over the last decade.

Otherwise, the key challenge faced by defence counsel – and by all of the key players in the youth justice system – related to the complexity of the YCJA. It has been widely acknowledged – including in several court decisions – how extraordinarily complex the YCJA is.[15] As examples, the YOA had 70 sections compared to the 157 sections of the YCJA. The YOA had a "Declaration of Principle," as does the YCJA (section 3), but the YCJA also has complementary statements of principle in relation to extrajudicial measures (section 4) and sentencing (section 38) that must be read in conjunction with the Declaration of Principle. The YCJA introduced very complex legal criteria in relation to pretrial detention decisions and sentencing, and added several new types of sentences, including reprimands, deferred custody orders and intensive rehabilitative custody, and supervision orders, along with "optional" sentences that the province could implement such as intensive support and supervision orders and attendance program orders. A formerly simple "truth in sentencing" type of custody order under the YOA (i.e., no remission or statutory release) was replaced under the YCJA by a system of custody and supervision orders with, usually, the final third of a sentence to be served in the community. This resulted in complex sentence calculation and release processes, while the processes and criteria for enforcement and review of new types of court orders – for example, probation versus conditional supervision versus supervision in the community – became much more varied and complex.

This far greater complexity under the YCJA directly affected not only defence counsel but also police, Crown counsel, judges, and probation officers. As discussed earlier, the latter state-operated or funded groups benefited from quite elaborate and extensive training programs that were mandatory, whereas private defence counsel had to rely on voluntary and much less extensive professional education programs. Hence there were perhaps greater challenges in adjustment in the initial years with defence counsel; however, with accumulated experience and increasing familiarity with the complexities of the YCJA over time, it appears that defence counsel, like other groups, adjusted fairly smoothly.

Youth Court Judges

The YCJA does not appear to have resulted in any significant changes in how youth court judges exercise their responsibilities regarding court procedures and sentencing, with the same exceptions as for others in relation to the infrequent cases of adult sentencing and the much greater complexity of the law described above. Perhaps the greatest change associated with the YCJA that judges – and Crown and defence counsel – have witnessed is the large reduction in the number of new youth court cases coming before the courts in British Columbia, as described in Figure 3.2.[16]

As Figure 3.2 indicates there has been a huge drop in the volume of new cases coming before the youth courts in the province, though this is not due to the YCJA. For example the number of new youth court cases declined by 36% in the five years immediately preceding the implementation of the YCJA in 2003, and continued to decline thereafter. Put another way, slightly more than one half of the decrease between 1997/1998 and 2011/2012 occurred before the YCJA was implemented. Accordingly, it cannot be said that the YCJA caused or even was

Figure 3.2 BC youth court cases

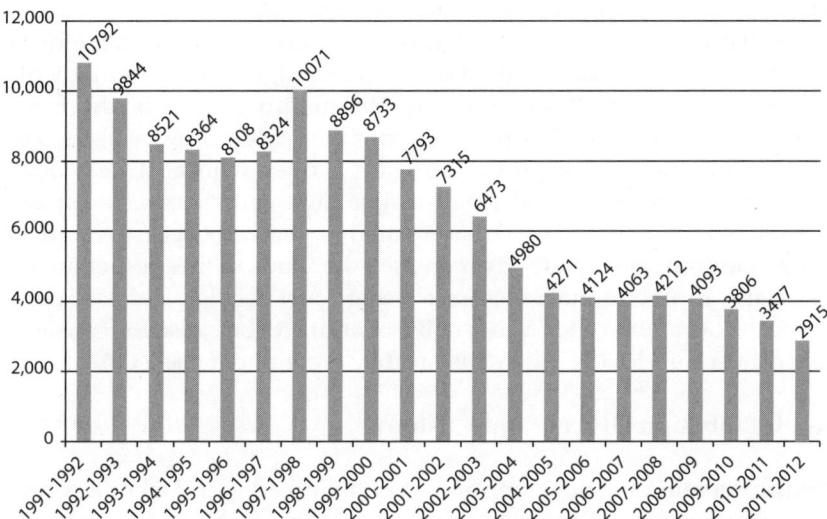

Source: Statistics Canada, Youth courts number of cases and charges by type of decision, Table 252-0064

directly associated with the reduction in youth courts cases (and other indicators); instead, it can only be said that pre-existing trends continued under the YCJA, which perhaps were reinforced or accelerated by the new legislation.

The decline in youth court cases appears to be principally related to two key factors: first, the considerable increases in the use of police diversion described earlier that were occurring long before the YCJA and second, the marked decrease in BC in the youth crime rate mentioned earlier. Regarding the latter, the police-reported per capita youth crime rate in the province has been progressively and sharply decreasing for more than 20 years and at a greater rate than in the rest of the country. For example, the youth crime rate (not shown) decreased by 73% between 1991 and 2013. Again, nearly half (49%) of these decreases occurred before the YCJA was implemented in 2003.[17]

Given the above, the explanation for the sharp reduction in the number of youth court cases heard by judges seems fairly straightforward: there are fewer youth committing crimes and of those, a much larger proportion are being dealt with informally by the police. Both trends were established long before the advent of the YCJA.

One would expect, perhaps, that such a sharp reduction in the number of cases coming before the youth courts might reap other benefits, such as making room for more expeditious processing of the fewer youth court cases. That has not been the case in BC,[18] however, because youth court judges are provincial court judges who also hear adult criminal, family court, and small claims civil court cases. It appears that the reduction in the workload related to youth court cases has been more than compensated for by increased demands in these other areas – especially adult criminal cases – such that court backlog and case delay in youth court (and other) cases in BC continue to be cause for considerable concern under the YCJA, just as they were under the YOA.

Youth Probation Officers and Custody

Youth probation officers continue to be involved – and play a central role – throughout the entire youth justice system in BC in various functions under the YCJA. Probation officers continued, as under the YOA, to provide screening and case management of "extrajudicial sanctions" (formerly alternative measures), and to carry out assessments and reports for the courts, along with bail supervision services, in relation to pretrial detention matters. The major changes experienced by probation officers relate to the substantial changes in the sentencing provisions of the YCJA.

Youth probation officers play, as they did under the YOA, a key role in sentencing through the preparation of pre-sentence reports, assessing youth, and advising the courts about sentencing options and resources available – especially community-based alternatives to custody – as well as being responsible for the case management, supervision, and enforcement of probation and other community orders. Community youth probation officers also retain youths on their active caseloads even when a young person is remanded or sentenced to custody, and continue to have the lead responsibility for preparing community release and transition plans from custody back to the community.

Equally important to the supervision and case management planning by probation officers, BC provides a number of community programs tailored towards the criminogenic needs of the youth, which include the following: day programs involving employment and life-skills training, specialized school programs, intensive support and supervision programs,[19] violent offence treatment programs, sexual offence treatment programs, as well as individual mental health assessments and counselling. In addition, BC offers full-time residential programs – mostly in family-based care arrangements – specifically for substance use, female youth, Aboriginal youth, rural wilderness challenges, and placements for youth who have committed a sexual offence. Most notably, for the past three decades BC has provided community residential bail beds as an alternative for those youths who would otherwise be remanded in custody.

The YCJA introduced substantive changes to sentencing, including the new post-adjudication adult sentencing process for a very small number of serious violent youth and complex new principles and sentencing criteria for all cases. Several new sentences were also added, including reprimands, attendance program orders, intensive support and supervision orders, deferred custody orders, and the intensive rehabilitative custody and supervision orders (IRCS) for serious violent offenders. As well, the new custody and supervision orders replaced the former "straight-time" custody sentences (i.e., no remission or parole) of the YOA with a new regime of two thirds of the sentence being served in custody and the final third being served under "supervision in the community," which, in effect, creates a system of court-ordered statutory early release.

These significant changes to sentencing brought about by the YCJA led to much greater complexity for youth probation officers and for other key actors in relation to the range and type of sentences to be imposed, the administration of orders – especially very complex new sentence calculation procedures – and the enforcement and review of a broader range of different types of community supervision orders (e.g., probation, conditional supervision, supervision in the community).

While it might be expected that youth probation officers would have had difficulty adjusting to the significant changes to sentencing, a BC study[20] indicated they were well prepared by Justice Institute training and workshops for these challenges: they appear to understand even the most conceptually elaborate sections of the YCJA, and have been able to understand and apply the substantive and procedural changes brought about by the new legislation.

Since they relate to serious violent offenders, adult sentences and IRCS orders are uncommon under the YCJA. During the past several years, British Columbia has had, on average, only a handful of adult sentence applications a year with a subset of those resulting in an adult sentence. As well, only 15 IRCS sentences have been imposed in BC since 2003.[21]

BC was well positioned to adapt to the changes in the sentencing provisions. For example, one key thrust of the YCJA is to reduce the reliance on youth custody and promote the use of community-based alternatives to custody, yet even before the YCJA, BC had a per capita rate of youth custody that was well below the national average and either the lowest or second lowest (to Quebec) in the country. The province had also established intensive support and supervision programs (ISSP) as well as community-based attendance programs, as alternatives to custody decades before the YCJA. The province used a substantial infusion of new program funding arising from the federal Youth Justice Renewal initiative in 2000 to significantly expand both types of programs. Since the YCJA has a particular focus on violent offences – obviously because youth violence is such an ongoing public policy and political concern – this new federal funding was also used to establish a specialized violent offence treatment program in youth custody centres and outpatient clinics across the province through Youth Forensic Psychiatric Services (YFPS), which is administered by the youth justice component of the Ministry of Children and Family Development. For decades, the YFPS has uniquely provided province-wide dedicated psychiatric assessment and treatment services for young offenders.

Another potential area for significant adjustment for youth probation officers related to the provisions for "conferences" (section 19), which afforded the courts the unfettered capacity to, for example, order restorative justice conferences, such as New Zealand-style family group conferencing, at sentencing hearings. In keeping with the general trend towards restorative justice measures in the decade or more before the YCJA and its restorative justice thrust, it was expected that there might be widespread use of court ordered restorative justice conferences under the YCJA. Accordingly, the province established 10 fully dedicated family group conferencing youth probation officer positions and trained generalist youth probation officers in victim-offender mediation so they would be prepared to meet the expected new demands of the court, which did not materialize.[22] While court ordered sentencing conferences do in fact occur under the YCJA, they are hardly a new wave and are infrequently ordered, most likely because such conferences can lead to an additional delay of several weeks in resolving cases, thereby aggravating ongoing concerns about a lack of timely resolution of youth court cases.

In keeping with the decreases discussed earlier, the caseloads of youth probation officers have also dropped a great deal; in fact, the total community youth justice caseload of 1,645 cases across the province in 2013/2014 was much less than one half of what it was a more than a

Figure 3.3 Average number of youth in custody in BC.

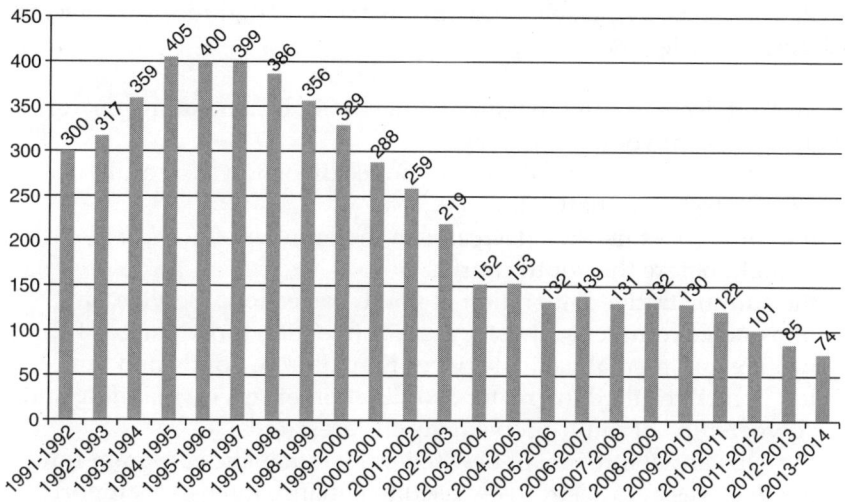

Source: Statistics Canada, Youth courts guilty cases by length of custody, Table 252-0069

decade before (4,150 cases in 2000/2001).[23] Similarly, the average number of cases that a probation officer carries has also progressively dropped, to an average of only 16 in 2013/2014.[24] Such low caseloads – accompanied by a fairly accessible and rich array of additional community supports such as ISSP and attendance programs, and outpatient youth forensic psychiatric treatment programs – obviously enables intensive case management and the mobilization of community alternatives to custody. The consequent impact on the use of youth custody has been remarkable, as is illustrated by Figure 3.3, which describes the average number of youth in custody in BC – including pretrial detention, and open and secure sentenced custody – from 1991/1992 to 2013/2014.[25]

As Figure 3.3 indicates, the average number of youth in custody in BC under the YCJA in 2013/2014 was slightly less than one-fifth of what it was at the peak in 1994/1995 under the YOA. As with the previously discussed indicators, however, the trend downward began under the YOA long before the implementation of the YCJA in 2003. In fact, more than one half (56%) of the total decrease in the custody population occurred before 2003 as a result of a progressive decline from 1994/1995 until 2003/2004, and which continued thereafter with the advent of the YCJA. These pre-YCJA changes appear to be related to several factors discussed earlier, including:

- marked decreases in the youth crime rate in BC, including decreases in the violent youth crime rate;
- substantial increases in the use of police diversion as a result of administrative initiatives;
- the consequent marked decreases in the number of new cases brought before the youth courts;
- the administrative integration of youth correctional services in 1997 into one government ministry responsible for a broad range of child welfare and mental health services for children, youth, and families, which resulted in greater coordination of service planning and "ownership" of multi-problem youth cases; and
- the substantial infusion of new federal youth justice program funding that was administratively used to enhance intensive support and supervision programs, community-based attendance programs, outpatient forensic psychiatric violent offence treatment programs, and restorative justice programs.

Obviously, the YCJA itself – especially with new principles and criteria restricting the use of pretrial and sentenced custody – had an impact from 2003 onward; however, these impacts are best described as a continuation and reinforcement of pre-existing trends that were principally the result of policy, administrative, and program initiatives taken by the province long before the advent of the YCJA.

The great reduction in the number of youth in custody resulted in the closure of four youth custody centres in the province, and reduction in the operating capacities of the three remaining centres in Burnaby, Victoria, and Prince George. While this has resulted in considerable cost savings for the province, a portion of those savings was re-allocated to enhance treatment and rehabilitative programs for youth in custody[26] as well as augment community-based alternatives to custody, which in turn may have fuelled even further reductions in the use of custody.

While the diminution of the youth justice caseload has contributed to a relatively greater level of rehabilitative programs and services being available for youth in custody and under community supervision, youth custody services have become much more centralized in BC. In addition to the closure of four small centres mentioned above, in 2014 the planned closure of a youth centre in Victoria, a major urban community, was announced. This change will leave youth custody services only available in Prince George and the Vancouver area. This announcement had also been preceded by the centralization of all girl's custody services to one youth custody centre in the Vancouver area. Consequently, some youths are now much farther from their homes, families, and usual service providers, which can create significant challenges in maintaining relationships and effective community transition planning.

The over-representation of Aboriginal youth in custody is also of continuing concern. Ironically, the average number of Aboriginal youth in custody steadily and substantially declined from a peak (95) in 1997/1998 through to the implementation of the YCJA, and thereafter to record low levels (35) in 2013/2014, yet Aboriginal youth comprised an increasing proportion of the youth custody population during this period, peaking at 47% of the youth custody population in 2013/2014.[27] The explanation for this, of course, is that the non-Aboriginal youth population has declined relatively more than the Aboriginal youth population.

Conclusion

There is little question that the YCJA has had an appreciable impact on all facets of the youth justice system in BC as a result of the introduction of new legal principles, mandated diversion processes, statutory decision-making criteria that limit the use of custody, new sentences, new post-adjudication adult sentencing processes, and a plethora of new procedures. Yet, when we examine the roles of key personnel and key justice system indicators, we find that the impacts of the YCJA are perhaps overstated. In keeping with new directions and substantive provisions of the YCJA, the use of police diversion in BC has nearly doubled so that it is now overwhelmingly the predominant response to police contact with youth. The number of new youth court cases has declined significantly, the number of youth on probation and other community supervision orders is less than half, and the number of youth in custody is dramatically less. But in every case, these trends began many years before the advent of the YCJA in response to administrative changes in policy and programs. In effect, the policy, programs, and youth justice culture in BC was already aligned with the general directions of the YCJA not only long before that legislation was implemented, but also long before it was even conceived. Simply put, changes to youth justice systems do not solely result from changes in law – even if those changes are substantive – but rather result from a complex inter-action of legal, policy, program, and organizational variables.

NOTES

1 Three of the four authors of this chapter were involved in different capac-ities with these reforms and with the implementation in 2003 of the YCJA. The lead author had been a long-standing academic critic of the YOA, and had also been involved with youth criminal justice in BC as the first chair of the Youth Program Committee, a legislated oversight body of non-governmental appointees mandated to review the operation of BC provincial legislation and programs, which at that time restricted the use of custodial institutions to more serious offenders and those with related high risk profiles for future serious offending. It was in this capacity that the lead author began a long collaborative research and publication rela-tionship with the second author, Alan Markwart, who became the senior BC policy lead and then assistant deputy minister responsible for youth justice services. The third co-author, Karla Gronsdahl, has led province-wide training initiatives under both the YOA and YCJA, and has conduct-ed research and published with the lead author about the impact of the YCJA on probation officer decision-making. Finally, the fourth co-author, Anne Kimmitt, has been a key provincial leader in youth justice policy and has been a provincial representative at federal/provincial/territorial youth justice policy and program forums. Both Markwart and the lead author, therefore, have been actively involved in BC youth justice policy and program development under the *Juvenile Delinquents Act* (JDA), the YOA, and the YCJA, while Gronsdahl and Kimmitt participated in the transition from the YOA to the YCJA and ongoing implementation thereafter.

2 See R. R. Corrado, Introduction in R. R. Corrado, N. Bala, M. LeBlanc, & R. Linden, Eds., *Juvenile Justice in Canada* (Toronto, ON: Butterworths, 1992).

3 R. R. Corrado, K. Gronsdahl, & D. MacAlister, "The Youth Criminal Justice Act: Can the Supreme Court of Canada Balance the Competing and Conflicting Models of Youth Justice?" (2007) 53(1) *Criminal Law Quarterly*, 14; R. R. Corrado, Introduction in R. R. Corrado, N. Bala, M. LeBlanc, & R. Linden, Eds., *Juvenile Justice in Canada* (Toronto, ON: Butterworths, 1992).

4 A. Markwart, "A Review of the Young Offenders Act and the Youth Justice System in Canada," in *Report of the Federal-Provincial-Territorial Task Force on Youth Justice*, August 1996 (Ottawa: Department of Justice Canada).

5 In September 1996, the BC government created the Ministry for Children and Families, launching a historical change in the delivery of social welfare, mental health, addictions, and youth justice services in the province. See "A. Armitage, Lost Vision: Children and the Ministry for Children and Families," (1998), 118 *BC Studies*; T. Gove (Hon. Judge), *Gove Inquiry into Child Protection, Final Report, Vol.1: Matthew's Story, Vol. 2: Matthew's Legacy* (Victoria, BC: Queens Printer, 1995); C. Morton, *British Columbia's Child, Youth and Family Serving System: Recommendations for Change* (Victoria, BC: Office of Transition Commissioner, 1996).

6 The second author, Alan Markwart, was the co-chair of the Federal-Provincial-Territorial Committee on Youth Justice Cost Sharing during this period and was succeeded as co-chair by the fourth author, Anne Kimmitt.

7 R. R. Corrado & A. Markwart, "The Evolution and Implementation of a New Era of Juvenile Justice in Canada," in R. R. Corrado, N. Bala, M. LeBlanc, & R. Linden, Eds., *Juvenile Justice in Canada* (Toronto, ON: Butterworths, 1992); A. Markwart & R. R. Corrado, "The Need to Reform the YOA in Response to Violent Young Offenders: Confusion, Reality or Myth?" (1994), 36(3) *Canadian Journal of Criminology*, 343.

8 More information on these programs can be found at: http:www.pssg.gov.bc.ca/crimeprevention/justice/index.htm#cap.

9 K. Roach, "The Role of Crime Victims under the Youth Criminal Justice Act" (2003) 40 *Alberta Law Review*, 965; D. Hillian, M. Reitsma-Street, & J. Hackler, "Conferencing in the Youth Criminal Justice Act: Policy Developments in British Columbia" (2004) 46(3) *Canadian Journal of Criminology and Criminal Justice*, 343. See also Calgary Community Conferencing, a long-standing collaborative partnership between justice, education and community-based organizations. Retrieved from http://calgarycommunityconferencing.com.

10 R. Munro, "Nanaimo Restorative Justice Program" (2006) 6 *Journal of the Institute of Justice and International Studies*, 47; J. E. Deukmedjian, "The Rise and Fall of RCMP Community Justice Forums: Restorative Justice and Public Safety Interoperability in Canada" (2008), 50(2) *Canadian Journal of Criminology and Criminal Justice*, 117.

11 P. J. Carrington & J. L. Schulenberg, *Police Discretion with Young Offenders* (Ottawa, ON: Department of Justice Canada, 2003). Retrieved from http://www.justice.gc.ca/eng/rp-pr/cj-jp/yj-jj/discre/pdf/rep-rap.pdf.

12 P. J. Carrington & J. L. Schulenberg, *Police Use of Extrajudicial Measures under the Youth Criminal Justice Act* (Ottawa, ON: Department of Justice Canada, 2006); M. Voula & N. Innocente, "Factors Influencing Police Attitudes towards Extrajudicial Measures under the Youth Criminal

Justice Act" (2008) 50(4) *Canadian Journal of Criminology and Criminal Justice*, 469.

13 Crime rates are based on youth accused (including those charged and diverted by the police) of *Criminal Code* offences, excluding traffic offences. The youth violent Crime Severity Index began to be measured in 1998. These data are publicly available through Statistics Canada's CANSIM (Crime and Justice) data tables at http://www5.statcan.gc.ca/cansim/a01?/lang=en.

14 For example, in 2004 the province of BC developed the Combined Forces Special Enforcement Unit, an integrated group of federal, provincial and municipal police officers to deal with gangs and organized crime groups. See http://www.cfseu.bc.ca.

15 See for example the following Supreme Court of Canada decisions: *R. v. C. (R.)*, [2005]; *R. v. D. (C.)* & *R. v. K. (C. D.)*, [2005]; *R. v. P. (B. W.)*, [2006]; *R. v. B. (D.)*, [2008]. For a more in-depth analysis of the Supreme Court of Canada's decision on the deterrence principle, see R. R. Corrado, K. Gronsdahl, D. MacAlister, & I. Cohen, "Should Deterrence Be a Sentencing Principle under the Youth Criminal Justice Act?" (2007) 85(3), *The Canadian Bar Review*, 539.

16 Source: Canadian Centre for Justice Statistics, Statistics Canada, CANSIM data tables, *supra* note 14.

17 *Ibid.*

18 In fact, Statistics Canada data indicate that the median number of days to process a youth court case has increased slightly under the YCJA. *Supra* note 17.

19 The intensive support and supervision program (ISSP) predates the YCJA as BC has made available one-to-one workers (historically called DARE workers) as supplementary rehabilitative support to probation officers for nearly 40 years.

20 R. R. Corrado, K. Gronsdahl, D. MacAlister, & I. Cohen, "Youth Justice in Canada: Theoretical Perspectives of Youth Probation Officers" (2010) 52(4) *Canadian Journal of Criminology and Criminal Justice*, 397.

21 Data current to July 2013.

22 D. Hillian, M. Reitsma-Street, & J. Hackler, "Conferencing in the Youth Criminal Justice Act: Policy Developments in British Columbia" (2004) 46(3) *Canadian Journal of Criminology and Criminal Justice*, 343.

23 Source: BC Ministry of Children and Family Development, Youth Justice and Forensic Services, 2014.

24 *Ibid.*

25 *Ibid.*

26 Youth Custody Centres in BC offer several core programs and specialized
    services to provide opportunities for youth to learn constructive skills and
    behaviours that will support healthy, pro-social developmental outcomes
    and increased resiliency to overcome challenges. The custody centres offer
    a wide variety of programs including educational and vocational/life-
    skills training, chaplaincy services, substance-use counselling, female
    youth programming, as well as services that connect youth to their identi-
    fied language, traditions, and culture, particularly Aboriginal programs.
    Finally, the custody centres offer specialized services that respond to the
    distinct needs of particular youth such as those who have committed a
    sexual and/or violent offence and youth who require mental health servic-
    es. While the aforementioned services are offered to the youth in custody,
    specific training programs regarding the impact of trauma on youth, un-
    derstanding female youth in custody, and therapeutic crisis intervention
    have been mandatory for all staff (e.g., senior management, youth super-
    visors, social workers, probation officers, admissions and discharge staff,
    nurses) employed at the custody centres. These strengths-based training
    initiatives are integral to the operational needs of the custody centres and
    act as an educational foundation for staff by providing an environment
    that is proactive, responsive, and supportive with youth.
27 Source: BC Ministry of Children and Family Development, Youth Justice
    and Forensic Services, 2014.

4 Youth Justice in Manitoba: Developments and Issues under the YCJA

RUSSELL SMANDYCH, MURRAY DYCK, COREY LA BERGE, AND JODI KOFFMAN

Introduction

In 1909, Manitoba became the first province to formally establish a juvenile court provided for in Canada's new child welfare-oriented *Juvenile Delinquents Act* (JDA) (Woloschuk, 2009). Over the past century, Manitoba's youth justice system has naturally evolved substantially from its humble beginnings in Winnipeg in 1909 as a single juvenile court. Indeed, per capita, it is probably one of the busiest provincial youth justice systems in the country today, if one takes into account measures such as youth court processing and custody rates; especially with Manitoba's anomalous status of having the highest provincial youth incarceration rate in the country in 2010–2011 (Manitoba Justice, 2011). Unlike most other provinces that have witnessed substantial decreases in youth incarceration since the introduction of the *Youth Criminal Justice Act* (YCJA), the Manitoba rate increased 38% from 2005 to 2011, with the province's youth remand rate increasing over this period to almost 5 times the overall national rate (Munch, 2012).

Despite the many questions that need to be answered about how the youth justice system has fared in Manitoba under the YCJA , it appears that little if any research aimed at generating baseline data to address such questions has been undertaken by either policy analysts in relevant branches of the government of Manitoba or criminologists and other researchers in Manitoba universities.[1] The purpose of this chapter is to begin to attempt to fill this gap in publically available knowledge about the effects of the implementation of the YCJA in Manitoba. We approach this effort in two ways. The first is by providing documentary and statistical evidence we have collected on youth crime prevention and the operation of the youth justice system in Manitoba since 2003. This includes data on how the government of Manitoba has attempted to implement the legislation through policy changes, as well as an analysis of available data on the effect of these changes. Second, we attempt, on a limited scale, to share with readers the views and experiences of youth crime prevention and justice professionals who have worked in Manitoba since 2003 and have had the opportunity to observe how the YCJA has been implemented in the province over the past decade. These first-hand experiences are drawn from interviews conducted by the first author with a small sample of youth justice-related professionals based mainly in Winnipeg, supplemented by the personal knowledge and insights of the other chapter co-authors who have worked more directly in Manitoba in the fields of policing and youth justice.[2] Given the limited scope of this research, our observations are necessarily preliminary. As we reveal in the information provided in this chapter, perhaps the most important and clear finding to date is that the implementation of the YCJA during its first 10 years in Manitoba has been difficult and challenging for youth justice professionals, while its benefits for youth at risk and young offenders are open to debate given the lack of systematically collected and reported data on prevention and intervention programs.

Youth Justice in Manitoba under the YCJA

The Manitoba Justice System

Manitoba Justice has the delegated responsibility for administering the YCJA in the province. Headquartered in Winnipeg, it has over 3,000 employees, and, in addition to administering the YCJA, it provides a wide range of justice-related services across the province. Within Manitoba Justice, the Manitoba Prosecutions Service is responsible for prosecutions under the YCJA. Also, within this service, there is a Youth Court Unit, located in Winnipeg, which has the primary responsibility for prosecuting charges laid against young persons in Winnipeg.[3]

Outside of Winnipeg, there are Regional Prosecution offices based in Brandon, Dauphin, Portage la Prairie, The Pas, and Thompson, where regional Crown attorneys prosecute all adult and youth offences arising in regional court locations. In addition, working in conjunction with lawyers from Winnipeg, adult and youth prosecutions are carried out in over 60 other communities throughout the province, often by way of rural and remote northern circuit courts. Through its Regional Courts Branch, Manitoba Justice also runs an Aboriginal Court Worker Program, which is aimed at helping Aboriginal people develop a better understanding of their rights and obligations in the criminal justice system, and employs Aboriginal court workers to assist and provide translation services for Aboriginal peoples who require them. Related programs have also been established in Aboriginal communities to promote the regular participation of community elders at sittings of the Provincial Court in their communities (Manitoba Justice, 2011). The mandate for administering "Youth Corrections" throughout the province, including custodial and community-based corrections, also falls within the overarching rubric of Manitoba Justice, and until 2012, most community-based youth crime prevention initiatives and programs were administered through Manitoba Youth Corrections.[4] Also, provincial court judges throughout the province are appointed to hear both adult and youth cases, meaning that there are very few, if any, judges who deal primarily or only with youth cases.[5] As we will see later in the chapter, these organizational arrangements have an important bearing on the way in which youth at risk and alleged young offenders, including, unfortunately, highly over-represented Aboriginal youth, are dealt with in the Manitoba youth justice system.

Like the provision of prosecutions services, policing in Manitoba is carried out across diverse urban, rural, and remote northern parts of the province. In addition, the responsibility for policing is shared by the RCMP, and municipal and First Nations police services. More specifically, outside of Winnipeg, which has its own municipal police force, most municipal and provincial policing in Manitoba is carried out under contract by the RCMP. Through its 84 rural and 22 municipal detachments across the province, the RCMP enforces federal, provincial, and municipal statutes and by-laws, and administers crime prevention programs in diverse smaller cities, towns, and villages that do not provide their own police services. In addition, the RCMP, along with the stand-alone Dakota Ojibway Police Service (DOPS), provide police services in First Nations communities across the province, which are cost-shared through a number of different First Nations policing programs and agreements negotiated by the Manitoba and federal governments (Manitoba Justice, 2011).[6] The division of responsibility for policing and diverse types of communities in which policing is carried out in Manitoba, along with the key role given to police in administering the YCJA, also pose significant implications for how young persons are dealt with in the Manitoba youth justice system.

Youth Crime Rates

Determining overall levels and patterns of youth crime in Canada is recognized to be a complicated task (Sprott & Doob, 2008; Winterdyk, 2012). This is even more the case when one tries to separate out provincial trends, given well-known long-standing interprovincial differences in how Canadian youth justice legislation has been applied (Bala, Carrington, & Roberts, 2012). However, it is important in the context of investigating the manner in which the YCJA has been applied in Manitoba, to provide a comparative discussion of Manitoba youth crime rates, based on information derived from federal annual *Juristat* reports.[7]

In general, reported data showed that rates of youth crime and youth charging are typically higher in Manitoba than in most other provinces. Consistent with earlier trends under the YOA, in 2003–2004, during the first year under the YCJA, the rate at which youths were brought to court in Manitoba was higher than any other province except Saskatchewan (Thomas, 2005, Table 7, p. 17; cited in Sprott & Doob, 2008, p. 623). This trend has remained the same since 2004, with Manitoba showing among the highest provincial rates of police-reported youth crime and youth charging under the YCJA. Although police-reported rates of youth crime have decreased across Canada over the past decade, they appear to be decreasing less in Manitoba than in most other provinces.

Trend data on Canadian youth (aged 12–17) police-reported crime between 2000 and 2010, show that the youth crime rate fell overall by 11% during this period, and by 7% from 2009 to 2010 (Brennan & Dauvergne, 2011, p. 19). With respect to Manitoba, data for 2009 and 2010 show that while the rates of specific property crimes (break and enter and motor vehicle theft) dropped by 5%, the rates of specific violent crimes (homicide, robbery, and serious assault) saw an overall increase of 1%; similar to the trend in Saskatchewan, which was the only other province to show an increase in violent youth crime (Brennan & Dauvergne, 2011, p. 37). Overall, compared to other provinces, Manitoba, along with Saskatchewan, had the lowest overall decline in youth crime (both at 4%). In addition, the data show that Manitoba and Saskatchewan had the highest scores on the youth Crime Severity Index that measures the seriousness of violent and non-violent youth crimes (Brennan & Dauvergne, 2011, p. 39; Winterdyk, 2012). Significantly, the higher reported youth crime rates in Manitoba are consistent with the self-reported data that Sprott and Doob (2008, pp. 630, 633) have gleaned from the Statistics Canada, National Longitudinal Survey of Children and Youth (NLSCY), published in 2007, which show that youth (aged 12–17) surveyed in Manitoba in 2004 reported among the highest violent and property crime rates.

While this comparative trend data is useful as a starting point for investigating methods that have been put into practice to respond to youth crime in Manitoba since the introduction of the YCJA, it also needs to be contextualized and considered in relation to the specific socio-economic, cultural, and political conditions that exist in the province, including, perhaps most importantly, the widely recognized problem of gang-related street crime and the vast over-representation of Aboriginal youth in Manitoba's child welfare and youth correctional systems. Before we turn to these issues, however, it is important to first highlight the range of youth crime prevention programs and strategies that have been put into place in Manitoba to keep youth out of the justice system.

Youth Crime Prevention

One of the guiding principles of YCJA is to prevent crime by addressing "the circumstances underlying a young person's offending behaviour." It does this by placing emphasis on the need to ensure "that a young person is subject to meaningful consequences for his or her offence" (YCJA, 3. (1)), and through recommending that communities, parents, and others concerned with the development of young persons should take steps to respond to the needs of young persons and "provide guidance and support to those at risk of committing crimes" (YCJA, Preamble). While the recent transfer of responsibility for overseeing community-based youth crime prevention initiatives from Manitoba Youth Corrections to the Department of Children and Youth Opportunities will likely have significant effects on the future restructuring and government funding of youth crime prevention initiatives, it is important to try to generate baseline information on how the implementation of the YCJA, and more generally existing federal-provincial funding arrangements, appears to have affected developments from 2003 to 2012.

In order to access how well the YCJA, and more generally government funding, is helping to support successful local youth crime prevention strategies, we need to start by highlighting the basic demographic characteristics of the province, and especially Winnipeg, where more than half of Manitoba's residents reside. According to Statistics Canada (2006 Census), Winnipeg's population differs from the national average in many ways. Winnipeg has a slightly higher percentage of youth (15–24 years old) in the population; 14.1% compared to the national average of 13.4%. Moreover, 10.2% of Winnipeg's population is Aboriginal, while the national average is 3.8%. In addition, the percentage of the population of Winnipeg who live on low incomes is also higher than the national average (15.7% versus 11.4%). Outside of Winnipeg, and in particular on First Nations reserves, the proportion of youth in the population is higher, as are low income and child poverty rates. For example, calculated on the basis of "Low Income Cut-Off as a measure of poverty, Manitoba's child poverty rate in 2007 was tied for highest in the country at 19%" (Curran, Bowness, & Comack, 2010, p. 8).

Within this demographic context, there are a variety of different primary, secondary, and tertiary youth crime prevention strategies that have been put into place both before and following the introduction of the YCJA, examples of which are highlighted below and in following sections on the use of extrajudicial and judicial measures under the YCJA.

Youth Serving Agencies

There are a number of youth serving agencies in Winnipeg and elsewhere in Manitoba that have the mandate of responding to the needs of youth in the general population and also those caught up in the criminal justice system. For example, the Youth Agencies Alliance (YAA), formerly called the Coalition of Community Based Youth Serving Agencies (CCBYSA), is a group of 18 Winnipeg-based agencies that meet regularly for the purpose of sharing information and developing strategies to better serve the needs of inner-city youth.[8] In 2010, researchers from the Department of Sociology at the University of Manitoba (Curran et al., 2010) conducted interviews with representatives of CCBYSA in order to learn about the work of and challenges faced by these agencies. Agency representatives identified gang involvement as one of the most urgent youth-related issues in Winnipeg, and frequently expressed the opinion that the main factors underlying gang involvement were broader systemic issues, such as poverty, dysfunctional families, unemployment, and discrimination (Curran et al., 2010, p. 7). CCBYSA representatives also included poverty as the biggest problem that affects all aspects of a young person's life, including school achievement and experiences in the family. The CCBYSA-, now YAA-, affiliated agencies are striving to offer Winnipeg inner-city youth resources that they need in order to overcome many of the poverty-linked problems they face, including crime involvement and victimization. However, they recognize that this is not an easy task since their own work is also greatly affected by government funding. In their assessment of formulae used by differ-ent levels of government to fund CCBYSA agencies, Curran et al. (2010, p. 26) note that the main characteristics of the existing system of fund-ing allocation "are increased accountability, short-term funding, hiring on contract, use of information and communication technologies, and forced partnerships, which reduces consistency and flexibility of pro-grams offered while increasing the work load of staff." It would appear from this that overall youth servicing agencies in Winnipeg are under-funded and, thus, simply struggling as best they can to meet the needs of inner-city youth at risk of crime and victimization. This also appears to be the picture that emerges if one examines funded youth crime pre-vention strategies in Manitoba more generally, with perhaps the excep-tion of those earmarked for priority funding by the federal government.

Funded Youth Crime Prevention Strategies

Manitoba has a range of funded primary, secondary, and tertiary youth crime prevention strategies that are similar to those in place elsewhere in Canada and in other Western countries, particularly the United States (Howell, 2009; Reid & Gilliss, 2012; Totten, 2012). One reason for this is the federal funding of youth crime prevention initiatives through the Canadian National Crime Prevention Centre (NCPC), which since 2006 has moved towards prioritizing the funding of initiatives targeted at com-bating youth gun- and drug-related crimes and violent crimes (Canada, Public Safety, NCPC, 2008, 2011; Vallée, 2010). Since 2006, the NCPC has moved in the direction of favouring strategies that take into account risk and protective factors related to youth crime and that are based on "best practice" models supported by "evidence-based" research. Towards this end, in 2009, it reformulated its mission statement to state that "NCPC's mission is to provide national leadership on effective and cost-efficient ways to both prevent and reduce crime by addressing known risk fac-tors in high-risk populations and places" (Canada, Public Safety, NCPC website; cited in Vallée, 2010, p. 44).[9]

Examples of the types of youth crime prevention programs in place in Winnipeg and across Manitoba are included in the following Table 4.1. The table highlights the extent to which each program falls into the category of primary (P), secondary (S), and/or tertiary (T) youth crime prevention, along with which of these strategies have been either partly funded or based on the types of "best practice" models and "evidence-based" interventions favoured by the NCPC.[10] Additional information on these and other currently funded youth crime prevention initiatives in Manitoba can be found in the sources cited in Table 4.1 and the following referenced reports and websites (MacDonald Youth Services, 2011; Manitoba Justice, Crime Prevention, online).

Table 4.1 provides a general picture of the various types of youth crime prevention programs that exist in Manitoba, though it does not reflect the degree of cooperation and interagency information sharing that exists between these and other agencies commonly concerned with youth crime prevention across the province. In an attempt to derive this type of information, in the context of examining best practices used by police agencies across Canada for dealing with chronic and persistent young offenders, in 2006 the Canadian Research Institute for Law and the Family (CRILF) carried out a study that involved contacting and interviewing personnel from police and other agencies in Manitoba who had experience in working with youth offenders (DeGusti et al., 2009). Based on the 14 interviews completed with representatives from Manitoba police and other agencies, the researchers offered a number of observations about the degree of cooperation that existed between police and other youth serving and youth crime prevention agencies operating in the province. The CRILF report gave particular attention to highlighting the work of the Brandon-based Multi-Agency Prevention Program (MAPP) as a model of one interagency approach that could be followed "to develop and implement effective intervention strategies for youth at risk" (DeGusti et al., 2009, p. 33). The report notes that, as of 2009, this interagency approach was also expanded to other communities in Manitoba, including Fisher Branch, Killarney, Oakbank, Thompson, and Swan River, where RCMP detachments were working with other agencies to monitor and address the needs of youth offenders who were at high risk of repeat offending. Although the findings of this research may be viewed as promising, it is also very preliminary and needs to be followed up with a more province-wide study in order to determine the extent to which these findings can be generalized.

Although not focusing specifically on Manitoba, in his overview of federal crime prevention initiatives since the mid-1990s, Michel Vallée makes a general point that also seems to have particular relevance to the province. Commenting specifically on "major changes" in the mission and role of the NCPC "that have occurred since the Harper Government came to power," he remarks that "[w]hile investing significant resources in evidence-based crime prevention interventions appears to be an appropriate strategy, it does represent a significant

Table 4.1 Funded youth crime prevention programs in Manitoba

Program	Type*	Description
Manitoba Aboriginal Head Start (a)	P	**Target**: Aboriginal children throughout Manitoba. **Aim**: to provide children with a positive sense of themselves as Aboriginal children and to build on the children's knowledge of their Aboriginal languages and experience of culture in their communities. Funding/Support: Health Canada.
Big Brothers/Big Sisters of Winnipeg – Ototema II Program (b)	T	**Target**: youth aged 7–18 who are in conflict with the law. **Aim**: a mentor program that matches youth with adult mentors who provide them with additional support through various activities. **Funding/Support**: Big Brothers Big Sisters of Winnipeg, Winnipeg Foundation, Justice Canada, Manitoba Justice.
Youth Advisory Committee – Brandon (c)	P	**Target**: youth residing in the City of Brandon. **Aim**: to develop youth recreational activities and address issues related to youth with input from community youth. **Funding/Support**: City of Brandon.
Choices Youth Program (d)	S	**Target**: Students in Grades 6–8 attending schools in the Winnipeg School Division. **Aim**: designed to give at-risk youth the tools they need to make healthy choices in their lives, through mentoring, life skills, and family support. **Funding/Support**: Winnipeg School Division, Winnipeg Police Service, Manitoba Justice (to 2012), Manitoba, Dept. of Children and Youth Opportunities.
Circle of Courage – Ka Ni Kanichick (e)	S/T	**Target**: Aboriginal youth between 12 and 17 years who are either involved in, or at high risk of involvement in, gangs. **Aim**: to reduce gang violence and criminal activity by providing intensive skill development and cultural reclamation programming along with education, counselling, and connections to multiple support services. **Funding/Support**: NCPC, Manitoba Gang Reduction Strategy, Neighbourhoods Alive! initiative.
Cross Lake Army Cadet Corps (f)	S	**Target**: Aboriginal youth aged 12–18 years, and their parents or caregivers. **Aim**: to provide a positive alternative to gang involvement, substance abuse, and other delinquent behaviours by encouraging positive lifestyle habits. **Funding/Support**: NCPC.
Winnipeg Auto Theft Suppression Strategy (g)	T	**Target**: high risk youth and adult offenders. **Aim**: monitoring and supervision of known youth and adult auto theft offenders. **Funding/Support**: Manitoba Justice, Winnipeg Police Service, Manitoba Public Insurance.
Just TV (h) – Broadway Neighbourhood Centre	S/T	**Target**: gang-involved Aboriginal youth and young adults aged 16–24 living in Winnipeg. **Aim**: to provide participants with alternatives to gang activity through art-based programming. **Funding/Support**: NCPC; Manitoba, Youth Gang Reduction Strategy.
Lighthouses – Neigbourhood Alive! initiative (i)	P/S	**Target**: offers various after-school activities for youth across Manitoba, operating out of approximately 70 urban and rural schools and community centres. **Aim**: to provide children and youth with recreation activities and mentoring. **Funding/Support**: Manitoba Justice (to 2012); Manitoba, Dept. of Children and Youth Opportunities.

Table 4.1 Funded youth crime prevention programs in Manitoba (*Continued*)

Program	Type*	Description
Link Crime Prevention Program (j)	S	**Target**: refugee youth in Winnipeg. **Aim**: to reduce and prevent involvement in gang activity. **Funding/Support**: NCPC.
Mediation Services – Winnipeg (k)	T	**Target**: young offenders who agree to participate in restorative justice programs. **Aim**: to provide restorative justice programs including community justice forums and family conferences. **Funding/Support**: Manitoba Justice, United Way of Winnipeg, City of Winnipeg.
Multi-Agency Preventative Program (MAPP) – Brandon (l)	S/T	**Target**: youth at risk of chronic and persistent offending. **Aim**: To develop a comprehensive interagency approach to dealing with youth at risk of chronic and persistent offending. **Funding/Support**: Partnering agencies, including Brandon School Division, Addictions Foundation of Manitoba, Child and Family Services of Western Manitoba, Manitoba Justice, Community and Youth Correctional Services.
Ogijita Pimatiswin Kinamatwin (OPK) (m)	T	**Target**: Aboriginal street gang members in North End, Winnipeg. **Aim**: to learn construction skills on the job through renovating houses. **Funding/Support**: Province of Manitoba, Winnipeg Partnership Agreement.
Onashowewin (n)	T	**Target**: victims, offenders, community members, and elders. **Aim**: an alternative Aboriginal justice program for both youth and adults charged with offences, using victim/offender mediation, community justice forums, and conciliation, as well as specific programs for offenders.**Funding/Support**: Manitoba Justice, Justice Canada Aboriginal Justice Directorate, Southern Chiefs Organization.
Ooskahtisuk (Youth) Club – Tataskweyak First Nation (o)	S/T	**Target**: youth aged 5–14 years. **Aim**: to prevent and reduce substance abuse, drug-related crime and interpersonal violence through after-school and family-based programs. **Funding/Support**: NCPC
Project O.A.S.I.S. – New Directions (p)	S/T	**Target**: designed to prevent at-risk, newcomer (refugee) youth aged 12–19 living in Winnipeg from joining gangs. **Aim**: provides newcomer, refugee youth and their families with gang prevention programming, including assistance in complying with criminal justice system conditions and exiting gangs. **Funding/Support**: NCPC, Manitoba Gang Reduction Strategy.
Project Venture – Norway House and Peguis Cree Nations (q)	S/T	**Target**: high risk Aboriginal youth 10–17 years. **Aim**: to prevent and reduce substance abuse, drug-related crime and interpersonal violence.**Funding/Support**: NCPC.
Triple P (r)	P/S	**Target**: positive parenting program. **Aim**: to teach current or future parents skills on how to deal with their children's developmental and behavioural problems. **Funding/Support**: Manitoba, Healthy Child Manitoba.
Turnabout Program (s)	S/T	**Target**: children under 12 years old who are in conflict with the law or are at risk of becoming involved in criminal activities. **Aim**: to connect at-risk children and their families with appropriate community resources that will support the family and turn around the child's behaviour. **Funding/Support**: Manitoba Justice (to 2012); Manitoba, Dept. of Children and Youth Opportunities.

Table 4.1 Funded youth crime prevention programs in Manitoba (*Continued*)

Program	Type*	Description
Turning The Tides – Ndinawe (t)	S/T	**Target**: at-risk youth aged 15–19. **Aim**: an intensive mentorship model designed to prevent youth joining and engaging in gang activities in Winnipeg's North End. **Funding/Support**: NCPC, Manitoba Gang Reduction Strategy.

Primary (P) = programs provided to a whole population group (e.g., such as all children through community-wide implementation)
Secondary (S) = programs provided to youth considered to be at risk of involvement in crime
Tertiary (T) = programs directed at young offenders aimed at reducing recidivism
* The inclusion of more than one type means the agency offers either single, combined, or coexisting separate programs that target youth and families who fit into more than one category.

Sources: (a) Manitoba Aboriginal Head Start. http://www.mbaboriginalheadstart.ca/ Program-Components page. Health Canada: Aboriginal Head Start on Reserve. http://www.hc-sc.gc.ca/fniah-spnia/famil/develop/ahsor-papa_intro-eng.php; (b) Manitoba Justice, *Annual Report 2010–2011*, p. 35; Big Brothers Big Sisters of Winnipeg. www/gov.mb.ca/justice/publications/annualreports/pubs/annual/annualreports1011.pdf http://www.bigwinnipeg.com/en/Home/mentoringprograms/ototema.aspx; (c) City of Brandon. http://brandonyouth.ca; (d) Aboriginal Council of Winnipeg, *Urban Gang Initiatives in the City of Winnipeg* (2010), pp. 26–28; (e) Aboriginal Council of Winnipeg, *Urban Gang Initiatives in the City of Winnipeg* (2010), pp. 23–26; (f) Public Safety Canada, NCPC, Backgrounder: Government of Canada Supports Crime Prevention Efforts in Manitoba, 2011. http://www.publicsafety.gc.ca/cnt/nws-riss/2011/20110318-2-eng-aspx; (g) Manitoba Justice, *Annual Report 2010–2011*, p. 35; (h) Aboriginal Council of Winnipeg, *Urban Gang Initiatives in the City of Winnipeg* (2010), pp. 5–10; (i) Manitoba Justice, *Annual Report 2010–2011*, p. 35; Manitoba Justice, Safer Communities, Lighthouses. http://www.gov.mb.ca/cyo/crime_prevention/lighthouses; (j) Public Safety Canada, Building the Evidence – Project Summaries – LINK (LINKing Refugee Youth and Families to Positive Social Supports) Crime Prevention Program. http://www.publicsafety.gc.ca/cnt/rsrcs/pblctns/lnkng/index-eng.aspx; (k) Mediation Services, Winnipeg. http://www.mediationserviceswpg.ca/programs/restorative-action-centre/; (l) DeGusti et al. (2009). *Best Practices for Chronic/Persistent Youth Offenders in Canada: Summary Report*, pp. 34–65; (m) Aboriginal Council of Winnipeg, *Urban Gang Initiatives in the City of Winnipeg* (2010), pp. 18–21; (n) Aboriginal Council of Winnipeg, *Urban Gang Initiatives in the City of Winnipeg* (2010), pp. 21–23; (o) Aboriginal Council of Winnipeg, *Urban Gang Initiatives in the City of Winnipeg* (2010), pp. 10–14; (p) Manitoba, Healthy Child Manitoba (2010). Triple P – The Positive Parenting Program: A Developmental Evaluation of Manitoba's Provincial Implementation. http://www.gov.mb.ca/healthychild/publications/triplep_implementation_fall2010.pdf; Manitoba, Healthy Child Manitoba, Positive Parenting Program (Triple P) website. http://www.manitobatriplep.ca/; (q) Manitoba Justice, Turnabout. http://www.gov.mb.ca/justice/safe/turnabout.html. (r) Aboriginal Council of Winnipeg, *Urban Gang Initiatives in the City of Winnipeg* (2010), pp. 14–18; (s) Manitoba Justice, Turnabout. http://www.gov.mb.ca/justice/safe/turnabout.html; (t) Aboriginal Council of Winnipeg, *Urban Gang Initiatives in the City of Winnipeg* (2010), pp. 14–18.

departure from previous community safety and crime prevention efforts." In particular, Vallée notes that one of the downsides of favouring "evidence-based" programs geared towards "at risk" youth, is that "it will limit financial support to communities who wish to test out new ideas and approaches directed toward their particular needs, as well as potentially limit the traditional support provided through the National Strategy to communities in need of capacity building if they are unable to put in place 'proven crime prevention programs,'" and that "[t]his is particularly true for northern and isolated communities as well as inner-city neighbourhoods faced with major social-economic and crime problems" (Vallée, 2010, p. 45).[11] Again, given the paucity of research on the topic to date, it is not yet possible to determine the extent to which the concerns expressed by Vallée regarding the trade-off between funding youth "at risk" measures and community capacity building strategies is reflected in the Manitoba experience since 2003.

The Over-representation of Aboriginal Youth

A troubling reality of the Manitoba youth justice system is that it is a system that, by default, exists primarily to deal with Aboriginal youth. It is important, of course, to take into account historical and systemic reasons for the over-representation of Aboriginal youth in Manitoba's and other Canadian provincial youth justice systems (see, for example, Minaker & Hogeveen, 2009; Greenberg, Grekul, & Nelson, 2012). In addition, in order to appreciate the specific challenges faced in implementing the YCJA in Manitoba, it is also crucial to see the degree to which youth justice professionals across the province are in place mainly to work with Aboriginal youth who are either with their original families and communities, or who are placed in the care of assigned provincial and Aboriginal child and family services (CFS) agencies.

It is all too common in Manitoba for Aboriginal children to be taken from their families and communities and put in child welfare placements. According to a recent government report, "Aboriginal children are over-represented among children cared for by CFS and the percentage of them in care has been steadily rising." More specifically, the report cites data on the increase in the percentage of Aboriginal youth in care from March 2002 to 2011, which shows that youth in care as a proportion of all youth in care increased from 81% to 85% during this period. Regarding specific numbers, it reported that of 9,432 children in care in Manitoba in March 2011, 6,301 were status Indian (66.8%), 877 were Metis (9.3%), 32 were

Inuit (0.3%), and 837 were non-status (8.9%). That is, "Aboriginal children, representing about 25 per cent of the child population in Manitoba,
comprised 85 per cent of the children in care population" (Manitoba 2012,
p. 55). In a Manitoba-based study on the relationship between child protection placement and later criminal involvement published in 2001, researchers found that 88% of Aboriginal inmates in the correctional system
in Manitoba (compared with 63.3% of non-Aboriginal inmates) "were
living outside their parental home at some point between the ages of 13
and 18 years," and that "Aboriginal inmates were not only more likely
to be placed in foster care throughout their childhood years," but "they
were also more likely to have been in a number of foster homes" (Skoog
& Perrault 2001). Provincial data for 2008 to 2009 indicate that 87% of
males admitted to sentenced youth custody in Manitoba were Aboriginal,
while 91% of sentenced females were Aboriginal. Overall, for both gen-
ders across all reporting provinces, 36% of youth admitted to sentenced
custody were Aboriginal (Calverley, Cotter, & Halla, 2010, pp. 5, 29).

One of the intentions of the YCJA was to reduce the number of youth
in courts and correctional institutions, including Aboriginal youth.
Tragically, this does not appear to be the case for Aboriginal youth in
Manitoba, who, as in the case of CFS placements, are still vastly over-
represented in the youth justice system, and particularly in remand and
sentenced custody. It also appears that the ratio of Aboriginal to non-
Aboriginal youth in courts and custody has increased in Manitoba since
the introduction of the YCJA. The unique demands placed on youth
justice-related professionals in Manitoba because of the complex social
factors and issues tied to the over-representation of Aboriginal youth in
the criminal justice system have been widely recognized and acknowledged by Manitoba Justice officials, as revealed in the cross-country
consultations on the proposed changes to the YCJA that were initiated
by the federal government in 2008 (Canada, Department of Justice, nd).
However, it is unfortunate that this level of sensitivity to the special circumstances and needs of Aboriginal youth is not promoted to any significant degree by Manitoba Justice and government officials in more
public policy statements on preventing and combating youth crime.

Following "Chargeable" and Convicted Youth through the System: Process and Issues

In the remaining parts of this chapter, we look more closely at data
on how the YCJA has been implemented in Manitoba. As part of this,

attention is given to showing how the implementation of the YCJA appears to be having differential effects on Aboriginal and non-Aboriginal youth. This discussion draws on available documents and statistical data in addition to information and first-hand views obtained from interviews with youth justice-related professionals in Manitoba who have had the opportunity to observe how the YCJA has been implemented in the province over the past decade.[12] Particular attention is given to reviewing information on the treatment of "chargeable" and convicted youth in Manitoba, including data on: the use of diversion (or extra-judicial measures), legal representation and the processing of cases through youth justice courts, remand and sentencing, and youth corrections. These data show that while, as in other provinces, the overall youth sentenced custody rates have fallen in Manitoba since the introduction of the YCJA, the implementation of the Act may also be having other less positive effects, including: a decline in the participation of volunteers in youth focused community justice committees; a decline in the direct participation of police in applying alternative/extrajudicial measures; the taxing of existing legal aid services and increased demands on defence counsel; the growing use of remand custody in lieu of sentenced custody; and the increased difficulties and disenchantment youth justice-related professionals have experienced in attempting to address the needs of at-risk and criminally-involved youth, particularly Aboriginal youth.

Diversion: From "Alternative" to "Extra-Judicial" Measures

In order to appreciate how the implementation of the YCJA has affected the use of youth diversion and other features of the processing of chargeable and convicted youth in Manitoba, it is necessary to start by providing some comparable data on how young offenders were dealt with in the province under the *Young Offenders Act* (YOA). In the late 1990s, Manitoba was one of the leading provinces in the use of alternative measures with young offenders.[13] At the time, it appears that alternative measures in Manitoba operated at both pre- and post-charge stages.[14] During the years the YOA was in effect, the Youth Corrections Branch of Manitoba also gave support to the use of alternative measures through community-based volunteer youth justice committees, and collected and shared both macro- and unique micro- (or disaggregated individual case and completion rate) data on their use across the province.[15] In addition, unlike in most other provinces, the Crown in Manitoba was given discretion to delegate to police "the authority to refer persons to alternative measures" (Kowalski, 1999, p. 4). Thus, under the YOA, police in Manitoba had the discretion to either divert youth informally on their own, or refer them directly to alternative measures under the authority delegated to them by the Crown.

What Happened to Youth Justice Committees?

The use of alternative measures was popular in Manitoba under the YOA, and it is known that youth justice committees even predated the YOA, going back to as early as 1977 (Canada, Department of Justice. *National Survey of Youth Justice Committees in Canada*, 2003, p. 34). In 1997–1998, Manitoba had the third-highest rate of the use of alternative measures in the country,[16] at 201 per 10,000 youth in the population, beat only by Alberta (with 359) and the Northwest Territories (with 312) (Kowalski 1999, p. 5).[17] Through the unique micro-data it generated, the province was also able to provide more detailed information on the types of interventions and completion rates associated with the use of alternative measures. These data showed that in 1998–1999, of the 1,760 alternative measures cases closed, 2,300 interventions were given, and that in these cases, 90% were closed as a result of the successful completion of the interventions.[18]

As part of an analysis of the possible effects of the YCJA on young offenders and the work of youth justice-related professionals in Manitoba, it is necessary to consider the effect it has had on youth diversion. One way of approaching this is to ask the question of what happened to youth justice committees (YJCs). Some baseline data for addressing this question is contained in the federal Department of Justice study that was conducted in 2003 during the transition from the YOA to the YCJA (Canada, Department of Justice, *National Survey of Youth Justice Committees in Canada*, 2003). As part of this study, Department of Justice researchers obtained permission from the Youth Corrections Branch of Manitoba to contact representatives from youth justice committees across the province, which at the time included 57 designated rural and urban-based provincial youth justice committees.[19] Of these designated YJCs, 28 completed and returned "short-form" mail-out questionnaires, and in-depth phone interviews "were conducted with four YJCs who indicated they would be willing to do an interview" (Canada, Department of Justice, 2003, p. 34).

Although limited, the findings of this study are revealing in what they indicate about the work and perceptions of YJC volunteers in Manitoba at the time of the transition from the YOA to the YCJA. In particular, the study found that the number of cases dealt with annually by YJCs was on average "quite small," with 20 out of 28 committees stating they had received fewer than 20 referrals in the past year. However, the caseloads were also quite variable, with the remainder indicating that they received more than 30 referrals annually, "including four who said they received more than 50 cases annually, and up to 100" (Canada, Department of Justice, 2003, p. 36). Briefly, the study also showed that: volunteer membership ranged from a low of four to a high of 15 among the 28 YJCs (with the median volunteer membership being 10 persons); over half (13) had either one or no members with any professional experience in youth justice or related fields; local probation officials provided a key liaison and support role; only 8 reported having a Board of Directors or advisory committee to guide their activities; only 2 had a paid position to assist with the activities of the volunteer members; and the annual provincial funding for each of the 28 committees was usually no more than $1,000.[20] Although the study did not report on the number of rural versus urban YJCs across the province, there were many urban-based YJCs operating in Manitoba prior to 2003, particularly in Winnipeg.

Despite their lack of professional supervision and training, under the YOA, YJCs dealt with a range of alternative measures cases. Specifically, the Department of Justice study found that just over half (16), received referrals at both the pre- and post-charge stages, while 5 received referrals at the sentencing stage, and almost equal numbers (12) indicated that either the police or the Crown referred most cases to them, while four indicated that most referrals came from the youth court. In addition, 22 of the YJCs rated the majority of cases they dealt with as "somewhat serious," while the rest rated cases as "not very serious." Overall, "the most frequently seen offences by most YJCs were theft under $5,000 (typically shoplifting) and mischief, with four YJCs also indicating that common assault was a frequent referral" (Canada, Department of Justice, 2003, p. 36). When questioned about the "sustainability and future" of YJCs in their communities, Department of Justice study respondents felt that although "sustainability was not a problem" given the long 26-year history of YJCs in Manitoba, "there was [also] some perception that Manitoba Justice [did] not adequately value the work of justice committees, in keeping cases out of the court system and in finding more appropriate measures for youth" (Canada, Department of Justice, 2003, p. 36).

Unfortunately, besides the cited federal Department of Justice study, there is still very little publicly available information on how youth and/

or community justice committees are constituted or how they have operated across the province since the implementation of the YCJA. Manitoba Justice currently operates a more general "Community-based Justice" program for both youth and adult offenders, whose website claims that "the Community Justice Branch supports over sixty justice committees and several community-based justice programs" across the province (Manitoba Justice: Criminal Legal Process, Community Justice, online).

However, other information we have obtained suggests that community justice committees (CJCs) dealing specifically with youth justice cases are much less active today than they have been in the past. For example, in Arborg-Riverton, which is one rural community that has a community justice committee, it was noted in a local community newspaper in March 2012, that the committee has seen an average of one youth per year in recent years, although local CJC members would like to see many more young offenders being dealt with locally through restorative justice measures. The chairperson of the committee, Kris Gudmundson, a retired school teacher, has attributed the meagre use of the committee to the lack of referrals from the local RCMP, noting that "We've had some real good success stories when you get the kids young. It's too bad that we don't get more of them. Maybe we could work more closely with the RCMP and things would get better." Similarly, Rob Jantz, a long-time member of the Gimli Community Justice Committee, also located in the Interlake region of Manitoba, has attributed the lack of referrals to the local RCMP and Prosecutions Services, noting that: "These cases only come our way if there's a referral from the Crown or the RCMP. Very few youth go through. I think there could be a lot more referrals" (Carey, 2012). Echoing this concern, when questioned about the use of police discretion in applying extrajudicial measures, one of the interview respondents for this chapter said, "I don't see police officers talking about diversion," their mindset is "charge him" or "turn the kid over to CFS," which "becomes the alternative measure." In this respondent's view, the police he/she was familiar with in Winnipeg took no initiative to have youth referred to diversion-based extrajudicial measures.

The number of youth-centred community justice committees in Manitoba has declined significantly since 2004, while the volume of cases being dealt with by those remaining also appears to have declined. According to the data provided by the Youth Corrections Branch for the Manitoba Justice annual report for 2010–2011, there were 47 "justice committees" operating in the province and approximately 200 volunteer members involved in administering "community justice (extrajudicial) measures" and providing "crime prevention and community education services in their communities" (Manitoba Justice, 2011, p. 38). Assuming, conservatively, and for our purposes as a general "guestimate," that the median volunteer membership of every YJC in Manitoba was 10 in 2003 (for a total of 570), a decline from 570 to 200 members in seven years is quite significant in itself. However, it may be the case that the number of volunteers participating in "justice committees" has declined even more dramatically than these numbers suggest. This is suggested in particular in the fact that while under the YOA urban-based YJCs in Winnipeg (which has over half the province's population), were busy and had many volunteers, since the introduction of the YCJA the operation of community justice committees (or former YJCs) has been discontinued in Winnipeg.[21] According to one interview respondent, who had experience working in the Manitoba youth justice system both before and after 2003, although under the YOA "Manitoba had a pretty extensive Youth Justice Committee network," since the enactment of the YCJA, YJCs have appeared to become "somewhat redundant."

Though more research is needed to determine the reasons for and extent of the decline of youth-centred community justice committees across Manitoba, there are a number of factors that might help to explain this apparent decline, along with the evident variation there now is in the use of CJCs in urban and rural communities. Government documents and the information provided by interview respondents indicate that since the introduction of the YCJA there has been a shift away from a community/volunteer approach towards a more formal/professional agency-based approach to administering alternative/extrajudicial measures in Manitoba. One place this is reflected is in the types of alternative justice and diversion programs provided for Aboriginal youth. In its *Annual Report 2010–2011*, Manitoba Justice (2011, p. 36) reported that it "provides funding to the Manitoba Métis Federation (MMF), Southern Chiefs' Organization (SCO) and Manitoba Keewatinowi Okimakanak (MKO) to support community justice alternative programming in their respective communities" and that ongoing support "was also provided to Onashowewin (a community-based Aboriginal justice program that provides community justice alternatives to both adult and young offenders) in Winnipeg, and the Community Holistic Circle of Healing in Hollow Water that delivers a holistic approach to address the community's justice needs including working with victims, victim support, offenders, offender support and the community." Although referred to by Manitoba Justice as "community-based" programs, unlike YJCs under the YOA, these Aboriginal-focused programs are not primarily volunteer-run programs, just as they are not necessarily youth-focused programs. The same is the case for other diversion programs run by prominent non-profit agencies in Winnipeg such as Mediation Services and the Salvation Army. These agencies also currently receive at least part of the funding for their diversion programs from Manitoba Justice on a per case basis, and have cases referred to them directly by Manitoba Prosecution Services, rather than the police or through referrals from probation officers, as was more often the case under the YOA.[22]

In Winnipeg, since the implementation of the YCJA, there has clearly occurred a shift from a more community-based volunteer (and police-involved) approach to youth diversion, to an agency-based approach to administering extrajudicial measures that is more centrally coordinated by Manitoba Prosecution Services. In fact, this move was undertaken quite clearly and openly in 2004 by Manitoba Prosecution Services in a publically circulated policy directive on "Extra-Judicial Community-Based Justice Programs" which stated, in relation to both adult and youth proceedings, that "[t]he ultimate decision as to whether a case is referred to a community-based justice program rests with the Crown Attorney" (Manitoba, Department of Justice Prosecutions, July 2004). In connection with youth diversion, the policy directive also stated that guidelines for "determining whether a referral to a community-based justice program is appropriate" should take into account "the special status of aboriginal people as set out in the *Youth Criminal Justice Act*" and provisions in the YCJA that require that "the victim should be consulted regarding the referral of the case to a community-based justice program." As noted earlier, in Winnipeg it is generally known that cases involving young persons are commonly referred to non-profit agencies with professional staff who run diversion programs. Given how little information we have so far been able to find on youth diversion in rural Manitoba, more research is clearly needed in order to begin to determine specifically how the introduction of the YCJA and coinciding changes in prosecution and police services' policy, along with the use of discretion by rural and First Nations police and probation officers, have affected young persons in conflict with the law in more rural and remote parts of the province.

While alternative measures were used widely in Manitoba under the YOA, it is also important, historically and comparatively, to recognize that in the late 1990s Manitoba reported the highest provincial rate of bringing chargeable cases to youth court, the lowest proportion of youth court convictions (at 58%), and the highest proportion of the use of stays of proceedings across the country (at 40%) (Sudworth & de-Souza, 2001). It also recorded the highest provincial rate of youth custody admissions (at 239 per 10,000 youth), and the highest rate of youth held in remand custody (at 168 per 10,000 Manitoba youth, or 70% of all youth held in custody).[23] At the same time, Manitoba reported rates of the use of secure custody that were below the national average (at 24, versus 32, per 10,000 youth), rates of open custody that were above the national average (at 46, versus 34, per 10,000 youth), and secure custody sentences than were longer than in any other province (at a median of 92 days) (Moldon & Kukec, 2000), along with transferring more youth cases to adult court than any other province (Canada, Justice, Background for YCJA, nd). In the following sections of the chapter, we examine data bearing on the extent to which the implementation of the YCJA has affected specific aspects of the processing of youth through the Manitoba justice system, along with the key issues and difficulties currently being experienced by youth justice-related professionals in the province.

Legal Services: Issues Relating to Legal Aid and Legal Representation

As in a number of other provinces, legal aid in Manitoba is provided through a mixed system of provincially paid staff and private bar lawyers. Legal aid services across Canada have long been criticized for being underfunded, so it perhaps comes as no surprise that over the last decade many issues have emerged in Manitoba surrounding the provision of legal aid services and legal representation for criminally charged youth. While other provinces may face similar issues, it is worthwhile to identify those that appear to be of particular concern in Manitoba.

As part of the interview-based research for this chapter, we have been able to canvas the views of a number of youth justice-related professionals in Manitoba who are familiar with youth legal representation within the framework of the YCJA. One of the recurrent themes that stem from this research is the common view that recent years have witnessed the taxing of existing legal aid services and increased demands on defence counsel. Although interview respondents mentioned a number of different factors they thought were contributing to the growing challenges involved in providing legal representation to criminally charged youth, one of the common themes to emerge was the feeling that this was partly related to the complexity of the YCJA. Another contributing factor identified by interview respondents were the serious challenges posed by high numbers of youths with special needs, such as fetal alcohol spectrum disorder (FASD) and mental health issues, who were being dealt with across child welfare and youth justice systems. At the same time, some interviewees suggested that the complexity of the YCJA can also open up opportunities for defence counsel to make strategic use of specific provisions of the Act.

How Youth Legal Aid Works in Manitoba

In recent years about 40% of legal aid work in Manitoba has been carried out by Legal Aid Manitoba (LAM) salaried staff lawyers, while 60% has been done by private bar lawyers who are paid a set fee for each specific type of case they handle (Manitoba, Legal Aid, *Annual Report 2011/2012*, p. 13).[24] Currently, LAM operates 18 Community Law Centres across the province and draws on the services of 219 private bar lawyers (LAM, *Annual Report 2011/2012*, p. 8, 11).[25] Approximately 23% of all criminal legal defences funded by Legal Aid Manitoba in recent years have related to youth criminal charges.[26] In addition, LAM funds the cost of duty counsel services for both adults and youth, including initial in-court and drop-in and phone assistance. Although LAM currently employs seven lawyers in its Winnipeg Criminal Duty Counsel Office, including a supervising attorney, four staff lawyers, and two articling students (LAM, *Annual Report 2011/2012*, p. 11), overall much of the duty counsel work carried out across Manitoba is done by private bar lawyers.

In its 2011/2012 annual report, LAM notes that due to shortfalls in funding, its low financial eligibility cut-off level for legal aid, which has remained unchanged since 2000, continues "to exclude many low-income Manitobans from accessing legal aid" and makes funding for legal aid an ongoing challenge (LAM, *Annual Report 2011/2012*, pp. 2, 4, 14). It also reports that, in order to manage with funding shortfalls, it has initiated several cost reduction and efficiency improvement measures in recent years, including a "complexity weighted productivity measure" which "requires LAM staff lawyers to bill all of their completed cases pursuant to the Legal Aid Manitoba Tariff." The aim of this measure is to "allow for an accurate analysis of service delivery efficiencies for both the private bar and staff lawyer delivery alternatives" (LAM, *Annual Report 2011/2012*, p. 4).

Another measure undertaken recently by the government of Manitoba to reduce the shortfall in legal aid funding is to make more parents pay for the criminal legal expenses of their children. While the

YCJA (section 25) formally obligates provinces to provide counsel to young persons, it also "includes a provision that recognizes the right of jurisdictions to look to parents of a young person to recover the costs of legal counsel" (Tustin & Lutes, 2012, p. 61). In line with this provision, in 2010, the government of Manitoba proposed amendments to *The Legal Aid Manitoba Act* that would "enable Legal Aid Manitoba to recover the cost of defending youth accused in criminal cases where their parents could have paid for their child's lawyer but refused to do so" (Justice Manitoba, 2011, p. 12). At the time the Attorney General of Manitoba, Andrew Swan, explained in a news release that the purpose of the proposed amendments was to recoup legal aid costs from the parents of youth who were not eligible for legal aid. He stated that the proposed bill, which "would be the first of its kind in Canada," was needed in light of statistics provided by Legal Aid Manitoba that showed that "the number of YCJA counsel appointments [had] been increasing," and that in the previous year there were approximately "200 cases where counsel was appointed for youth whose parents did not meet legal aid's financial eligibility guidelines, with an estimated cost of over $100,000" (Manitoba, 2010). Although Tustin and Lukes (2012, p. 61) point out that few, if any, youth legal aid "cost recovery" programs exist across Canada, Manitoba, at least in theory, now has one provided for in recent amendments to *The Legal Aid Manitoba Act* (primarily in section 17.2(2)), on the "Responsibility of parent[s] for legal services".[27] However, whether it will do much to reduce the burden of funding legal counsel for criminally charged youth in Manitoba seems doubtful.[28]

The problem faced by Legal Aid Manitoba, and the youth justice system more generally in Manitoba, is not the number of rich kids from the city suburbs and rural "mega-rich farms" whose parents refuse to pay their legal expenses, but rather the far too many poor, marginalized, homeless, and minority youth who lack the supports needed to keep them out of the criminal justice system. Respondents interviewed for this chapter pointed out, in their often impassioned pleas for change, that kids and parents need "jobs and housing," not punishment; 80% of youth in diversion programs are in CFS and group homes; most kids are marginalized and feel they "have nothing to lose by going to jail"; "FASD is a bigger problem" than youth crime in Manitoba; and that "lots of crime is survival crime." These are the more typical backgrounds and circumstances of youth who are charged with crimes in Manitoba and end up being processed through the youth criminal justice system.

It is also of course significant that most of the youth processed through the Manitoba criminal justice system are Aboriginal youth. Although the problem of the growing disproportion of Aboriginal youth in courts and custody since the introduction of the YCJA was pointed to earlier in the chapter, it is important to also look beyond statistical indicators of the problem to how youth justice-related professionals themselves perceive and attempt to cope with it in their daily work lives. In an attempt to get at this, interview respondents were asked what their views were on how the implementation of the YCJA has affected the sentences received by Aboriginal young offenders in Manitoba, in light of the fact that the Act requires that the special circumstances of Aboriginal youth be taken into account by the court at the time of sentencing. The responses to this question were often detailed and pointed, and showed that there is widespread and deep concern about what is happening to Aboriginal youth in the Manitoba criminal justice system. For example, one respondent lamented that: "I don't think it's done anything. You can add a *Gladue* component to a sentence … but it doesn't make any difference … It doesn't speak directly to why kids are in the system," and since almost all of the kids in the system are Aboriginal, "judges already know … so it doesn't need to be spelled out." Another said: "I haven't seen it – I've heard of programs up North – sentencing circles." In Winnipeg, however, "none of the [Aboriginal] kids I've worked with have benefited from this part of the YCJA." Sadly, several respondents pointed out that the section of the YCJA that includes the *Gladue* component often has no effect except to lengthen the time Aboriginal youth spend in remand custody, since it usually takes a number of extra weeks for *Gladue* reports to be prepared.

The Complexity of the YCJA and Legal Representation

It is widely acknowledged that the YCJA is considerably more complicated than the YOA and that it is not even fully understood by many legal professionals who work with it on a day-to-day basis (Bala, 2003; Tustin & Lutes, 2012). In provinces, such as Manitoba, that have few or no provincial court judges who preside in youth justice courts full time, and that have many private bar lawyers doing youth legal aid work who also usually do not specialize in youth justice law, the challenges of administering such a complicated Act may be even more serious. This appears to be the sentiment of a number of youth justice-related professionals in Manitoba interviewed for this chapter who are familiar with youth legal representation within the framework of the YCJA.

One of the key challenges youth justice-related professionals in Manitoba face in administering the YCJA involves the issue of how to interpret and apply sections of the Act dealing with the "breach of conditions" of court orders and imposed sentences.[29]

One of the points made by the interview respondents was that far too many youth were being "breached" for violating conditions attached to probation orders and other community-based sentences, which was leading to more youth in remand custody. A stated aim of the YCJA, of course, is to reduce the use of youth custody; both remand custody and sentenced custody. However, unlike most other provinces that have witnessed substantial decreases in youth incarceration since the introduction of the YCJA, the overall youth custody rate in Manitoba increased 38% from 2005 to 2011, while the province's youth remand custody rate increased over this period to almost 5 times the overall national rate (Munch, 2012). This has led to Manitoba being in the peculiar situation of having by far the highest provincial rate of remand custody and one of the lowest provincial rates of the use of sentenced custody.

When interview respondents were asked for their thoughts on why this might be happening, they often replied that the increase in the use of remand custody was likely tied to the more frequent remanding of youth for "breaching" previous court conditions received as part of earlier community-based sentences for less-serious offences. Several respondents pointed out a pattern of how this works: typically young persons who fail to comply with court orders on a repeated basis are in turn given increasingly more strict court-ordered conditions of release. After a course of numerous breaches, each followed by more strict court orders, youth are eventually remanded in accordance with enabling sections of the YCJA (sections 39, 97, and 102). In turn, this leads to a cycle of youth being repeatedly remanded, sometimes for only a few days, but sometimes also for many months. Interview respondents for the most part were not previously aware of the fact that Manitoba reported the lowest sentenced custody rates in the country at the same time as it reported the highest remand custody rates. However, when this was pointed out to them, several recognized from their experience that what appeared to be happening in Manitoba was that more youth were now serving time in remand custody in lieu of sentenced custody and community-based court orders. It is important to make it clear that this is not a hidden judicial practice or departure from the appropriate application of the YCJA, since it is well known and accepted among youth-justice professionals in Manitoba, including sentencing judges, that the time a youth spends in remand custody awaiting trial and sentencing will be taken into account and deducted at the time of sentencing at a rate of 1.5 days of sentenced custody for every one day of remand custody. Knowing this, it is not as surprising as it might at first appear to find that Manitoba has the lowest youth sentenced custody rate in the country, while having the second highest count of youths in custody on any given day in 2010–2011 (Munch, 2012).[30]

Whether appropriate or not, a great deal of concern was expressed by interview respondents about whether the YCJA should be applied in this way. In particular, respondents voiced concerns about the frequent "breaching" of youth, which leads to additional criminalization, and the implications for custody-based youth correctional programming linked to the fact that youth detention centres in Manitoba are now primarily used for holding youth in remand custody. According to one respondent, "the YCJA sets youth up for onerous conditions – sets them up to fail. Most kids are in custody for breaches" for failing to meet the increasingly "strict conditions" imposed by judges – "of course they are going to breach." Other respondents echoed these concerns, lamenting that "breaches are massive," "every kid breaches," kids are doing "more community service hours," and some kids are even doing "community service hours while in custody." In addition, respondents involved in working in treatment programs noted how frustrating it was to see youth in treatment programs "going in and out of MYC [the Manitoba Youth Centre] for breaches," and "kids who have a multitude of problems and conditions," like addictions and FASD, "constantly being re-criminalized" and "lumped in" with other youth who "don't have the same issues." However, the growing use of remand custody in Manitoba is also probably being contributed to by factors other than how the YCJA is being interpreted and applied by youth justice professionals. It may also be happening partly, as one respondent pointed out, because of the fact that there is "nowhere [else] for some kids to go," when "CFS is overloaded," when CFS kids are being placed in hotels, and when kids "can't be let out on bail since they can't go home [and there are] no placements in the community."

The High Numbers of Youth with Special Needs

The challenge of dealing with youth in the criminal justice system with special problems and needs, including those with FASD[31] and mental health-related disorders, is not unique to Manitoba. It is also an issue that, at least on the surface, is not directly tied to the implementation of the YCJA. However, respondents interviewed for this chapter commonly voice the concern that the high numbers of youth with special needs being drawn into the youth justice system in Manitoba is a tragic problem that urgently needs to be addressed.

One reason for these high numbers is the prevalence of FASD in Aboriginal communities, and the widely observed connection between youths with FASD and their involvement in the criminal justice system as both offenders and victims (Bracken, 2008; Totten, 2010). Not surprisingly, Aboriginal youths with FASD also appear over-represented in the CFS placements (Burnside 2012; Manitoba, Office of the Children's Advocate, 2012). The issue of the linked over-representation of Aboriginal and FASD youth in CFS and youth justice systems has been addressed widely in the province at different levels of government, the justice system, and the media. In the context of youth justice, youth defence counsel have been especially vocal in their criticism of the lack of adequate programming for FASD young offenders, and even provincial court judges have spoken out in public on this issue. An example of this is captured in the newspaper article "Youth program battles 'sausage-factory justice'" in the *Winnipeg Free Press* in April 2010, which describes the challenges faced by the government-funded "FASD Youth Justice Program" operating in Manitoba. The article noted that although at the time more than 300 accused young offenders were "waiting to get diagnosed" through the FASD Youth Justice Program operating through the Manitoba courts, in the previous five years only 72 youths were diagnosed with FASD through the program, while "judges, lawyers, probation officers and other court officials have referred about five times that many kids to the program." Speaking publically on this issue, Judge Mary Kate Harvie stated that while "We're very good at the sausage-factory justice, the Kentucky Fried Justice, the millions and millions served," the task of diagnosing FASD in young offenders is nonetheless "worth the investment" (Welch, 2011, p. A9). Until recently, one of the most prominent defence counsel in Manitoba involved in providing legal representation to criminally charged FASD youth was Corey La Berge, who worked with Manitoba Legal Aid as "Accommodation Counsel for Youth Living with FASD," which was a three-year project, funded by the Department of Justice Canada and the Province of Manitoba (South First Nations, Network of Care, Partnerships, nd). In this capacity, La Berge also took advantage of opportunities to provide public education on FASD and advocate for FASD youth through the media, highlighting the findings of studies on the connection between the victimization experiences of youth with FASD and their involvement in crime, and the need for more adequate services and programs for FASD youth caught up in the criminal justice system (Rabson, 2011).

In addition to advocating on behalf of FASD youth, La Berge has also been an outspoken critic of the Manitoba justice system and its treatment of youth suffering from mental health disorders; in one case arguing that a charge laid against one of his clients for "a weapons breach after cutting herself with a kitchen knife" was an act akin to child abuse. After trying to harm herself, the girl was shackled in her detention cell. Prior to the "weapons breach" with the "kitchen knife," the youth had been "breached" on several occasions for violating court conditions related to a conviction for being unlawfully in a dwelling house, as well as the failure to comply with previous court conditions. This case, La Berge noted, offered yet another example of the fact that Justice Manitoba seemed "to be endorsing the criminalization of a young person, a young, vulnerable person for having a disability and mental-health problems" (Giroday, 2011). This case also mirrors many other similar cases that have been described to the first author of this chapter by other youth justice professionals in Manitoba of the continuous "breaching" of youth for bail and probation condition violations, and recurrent remanding of these youth, even though many are suffering from personal, familial, and mental health problems that make it difficult if not impossible for them to meet the conditions of their bail and/or probation agreements. Partly in response to the specific case made public in the media by La Berge in 2011, Louis Goulet, the executive director of youth correctional services for Justice Manitoba, announced that a new program would be adopted in youth centres for treating girls suffering from mental health problems (Giroday, 2011), and in its annual report for 2010–2011, Manitoba Justice (2011, p. 38) stated more generally, regarding program development initiatives for special needs youth, that "[i]n an effort to better understand and effectively deal with youth with complex needs, Youth Corrections [had recently] trained staff at the Manitoba Youth Centre and Agassiz Youth Centre in Trauma Informed Care, Mental Health First Aid and Fetal Alcohol Spectrum Disorder (FASD)." This arguably speaks volumes about the ad hoc nature of policymaking and training in Manitoba Youth Corrections, and the continuing piecemeal manner in which the needs of FASD and mentally disordered accused and convicted youth are being dealt with in the community and in custody under the YCJA.

The Strategic Use of the YCJA by Defence Counsel

It is also important to recognize that because of its inherent complexity, and continuing reinterpretation by the courts, various sections of the YCJA can be used selectively by defence counsel on behalf of their clients. An example of this in Manitoba is the way in which defence counsel advocate on behalf of their clients at sentencing to ensure that the sentence they receive has "meaningful consequences." In general, they recognize that while judges have a huge amount of discretion, it was not consistently or uniformly applied. In addition, they know that it is sometimes the case that judges who "fill in," or are temporarily assigned to hear youth cases, may not be as familiar with the YCJA as other judges, and may be less sympathetic to the case they are arguing. The common perception among defence counsel interviewed for this chapter is that since "sections of the YCJA are confusing," the outcome of the case often "depends on the judge."

Arguing for "Meaningful Consequences"

Section 38(1) of the YCJA states that the purpose of youth sentences is "to hold a young person accountable for an offence through the imposition of just sanctions that have meaningful consequences for the young person and that promote his or her rehabilitation and reintegration into society, thereby contributing to the long-term protection of the public." In 2012, the range of considerations judges could take into account in deciding on what were "just sanctions" and "meaningful consequences" was expanded by the federal government of Canada through the implementation of Bill C-10, which added "specific deterrence" and "denunciation" to the sentencing justifications that might be considered by youth court judges. While criminologists and lawyers from across Canada have expressed concern about the possible effect Bill C-10 may have on youth potentially receiving considerably more harsh but ineffective sentences (Green, 2012; Bala et al., 2012), youth justice professionals in Manitoba who are familiar with past sentencing practices question whether Bill C-10 will make any real difference. In particular, some defence counsel claim that in their experience, even before Bill C-10, at least some judges implicitly took into account specific deterrence and denunciation at sentencing under the general umbrella of "meaningful consequences." Consequently, these defence counsel maintained that one of their most important roles at sentencing was to remind judges that harsh sentences were often not necessarily "just" or "meaningful." They also often expressed the belief that because some judges were known to subscribe to a more conservative view of what constituted "meaningful consequences," at least in the court settings they worked in, "judge shopping" mattered.

2.9. Issues in Youth Corrections

Given what we have already learned in this chapter, it is easy to understand some of the difficulties and disenchantment youth justice-related professionals experience in attempting to address the special needs of at-risk and criminally involved youth in Manitoba. This, arguably, may especially be the case for youth justice professionals working in youth corrections in Manitoba. What we have seen happen in Manitoba since the introduction of the YCJA is the virtual stripping of Manitoba Youth Corrections of its mandate to serve as an agency for promoting youth crime prevention and the "rehabilitation" and "reintegration" of young offenders. As was noted earlier in the chapter, in 2012 Youth Corrections was required to give up its long-time role in implementing community-based youth crime prevention programs to the newly formed Department of Children and Youth Opportunities. We have also seen how, over the last decade, that Youth Corrections, which had been a national leader in promoting the use of alternative measures under the YOA, has given up much of the responsibility it could have taken on for administering extrajudicial measures (if youth justice committees were given more support) to Manitoba Prosecution Services and non-profit alternative and restorative justice agencies. While it appears that youth probation services is still an important service that operates under the umbrella of Manitoba Youth Corrections, we have also seen how the rehabilitative and reintegration role of youth probation officers has been undermined by the fact much of the attention of probation officers is now spent "breaching" youth for failing to comply with court orders and overseeing the production of pre-sentence and *Gladue* reports. And finally, and perhaps most distressingly for rehabilitative-oriented youth corrections workers, we have seen youth custody facilities in Manitoba turned into serving primarily as youth remand custody centres, where it is no doubt becoming increasingly difficult to run effective treatment programs for sentenced young offenders. In light of these developments, it might be prudent for the government of Manitoba to look at, and perhaps follow, the experience of other provinces, such as British Columbia and Quebec, that have traditionally given their government ministries of Children and Family Development and Health and Social Services responsibility for providing services to young offenders and their families (Cournoyer et al., 2012; Morrison & Pawlychka, 2012; see also chapters by Alain and Corrado et al. in this volume).

Conclusion

Most of the research carried out to date on the implementation of the YCJA at a national level drawing on aggregate level data has pointed to the apparent positive effects it has had in increasing the use of alternative/extrajudicial measures and lowering the use of sentenced custody (Bala et al., 2012). Drawing on this type of evidence, most criminologists have concluded that overall the YCJA seems to be working reasonably well (cf. Doob & Sprott, 2006). On the other hand, however, some have taken a more sceptical stance, pointing to "the continuing potential for the YCJA, and its possible perceived failures, to be used to justify more punitive responses to various types of broadly defined 'youth violent crime' and 'serious violent offenders'" (Smandych, 2012, p. 20; citing Hogeveen, 2005a, 2005b; and Smandych, 2006). Essentially, these more critical criminologists argue that adequate resources may not be put into place to allow for the proper implementation of the YCJA in already disadvantaged communities (such as Aboriginal communities), and if this happens communities themselves may be unfairly blamed for the perceived failures of the Act.

The findings reported in this chapter suggest that the implementation of the YCJA in Manitoba has been difficult and led to many challenges and issues. However, they do not provide evidence of the inherent failure of the legislation itself. On balance, the youth justice-related professionals in Manitoba interviewed for this chapter felt that while the YCJA may be an adequate piece of written legislation, the specific political, socio-economic, and demographic characteristics of the province made it difficult to implement. One thing that is certain is that we need more research that can help us understand what youth justice-related professionals, and other concerned Manitobans, think about how well the YCJA is working in the province and about what they feel can be done to improve the way in which youth justice is administered. Document-based and statistical evidence provides a useful starting point for attempting to shed light on how the YCJA has been implemented provincially and at a national level. However, it is only through systematic research aimed at collecting the first-hand accounts of professionals and volunteers working in the various "trenches" of the youth justice system, that a more complete picture of the effects of the YCJA in diverse provinces, like Manitoba, can be developed. This chapter offers a beginning step in this direction.[32]

NOTES

1 To our knowledge, this chapter represents the first focused study written specifically about the introduction of the YCJA in Manitoba and its apparent impacts on youth at risk, young offenders, and the provincial youth justice system.
2 All of the co-authors of the chapter except for Russell Smandych have extensive first-hand experience with the youth justice system in Manitoba. However, the specific views held by these co-authors are not individually identified in the chapter, nor do any of the views and opinions offered in the chapter represent the views or formal positions of the agencies where they are now employed or have been employed in the past.
3 As of 2011, approximately 55% of Manitobans (691,800) lived in Winnipeg, while the rest (558,800) lived in smaller urban, rural, and remote northern parts of the province; Winnipeg (2012), online.
4 In 2012, the responsibility for implementing community-based youth crime prevention programs was transferred to the newly formed Department of Children and Youth Opportunities. See Manitoba, *Department of Children and Youth Opportunities Annual Report, 2012,* available online. The youth crime prevention mandate of this new department has also been broadened to include "promoting and raising awareness of best practices in crime prevention and collaborating with communities to undertake evidence based activities"; "promoting reconciliation between children under 12 in conflict with the law and the community" and "the coordination of services for these children and their families."
5 There are currently 44 provincial court judges appointed in Manitoba, 33 of whom are based in Winnipeg, with the remaining judges based in Thompson (3), Brandon (3), Dauphin (2), The Pas (2), and Portage la Prairie (1) (Manitoba, Manitoba Courts, Provincial Courts – Judges, online).
6 The Dakota Ojibway Police Service, which is the only stand-alone Aboriginal police service in Manitoba, provides policing services to five First Nations communities in southwestern Manitoba, while the RCMP

oversees First Nations policing in the remaining 58 First Nations communities across the province.

7 It is important to note that the attempt to determine longer-term trends in youth crime, both at individual local and federal levels is further complicated by the fact that since 2003, under the YCJA, the police-reported youth crime rate includes all "chargeable" or "apprehended" young persons (including those diverted from courts) "who have been identified by police as offenders and against whom a charge could be laid" (Bala, Carrington, & Roberts, 2012, p. 84).

8 Youth Agencies Alliance website.

9 See also Canada, Public Safety, NCPC Publications – Building the Evidence, online.

10 Following common practice among criminologists, we define *primary prevention programs* as programs provided to a whole population group, such as all children through school-wide implementation, while *secondary programs* focus on at-risk populations and *tertiary programs* are provided to people, including youth, who are already involved in crime and caught up in the criminal justice system (Howell, 2009, pp. 335–337).

11 Further evidence of the preoccupation of both federal and provincial Manitoba governments with youth crime prevention initiatives related to guns, gangs, and violence are other programs supported by both levels of government including the expansion of the province's Gang Response and Suppression Program (GRASP) in 2011. GRASP is an integrated initiative on the part of "police, prosecutions and probation to coordinate a community risk management plan" for the "intensive supervision of gang members and high risk offenders on bail or probation in order to ensure their compliance with court order conditions and to detect breaches." Manitoba Justice has also continued to support a gang suppression and prevention initiative called "Spotlight," which is "designed to combine close supervision and swift consequences with collaborative community services to help youth deal with substance abuse, stay in school or find a job" (Manitoba Justice, 2011, p. 35). Another indication of the priority given by the federal government to these types of initiatives is the Harper government's announcement in Winnipeg in February 2012, on the renewal of the NCPC, Youth Gang Prevention Program (Canada, Public Safety, Harper Government Launches Next Phase of Youth Gang Prevention Program, online).

12 As set out in the University of Manitoba Research Ethics Protocol that was approved to carry out these interviews, a research instrument consisting of 10 open-ended interview questions was used to gather information and opinions from 15 to 20 interview respondents. In order to protect

confidentiality, especially in the context of the small size of the sample and
the small community of youth justice-related professionals in Manitoba,
no identifying information is provided regarding interview respondents'
current professional occupations, beyond referring to them as working
in one of the broad fields of youth crime prevention, legal representation
(defence counsel), youth treatment, and youth justice.

13 Under the YOA, alternative measures were defined as "formalized programs
across Canada to which young persons who would otherwise proceed to
court are dealt with through non-judicial, community-based alternatives"
(Kowalski, 1999, p. 1).

14 Kowalski (1999, p. 3) states that alternative measures operated in
Manitoba at the pre-charge stage, while Sanders (2000, pp. 3, 12) states
that in Manitoba alternative measures were initiated at the post-charge
stage. Further research is required to clarify which if either of these was
the case, or whether both pre- and post-charge alternative measures were
used in Manitoba under the YOA as they were in a number of other provinces (Kowalski, 1999). In any event, as we shall see shortly, after the YCJA
came into effect in Manitoba extrajudicial measures were (re-)designed to
operate at both pre- and post-charges stages.

15 From 1998 to 1999, Manitoba was the only jurisdiction in the country to
submit disaggregated micro-data on youth alternative measures to the
Canadian Centre for Justice Statistics, which enabled more detailed data
analysis and comparison (Engler & Crowe, 2000, p. 11).

16 Excluding British Columbia, for which data were unavailable.

17 Although the following year, Manitoba recorded a drop from 201 to 155
per 10,000, which lowered it to the fourth highest reported rate of the use
of alternative measures across the country (Engler & Crowe, 2000, p. 6).

18 The most common interventions were caution letters, apologies and essays, presentations, or referrals. Notably, also, "although 90% of cases were
successfully completed, 99% of the individual interventions were completed. Therefore, in most cases at least some of the interventions were completed" (Engler and Crowe, 2000, p. 11).

19 The study noted that at the time, Manitoba also had "Aboriginal committees" under the umbrella of the Manitoba Keewatinowi Okimakanak organization that were not provincially designated, and therefore were not
included (Canada, Department of Justice, 2003, p. 5). A number of these
committees, located in First Nations communities, are funded through the
First Nation Justice Strategy (FNJS), which is a joint initiative of Manitoba
Justice, the Department of Justice Canada, and Manitoba Keeawtinowi
Okimakanak Inc. (MKO), which represents 16 northern and remote First
Nations communities (Manitoba Keeawtinowi Okimakanak Inc., Justice,

online). In 2011, an external evaluation was conducted of the community justice initiatives run through MKO that involved interviews "with program managers, community justice workers, offenders/victims, [and] court personnel (Crowns, RCMP, and Probations)," as part of its application for funding renewal; however, besides reporting that the outcome of the evaluation was positive, the MKO website provides sparse information on its community justice initiatives and no links to the evaluation itself or the company that was hired to conduct it.

20 This included an automatic $200 for small administrative requirements such as postage, and a possible additional $800 that could be requested in a proposal for resources and training, including items like videos and expenses for training courses provided by Mediation Services (Canada, Department of Justice, 2003, p. 35).

21 Information provided by interview respondents.

22 Information provided by interview respondents.

23 Sixty-nine per cent of these youth admissions to remand were identified as being Aboriginal, while 75% of youth admissions to sentenced custody were identified as Aboriginal, whereas at the time only 16% of Manitoba's youth population were Aboriginal (Moldon & Kukec, 1998, pp. 7, 9).

24 More specifically, in 2010/2011, the ratio of private bar to staff services was 58:42, while in 2011/2012 it was 61.39 (Manitoba Legal Aid, *Annual Report 2011/2012*, p. 13).

25 In 2011/2012, 83 legal staff were employed in Community Law Centres, including 16 supervising attorneys, 42 staff lawyers, 7 paralegals, and 17 articling students.

26 This is calculated from LAM statistics for "criminal adult" and "criminal youth" cases opened and closed in Manitoba in 2010/2011 and 2011/2012 (Manitoba Legal Aid, *Annual Report 2011/2012*, p. 12).

27 Which reads:

> 17.2(2) In the following circumstances, the cost of legal aid provided to a child constitutes a debt due and owing from the parent of the child to Legal Aid Manitoba recoverable in any court of competent jurisdiction:
>> (a) a child is charged with an offence;
>> (b) the child is ineligible to receive legal aid because of the income or other financial resources of the child's parent or parents, or the refusal or failure of the child's parent or parents to provide information to determine the child's eligibility for legal aid;
>> (c) the child's parent or parents refuse or fail to retain legal services on behalf of the child;

> (d) Legal Aid Manitoba provides legal aid to the child as the result of a direction made under section 25 of the *Youth Criminal Justice Act* (Canada).

In the revised 2012 Legal Aid Manitoba "Area Directors' Manual' nothing is mentioned specifically regarding how youth legal aid cost recovery amendments to *The Legal Aid Act of Manitoba* have been put into effect in practice. However, it does state (somewhat ambiguously) under: "5.2 Merit in Criminal Matters: Practices Notes, Court Appointed Counsel Under Section 25(4)(b)" that: "Where the court appoints counsel under section 25(4)(b) of the YCJA, and the parents do not qualify due to excess income, a staff lawyer will be appointed, since choice of counsel is otherwise available to the client through private retainer" (Manitoba, Legal Aid Manitoba, Area Directors' Manual, Revised May 22, 2012, p. 27, online).

28 The effectiveness of this amendment also seems doubtful and problematic since the definition of "parent" for the purpose of applying the law may also arguably (and ironically) include the Child and Family Services branch of the government of Manitoba, as the legal guardian of children under CFS care: view of interview respondent.

29 YCJA, section 97(1) (2), "Conditions to be included in custody and supervision order," and "Other conditions." Section 102(1), "Breach of conditions"; Tustin and Lutes (2012, pp. 186–198).

30 In addition, it is possible that the current manner in which remand custody is used in Manitoba may be having an effect on how frequently youth prosecutors across Manitoba request adult sentences upon conviction, since hypothetically it may be the case that the time the convicted youth has already spent in remand is equivalent to an adult sentence.

31 FASD is the term used to categorize several possible medical conditions that are the result of central nervous system irregularities caused by prenatal exposure to alcohol, including fetal alcohol syndrome (FAS), partial FAS, and alcohol-related neurodevelopment disorder (ARND) (Brown et al., 2012, p. 770). The prenatal brain damage caused by this exposure has been linked to the inability of young people suffering from FASD to "connect unacceptable behaviour with consequences"; comprehend and follow institutional rules; and avoid "the risk of negative influence through association with criminal peer models" (Conry & Fast, 2000, pp. 69–73; Green, 2012, p. 73).

32 The authors would like to thank research assistants Mateja Carevic and Ermina Delalic for the work they did gathering document- and statistic-based information for this chapter.

REFERENCES

Aboriginal Council of Winnipeg. (2010). *Urban gang initiatives in the city of Winnipeg*. Winnipeg: Aboriginal Council of Winnipeg. Retrieved from http://www.abcouncil.org/PDF/ACWI%20 Gang%20Prevention%20Programs%20Community%20Resource%20Guide.pdf.

Bala, N. (2003). *Youth criminal justice law*. Toronto, ON: Irwin Law.

Bala, N., Carrington, P., & Roberts, J. (2012). Implementing youth justice reform: Effects of the Youth Criminal Justice Act. In J. Winterdyk & R. Smandych (Eds.), *Youth at risk and youth justice: A Canadian overview* (pp. 80–103). Toronto, ON: Oxford University Press.

Bracken, D. (2008). Canada's Aboriginal People, fetal alcohol syndrome and the criminal justice system. *British Journal of Community Justice 6*(3): 21–33.

Brennan S., & Dauvergne, M. (2011). Police-reported crime statistics in Canada, 2010. *Juristat* (July): 1–39. Retrieved from http://www.statcan.gc.ca/pub/85-002-x/2011001/article/11523-eng.pdf.

Burnside, L. (2012). *Youth in care with complex needs. Special report for the Office of the Children's Advocate of Manitoba*. Retrieved from http://www.childrensadvocate.mb.ca/wp-content/ uploads/Youth-with-Complex-Needs-Report-final.pdf.

Carey, T. (2012). Community Justice Committee should be utilized more. *Interlake Spectator*, 29 March. Retrieved from http://www.interlaketoday.ca/2012/03/19/community-justice-committee-should-be-utilized-more.

Canada, Department of Justice. (2003). *A national survey of youth justice committees in Canada*. Retrieved from http://www.justice.gc.ca/eng/rp-pr/cj-jp/yj-jj/rr03_jj7/rr03_yj7.pdf.

Canada, Department of Justice. (n.d.). Background for YCJA, Part C: Transfers to adult court. Retrieved from http://www.justice.gc.ca/eng/rp-pr/cj-jp/yj-jj/back-hist/partc.html.

Canada, Department of Justice. (n.d.). *Comprehensive review of the Youth Criminal Justice Cross Country Roundtable Report*. Obtained through Access to Information and posted only by W. Campbell, April 4, 2011. http://www.loosehttp://www.loosefiles.ca/?p=191files.ca/?p=191.

Canada, Public Safety, NCPC. (2008). Promising and model crime prevention programs. Volume 1. Retrieved from http://www.publicsafety.gc.ca/cnt/rsrcs/pblctns/prmsng-mdl-vlm1/index-eng.aspx.

Canada, Public Safety, NCPC. (2011). Promising and model crime prevention programs. Volume 2. Retrieved from http://www.publicsafety.gc.ca/cnt/rsrcs/pblctns/prmsng-mdl-vlm2/index-eng.aspx.

Calverley, D., Cotter, A., & Halla, E. (2010). Youth custody and community services in Canada, 2008–2009. *Juristat* (April): 1–29. http://www.statcan .gc.ca/pub/85–002-x/2010001/article/11147-eng.pdf.

Cournoyer, L-G., Dionne, J., Goyette, M., & Hamel, P. (2012). Quebec's experience in keeping youth out of jail. In J. Winterdyk & R. Smandych (Eds.). *Youth at risk and youth justice: A Canadian overview* (pp. 335–357). Toronto, ON: Oxford University Press.

Curran, A., Bowness, E., & Comack, E. (2010). *Meeting the needs of youth: Perspectives from youth-serving agencies.* Winnipeg, MB: Canadian Centre for Policy Alternatives-Manitoba.

DeGusti, B, MacRae, L., Vallée, M., Caputo, T., & Hornick, J. (2009). *Best practices for chronic/persistent youth offenders in Canada: Summary report.* Calgary, AB: Canadian Research Institute for Law and the Family and Centre for Initatives on Children, Youth and the Community. Retrieved from http:// www.publicsafety.gc.ca/cnt/rsrcs/pblctns/prstnt-ffndrs/index-eng.aspx.

Doob, A., & Sprott, J. (2006). Punishing youth crime in Canada: The blind men and the elephant. *Punishment and Society 8*(2): 223–233.

Giroday, G. (2011, January 6). Girl who abuses self charged: Lawyer says approach akin to child abuse. *Winnipeg Free Press.*

Green, R. (2012). Explaining the Youth Criminal Justice Act. In J. Winterdyk & R. Smandych (Eds.), *Youth at risk and youth justice: A Canadian overview* (pp. 54–79). Toronto, ON: Oxford University Press.

Greenberg, H., Grekul, J., & Nelson, R. (2012). Aboriginal youth crime in Canada. In J. Winterdyk & R. Smandych (Eds.), *Youth at Risk and Youth Justice: A Canadian Overview* (pp. 228–252). Toronto, ON: Oxford University Press.

Hogeveen, B. (2005a). Toward "safer" and "better" communities? Canada's Youth Criminal Justice Act, Aboriginal youth and the processes of exclusion. *Critical Criminology 13*: 287–305.

Hogeveen, B. (2005b). If we are tough on crime, if we punish crime, then people get the message: Constructing and governing the punishable young offender in Canada during the late 1990s. *Punishment and Society 7*(1): 73–89.

Howell, J. (2009). *Juvenile delinquency: A comprehensive framework.* 2nd Edition. Thousand Oaks, CA: Sage.

Kowalski, M. (1999). Alternative measures for youth in Canada. *Juristat* (June): 1–11. Retrieved from http://publications.gc.ca/collections/Collection-R/ Statcan/85-002-XIE/0089985-002-XIE.pdf.

MacDonald Youth Services. (2011). *MacDonald Youth Services, 2010– 2011 Annual report.* http://cms.tng-secure.com/file_download. php?fFile_id=18967.

Manitoba, Department of Justice Prosecutions. (2004). Policy directive. Subject: Extra-judicial community-based justice programs, Guideline No. 5: COM:1.1, July. Retrieved from http://www.gov.mb.ca/justice/prosecutions/policy/pdf/extra_judicial_community_based_justice_alternatives.pdf.

Manitoba Justice. (2011). *Annual Report 2010–2011*. http://www.gov.mb.ca/justice/publications/annualreports/pdf/annualreport1011.pdf.

Manitoba Justice. (n.d.). Crime prevention. http://www.gov.mb.ca/cyo/crime_prevention/index.html.

Manitoba Justice. (n.d.). Criminal legal process, community justice. http://www.gov.mb.ca/ justice/criminal/communityjustice.html.

Manitoba, Legal Aid Manitoba. (2012). *Annual report 2011/2012*. Retrieved from http://www.legalaid.mb.ca/pdf/2012_annual_report.pdf.

Manitoba, Legal Aid Manitoba. (2012). Area directors' manual, p. 27. http://www.legalaid.mb.ca/pdf/ADManual_May22_12.pdf.

Manitoba. News Release. (2010). Legislation proposed to help legal aid recover costs from parents who won't pay. November 24. Retrieved from http://news.gov.mb.ca/news/ index.html?item=10251.

Manitoba, Office of the Children's Advocate. (2012). *Strengthening our youth: Their journey to competence and independence, a progress report on youth leaving Manitoba's child welfare system*. Retrieved from http://digitalcollection.gov .mb.ca/awweb/ pdfopener?smd=1&did=20935&md=1.

Minaker, J., & Hogeveen, B. (2009). *Youth, crime, and society: Issues of power and justice*. Toronto, ON: Pearson.

Moldon, M., & Kukec, D. (2000). Youth custody and community service in Canada, 1998–99. *Juristat* (September): 1–15. Retrieved from http://www.statcan.gc.ca/pub/85-002-x/85-002-x2000008-eng.pdf.

Morrison, B., & Pawlychka, C. (2012). Juvenile justice and restorative justice: Reflecting on developments in British Columbia. In J. Winterdyk & R. Smandych (Eds.), *Youth at risk and youth justice: A Canadian overview* (pp. 358–378). Toronto, ON: Oxford University Press.

Munch, C. (2012). Youth Correctional Statistics in Canada, 2010/2011. *Juristat* (October): 1–22. Retrieved from http://www.statcan.gc.ca/pub/85-002-x/2012001/article/11716-eng.pdf.

Rabson, M. (2011). Likelihood of FASD leading to victimization overlooked. *Winnipeg Free Press*, 3 November.

Reid, S., & Gilliss, S. (2012). Key challenges in hearing the voice of youth in the youth justice system. In J. Winterdyk & R. Smandych (Eds.), *Youth at risk and youth justice: A Canadian overview* (pp. 379–399). Toronto, ON: Oxford University Press.

Skoog, D., & Perrault, S. (2001). *Child protection and criminal involvement: An empirical study,* Winnipeg, MB: University of Manitoba.

Smandych, R. (2006). Canada: Repenalization and young offenders' rights. In J. Muncie & B. Goldson, (Eds.), *Comparative youth justice.* London, UK: Sage.

Smandych, R. (2012). From "misguided children" to "criminal youth": Exploring historical and contemporary trends in Canadian youth justice. In: J. Winterdyk & R. Smandych (Eds.), *Youth at risk and youth justice: A Canadian overview* (pp. 3–25). Toronto, ON: Oxford University Press.

South First Nations, Network of Care. (n.d.). Partnerships. Retrieved from http://www.southernauthorityfasd.org/ partnerships_accommodation_counsel.php.

Sprott, J., & Doob, A. (2008). Youth crime rates and the youth justice system. *Canadian Journal of Criminology and Criminal Justice 50*(5): 621–639.

Sudworth, M., & deSouza, P. (2001). Youth court statistics, 1999/2000. *Juristat* (May): 1–18.

Thomas, J. (2005). Youth court statistics, 2003/4. *Juristat* (June): 1–19.

Totten, M. (2010). Investigating the linkages between FASD, gangs, sexual exploitation and women abuse in the Canadian Aboriginal population: A preliminary study. Native Women's Association of Canada. Retrieved from http://journals.sfu.ca/fpcfr/index.php/FPCFR/article/view/89/154.

Totten, M. (2012). An overview of gang-involved youth in Canada. In J. Winterdyk & R. Smandych (Eds.), *Youth at risk and youth justice: A Canadian overview* (pp. 253–278). Toronto, ON: Oxford University Press.

Tustin, L., & Lutes, R. 2012. *A guide to the Youth Criminal Justice Act.* Markham, ON: LexisNexis.

Vallée, M. (2010). An historical overview of crime prevention initiatives in Canada: A federal perspective. *International Journal of Child, Youth and Family Studies 1*(1), 21–52.

Welch, M. (2011). *Corrections: A critical approach.* Oxford, UK: Routledge.

Winterdyk, J. (2012). Nothing but the facts: Measuring youth crime in Canada. In J. Winterdyk & R. Smandych (Eds.), *Youth at risk and youth justice: A Canadian overview* (pp. 80–103). Toronto, ON: Oxford University Press.

Woloschuk, C. (2009). Protecting and policing children: The origins and nature of juvenile justice in Winnipeg. In E. W. Jones & G. Friesen (Eds.), *Prairie metropolis: New essays on Winnipeg social history* (pp. 63–81). Winnipeg, MB: University of Manitoba Press.

5 Youth Justice in New Brunswick

SUSAN REID

Professor Daniel Hurley, of the Faculty of Law at the University of New Brunswick, suggested that New Brunswick has never had the luxury of vast resources as other provinces have when implementing their youth justice systems, and uses the metaphor describing the New Brunswick system as an "under-serviced delivery van" compared to the "Cadillac smoothness" of some of the other provincial jurisdictions (Hurley, 1992, p. 2). The services for young persons in New Brunswick under the *Youth Criminal Justice Act* (YCJA), the lack of resources for training, inconsistency of programs across vastly different geographic regions, and reliance on federal funding for innovative programs, has meant that the province continues to work with meagre resources provided through federal-provincial transfer arrangements. In 2008, as part of the federal government's comprehensive review of the YCJA, the minister of justice invited provincial and territorial ministers to join him in hosting consultations about the successes and challenges of the legislation. The round-table discussion groups, held in each province and territory, included members of the judiciary, prosecutors, defence counsel, police, academics, non-government organizations, mental health programs, as well as municipal and provincial government official. Consistently across all provinces and territories, the government was told that the YCJA was a "long and thoughtful process based on research evidence. As indicated in the final report,[1] "legislation cannot prevent crime, reduce crime or protect the public" was echoed across the country. All provinces and territories identified a lack of sustainable resources to implement the programs and services necessary to fully embrace the YCJA. In the New Brunswick round-table, in which the author participated, the report captured a recurring theme of a lack of resources: "Federal and provincial governments should share the responsibility for resources to support the Act" (p. 16) and "A lot of the necessary resources to fulfil the YCJA implementation have not been put into place" (p. 17).

Despite a lack of financial resources to support youth services in New Brunswick, a number of innovations have been developed that have drawn on the strength of community agencies and partnerships throughout the province. While there have been some challenging situations within the youth system over the past decade, New Brunswick continues to strive for opportunities to replace worn out parts of the system with the infusion of new energy from integrated partnerships between government departments, police, and community agencies.

This chapter will outline the history of youth justice in the province providing a backdrop of the continuing struggles to deliver a high quality program for youth in a province with a small population base and a large geographic boundary. Some of the initiatives that have been developed over the past few years under the YCJA will be highlighted to show the strength of partnerships at the community level and the attempt to close the gap in services for youth despite continuing fiscal restraint. The author will be drawing on a series of interviews and focus groups that have been conducted with community agencies, criminal justice professionals, and young people involved in the system to ensure that the discussion of these key issues is framed within the voices from the field.

New Brunswick is the largest of the three Maritime provinces covering approximately 242 kilometres (150 miles) from east to west and 322 kilometres (200 miles) north to south. Despite its physical size, the population of New Brunswick in 2012 was 755,950, which is almost 200,000 less than its neighbour Nova Scotia.

One of the challenges faced by those working in the province with young persons under the YCJA, is the geographic constraints experienced by a largely rural population. The largest cities are in the southern part of the province. While there are regional offices throughout the province, the head office for the RCMP, the Department of Public Safety, and the Attorney General are all in the capital of Fredericton. Policing in New Brunswick is a blend of municipal and city police forces as well as the RCMP. Due to the largely rural nature of the province, the RCMP is responsible for a good deal of the policing with 12 district offices and 57 satellite offices. There are also eight municipal (Bathhurst, Edmundston, Fredericton, Miramichi, Saint John, Rothesay, Woodstock, and Grand Falls) and one regional force in the north. The cities of Moncton and Dieppe are policed by the Codiac Regional detachment of the RCMP. The provincial Department of Public Safety is responsible for Corrections and Community Services for both youth and adult offenders.

Early History of Youth Corrections in New Brunswick: Overcrowding and Institutional Abuse

Between 1846 and 1857 more than 300 young people, convicted of drunkenness, theft, and vagrancy, were sentenced to the New Brunswick prison in Saint John (Department of Justice Canada, 2004, p. 11). When a new penitentiary was opened in Dorchester, the province opened an industrial home for boys on the site in 1893 (Department of Justice Canada, 2004). By the time the *Juvenile Delinquents Act* (JDA) (1908) was proclaimed, the Boys' Industrial Home in Saint John had been admitting boys from across the province for 15 years. A report of the Canadian Council on Child Welfare in 1929 criticized the boys' home for its emphasis on incarceration over rehabilitation, as well as the tendency to crowd beyond its capacity of 45 youth (Marquis & Boudreau, 2010). The home was closed and a new facility was opened just outside of Fredericton in 1962. The Kingsclear Training School housed up to 65 male residents who were sent there under the New Brunswick *Training School Act* (R.S.N.B. 1973, c.T-11) as either a child in need of protection for child welfare concerns or as a juvenile delinquent under the *Juvenile Delinquents Act*.

The Kingsclear Training School became a place of secure custody under the *Young Offenders Act* (YOA) (1984) and remained open until January 1998 when it was closed and youth were transferred to a unit of the Saint John Regional Correctional Centre until a new facility in Miramichi (New Brunswick Youth Centre) opened later that year. The closing of the Kingsclear Training School happened amid a highly publicized trial and subsequent public inquiry regarding sexual offences against former residents of the school (Kennedy, 2007). Karl Toft, employed as a correctional officer, was transferred out of the training school in 1985 after allegations of sexual molestation were reported by a counsellor at the centre. With no substantiated evidence, Toft was rehired as a summer camp counsellor at the facility. He was charged, and the following year pled guilty, to 34 sexual offences against children, and was sentenced to 13 years.

Following the sentencing of Toft, a Commission of Inquiry was established under the Honourable Richard L. Miller, who was a former justice of the New Brunswick Court of Queen's Bench, to investigate not only the allegations at Kingsclear, but to also consider allegations of physical and sexual abuse at the former Boys' Industrial Home in Saint John (Miller, 1995). The investigation and subsequent compensation packages for victims of institutionalized abuse was far too common throughout this period as evidenced by the number of commissions of inquiry throughout Canada. Kaufman (2002) in his report on an investigation into institutional abuse in the province of Nova Scotia chronicles similar investigations not only in the Maritimes, but across Canada (Newfoundland and Labrador, Ontario, British Columbia). The safeguards of due process and the increased attention to appropriate training and professional development of officers responsible for the care and custody of youth in institutionalized settings was underscored in a publication by the Law Commission of Canada (2000), which asked that the government ensure that victims of such abuse were given fair compensation, counselling, and support.

The issue of sexual abuse of children gained primacy during the 1980s with the release of a Royal Commission of Inquiry into sexual offences against children in 1984 (Badgely, 1984). Prior to the 1970s, there was very little research on the prevalence of the issue, and as Hornick and Morrice (2007) point out the lack of professional and public knowledge in these early years meant that it was not until the 1980s and 1990s that a significant body of research had been accumulated on the long-term effects of child sexual abuse on victims. It was not until 1995 that the first comprehensive manual on the investigation of child sexual abuse was published (Hornick & Paetch, 1995). The lack of knowledge about sexual offences against children in cases of institutional abuse was evident in the recent apology by Scouts Canada to former victims who suffered abuse, which was uncovered in a forensic investigation, known as the Miller Inquiry, of 486 files spanning a 64-year history of the organization (Kent, 2012).

One of the recommendations of the Miller Inquiry (1995) was to replace the Kingsclear Training Centre with a new facility that would provide more appropriate services to young offenders. The province of New Brunswick retained the Portage Program for Drug Dependencies Inc. on contract to determine the best way to approach programming at the new centre in the Miramichi. Portage had been developing programs for youth and adults since 1970, and the government felt that the focus on techniques of a " Therapeutic Community" would assist the new facility in providing appropriate intervention that focused on peer support and positive role modelling (Richard, 2008).

Therapeutic Community Model for Youth Custody, 1998

The contracting of Portage to assist in the design and implementation of the new youth centre was based on the organization's history of developing 21 therapeutic-based prison programs in the United States and its involvement in the provision of services for young offenders serving open custody sentences in Elora, Ontario, and Cassidy Lake, New Brunswick. The Therapeutic Community model is based on the premise that peer support within an institutional culture, which builds on the development of relationships between staff and residents, will assist youths to take responsibility for their own actions. Within the program are strict and explicit behavioural norms, as well as sanctions for negative behaviour, delivered within an institutional structure where both residents and staff serve as role models. The goal of the program is to assist other members of the "community" to work within an organized structure and foster respect for authority (Richard, 2008, p. 13).

Part of being responsible to the community is a requirement for group meetings where residents share positive experiences, gain insight into their own and others therapeutic and program goals, and point out inappropriate behaviours. These meetings are held on the units daily with the whole institution gathering in the community room in the morning a few times during the week. The hierarchy of leaders who have mastered the skills of early stages of the program leads to added privileges for that young person and an opportunity to take on more leadership responsibilities in the institution. Sanctions for negative behaviour include restrictions on privileges as well as "time outs" where youth are either locked in their cells or placed for a period of time in "therapeutic quiet" (segregation).

The New Brunswick Youth Centre (NBYC) adapted the Therapeutic Community Model in the first year the centre was opened and during the early implementation and monitoring of the program by Portage. It became clear that many of the elements of the program were beneficial to the youths who were working on their own personal goals through plans of care with their key workers, though some of the elements of the program were not conducive to ensuring their needs. In particular, the emphasis on a hierarchical arrangement of youth leaders responsible for the imposition of sanctions on other youth contributed to institutional bullying, as reported by some youths at the institution. Staff had to respond to crises on the units on a regular basis, which increased the number of youths removed from the unit and placed in segregation. In order to achieve a balance between the therapeutic intent of the model to assist young people using a peer-helping framework, while maintaining an operational mandate to ensure the safety of all youth and staff, clearer operational guidelines were developed to address rising concerns over the number of incidents.

The NBYC has also adopted a number of strategies to enhance the participation of youths in their own goal setting and planning by introducing competency webs that are completed by the youth and his or her primary worker. Building on a strengths-based approach to intervention, these tools assist young people to consider their own skills and talents and work towards positive outcomes both while in the institution and upon release into the community. In speaking to the youths at the NBYC who have used these competency webs, they indicated that they were able to complete them with their primary worker, but may not follow up on the goals that are set out due to a lack of resources, goals that may be beyond the capacity of the institution to deliver, or a lack of opportunity to work more specifically on individual programs within the constraints of the institution.

Increasingly, youth who are sentenced to closed custody present with a myriad of mental illnesses, which may not be amenable to the Therapeutic Community Model. These more complex cases require intensive therapeutic intervention delivered by trained professionals. This point was perhaps most clearly articulated in two systemic reviews, completed by the New Brunswick Office of the Ombudsman and Child and Youth Advocate (Richard, 2007, 2008), of youth with complex needs being dealt with under correctional services. The reports concluded that youth with mental illness had highly complex needs, and there was a need to develop a continuum of clinical services for them (Richard, 2008, p. 36). Around the same time these reports were released, Judge Michael McKee chaired a task force on the future of mental health in the province, which also recommended strategies to deal with the number of young people who presented with mental illness in the youth justice system (McKee, 2009).

In its response to these reports, the government of New Brunswick has established a Youth Treatment Program Team through a memorandum of agreement between the departments of Health and Public Safety, which provides assistance to correctional staff through a clinician on site who is able to access and deliver more intensive mental health interventions (New Brunswick, 2009). Further, the Department of Public Safety has provided training to correctional staff using the mental health training developed by the Correctional Services of Canada, as well as training on a best practices model of motivational interviewing. As of this writing, all probation staff in the province, as well as programmers at the NBYC, have received training on motivational interviewing, and plans are underway to ensure that all staff receive such training over the next year. Further, the policy with respect to secure custody for youth has eliminated the term "therapeutic quiet" and defines segregation in terms that limit its use for only those youth who are not experiencing mental health problems. The issue of segregation is further exemplified in the case of Ashley Smith who was kept for long periods of time in segregation both while in the youth system and once she was transferred to the adult system. This policy, which places clear limits on the use of segregation, is a direct response to the problems experienced in this case.

Lack of Resources to Treat Youth with Mental Illness: The Case of Ashley Smith

Ashley Smith, a 19-year-old woman from Moncton, New Brunswick, committed suicide while in an adult penitentiary after being transferred less than a year before from the youth system. One might assume that Ashley had committed a heinous offence to warrant transfer to an adult institution, but this was not the case. She had exhausted the alternatives that had been provided to her, had somehow managed to fall through the cracks of the system, and was left undiagnosed for underlying mental health problems.

During early adolescence, her parents reported a change in her behaviour that was also being witnessed in the school system. At age 12, Ashley received a six-week suspension after she and a friend were caught buying marijuana at school. The following year, reports from school indicate disciplinary actions for bullying, verbal threats, a disrespectful attitude, and non-compliance. She was banned from most public areas including the public transit system, the mall, and her school. Her parents reported that their relationship was strained as Ashley defied rules at home. Her mother sought the help of a private psychologist who reported no signs of mental illness but clear indications of behavioural problems.

Ashley's trouble with the law began in March 2002, at the age of 14, with offences related to public disturbances and trespassing. A youth court ordered one-year probation and, due to the number of offences, a referral to the province's Intensive Support Program (ISP). Despite the additional reporting and intervention, she continued to have problems following rules and accrued additional charges. She was referred for a 34-day assessment at the six-bed residential program Pierre Caissie Centre in Moncton. The psychological assessment recommended that the parents receive counselling sessions on how to deal with an "oppositional defiant youth" and that everyone work together in dealing with Ashley's behaviour. Her behaviour while resident at the centre escalated, and the police were called twice after her assaults on staff. A very small facility, the centre decided that her outbursts impacted on the assessments being conducted on the other five residents, and her stay was reduced to 27 days. She was remanded to the New Brunswick Youth Centre (NBYC) for one month where she accumulated over 30 recorded incidents ranging from refusing staff orders and becoming aggressive, to making threats of self-harm. This resulted in Ashley being charged institutionally and placed in isolation (aka "Therapeutic Quiet").

Upon release, she was charged with throwing crab apples at a postal worker who she believed was responsible for the late delivery of welfare payment cheques. Recognizing the difficulties that Ashley had in secure custody, she was placed in open custody only to be returned to the NBYC for her own safety after a number of incidents of self-harm. In less than three months, she was in and out of the NBYC five times. She would be released on community supervision and then either breach her conditions or commit a new offence that would send her back to remand. Ashley spent approximately three years in custody at the NBYC where she had over 800 incident reports leading to institutional charges in over 500 of these incidents. As reported by Richard (2008, p. 19) "it was nothing out of the ordinary for Ashley to have anywhere from one to five reported and documented incidents per day." Ashley had 158 self-harm incidents and acquired 50 criminal charges while at the NBYC.

In January 2006, she turned 18, which meant that if she committed any new offences she would be treated as an adult offender, and this was explained to her by senior staff of the institution. The superintendent of the NBYC decided to make an application under section 92 of the *Youth Criminal Justice Act* to transfer Ashley to the adult system. In the two court hearings regarding this transfer, information was provided about the opportunity for Ashley to attend more programs in the adult system that would assist her in her rehabilitation. The court was also told about Ashley's fear of entering the adult system:

Although I know that my record looks bad, I would never intentionally hurt anyone. I am really scared about the thought of going to an adult facility with dangerous people (Richard, 2008, p. 26).

The judge decided that Ashley should be transferred to the adult system and within a few hours of her transfer to the Saint John Regional Correctional Centre (SJRCC), Ashley was sent to segregation and threatened with both pepper spray and a taser for non-compliance with institutional rules.

Ashley had 34 incident reports over the 26 days that she was held at the SJRCC, and spent most of this time in segregation. On October 24, 2006, she appeared in adult court to answer to the criminal charges that had been laid while at the NBYC, where she received an additional 348 days of custody. When the new custody was added to the already existing 1,455 days left of her youth sentence, it meant that Ashley's time exceeded the provincial requirement of two years less a day and she had to be transferred to a federal institution. At the age of 18, she entered the Nova Institution for Women in Nova Scotia.

In less than 12 months in federal custody, Ashley was moved 17 times between three federal penitentiaries, two treatment facilities, two external hospitals, and one provincial correctional facility across four of the five Correctional Services of Canada regions (Nova Scotia, Quebec, Ontario, and Saskatchewan). Howard Sapers, the federal correctional investigator, reported that "In the last 11 months of her life, her name appeared on at least 150 'situation reports'" filed by federal penitentiaries detailing her attempts to hurt herself or others (Sapers, 2008, p. 6). Ashley was continuously housed in administrative segregation (i.e., solitary confinement). According to Sapers (2008, p. 7) administrative segregation status is a highly restrictive and, at times, inhumane regime, and as such is to be subject to review every 60 days. However, her status was "lifted" whenever she was physically moved out of one institution to be placed in another, thereby, circumventing the requirement for a 60-day review. This meant Ashley spent all of her time alone and in a security gown to protect her from self-harm. A psychologist who examined the case interpreted some of Ashley's self-injurious behaviour as a means of drawing the staff into her cell "in order to alleviate the boredom, loneliness and desperation she had been experiencing as a result of her prolonged isolation" (Sapers, 2008, p. 8).

Ashley Smith took her life in the early morning of October 19, 2007, less than one year from the time she was placed in the adult correctional system (Reid, 2012). The coroner's inquest continued for six years after her death. The jury ruled in December 2013 that the case was a homicide and provided over 100 recommendations for policy and procedures to be developed for inmates who present with mental health issues.

This case is an example of the problems inherent in the youth correctional system being used to deal with highly complex cases because there are no other available resources or options. While the case shows the effort taken to abide by the principles of the *Youth Criminal Justice Act* in using alternatives to the formal youth justice system whenever practical, it is clear that it was necessary to also consider the mental health treatment needs of this young woman. Since that time, there have been a number of changes with respect to clinical intervention with youth who present with highly complex needs, but as noted by Richard (2008) more has to be done to ensure that youth do not fall through the cracks.

One of the responses to the issue of tracking and providing seamless services to youth is the development of an integrated service delivery system that is being piloted in two communities over the next three years. The system, which would have information sharing protocols between the applicable government departments, would streamline opportunities to ensure that assessments are completed in a timely fashion and tracked through records of the departments of Education, Health, Public Safety, and Social Development (New Brunswick, 2009). The province has recently been awarded multi-year funding through a national network, Transformational Research in Adolescent Mental Health (TRAM), which will further assist the creation and development of mental health services for youth in the province.

Following the highly publicized trial and public inquiry regarding the Kingsclear Training School, there was a slight decline in the use of custody: from 1997 to 1998 there was a year-to-year decline of 9%. However, by 1999, the percentage of youth receiving custody returned to the same percentage as the year prior to closing the training school.

As has been pointed out throughout this book, the creation of the *Youth Criminal Justice Act* was, in particular, a response by Anne McLellan, the then minister of justice, to the embarrassing rates of youth incarceration in Canada. On February 14, 2001, McLellan rose in the House of Commons to speak on the first reading of Bill C-7, the proposed *Youth Criminal Justice Act* (YCJA):

... the existing YOA has resulted in the highest youth incarceration rate in the western world, including our neighbours to the south, the United

States. Young persons in Canada often receive harsher custodial sentences than adults receive for the same type of offence. Almost 80 percent of custodial sentences are for non-violent offences. (House of Commons Debates, 2001, p. 1,530)

The philosophy and principle of the YCJA are consistent with the academic research that shows that incarcerating young people can do more harm than good, and that our most successful interventions should be doing less criminal-justice processing for the majority of those who present as low-risk, low-need offenders (Petrosino, Turpin-Petrosino, & Guckenburg, 2010). Looking at the statistics regarding youth incarceration, it appears that the YCJA is meeting its objective of reducing the use of incarceration.

For all of Canada, the youth incarceration rate, at 8 per 10,000 youth population, fell 5% between 2009/2010 and 2010/2011, the third consecutive annual decline (Munch, 2012). For New Brunswick, the youth incarceration rate was right at the national average of 8.2 per 10,000 youth population. This rate also fell from the previous year, but at a much more substantial rate (22%) after showing a 9% increase between 2008/2009 and 2009/2010. Over the past five years, however, the youth incarceration rate in New Brunswick has declined by 25%. On any given day in 2010/2011, just over 1,500 youth, or about 10% of those in the correctional system, were in custody. Of these, just over half (54%) were in remand and 44% were in sentenced custody. Of youth in sentenced custody, 53% were in secure custody, while 47% were in open custody (Munch, 2012). However, in New Brunswick, there were 57% of youth in sentenced custody on any given day and 43% for remand. It is difficult to ascertain the reasons for a lower proportion of cases on remand in New Brunswick without having access to the data that provide a breakdown by offence type or reason for detention. One might speculate that there are fewer cases coming to the attention of the formal youth justice system as a result of the greater use of extrajudicial measures and sanctions, but this cannot be calculated with the data as retrieved from Statistics Canada.

The following figure provides an overview of the declining rates of youth custody in New Brunswick since the implementation of the YCJA. The rates per 100,000 show a standardized pattern of any changes in the number of cases coming to court and in the proportion of cases with a finding of guilt. The percentage of sentenced youth who received custodial sentences for their guilty conviction is standardized based on the

Figure 5.1 Rates and proportion of custodial sentences in youth court, New Brunswick, 2000–2011.

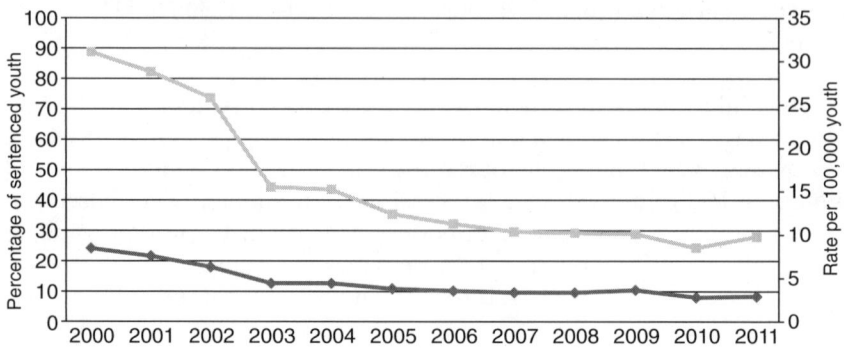

Source: Statistics Canada. Figure 251-0014. Youth Custody and Community Services (YCCS) admissions to sentence custody. CANSIM (database).

total number of sentences handed down. This data includes only those cases of youth serving a custodial sentence (either open or secure) following conviction, and do not include the remand population pretrial.

The per capita rate of custodial sentences dropped 20% from 2002 to 2003, when the YCJA was introduced. While no change was experienced in rates in 2003–2004, further declines have resulted in a 10% decline over the next five years. The proportion of sentenced cases in New Brunswick that received custodial sanctions also declined over this period, from 24% in 2003 to 9% in 2010–2011.

Police Charging Practices

One of the stated purposes of the *Youth Criminal Justice Act* was to increase the use of alternatives to the formal youth justice system in order to reduce the rate of youth being charged for minor criminal offences. Wilson and Hoge (2012) suggest that the term "true diversion" refers to pre-charge caution programs because they are the most likely to limit exposure to the criminal justice system. The YCJA sets up a series of responses that must be considered by the police pre-charge under extrajudicial measures. Nationally, the YCJA has had the effect of dramatically reducing the number of young people who are charged for criminal offences with Brennan (2012) reporting that in 2011, 57% of youth were diverted from the justice system while 43% were formally charged.

Figure 5.2 Rates of police-reported youth crime in New Brunswick, 2000–2011.

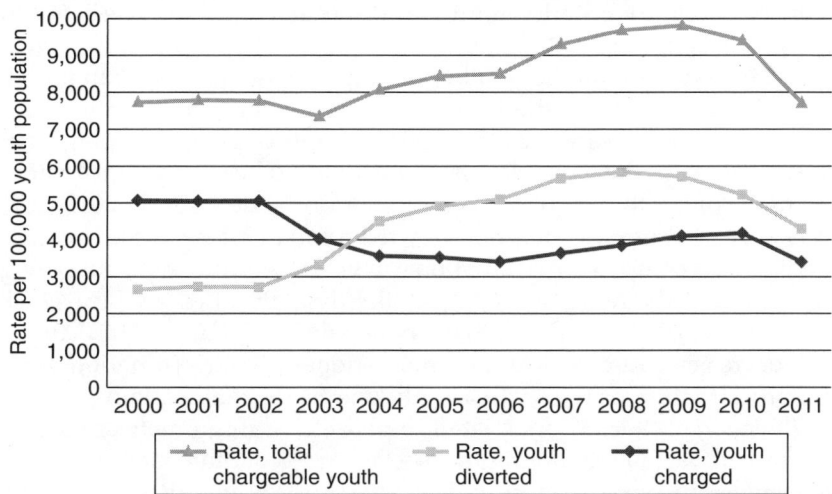

Source: Statistics Canada. Table 252-0051. Incident-based crime statistics by detailed violations. CANSIM (database).

Looking at New Brunswick specifically, a similar reduction in charging by the police can be observed when the Act was first implemented, but the year-to-year rates do not reflect the national practices since the proclamation of the Act. As was pointed out earlier, New Brunswick relied on post-charge diversion for its community-based alternative programs, and this has been the reason for it taking a considerable amount of time for the police to alter their practices of laying charges.

Between 2010 and 2011, the national youth crime rate and the Crime Severity Index (CSI) both decreased by 10%. In New Brunswick the youth crime rate declined by 22% from the previous year while the CSI dropped 21% (Brennan, 2012). With greater declines in the CSI in New Brunswick, the increase in the number of youth being diverted out of the formal court system should also correspond. The decline in the crime rate is reflected in the total chargeable youth, however, the number of youth charged and diverted should show an increase if diversion practices were increasing. The explanation for this lower number is due to a change in policing practices whereby more youth are being dealt with under extrajudicial measures.

This figure shows the change in the police charging rates from two years prior to the legislation until the most recent data. The rate of youth charged dropped from 2,362 per 100,000 in 2003 to 1,784 per 100,000 in 2011. The reduction in the number of youth charged showed an immediate decline following the introduction of the legislation with a 12% reduction in charges from 2003 to 2004. The rate of police charging from 2004 through 2009 was stable with some mild fluctuation year to year in the range of 3% to 4%, followed by a substantial decrease in 2010–2011 of 19%. New Brunswick has not shown a comparable decrease in charging practices compared to the national average as found in the following figure, where the rate per 100,000 is slightly higher in New Brunswick (3,620 per 100,000) compared to the national rate (3,150 per 100,000).

A decreasing rate of youth crime, nationally, over the period since the proclamation of the YCJA is only one factor that explains the use of diversion. Other factors related to police charging practices include changes in various demographic, social, and economic factors as well as changes in police service policies and procedures (Brennan, 2012; Bala, Carrington, & Roberts, 2012). In New Brunswick, the use of diversion had historically been done only as a post-charge option and changing police practices to include extrajudicial measures has taken a great deal of police training.

Diversion in the Province of New Brunswick

There has been a growing body of research that demonstrates that the further youth are involved in the juvenile justice system, the greater the likelihood of increased offending behaviour (Becker, 1963; Farrington, 1977; Smith, Goggin, & Gendreau, 2002; Andrews & Bonta, 2003; Bernberg, Krohn, & Rivera, 2006; Lipsey, 2009; Petrosino, Turpin-Petrosino, & Guckenburg, 2010; Loeber, Hoeve, Slot, & Van Der Laan, 2012). Diversion programs were developed to respond to the research evidence that suggests that keeping youth in their family and communities supported by a package of services aimed at their individual needs has been shown to have a positive effect on reducing recidivism (Lipsey, Wilson, & Cothern, 2000; Latimer, 2001). Keeping youth in their community allows for a "holistic intervention approach" focused on identifying individual, family, and community risks and strengths, and treating them comprehensively (Sullivan, Veysey, Hamilton, & Grillo, 2007). Cohen and Piquero (2009) argue that when offenders are identified early, the costs to society in economic and social terms are reduced through the use of effective diversion practices.

Figure 5.3 Rates of police use of extrajudicial measures, Canada and
New Brunswick, 2002–2011.

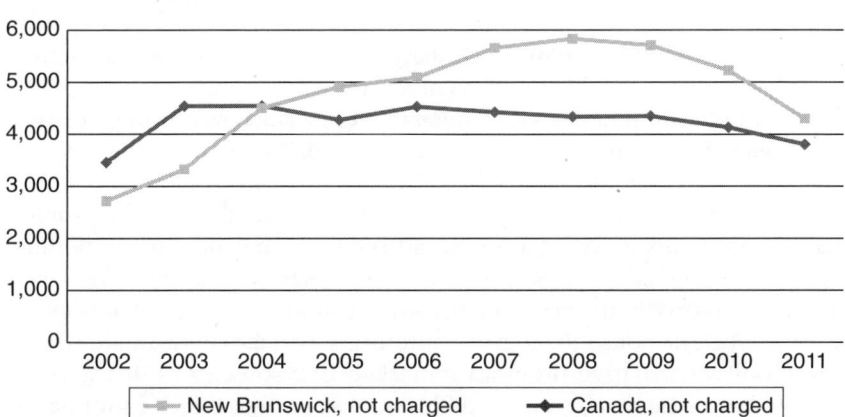

Source: Statistics Canada. Figure 252-0051. Incident-based crime statistics
by detailed violations. CANSIM (database).

In New Brunswick, the Saint John Juvenile Diversion Project started in 1978 prior to the introduction of the *Young Offenders Act* in 1984.
Since this program had been implemented for a number of years, it
was an easy transition to change the name to an alternative measures
program under the YOA. Changes to the *Criminal Code* in 1996 led to
the development of an ancillary program for adults that was modelled
on the existing youth alternative measures program in 1998 (Ballucci
& Rossignol, 2011). It has been noted both by Reid (2009) and Whalen
(2011) that the UN *Convention on the Rights of the Child* (1989) calls for
the establishment of separate programs for youth and adults who come
in conflict with the criminal justice system. In the audit of extrajudicial measures and sanctions, Ballucci and Rossignol (2011) also pointed
out the need to ensure that diversion programs in the province were
distinct for youth and adults. Despite the need for separate programs
with their own dedicated staff and service provisions, the creation of
the adult alternative measures program based on the successful youth
diversion program is testament to the legacy of alternative processes
for youth within the province.

In a report commissioned by the New Brunswick Department of
Public Safety, a series of interviews and focus groups were conducted
by this author with police, criminal justice professionals, and service

agencies throughout New Brunswick (Reid, 2009). One participant re-marked that alternatives to the formal youth justice system means:

> Any program/initiative in which the youth is able to embrace account-ability and responsibility for criminal acts while achieving an enhanced or new set of skills and a sense of value to their position as a youth, family member and member of their community. (Reid, 2009, p. 11)

However, there were a number of front-line professionals who pointed out the problems with the amount of time that was taken from the time the police received a file on a young person who was being considered for an alternative to the youth justice system, and the implementation of a youth justice response through a community panel. A coordinator of the community alternative program remarked that sometimes it was up to 30 days before he would receive a file and there "were three or four hands on the file before it ever went to alternative measures." (Reid, 2009, p.15)

The concept of accountability and responsibility is clearly under-scored when we consider the principle of the YCJA in section 3 of the Act and further define the strategies outside of the formal youth justice system. However, in our haste to hold young people accountable, we must focus on not only identifying the young person's risk to recidi-vate, but also ensure that we have placed appropriate resources that give youth the opportunity to recognize their skills, talents, and abili-ties so that they can become integral members of our communities.

Identifying Risks: Screening Youth for Diversion

The assessment of offenders for risk to reoffend has garnered consider-able research evidence over the past 10 years (Andrews & Bonta, 2003). Known as the risk-need-responsivity (RNR) model, the premise is that if we are able to effectively screen out low-to-moderate risk offenders us-ing standardized assessment tools, we can then concentrate on the high-er risk offenders who will benefit from more intensive interventions. As Hoge, Guerra, and Boxer (2008) have argued, we need to be mindful of how to determine what works for whom and under what circumstances, and the creation of screening tools to determine the level of risk and needs, which appear to be gaining prominence throughout Canada.

Perhaps the most widely used risk assessment tool is the *Youth Level of Service/Case Management Inventory* (YLS/CMI) (Hoge & Andrews, 2003). This 42-item assessment considers eight domains present in the youth and his or her circumstances that have been shown to impact on youth recidivism (i.e., criminal history, family circumstances, education and employment, peer group association, substance use, leisure or recreation, personality or behaviour and attitudes, or criminal orientation). The YLS/CMI has demonstrated its effectiveness in predicting overall rates of recidivism for young offenders (Olver, Stockdale, & Wormith, 2009), and has been seen as a useful tool to assist in case management and measurement of change over time. However, the assessment is not a diagnostic tool and as Holsinger, Lowenkamp, and Latessa (2006) point out, it is essential that a full assessment using other measures is needed if any one of the domains in the assessment tool are of clinical concern in order to determine appropriate treatment interventions.

A screening version of the YLS/CMI was developed by Hoge and Andrews (2004) and is known as the *Youth Level of Service/Case Management Inventory: Screening Version* (YLS/CMI: SV). This version contains the same eight domains on the longer 42 assessments, but only contains eight items. The New Brunswick RCMP program has been modelled after the Ottawa Police Services Program, where the screening tool was piloted and standardized (Hall, Logue, & Shaw, 2011). Front-line officers complete the screening tool for all chargeable youth (Shaw et.al, 2011).

As pointed out by Savignac (2010, p.11), it is important to recognize that risk assessment tools, while based on a scientific foundation, are "neither a panacea nor a predictor of future behavior." It is essential that training is provided for the proper administration of this assessment tool and, as Bonta (2002, p. 374) argues, that training should be a minimum of two full days for those with prior knowledge of the treatment and risk prediction literature, and five days for all others. The interpretation of the results of the assessment by untrained youth practitioners may lead to not only differential and unequal treatment, but may inadvertently screen youth who would not benefit from an intensive intervention into a therapeutic program.

A recent meta-analysis of diversion programs was conducted by Wilson and Hoge (2012) and found that the programs that were primarily police caution programs were most effective in reducing recidivism for low-risk offenders, compared to programs that provided some form of intervention. They report that "low risk youth referred to caution programs were 2.44 times less likely to reoffend" while the same low-risk youth who were referred to an intervention program were only "1.49 times less likely to reoffend" (Wilson & Hoge, 2012, p. 11). In applying this knowledge to the use of the YLS/CMI: SV tool being used throughout detachments of the RCMP in New Brunswick, it is essential that the training of those using the instruments underscores this important fact.

In an evaluation of the implementation of the use of the YLS/CMI: SV throughout RCMP districts in New Brunswick, Dyck and Campbell (2011) reported that over 200 screening tools had been completed and returned to J Division headquarters over the two- year implementation. The majority of these assessments (74%) were completed by RCMP officers, while some had been referred on to the community program officer (CPO) who is a civilian RCMP member responsible for crime prevention and community engagement. When RCMP officers were interviewed for the review, only 62% of them indicated that they had received training on the YCJA, and only 52% indicated they had received specific training on the YLS/CMI: SV (Dyck & Campbell, 2011, p. 37). The officers were quick to point out, however, that not all districts were using the YLS/CMI: SV as it was not mandatory at that time. As of August 30, 2012, a province-wide policy has been developed by J Division requiring each district to show that they have established a recognizable intervention and diversion process. While there is some opportunity for districts to utilize other processes, the policy encourages members to use the screening tool (J Division Operational Manual 39.6 Extrajudicial Measures and Sanctions, 2012). According to the 2011–2012 *RCMP New Brunswick Annual Report* (Lang, 2012), through a significant funding contribution from the federal Department of Justice, over 640 police officers, provincial partners, and community service providers were trained in workshops on youth diversion, including issues of mental health, addictions, and motivational interviewing. Further evidence of an increase in the training of officers in the districts can be found in the short summaries included in the report where seven of the nine districts mention that officers had received training on the risk assessment tool in the past year.

Youth Justice Committees

In his testimony to the Standing Committee on Justice and Human Rights regarding Bill C-10, the acting Child and Youth Advocate stated that New Brunswick "has not established any of the Community Youth Justice Committees (YJC) called for under section 18 of the *YCJA*" (Whalen, 2011, p. 3). The provision to establish YJCs existed under section 69 of the former *Young Offenders Act*, and as reported by Hann & Associates (2003), there were variations both in the number of committees operating within provinces and across provinces. Quebec, New Brunswick, Nova Scotia, and Prince Edward Island had not officially designated any committees while Newfoundland and Labrador had 32 such committees. Hann & Associates (2003) note that there was "some concordance between the annual budget and the number of referrals" made to each committee.

Under section18 of the YCJA, the Attorney General of the province makes provisions to establish YJCs. In addition to assisting with extrajudicial sanctions, such committees may also provide advice to the provincial and federal governments on matters related to youth justice, monitor whether youth rights are being adhered to under the Act, coordinate services for youth, and provide information about youth justice to the community. New Brunswick has not established any formal Youth Justice Committees. However, J Division of the RCMP has created Youth Intervention and Diversion Committees (YIDCs) that are defined as "a committee made up of community service providers and others who will conduct a broad risk assessment and develop recommendations related to an intervention and diversion plan for a YP who is referred for EJM by a member, under the mandate of section 19 of the YCJA" (J Division Operational Manual 39.6 Extrajudicial Measures and Sanctions, 2012).

In the evaluation of the strategy being implemented by the RCMP, Dyck and Campbell (2011) indicated that in many areas throughout the province, these committees included a civilian RCMP member, known as a Community Program Officer (CPO). Within New Brunswick, the RCMP employs 12 CPOs who are civilian employees who are responsible for community engagement and to establish and foster relationships with the community to "make an impact on crime prevention" (Gervais, 2008, p. 3). The CPO positions are seen as valuable assets to the RCMP both in terms of assisting with the implementation of the Youth Intervention and Diversion Program and informing the community about early intervention, but also in terms of providing intelligence to the regular members of the force with respect to knowledge of "firsthand pieces of information that may be shared with police officers (i.e., gang hangouts, main areas for drug use and sales, suspected crack houses)"(Gervais, 2008, p. 13). Those CPOs who were interviewed for the review of the intervention and diversion program were generally enthusiastic with the implementation of the strategy, but indicated the need for additional training for community members and regular members of the RCMP. Workload issues were seen to be a problem for some of the CPOs indicating that the paperwork involved in handling the large number of cases referred to the committees was too much for one person to handle. Discussion was underway to determine whether a volunteer community member might be able to take over the paperwork responsibility.

As discussed the interpretation of the results of an assessment is important, and it is to be hoped that those assigned to do this work will receive sufficient training. While individuals who were interviewed by Dyck and Campbell (2011) indicated that they had some knowledge of the risk assessment process, those who were community members had a great deal of difficulty delineating criminogenic risks and criminogenic needs when asked. In light of the need for appropriate training on the use and interpretation of risk assessment tools outlined above, if the RCMP continues to work with these YIDCs, there will be an ongoing need for training.

The opening paragraph of this chapter pointed out that in a small province with few resources, the reliance on others to provide training and assistance is paramount. The RCMP has received funding to establish the intervention and diversion strategy under the federal Department of Justice's anti-drug funding. While the YIDCs do not necessarily focus on substance abuse, there has been a focus on training individuals for a substance abuse program in the past year (Lang, 2012). A continued focus on substance-disordered youth, which matches the mandate of the anti-drug strategy, is a positive contribution to the province of New Brunswick in light of the results of a recent longitudinal study. Hoeve et al. (2013) found youth with substance disorders were particularly at risk for further offending behaviours, particularly in cases of property offenders. The study also found that the more formal system processing, the higher the likelihood of more severe future offending. Youth who were held in pretrial detention were more likely to reoffend with increasing severity than those who were on probation. The results of this study underscore that interventions at an early stage of youth justice processing for substance abuse disorders may prevent an escalation of crime and likely affect future public safety (Hoeve et al., 2013, p. 300).

Provincial Extrajudicial Measures and Extrajudicial Sanctions: The Diversion Charter

While the RCMP is interested in having its YIDCs also receive referrals from Crown attorneys for Crown cautions and provide programming for extrajudicial sanctions, the program has not been designated by the NB attorney general. New Brunswick utilizes a post-charge extrajudicial sanction option as its program under the YCJA, which is overseen by senior Community and Correctional Services (CCS) management at the Department of Public Safety. There are 28 extrajudicial sanctions committees (EJS) composed of volunteers, probation officers, police, mental health and addictions workers, and social workers throughout the province. While these EJS committees are not designated Youth Justice Committees, they perform most of the activities related to extrajudicial sanctions outlined in section 19 of the Act.

Following the review (Reid, 2009) and subsequent audit (Ballucci & Rossignol, 2011) of extrajudicial measures and sanctions (EJM/EJS), a number of changes have taken place with respect to the management of these committees and the oversight of these programs. Training has been ongoing throughout the past two years for all probation and community staff in the techniques of motivational interviewing. Further, the government has purchased videoconferencing capabilities to ensure that staff and volunteers in more rural areas of the province can be linked for conferences and advice on ways to proceed. Many staff from the Department of Public Safety have also participated in the training offered by the RCMP on addictions, mental health, and diversion. The ongoing work within the Department of Public Safety in response to *125 Warnings* and the audit of extrajudicial measures and sanctions is reflected in the recently signed *Charter for Improvements to Diversionary Practices for Youth* signed by the departments of Public Safety, Justice, and the Attorney General, the RCMP, and the Association of NB Chiefs of Police (October, 2012):

> Several New Brunswick reports point to inconsistencies in the application of diversionary approaches for youth, and levels of stakeholder involvement in these activities. These reports make several recommendations to achieve effective, efficient and provincially consistent diversionary practices that can result in better outcomes for New Brunswick youth in conflict with the law.

As part of the vision for this Charter, there is a recognition of the need for collaboration that will "optimize opportunities for success for all those affected by crime." This vision clearly articulates a way to work through the inconsistent application of extrajudicial measures and sanctions between police agencies and communities in New Brunswick, and affirms a commitment to working together. The Charter also provides a commitment to ensure that decisions are made "based on the best available information and tools," and that research guides the selected remedy with the use of "current" and "meaningful" interventions.

The Charter also responds to criticisms about the lag time between a young person committing an offence and it being handled through an extrajudicial measure or program, which was found to be a problem in both reports (Reid, 2009; Ballucci & Rossignol, 2011). The Charter presents guiding principles that have elements of restorative justice in keeping with the already existing community groups who have been delivering such practices. The objectives of this Charter include provisions for ongoing collaborative meetings among the stakeholders to evaluate and monitor the effectiveness of the program, as well as to promote formal evaluations to be completed on a regular basis "in order to maintain program integrity, prevent program drift and effectively address crime and public safety."

The focus on partnerships and collaboration has also been seen in the creation of a provincial round-table on crime prevention, which includes a variety of stakeholders. In December 2012, the Department of Public Safety released their Crime Prevention and Reduction Strategy, which identifies "at risk youth" as a top priority. Reiterating the research that has already been discussed throughout this chapter, the strategy argues that "early identification and targeted prevention and intervention efforts" with youth at risk can "decrease risk, build resiliency and greatly decrease the likelihood that they will offend" (p. 10).

Creating Youth Adult Partnerships in Closed Custody Settings

There is a body of literature known as *positive youth development* which has shown that youth-adult relationships are integral for the developmental transitions through adolescence to young adulthood (Zeldin et al., 2005; Zeldin & Collura, 2010; Wong, Zimmerman, & Parker, 2010). These relationships are essential as a protective factor for youth who may be enmeshed in the youth justice system (Langdon, Cosgrave, & Trannah, 2004; Lipsey, 2009). When looking at secure custody facilities for youth, there have been some recent attempts to assess the relationships between staff and youth. Sedlak and McPherson (2010) reported on a survey of over 7,000 youth in juvenile custody institutions in the United States, where 43% of the respondents indicated that relations with staff were poor. While almost half of the respondents (48%) described staff as friendly and helpful, 40% of youth indicated that staff were hard to get along with and 38% described staff as disrespectful.

Schubert et al. (2012) reported that youth who do not feel that they can go to staff for help within the institution are more likely to have difficulty in post-release outcomes. Conversely, Marsh and Evans (2009) found that when youth in a closed custody setting were asked to determine the qualities of a staff member they respected, those staff with high levels of trust, positive affect for the youth, high levels of engagement, and effective problem-solving skills were seen as the most respected. The youths who nominated staff in this category were also more likely to self- report that they believed that they would experience high levels of success following incarceration with respect to their substance abuse issues, the creation of positive social networks, and their desistance from crime.

Over the past year, this author has been working with a group of university students to deliver adult ally training to all youth correctional officers, clinical staff, and senior management at the New Brunswick Youth Centre (NBYC). The half-day workshops are delivered in an interactive manner by the young people. Content includes exploration of the qualities of an effective adult ally in a correctional centre, definitions of youth engagement, and a retrospective look at their own experiences as youths. By focusing on the youth-adult relationships in a closed custody setting, the participants share experiences that have been positive as well as negative within the setting's confines. Themes emerging from these conversations with staff at the New Brunswick Youth Centre focus on the importance of patience, tolerance, listening skills, being able to interact in a positive manner, communication, and respect (Reid, 2012). Effective problem-solving skills were illustrated by one officer who reported that after listening to the young person, he was able to effectively facilitate a plan for a youth: "I had a conversation with an "at risk/ young offender" about him going to __. He told me I was the first person to suggest it, and that he might even consider it."

Another example of facilitating decision-making with a young person at NBYC was: "When a youth did not want to go to school we discussed reasons why they should and shouldn't. In the end youth decided to go."

Positive affect and regard for the young person was provided in the following example from a correctional officer: "I helped a young person feel better about themselves after they had an upsetting phone call from a family member who told them they were nothing."

The officers reported in the evaluation of the training that they learned another way to look at youth engagement beyond the group activities they implement on the units: "This shows how we interact with youth everyday." Others indicated that as a result of participating in the workshop they will "take a second look "at how they are engaging with the youth and ask, "Could I have been more supportive? Am I being biased by my own views?"

As indicated in previous literature, the social climate of the institution can have a dramatic impact on the way that youths adapt not only to the environment of the closed custody setting, but also in terms of their release success. In order to change the environment for the young persons, training, such as the adult ally initiative delivered by young people, is an essential component for working on the integration of services within the setting. When officers work collaboratively and share in the engagement process it will have a beneficial impact on the youth. Further work is underway with research exploring the dynamics and contexts of adult-youth partnerships within this institution and in a community setting with at-risk youth. Additional adult ally training is being developed with plans to deliver the program designed in New Brunswick with youth correctional officers in Ontario.

Creation of Youth Leadership Team at New Brunswick Youth Centre

Bessant (2005, p. 5) argues that the problem with current discussions about youth policy is that adult policymakers try to "imagine what young people want or what they believe they ought to want or need." Youth need to be invited to the conversation as they are an important source of information and it is an obligation under articles 12, 13, and 14 of the UN *Convention on the Rights of the Child*, which states the rights of children under 18 years of age to fully participate in decisions that affect them, to be able to express their ideas and concerns in any way that is appropriate for them, and to have access to full information about situations that affect them (Reid & Gilliss, 2012).

Schubert et al. (2012) stress the importance of speaking to youth in custodial settings about the programs they are attending, because there may be aspects of adult-designed programs that are perceived differently than they were conceived. There is a tendency to see juvenile offenders as an "'invisible population" (Inderbitzin, 2006) because few people have taken the time to listen and understand their incarceration experiences. Walters (2006) concurs and suggests that many people ignore or dismiss the opinions of young offenders because of scepticism about the value of their viewpoint.

Over the past year, Youth Matters, a university student-led organization that delivers youth conferences, conducts training with high school and middle school youth, and is actively involved as youth co-researchers to the Centre for Research on Youth at Risk at St. Thomas University, has been working closely with a group of young persons resident at the NBYC to deliver conferences inside the facility on substance abuse, institutional bullying, and reintegration planning. The origin of this group came as a result of two of the residents participating in a Youth Matters conference held in the community while on escorted day passes. They were so moved by their youth conference experience that they asked if we might support them to develop a conference for their peers inside the institution, so that others might benefit from the engagement that they had experienced. This set in motion a year-long planning process with the young people and included the delivery of a two-day conference this past summer with all but one resident of the institution attending. The two youths were joined by three other youths identified by staff as showing positive leadership skills, and the group worked together with university students and NBYC staff over the course of about six months. The group identified two topics of interest for the conference, and with assistance from university students, found relevant literature on substance abuse and institutional bullying. The youths participated for two full days in the conference outside of their units, with the other university student facilitators assisting the youth leadership team from NBYC to deliver discussion groups on these topics. Recommendations were developed at the end of each day and presented by the youths from the centre to all the institution's staff and senior managers during a morning forum.

Since the initial conference, the youth leadership team has been working with Youth Matters to create a film for newcomers to the institution on the problems of institutional bullying. Their intent is for all youth that are admitted to the institution to view this video before arriving on a unit so that they will be more informed of the problems that they may experience and how to deal with them. The desire for the youth leadership team to assist their peers in identifying other issues of concern continues, and another full-day forum on reintegration planning was held in December 2014. As Abrams (2006) has pointed out, listening to youth offenders and integrating the feedback into efforts to improve institutional settings can lead to better outcomes. The work of the Youth Matters leadership team on the creation of a video has received positive feedback from senior administration at the NBYC.

The success of the Youth Matters leadership team within the New Brunswick Youth Centre may be attributed to a number of factors. The senior management of the centre saw the value in providing training to staff by young people, and made arrangements for all staff to receive adult ally training. This provided officers and other staff with more insight into what the young people were engaged in during the Youth Matters meetings, and created a more accepting climate for conferences and meetings to take place. The youth who have taken on the leadership roles are well supported by Intensive Rehabilitation and Custody Support (IRCS) staff, who work specifically with high risk youth.

The principles of effective treatment apply to the creation of this leadership team in that the most intensive intervention (i.e., ongoing participation in Youth Matters) is being applied to the highest risk offenders. The approach also builds on the tenets of a positive youth development approach in that the youths who are taking responsibility for the leadership team within the institution are also building on their strengths, talents, and abilities. They have received incentives for their work with other youths in the institution by being escorted to other Youth Matters events outside of the institution. As co-facilitators at other youth conferences, and as active participants within strategic-planning sessions held at St. Thomas University, these "at-risk" leaders have begun to recognize their abilities in assisting their peers at the NBYC. Recently at a leadership team meeting at the NBYC, one youth reported that a peer had been visibly upset upon being remanded for a breach of conditions when arrested wearing a Youth Matters T-shirt from the institutional conference. The impact of this suggests that, like the name of the group, this youth "mattered," felt part of something positive, and did not want the organization to be tarnished in the eyes of the community. Perhaps "mattering" was what Ashley Smith wanted in her life at the NBYC. Had this opportunity for youth engagement and leadership been available to her, with supports from staff such as the IRCS professionals who assist with the delivery of the program, she may have had less distress. The institution should be congratulated for taking the risk to bring in outside youth mentors to assist in the delivery of programs. The model developed in New Brunswick creating youth-adult partnerships and building on the strengths of the youth through leadership training opportunities supported by appropriately trained staff, was piloted in Ontario in 2015. This positive approach to working with the most at-risk youth may ensure that all youth recognize that they "matter" thereby making their reintegration to community more successful.

Future Directions

The signing of the *Diversion Charter* by the province, the NB Association of Chiefs of Police, and the RCMP is indicative of the commitment to providing a coordinated and collaborative process to ensure that New Brunswick utilizes whatever means necessary to reduce the number of youth who are brought into the formal youth justice system. The Department of Public Safety has recently selected diversion for youth and adults as its baseline for improvement in the provincial government's initiative to provide a scorecard on improvements within the province. This underscores the commitment outlined in the Charter.

Additional funding has been secured by the RCMP for training on the risk assessment screening tool, and plans are underway for additional workshops and training opportunities with both RCMP members and the community partners. This will provide a much needed resource for those working with young persons throughout the province.

The concluding observations of the UN Committee on the Rights of the Child (2012), following deliberations on the monitoring report on the implementation of the UN *Convention on the Rights of the Child*, remarked on the need for Canada to strengthen its commitment to training youth justice professionals:

> Art.26 – In particular, the Committee is concerned that personnel involved in juvenile justice, such as law enforcement officers, prosecutors, judges, and lawyers, lack understanding and training on the Convention.

The training hosted by the RCMP in collaboration with the Child and Youth Advocate over the past number of years will provide continuing training opportunities in this area. Further, the work of Youth Matters in the provision of adult ally training with adult professionals in the youth justice system provides a much needed outlet to answer this call.

The *Crime Prevention and Reduction Strategy* released in December 2012, also prioritizes youth at risk as one of its three initiatives. The Working Group on At Risk Youth is considering ways to measure the success of diversion and crime reduction through existing data both within the province and through Statistics Canada. Action plans will be developed to address the priorities created within the Working Group and approved by the province. It is hoped that there will be ongoing support for the creation of training and development opportunities for New Brunswickers to gain more knowledge about the YCJA and ways to provide opportunities for youth that will not only prevent youth crime but assist those who are reintegrating into their communities from custody.

The involvement of Youth Matters with the New Brunswick Youth Centre in creating a training package and model for the creation of youth-adult partnerships in closed custody settings will be piloted in Ontario in 2015. This model will be refined and additional training modules for the creation and support of youth leadership teams within secure custody facilities will be developed with the New Brunswick team taking the lead in disseminating the model in other provinces.

While New Brunswick continues to struggle with a lack of resources, there continues to be occasions to collaborate and develop unique opportunities through the relationships and partnerships that have been nourished with the infusion of resources that have provided much needed "detailing" for our service van!

NOTE

1 The final report on the round-table was not released to participants. Refer to a copy accessed under Freedom of Information at www.loosefiles.ca.

REFERENCES

Abrams, L. S. (2006). Listening to juvenile offenders: Can residential treatment prevent recidivism? *Child and Adolescent Social Work Journal, 23*, 61–85.

Andrews, D. A., & Bonta, J. (2003). *The psychology of criminal conduct, 3rd edition.* Cincinnati, OH: Anderson Publishing Co.

Andrews, D. A., & Dowden, C. (2007). The Risk-Need-Responsivity model of assessment and human service in prevention and corrections: Crime-prevention jurisprudence. *Canadian Journal of Criminology and Criminal Justice, 49,* 439–464.

Badgley, R. F. (1984). *Sexual offences against children: Report of the Committee on Sexual Offences Against Children and Youth, Volume 1.* Ottawa, ON: The Minister of Justice and Attorney General of Canada, and The Minister of National Health and Welfare.

Bala, N., Carrington, P., & Roberts, J. (2012). Implementing youth justice reform: Effects of the Youth Criminal Justice Act. In J. Winterdyk &

R. Smandych (Eds.), *Youth at risk and youth justice: A Canadian overview* (pp. 80–103). Toronto, ON: Oxford University Press.

Ballucci, D., & Rossignol, A. (2011). *Alternative measures and extrajudicial sanctions program audit: Grasping policy and procedure in New Brunswick, Final Report.* New Brunswick Department of Public Safety, May 31, 2011.

Becker, H. (1963). *Outsiders: The sociology of deviance.* New York: Free Press.

Bernburg, J. G., Krohn, M. D., & Rivera, C. J. (2006). Official labeling, criminal embeddedness and subsequent delinquency: A longitudinal test of labeling theory. *Journal of Research in Crime and Delinquency, 43*(1), 67–88.

Bessant, J. (2005). Principles for developing youth policy. *Policy Studies, 26*(1), 103–116.

Bonta, J. (2002). Offender risk assessments: Guidelines for selection and use. *Criminal Justice Behavior, 29*(4), 355–379.

Brennan, S. (2012). Police-reported crime statistics in Canada, 2010. *Juristat* (July): 1–39. Retrieved from http://www.statcan.gc.ca/pub/85-002-x/2012001/article/11692-eng.pdf.

Cohen, A. M., & Piquero, A. R. (2009). New evidence on the monetary value of saving a high-risk youth. *Journal of Quantitative Criminology, 25,* 25–49.

Department of Justice Canada. (2004). *Evolution of juvenile justice in Canada.* Retrieved from Department of Justice: http://www.justice.gc.ca/eng/abt-apd/icg-gci/jj2-jm2/jj2-jm2.pdf.

DuBois, D. L., Holloway, B. E., Valentine, J. C., & Cooper, H. (2002). Effectiveness of mentoring programs for youth: A meta-analytic review. *American Journal of Community Psychology, 30,* 157–197.

Dyck, H., & Campbell, M. A. (2011). *Implementation review of the youth intervention and diversion strategy: J Division.* RCMP: J Division (unpublished manuscript).

Farrington, D.P. (1977). The effects of public labelling. *British Journal of Criminology, 17,* 112–125.

Gervais, E. (2008). *Community program officer – Research and interpretation.* RCMP: J Division Report to Inspector Rick Shaw (unpublished manuscript).

Government of New Brunswick. (2009). *Reducing the risk, addressing the need: Being responsive to at-risk and high complex children and youth.* Government report.

Hall, S., Logue, L., & Shaw, R. (2011). The rural approach to youth diversion: No easy fix. *Gazette, 74*(1).

Hoeve, M., McReynolds, L. S., Wasserman, G. A., & McMillan, C. (2013). The influence of mental health disorders on severity of reoffending in juveniles. *Criminal Justice and Behavior 40,* 289–301.

Hoge, R. D., & Andrews, D. A. (2003). *Youth Level of Service/Case Management Inventory (YLS/CMI)*. Toronto, ON: Multi-Health Systems.

Hoge, R. D., & Andrews, D. A. (2004). *Youth Level of Service/Case Management Inventory (YLS/CMI) – Screening Version*. Toronto, ON: Multi-Health Systems.

Holsinger, A. M., Lowenkamp, C. T., & Latessa, E. J. (2006). Predicting institutional misconduct using the Youth Level of Service/Case Management Inventory. *American Journal of Criminal Justice, 30*, 267–284.

Hornick, J. P., & Morrice, C. (2007). *A historical review of the evolution of police practices, policies and training regarding child sexual abuse.* Calgary: Canadian Research Institute for Law and the Family.

Hornick, J. P., & Paetsch, J. J. (Eds.). (1995, updated). *A police reference manual for cases of child sexual abuse.* Ottawa, ON: Solicitor General Canada.

Hurley, D. M. (1992). The Young Offenders Act: Juvenile justice or societal protection – An elusive web. Presentation to annual meetings of the Canadian Sociology and Anthropology Association, June 2, 1992. Charlottetown, PEI.

Inderbitzin, M. (2006). Growing up behind bars: An ethnographic study of adolescent inmates in a cottage for violent offenders. *Journal of Offender Rehabilitation, 42*(3), 1–22.

Kaufman, F. (2002). *Searching for justice: An independent review of Nova Scotia's response to reports of institutional abuse.* Province of Nova Scotia.

Kennedy, P. (2007). *Kingsclear investigation report – public interest investigation into RCMP investigations of the New Brunswick Training School.* Commissioner of Public Complaints Against the Royal Canadian Mounted Police, Canada. Ottawa, ON: Royal Canadian Mounted Police.

Kent, S. (2012) *Scouts Canada child and youth safety update. (KPMG Report).* Retrieved from http://www.scouts.ca/cys/SC-CYS-Update-2012.pdf.

Lang, W. (2012). *RCMP New Brunswick year in review – 2011–2012, Building on our momentum,* RCMP: New Brunswick Chief Commanding Officer.

Langdon, P. E., Cosgrave, N., & Tranah, T. (2004). Social climate within an adolescent medium-secure facility. *International Journal of Offender Therapy and Comparative Criminology, 48*, 504–515.

Latimer, J. (2001). A meta-analytical examination of youth delinquency, family treatment, and recidivism. *Canadian Journal of Criminology, 43*(2), 237–253.

Law Commission of Canada. (2000). *Restoring dignity: Responding to child abuse in Canadian institutions.* Ottawa, ON: Minister of Public Works and Government Services.

Lipsey, M. W. (2009). The primary factors that characterize effective interventions with juvenile offenders: A meta-analytic overview. *Victims and Offenders, 4*, 124–147.

Lipsey, M. W., Wilson, D. B., & Cothern, L. (2000). *Effective intervention for serious juvenile offenders*. Washington, DC: OJJDP.

Loeber, R., & Farrington, D. (1998). *Serious and violent juvenile offenders: Risk factors and successful interventions*. Thousand Oaks, CA: Sage.

Loeber, R., Hoeve, M., Slot, N. W., & Van Der Laan, P. H. (2012). *Persisters and desisters in crime form adolescence into adulthood: Explanation, prevention and punishment*. Surrey, UK: Ashgate Publishing Ltd.

Marquis, G., & Boudreau, M. (2010). *Young people and the law: History of crime in New Brunswick, Retrieved from* http://www.unb.ca/saintjohn/arts/projects/crimepunishment/legal/youth.html.

McKee, M. (2009). *Together into the future: A transformed mental health system for New Brunswick*. Department of Health, Province of New Brunswick. Retrieved from http://www.gnb.ca/cnb/Promos/MentalHealth/NBMHS-e.pdf.

Munch, C. (2012). "Youth correctional statistics in Canada, 2010–2011." *Juristat* (October): 1–29. Retrieved from http://www.statcan.gc.ca/pub/85-002-x/2012001/article/11716-eng.pdf.

Olver, M. E., Stockdale, K. E., & Wormith, J. S. (2009). Risk assessment with young offenders: A meta-analysis of three assessment measures. *Criminal Justice and Behavior, 36*, 329–353.

Petrosino, A., Turpin-Petrosino, C., & Guckenburg, S. (2010). Formal system processing of juveniles: Effects on delinquency. Campbell Systematic Reviews.

Reid, S. A. (2009). *125 warnings: A review of extrajudicial measures and extrajudicial sanctions for youth in New Brunswick*. Department of Public Safety.

Reid, S. A. (2012). *Creating youth-adult partnerships in closed custody settings*. Centre for Research on Youth at Risk, St. Thomas University.

Reid, S. A., & Gilliss, S. (2012). Key challenges in hearing the voice of youth in the youth justice system. In J. Winterdyk & R. Smandych (Eds.) *Youth at risk and youth justice: A Canadian overview* (pp. 379–397). Toronto, ON: Oxford University Press.

Reid, S. A. (2012). Case study – Ashley Smith. In K. O'Regan & S. A. Reid (Eds.), *Thinking about criminal justice in Canada*. Toronto, ON: Emond Montgomery.

Richard, B. (2008). *The Ashley Smith report*. Fredericton: New Brunswick Ombudsman and Child and Youth Advocate. Retrieved from http://www.gnb.ca/0073/PDF/AshleySmith-e.pdf.

Sapers, H. (2008). A preventable death: Report of the Correctional Investigator of Canada, June 20, 2008. Retrieved from http://www.oci-bec.gc.ca/cnt/rpt/pdf/oth-aut/oth-aut20080620-eng.pdf.

Savignac, J. (2010). *Tools to identify and assess the risk of offending among youth.* Ottawa, ON: National Crime Prevention Centre. Retrieved from https://www.publicsafety.gc.ca/cnt/rsrcs/pblctns/tls-dntf-rsk-rprt/tls-dntf-rsk-rprt-eng.pdf.

Schubert, C.A., Mulvey, E. P., Loughran, T. A., & Losoya, S. H. (2012). Perceptions of institutional experience and community outcomes for serious adolescent offenders. *Criminal Justice and Behavior, 39*(1): 71–93.

Sedlack, A. J., & McPherson, K. S. (2010). *Conditions of confinement: Findings from the survey of youth in residential placement.* Washington, DC: US Department of Justice.

Shaw, R., Hornick, J., Davidson, R., Petelski, K., & Waller, I. (2011). What's the best approach to reducing youth crime? *Gazette, 73*(2), 12.

Smith, P., Goggin, C., & Gendreau, P. (2002). *The effects of prison sentences and intermediate sanctions on recidivism: General effects and individual differences.* Ottawa, ON: Solicitor General Canada User Report 2002-01.

Sprott, J., & Doob, A. (2008). Youth crime rates and the youth justice system. *Canadian Journal of Criminology and Criminal Justice 50*(5): 621–639.

Sullivan, C. J., Veysey, B. M., Hamilton, Z. K., & Grillo, M. (2007). Reducing out-of-community placement and recidivism: Diversion of delinquent youth with mental health and substance use problems from the justice system. *International Journal of Offender Therapy and Comparative Criminology, 51,* 555–577.

Tolan, P., Henry, D., Schoeny, M., & Bass, A. (2008). *Mentoring interventions to affect juvenile delinquency and associated problems.* The Campbell Collaboration.

Tustin, L., & Lutes, R. (2012). *A guide to the Youth Criminal Justice Act.* Markham, ON: LexisNexis.

UN Convention on the Rights of the Child. (1989). Retrieved from www.ohchr.org/en/professionalinterest/pages/crc.aspx.

UN Committee on the Rights of the Child. (2012). *Consideration of reports submitted by states parties under article 44 of the Convention, concluding observations: Canada.* Sixty-first session, September 17–October 5, 2012. Retrieved from http://rightsofchildren.ca/wp-content/uploads/Canada_CRC-Concluding-Observations_61.2012.pdf.

Walters, G. D. (2006). Risk-appraisal versus self-report in the prediction of criminal justice outcomes: A meta-analysis. *Criminal Justice and Behavior, 33,* 279–304.

Whalen, C. (2011). *Submission to Standing Committee on Justice and Human Rights, Bill C-10,* (Acting Child and Youth Advocate, New Brunswick) November 9, 2011. Retrieved from http://www.gnb.ca/0073/Child-YouthAdvocate/PDF/Bill/Soumission-e.pdf.

Wilson, H.A., & Hoge, R. D. (2012). The effect of youth diversion programs on recidivism: A meta-analytic review. *Criminal Justice and Behavior.* doi: 0093854812451089. First published October 15, 2012.

Wong, N. T., Zimmerman, M. A., & Parker, E. A. (2010). A typology of youth participation and empowerment for child and adolescent health promotion. *American Journal of Community Psychology, 46,* 100–114.

Zeldin, S., & Collura, J. (2010). *Being Y-AP savvy: A primer on creating and sustaining youth-adult partnerships.* Ithaca, NY: ACT for Youth Center of Excellence.

Zeldin, S., Larson, R., Camino, L., & O'Connor. (2005). Intergenerational relationships and partnerships in community programs: Purpose, practice, and directions for research. *Journal of Community Psychology, 33*(1), 1–10.

6 The Implementation of the *Youth Criminal Justice Act* in Newfoundland and Labrador: No Problem?

ANNE MORRIS AND MALIN ENSTRÖM

Introduction

The *Youth Criminal Justice Act* (YCJA) was introduced in April 2003 and was accepted by all Canadian provinces. The YCJA was intended to reduce the high levels of incarceration taking place under the *Young Offenders Act*, to deal with youth who committed minor crimes in a less severe manner, and to ensure that the most serious responses were reserved for youth who had committed violent crimes. As a result, only the most violent and serious repeat offenders would receive custodial sentences (Davis-Barton, 2009, p. 65, as cited in Winterdyk & Smandych, 2012, p. 56).[1] Since 2003, there has been an overall decrease in numbers of youth being arrested and charged, going into the courts system, and entering into custody in Canada in general and in Newfoundland and Labrador (NL) in particular.

The purpose of this chapter is to investigate the extent to which the new legislation contributed to the decreasing numbers compared to other factors. The chapter also looks at how the YCJA has affected the various components of the criminal justice system (CJS) and community-based programs for youth. It is over 10 years since the YCJA was introduced, and little has been written about these effects on the youth justice system in Newfoundland and Labrador.

The information in this chapter is mainly descriptive in nature, based on a review of provincial statistics and interviews with several people working in the youth justice system. Federal and provincial government documents, and statistical information from the Royal Newfoundland Constabulary (RNC) and the Royal Canadian Mounted Police (RCMP) are reviewed. The chapter is also informed by: informal interviews with, and surveys of, police officers; site visits to the Newfoundland and Labrador Youth Correction Facilities in St. John's and Whitbourne and interviews with staff; interviews with youth court officials and staff in youth corrections; interviews with managers in the provincial Department of Child, Youth and Family Services; interviews with social workers who coordinate pretrial services and extrajudicial measures/sanctions programs; and interviews with individuals involved in a number of community groups who work with youth in the criminal justice system.

The Province of Newfoundland and Labrador

The province of Newfoundland and Labrador covers a vast geographic area with most of the population centred on the Avalon Peninsula, mostly in the northeast, which includes the St. John's Metropolitan Area (196,966). The next largest population centres are Corner Brook (19,886) and Stephenville (6,719) on the west coast, Gander (11,054) and Grand Falls-Windsor (13,725) in the central part of the island, and Happy Valley-Goose Bay (7,552) and Labrador City (7,367) in Labrador.[2] There are 12 additional population centres with a population of over 3,000, and more than 200 smaller and very small communities distributed mainly along the coast. Geography and the organization of policing in the province have an influence on how the youth justice system is organized and administered.

Over the last two decades Newfoundland and Labrador has gone from being a have-not to a have province. In a province traditionally dependent on natural resources in fishing, mining, and forestry, the major economic driver is now the development of the offshore oil industry and supporting infrastructure, as well as new hydroelectric and mining projects. At the overall provincial level, economic conditions in Newfoundland and Labrador are currently strong but unequally distributed among the population and the different regions of the province.

Employment was expected to reach record levels in 2013, and the unemployment rate was expected to decline to the lowest rate since 1973. Sales of retail goods, including cars, and expenditures on services have all experienced solid growth according to the Provincial Economic Review for 2013.[3] The province achieved the best high school graduation rate ever recorded for the year 2012–13, with 94.2% of eligible graduates earning a diploma.[4] In addition, the unemployment rate for youth was at an all-time low of 16.7% in 2013.[5] In 2013, labour force participation rates for youth were 15.9%, slightly lower than 2012, but higher than any other year since 1976.[6]

Table 6.1 Youth population in Newfoundland and Labrador[7]

Year	1971	1990	2000	2006	2012
Age: 10–14	65,658	51,003	36,025	29,289	26,501
Age: 15–19	60,591	55,966	40,845	34,134	28,804
Total youth	126,249	106,966	76,879	63,423	55,305

These high rates of employment are due, in part, to past trends of large numbers of young people leaving the province to find work elsewhere in Canada. This trend, combined with a declining birth rate and low rates of immigration, have resulted in a decrease of the youth population in Newfoundland and Labrador by more than 50% over the last 15 years (see Table 6.1). This is one clear contributor to the lower absolute numbers of young people coming into the criminal justice system today.

An interesting question arises from these trends. Have the decreasing number of youth, increasing educational attainment, rates of employment and income, and [uneven] economic boom circumstances of the province affected rates of crime among youth and the number of youth offenders? The following sections of this chapter look at crime rates among youth in Newfoundland and Labrador mostly over the last decade.

Youth Crime in Canada and Newfoundland and Labrador

According to Statistics Canada (2012), the Youth Accused Rate (YAR) and the youth Crime Severity Index (CSI) declined in almost every province and territory, and Newfoundland and Labrador was no exception. The Police-Reported Youth Accused Crime Rate in NL,[8] along with the youth Crime Severity Index,[9] both showed a steady decrease for the third consecutive year. For example, Newfoundland and Labrador, along with Quebec, had the sharpest decline in 2012 with −5% for both provinces.[10]

These numbers only reflect youth offenders identified by the police. In NL, the numbers of youth arrested and the numbers of youth charged has decreased considerably. The number of youth going to court or into custody has also declined. As with many other provinces and territories, half of the youth accused of crime were accused of: theft of $5,000 or under, mischief, Level 1 assault, or possession of cannabis. In addition, most charges are for less serious violent offences or for multiple breaches (administrative offences).[11]

Policing in Newfoundland and Labrador

The organization of police services in Newfoundland and Labrador is structured in a unique way compared to other provinces in Canada. The Royal Newfoundland Constabulary (RNC) is the provincial police force and provides policing services to several larger centres including most of the St. John's Metropolitan Area, Corner Brook, and Labrador City, as well as Wabush and Churchill Falls in Labrador. The Royal Canadian Mounted Police (RCMP) polices the remaining areas of the province.

This division of jurisdictions is significant for policing youth for a couple of notable reasons: youth may need to travel to other towns for court dates, and community-based services are more available to youth in the larger centres. This in turn may influence the types of dispositions that youth receive. The division of jurisdictions between the RNC and RCMP also has an impact in terms of sharing information regarding the issuing of warnings.

Police Assessment of YCJA

We surveyed and interviewed senior police officers from the RNC (n = 8) and the RCMP (n = 6), representing a range of rural and urban locations across the province, to assess their impressions of the changes that have occurred since the implementation of the YCJA. Police are the first line of contact with the CJS for most youth. They often determine what happens next. We wanted to know how they interpreted the available statistical data, which reports that police charge rates have decreased dramatically since the implementation of the YCJA in terms of the reality of youth criminal activity.

The years of policing experience for these officers range from nine to 26 years and most of them had worked in several locations. The findings from these surveys and interviews indicate several themes. All of the participants agreed that they liked the YCJA, particularly for having greater discretion in dealing with youth who commit minor offences. The participants also agreed that they supported the issuing of warnings, and that these were used frequently for many different types of minor offences. However, one concern that was raised was that while most centres do record warnings, recording is not done in a consistent manner. Furthermore, warnings are not commonly shared between the RNC and RCMP police forces that work in adjacent areas.

The respondents also indicated that there are important points to consider related to the implementation of the YCJA; in particular, section 6(1) of the YCJA, which *requires* police officers to consider if a warning is a sufficient response to a youth's behaviour. It states "a police officer shall" before starting judicial proceedings or taking any other measures under the YCJA against a young person alleged to have committed an offence, consider whether it would be sufficient to: (a) take no further action, (b) warn the young person, (c) administer a caution, (d) refer the young person to a program or agency in the community that may assist the young person not to commit offences.[12] In addition, the province has not introduced a formal police or Crown cautions program, and the province has not introduced a formal police-warning program.[13]

Among police districts, the policy is usually to issue one warning and then to charge on a subsequent offence; however, our participants reported that multiple warnings are sometimes issued for minor offences. One officer stated: "*Some of the youth warned, learn from the incident but for the most part I find that the warnings are taken for granted and quite regularly we deal with the youth again in the near future.*" The statistical information suggests a significant decline in youth being charged by the police. Although this may be the case, the majority of the police officers who participated in our survey did not believe that youth crime has, in fact, decreased. Many of the participants instead stated that what has really changed is the number of youth who actually get charged and the types of encounters they have with youth.

The RCMP tracks chargeable offences and instances where charges have been laid. Their statistics for 2009 to 2012 show a downward trend in the number of chargeable youth, and also a significant decrease in the number of youth charged. For the last four years, the percentage of youth charged for violent offences was between 29% and 36%, and for property offences between 23% and 27%. The situation is a little different in some settlements in Labrador where there is a slight upward trend in the number of youth charged. In most cases, chargeable youth are being given warnings or diverted from the system.[14]

The majority of officers indicated that although many of the crimes that youth commit are the same as they were 15 years ago, they see more serious youth crime than they did in the past. For example, there is more crime involving the use of weapons and more violent youth crimes, and as one officer stated:

I feel that youth are committing more serious offences more frequently today than they were 15 years ago, i.e., robbery, assault with a weapon, and aggravated assault. Another said: I believe we have observed an increase of violence among youth since I first entered policing in the later 1990s.

This impression was supported by most of the other officers and about half of the officers who responded also said they think more female youth are involved in crime than in the past. Two of the officers suggested this might be related to cultural issues in areas that they police.

However, there was a feeling that the YCJA was having a positive impact in general, especially for minor offenders, most of our participants did not think that youth who commit serious crimes receive adequate sanctions. One officer commented:

> If I were to put it bluntly, I think youth are getting away with too much and getting off too easy. I do like the concept of the verbal warning, because it gives youth who make an error in judgement, on that particular day or during a particular incident, the chance to reflect on what they have done and hopefully never make the error in judgement again, without getting tied up with court proceedings or getting a criminal record. Another said, I feel youth know there are no real consequences for getting in trouble the first few times they break it. An officer with over 20 years of experience said, I'm not a huge fan of the YCJA. A lot of youth we deal with think the whole thing is a joke. They commit crime because they know there are little to no repercussions, and their youth criminal record will not follow them. I see time and time again, offenders being given a minimal sentence for repeat breaches of court orders and repeat offences. It can be extremely frustrating for law enforcement and the victims in the community. Another officer state: The courts rely too heavily on court orders to deal with serious offences. You can have a youth who is on several orders for different matters.

The term "probation inflation" was used by some police officers when referring to probation as the most common type of sentence that youth receive.

Further concerns were also raised around another issue. According to one officer:

> My fear is that because of the YCJA the police are often verbally warning, or worse not even investigating crimes, because they know that youth are involved and that "nothing will be done about it". I have often heard from community members and victims that they chose not to report crimes against them because the suspect is a youth and they will "get nothing for it." A big challenge for police is that victims of the crimes often feel like

they get the short end of the stick. The youth very seldom see the inside of a police station for most offences and are usually arrested and released on scene, at the school, or even at their own home with their parents present. Victims regularly complain that not enough is being done to deter these youth from committing the same crime again. They believe there should be harsher penalties for youth who commit crimes, until of course that youth is their child, then the opinion changes.

A general feeling of many officers towards the new YJCA is that youth think they can get away with crime. One police officer commented:

> The biggest challenge of policing youth is knowing that they will not, for the most part, be punished for the crime. A lot of youth know this and have no respect for the court process or warnings from police.

Another officer expressed that he did not think the type of offences had changed, as much as youth attitude towards and fear of police and/or the justice system since the YOA:

> I have noticed that youth are less fearful of the consequences of criminal behaviour and hold less respect for police and their powers to deal with youth. This leads to an interesting consideration ... if youth do not re-spect/fear the justice system as young men and women, will they sud-denly gain a respect for the system or for the police on their 18th birthday, when they are now dealt with as an adult? My guess would be NO.

Two officers expressed concerns with the paperwork under the YCJA and logistics of arresting, interviewing, charging, and dealing with youth in court: "It is frustrating under the current system. I think most officers would prefer to use verbal, written warnings and alternative measures before charging ANY youth."

Some of the key reasons that youth get in trouble with the law were echoed by officers and are covered in the following quote.

> Lack of parental supervision/interest is primary and lack of access to local community activities or sports. Drugs are an issue. We see kids commit-ting property crimes to obtain funds to buy drugs. We also see second-generation criminals – a way of life taught by one or both parents. A sense of entitlement. "I want it, but I don't want to have to work for it, so I will just take it" attitude.

Police expressed concerns about youth involvement with more serious drugs than in the past – like cocaine and ecstasy – and they are seeing more youth with mental health issues.

Most officers work well with others in the CJS and with community groups who are working with youth. They like extrajudicial measures programs and feel they are very beneficial for most youth. Information from some police officers seems to contradict the official statistics that tell us that youth crime is on the decrease and that the severity of youth crime is declining. What they suggest is that fewer youth are being charged, arrested, and coming into the system. They suggest that youth crime seems to be at the same levels as in the past with the suggestion that the crimes seen today are more serious than in the past. The most common crime with which youth were charged by the RNC in 2013 was minor assault. It was followed by administrative breaches, then shoplifting and mischief. Despite the general notion expressed that youth crime was leaning towards a more violent nature, mostly all maintained a very positive attitude towards youth in general. As one officer told us: "The positive aspect of policing youth is the opportunity to have a positive influence on them, and to show them that there is hope for them."

In regards to the YCJA, most police officers opinions reflect the statement of one officer who feels that the YCJA has "provided greater flexibility of options for the justice system to use in order to get youth on the right track to succeed in society." They feel that the use of discretionary power and warnings are very beneficial for many youth, especially those who are first-time or minor offenders and those who are likely to learn from their encounter with the police. They do have concerns about how the court deals with repeat offenders and those who commit more serious offences. They are concerned about the reasons why youth get in trouble and the lack of support structures for many youths and their families in many communities. They like that the YCJA allows them to "look beyond the offence" and look at the situation of young people who themselves have been victims of abusive family situations, the child welfare system, and those who have no one to care for or support them.

Although the officers feel they are seeing just as many youth as they did in the past, it appears that they are sometimes seeing them in a different capacity and dealing with them differently. Many of the youth who might have been charged in the past are not being charged now. They are being given warnings, taken home to parents, referred to community services, or dealt with by way of extrajudicial measures. They are also seeing youth for non-criminal matters – such as youth in care missing curfews at group homes and then being reported missing. They are dealing with altercations between parents and youths in their homes and settling them with mediation and referrals.

Both police services in the province are committed to working in a positive manner with youth. The RNC and RCMP offer many community services programs aimed at youth, youth at risk, and youth in trouble with the law. All RNC officers are now trained through the university and part of their program includes a sociology course on youth justice as well as other courses in mental health, forensic psychology, and abnormal psychology. By taking courses they have a better understanding of the issues facing many young people and also learn about the history and background of legislation dealing with youth in Canada, which in turn may influence how they deal with youth. The RCMP operates a youth crime prevention website, is introducing a new youth policing model in the province and runs many other programs for youth. Information about these programs can be found on the RNC and RCMP websites.

Youth Court

The number of cases in youth court in Canada has declined considerably (−32%) over the last 10 years,[15] The majority of cases completed in youth court in 2010/2011 were non-violent offences, more specifically property offences, administration of justice offences, other *Criminal Code* offences, traffic offences, and other federal statute offences (e.g., drug offences) accounted for close to three quarters (73%) of all cases completed in youth court. Violent offences accounted for the remaining 27% of youth court cases. Older youth (ages 16–17) appear most often in court, and in 2010/2011 cases involving male youth accounted for 77% of cases.[16]

There are 10 court centres in locations throughout Newfoundland and Labrador (see Table 6.2). In addition to sitting in its principal locations, the Provincial Court conducts circuits to various rural and remote communities. Youth cases are heard in all of these locations.

As previously stated, the location of the courts is significant because youth often have to travel to court, which could be some distance from their home. Youth court cases comprised 7.9% of NL provincial court cases in 2011–2012. The total number of cases was 2,335. The majority of these cases were heard in St. John's (1,249), with 337 being heard in Corner Brook and 203 in Happy Valley–Goose Bay. Court proceedings for the last 10 years show a steady decline in the number of youth

Table 6.2 Court locations and circuits[17]

Location	Judge(s)	Staff	Circuits
Clarenville	1	3	Bonavista
Corner Brook	3	9	Port au Choix, Rocky Harbour, St. Anthony
Gander	2	5	None
Grand Bank	1	3	None
Grand Falls–Windsor	2	5	Baie Verte and Head of Milltown–Bay d'Espoir
Happy Valley–Goose Bay	2	8	Hopedale, Makkovik, Naini, Natuashish, Port Hope Simpson, Postville, Rigolet
Harbour Grace	1	3	Placentia
St. John's	1 CJ, 1 ACJ, 1SCJ, and 6 judges	28	None
Stephenville	1	4	Port aux Basques
Wabush	1	2	None
Corporate Services	0	12.5	None
Total	23	82.5	15

appearing in court with the sharpest decline from 2008 to 2013 (see Table 6.3). The caseload now appearing in youth court is less than half of what it was 10 years ago.[18]

Table 6.4 outlines the types of cases appearing in court in Newfoundland and Labrador for 2011–2012 and the associated decisions.

The majority of cases coming to court were for property offences (255), with the most common being theft, break and enter, and mischief. These made up 43% of the overall number of cases. Crimes against persons amounted to 206 or 35% of the total number of offences with common assaults (93) making up 45% of these. Uttering threats and major

Table 6.3 Cases appearing in court:
Newfoundland and Labrador, 2003–2013[19]

Fiscal year	Youth cases
2003–04	4,967
2005–06	3,617
2007–08	3,724
2009–10	3,222
2010–11	2,791
2011–12	2,618
2012–13	2,335

Table 6.4 Court youth cases by decision: Newfoundland and Labrador, 2011–2012[20]

	Total all decisions	Guilty	Acquitted	Stayed or withdrawn	Other
Total offences	587	419	2	164	2
Total CC offences	521	385	2	152	2
Crimes against persons	206	141	2	62	1
Homicide	0	0	0	0	0
Attempted murder	0	0	0	0	0
Robbery	8	6	0	0	0
Sexual assault	11	7	1	3	0
Other sexual offences	4	3	0	1	0
Major assaults	41	30	0	11	0
Common assaults	93	63	1	29	0
Uttering threats	47	31	0	16	0
Criminal harassment	0	0	0	0	0
Other crimes against persons	2	1	0	1	0
Property crimes	255	177	0	1	1
Theft	82	56	0	26	0
Break & enter	83	59	0	23	1
Fraud	11	7	0	24	0
Mischief	51	33	0	18	0
Possession of stolen Goods	23	18	0	5	0
Other property crimes	5	4	0	1	0
Administration of justice	44	36	0	8	0
Other CC offences	8	3	0	5	0
CC traffic	8	8	0	0	0
Impaired driving	2	2	0	0	0
Other CC traffic	6	6	0	0	0
Other federal statues	66	54	0	12	0
Drug possession	7	7	0	0	0
Other drug offences	7	3	0	4	0
YJCA	49	41	0	8	0
Residual federal statues	3	3	0	0	0

Note: A case that has more than one charge is represented by the "most serious charge." In Newfoundland and Labrador acquittal and dismissed are used interchangeably, resulting in an undercount of acquittals. 1. Includes final decisions of found not criminally responsible and waived out of province or territory. This category also includes any order where a conviction was not recorded, the court's acceptance of a special pleas, cases that raise Charter arguments and cases where the accused was found unfit to stand trial. Source: Statistics Canada, CANSIM.

assaults were the next highest in number. Administrative offences (44), other federal statutes (66), and YCJA violations (49) made up 27% of the total. Although most cases that appear in court are found guilty (71%), a large number are also stayed or withdrawn (28%).

Court Officials

Historically there was a particular judge assigned to youth court, but when the numbers of cases going to court dropped, the situation changed. Judges in Newfoundland and Labrador rotate through provincial youth court, although one judge in particular gets most of the cases. This is similar to the process in adult court, and most feel it works very well. The purpose of sentencing under the YCJA is set out in section 38. The judge is required to follow these guidelines, which reflect the philosophy of holding a young person accountable for an offence through the imposition of just sanctions that have meaningful consequences for the young person, and that also promote his or her rehabilitation and reintegration into society, thereby leading to the protection of the public. (YCJA [S.C. 2002 c.1]) As well, section 38(2) (d) states that all available sanctions, other than custody, that are reasonable in the circumstances should be considered for all young persons, with particular attention to the circumstances of Aboriginal young persons.[21] These guidelines strongly influence the types of sentences that judges give.[22] Although the provision is available under the YCJA, conferencing involving judges is rare in NL; but if requested it seems to operate well.

Within the Newfoundland and Labrador court system there is usually a dedicated Crown attorney and a duty counsel, who both operate in what is described by a Crown prosecutor as a *collaborative model,* which discusses the process in terms of what is in the best interests of the youth. The Crown prosecutor who works in youth court receives training specific to the YCJA. There are also carefully set guidelines in the *Crown Attorney's Handbook.* The Crown assesses the charges from the police based on the strength of the case and likelihood of conviction, and then determines whether the public interest requires a prosecution. A full-time legal aid defence counsel is assigned to youth court. From discussions it appears that only about 15 to 20% of youths have private lawyers. Most young persons have a lawyer from legal aid appear on their behalf. There are about 16 to 20 cases going to court each week in St. John's. It is important that youth justice happens in a speedy manner. Youth who are arrested have to appear before a justice in 24 hours, a first appearance usually happens within 4 to 6 weeks and if a trial is necessary that usually happens within 2 to 3 months.

Discussions with officials in youth court suggest that fewer youth are coming to court and that cases do not appear to be more serious than in the past. Most youth are appearing in court for property types of offences including shoplifting, disturbances, and small frauds. Other types of offences include minor assaults and minor weapon possession offences. There does seem to be a trend towards more assaultive behaviour by females. This may be a reflection of society becoming more gender neutral or that the police are taking it more seriously.

It also sometimes appears that while there are fewer crimes going to court, and property crimes are still the most common types of crime committed by youth, the cases are more complex. The youth have multiple issues and need different types of interventions. Common offences include assaults on school property for which there is a zero tolerance policy. Domestic assaults in the home and group homes are concerning. Common assaults and uttering threats make up a large number of the cases going to court. Concern with these types of cases was also expressed by social workers working with various community organizations. There does not seem to be as many break and enters as in the past, and very few drug cases appear in court although social workers in community groups do mention drug use and addiction as a common problem with youth. It is possible that the federal prosecutor often sends drug cases to extrajudicial sanctions programs.

The Crown makes the decision to refer the youth to extrajudicial sanctions programs, and sometimes the police will make a recommendation. Youth are referred depending on their age and the sophistication of the offences. It does not have to be a first-time offence; it depends on the circumstances.

Based on information from interviews, it appears that extrajudicial sanctions programs are very popular and used whenever possible. These programs are seen as restorative, educational, and punitive. They can be used more than once and apparently are sometimes referred to by youth and officials in the CJS as a "degree in diversion." They can involve community service, restitution, or writing an essay on a related topic. Probation with supervision is the most common disposition handed down in youth court. Deferred custody and supervision is often given if the youth have a stable home environment. The sentences reflect a supportive attitude. With regards to custodial dispositions, the court takes a measured approach, and there is a qualifying threshold.

Cases involving violence resulting in bodily harm and indictable offences with a history of breaches are more likely to end up in custody. This is similar to the rest of Canada (Brennan, 2010–2011).

An important issue raised is the number of youth appearing in court for administrative offences. These include breaches of probation, curfews, and various other conditions. As one court official said, "these can become the entire record for some youth and may eventually put them in secure custody." The option not to charge is available, and it can be up to the youth worker to decide. They usually charge if there is a safety issue. Pre-trial services (discussed later) seem to be crucial to the court process under the YCJA in helping young people adhere to their release conditions while awaiting trial.

Custodial sentences are used a lot less and usually as a last resort. Open custody is preferred but often even the open custody facilities are not full. Because there are only two open custody facilities, one in St. John's and one in Corner Brook, there is the chance that youth who receive this disposition might be sent far away from family support. Other considerations in terms of custody include the introduction of Bill C-10, which makes specific deterrence and denunciation part of the YCJA. To date, no difference has been noted.

The other key players in the courtroom are social workers from pretrial services, child, youth, and family services, and youth corrections. All these individuals work together with the judges and lawyers in the best interests of the youth appearing in court. From discussions with court officers, it seems an improvement in the system under the YCJA is the flexibility in avoiding criminalizing youth behaviour. There are still some issues with coordination of services, sharing of information, and access to medical and psychiatric assessment. Other important issues for youth in court are mental health concerns. A major concern is youth who commit minor criminal acts and are released by the courts but do not have a stable home environment to go to, and sometimes, there is nowhere for youth to go. Waiting lists for resources can be long. Parents are desperate; they don't have the skills or resources to provide for their families. There may be no food in the house, and youth end up coming into the system for child protection issues. They are shop-lifting every lunchtime, hungry, and neglected. According to a court official, "sometimes youth are really in need of protection and corrections is sometimes being used as a parking lot." There are concerns about the health and social needs of these youth and referrals have to be made to Child, Youth and Family Services (CYFS) to try to find places for them to go.

Generally people who work in the court system seem happy with the YCJA. They feel that too many youth were going into custody for minor offences before the Act, and that with increased funding more services are available to support young people through the court process. They work with some very good community-based programs that support youth. The Provincial Court of Newfoundland and Labrador has put considerable effort into educating youth and the general public about the *Youth Criminal Justice Act*. Its website contains links to useful sites from how to find a lawyer, to what the rights of the young person are and what they can expect going through the court process. The Public Legal Information Association of Newfoundland and Labrador also has several publications and produced a kit that volunteers used to explain the Act to young people in schools, to university classes, and interested community groups.

Corrections

The responsibility for youth corrections in Newfoundland and Labrador is divided between the provincial Department of Justice, which is responsible for remand and secure custody services, and the provincial Department of Child Youth and Family Services, which is responsible for all the community-based services. Some key points related to Newfoundland and Labrador's implementation of the *Youth Criminal Justice Act* are that: (a) as no formal program exists referral to an attendance program, under section 42.2 (m) of the Act, is not available as a sentencing option; (b) as no formal program exists, an intensive support and supervision order, as per section 42.2(l) of the Act, is not available as a sentencing option; (c) intermittent custody is not available as a sentencing option.[23]

Pre-trial Services

The Pre-trial Services Program comes under the Department of Justice, Secure Custody Division and serves the St. John's youth court. It was introduced in January 2002, in anticipation of the implementation of the YCJA, to help provide an alternative to the pretrial detention of youths. It operates seven days a week from 9 a.m. to midnight. The program takes referrals from the judge, Crown prosecutor or defence counsel. The program[24] provides the court verified information on the status of a youth with respect to acceptance into the Pre-trial Services Program at his /her bail hearing, provides community supervision as per the guidelines of the program for a youth released on judicial interim release order, as directed by the Youth Justice Court, and provides support and information to a detained youth for the purpose of applying for a judicial review of variation or review of the detention order.

The functions of the program are:[25]

- Verification: Determines the eligibility of the youth for the program by verifying the information the youth is providing to the court through collateral contacts in his/her application for bail.
- Supervision: Is provided following the release of a youth on bail with a court-ordered supervision condition to the Pre-Trial Services Program to ensure the youth's compliance with the conditions of the release order; to ensure the youth follows the daily program that has been developed; to ensure the community safeguards are continuing to be met; and to monitor that the regime of supervision is acceptable.
- Review: Should a youth be denied bail, reviews assist and facilitate a judicial review of the youth's detention should circumstances change and/or mandatory review dates are reached.

A social worker from Pre-trial Services comes to the first court appearance and offers suggestions to help keep youth out of custody, provide intensive supervision to the youth, and offers support to families. Social workers run parenting groups, anger management groups, mediate with school, and help youth with transportation as well as providing whatever supervision and support is necessary to keep them out of custody while awaiting trial. The main focus of the program is to develop relationships with young people and their families, and act as an advocate for youth. The workers try to avoid a security mentality, and information from individuals who work in the YJS suggests that the majority of youths who participate do not breach conditions.It appears that except for the year of 2011/12, the numbers of youth taking part in Pre-trial Services in Newfoundland and Labrador has been fairly consistent since it was put in place (see Table 6.5). This is interesting given the decreased numbers of youth being arrested and going to court. It is probably a contributing factor to the reduced numbers of youth going into remand (which are lower in Newfoundland and Labrador than in the rest of Canada) and secure custody. A positive aspect of the program is that it can respond quickly to youth who breach their conditions. The

Table 6.5 Average number of youth on pre-trial services program by selected months of fiscal year[26]

Year	April	June	August	October	December	February	March	Year totals
2002/03	10	10	12	9	11	9	12	119
2004/05	11	16	14	16	15	10	10	167
2008/09	10	13	15	14	13	15	17	164
2010/11	13	18	15	17	14	7	8	156
2011/12	7	6	13	8	8	5	4	92
2012/13	5	9	11	18	17	19	19	157

social workers can assess the situation and call the police if necessary before any harm is done. From all accounts, the initiative seems to have been successful in keeping youth out of pretrial detention.

Community Youth Corrections

The Department of Child, Youth and Family Services is responsible for three primary areas of service delivery under Youth Corrections; extrajudicial sanctions, community supervision, and open custody. Tables 6.6, 6.7, and 6.8 outline the number of programs in different areas of the province in 2013.

The majority of programs exist in the eastern part of the province, with St. John's being the community having the largest number overall. St. John's has almost all of the extrajudicial sanctions programs. The majority of participants are male with the percentage of females approximately 32%. The percentage of Aboriginal youth is approximately 9%. The total number of 385 is an increase from 2010/2011 when 359 youth were sentenced to community supervision program. At the time that was a change of −32% from 2005/2006.

Extrajudicial Sanctions

This program formerly referred to as Alternative Measures, acts as an alternative to the court system while allowing youth to make amends for their criminal act without receiving a criminal record. It is most often used for first-time offenders who have committed non-violent offences, although in some cases youth who have committed prior offences and

Table 6.6 Program statistics, community youth corrections, (March 31, 2013)[27]

Service	Central/East	Metro	Labrador	Western	Provincial total
Community youth corrections	100	90	30	110	330
Extrajudicial sanctions	< 5	45	0	< 5	50
Open custody	< 5	< 5	0	< 5	10
Total	105	140	30	110	385

Table 6.7 Youth correctional statistics by gender (March 31, 2013)[28]

	Community corrections	Extrajudicial sanctions	Provincial total
Male	245	30	275
Female	70	20	90
Gender not indicated	15		15
Total	330	50	380

Table 6.8 Sanctions according to youth status

	Number of youth by Aboriginal status (March 31, 2013)[29]		
Aboriginal	35	< 5	35
Not Aboriginal	275	50	325
	Community corrections	Extrajudicial sanctions	Provincial total
Not indicated	20	0	20
Total	330	50	380

those who have committed violent offences may be considered, depending on the circumstances of the offences and the recommendation of the Crown prosecutor.

There are some key points related to Newfoundland and Labrador's implementation of the *Youth Criminal Justice Act* regarding extrajudicial sanctions (EJS): (a) extrajudicial sanctions are delivered through the mechanism of volunteer youth justice committees; (b) referrals to youth justice committees are primarily through Crown prosecutors; (c) social workers, employees of the Department of Child, Youth and Family Services, are delegated all authorities – tasks of the "youth worker" as defined by the Act, (d) roles-functions-authorities of "Provincial Director" as defined by the Act have been delegated to various positions within the department.[30]

Apparently at its peak capacity, the EJS program was composed of 35 committees located throughout the province. Over the last several years the number of referrals has decreased considerably (Table 6.9). As of the fiscal year 2013/2014, five of these committees are considered inactive because there is not at least one volunteer to accept a referral. Suggestions on what is driving the change include a declining youth population, especially in rural parts of the province, a decrease in Youth Corrections caseloads, and a decline in the number of youth receiving custody. There appears to be larger issues beyond new legislation affecting the caseloads.[31]

Table 6.9 Comparison of number of referrals to volunteer extrajudicial sanctions youth justice committees for select fiscal years[32]

Fiscal year	Number of referrals
1995–1996	931
1996–1997	989
1999–2000	771
2000–2001	729
2007–2008	398
2008–2009	412
2009–2010	353
2010–2011	307
2011–2012	268

According to information from workers in Youth Corrections, it appears the transition from YOA to YCJA as it relates to extrajudicial sanctions was a relatively smooth one. The new Act resulted in a name change, but the model remained the same as it was under the YOA. The programs are pre-charge; the Crown makes a referral to members of a volunteer EJS committee. The province's attorney general authorizes the committees, which follow program standards put in place by the province and established a list of offences for which they accept referrals. There were a few significant changes to the program after the introduction of the YCJA. Along with a gradual decrease in the number of referrals to EJS programs mentioned above, there has also been a more recent decline in the number of committees actively accepting referrals.[33]

As seen in Table 6.10 below, the most common offence for which youth are referred is theft under $5,000. The next most common offences are for property damage, mischief, and assault. In the year 2012/2013,

Table 6.10 Types of offences

Most common types of offences for which youth are referred[34]		
2010–2011	Theft under $5,000	28
(111 referrals)	Property/mischief	13
	Assault	12
	Trespassing at mall	11
	Fraud	10
	Break & enter	7
	Uttering threats	6
	Possession of controlled drug/substance	1
2011–2012	Theft under $5,000	39
(130 referrals)	Property/mischief	15
	Assault	14
	Trespassing at mall	10
	Uttering threats	9
	Police-related offences	8
	Possession of controlled drug/substance	7
	Break & enter	6
2012–2013	Theft under $5,000	45
(149 referrals)	Malicious damage to property	33
	Assault	11
	Failure to comply with a condition or undertaking	9
	Police-related offences	6
	Uttering threats	5

it appears more youth were referred for failure to comply with conditions. A small percentage are charged with drug offences, the most in 2011/2012 with seven referrals.

For the last three years the majority of youth referred were male: 78 males and 33 females in 2010/2011, 90 males and 40 females in 2011/2012, and 94 males and 55 females in 2012/2013. Although there were a small number of youth aged 12, the majority of participants were between 15 and 17 years of age. Most programs are for a period of six months. The EJS program has approximately a 75% success rate with those who break their contract being sent back to the court system.[35]

The program liaison social worker carries out a case management role and sets up a contract with each youth who enters the program. The contract is based on the offence committed and the needs of the individual. It may involve writing an apology to the victim, doing community service work, going to drug and/or general counselling sessions or an education program. About 30% of the contracts involve community services work. Members of the board and staff also conduct victim/offender mediation sessions when appropriate.

The EJS program partners with various organizations in the community and provides the opportunity for youth to participate in several education programs. Some are run by the RNC, including Crimes of Disorder Educational sessions with youth who are charged with resisting arrest, causing a disturbance in public, obstructing justice, or assaulting a police officer. There are also programs addressing adolescent health issues, anger management, and drug problems. These multitudes of education programs help youth learn how to "think before they act."

A number of young people who attend the EJS program have multiple problems. Many are from single parent families. Many have difficulty in the school system. They come from all social classes. The problems seem more complex in nature in recent years with more mental health issues present. The social workers often see the same youth more than once. Most of the youth who end up in the corrections system have been through diversion first. The major selling point of the program is that there will be no criminal record if a youth successfully completes the extrajudicial sanctions program.

Community-Based Supervision

Some type of non-custodial order is the most common disposition that young people receive. The type of community supervision is determined by the type of order issued by the Youth Justice Court, the duration of the order, the specific conditions attached and contact and service standards connected to the application of the Youth Level of Service/Case Management Inventory, and any specific standards for contact connected to a specific sentence. All these orders are supervised by registered social workers. The most common type of community disposition is supervised probation. Other sentences with supervision and preventive services are: community service order (work for the community), personal service order (work for a victim), custody and supervision order, and deferred custody and supervision order.

Community Corrections services are provided by social workers with Child, Youth and Family Service (CYFS). They prepare pre-sentence reports, progress reports for non-custodial reviews, suspension reports for community supervision, and deferred custody as well as documentation leading to "failure to comply" charges. Each youth corrections case is assessed using the *provincial risk/need classification model,* and a plan is developed based on the young person's needs. The youth corrections social worker manages the case and provides direct services as well as coordinating any other services the young person needs. This can include a number of activities, such as crisis intervention, family support and counselling, individual counselling, referrals to specialized services, financial assessment to access programs, assistance with housing, and several other services. Social workers may also provide preventive services to young persons at risk and after-care services to youth who have been released from custody. These services are offered on a volunteer basis.[36]

Table 6.11 Average days and supervised probation counts[37]

Fiscal year	Male	Female	Not stated	Total of average days
2003–2004	456	114		570
2005–2005	382	71		453
2007–2008	277	69		358
2009–2010	236	51		287
2011–2012	212	57	3	271

As noted, supervised probation is the most common community-based sentence. The following table outlines the numbers of youth on supervised probation for a sample of years between 2004 and 2012. We see a steady decline in total numbers from 570 to 271.

Similar to the decline of youth arrests, there has been a steady decline in the number of youth being sentenced to supervised probation. The total number in 2011–2012 is less than half the number for 2003–2004. As can be seen in the next table, there is a slight increase in probation numbers in 2013. The male/female ratio is fairly consistent. According to Statistics Canada 2012, the average length of time for a youth to be on probation in Newfoundland and Labrador is approximately 365 days. That is similar to the Canadian average.[38]

Table 6.12 outlines the most common court orders given in Newfoundland and Labrador to youth for 2013. These reflect the most common sentence in most other provinces and Canada in general.

Open Custody Residential Services

Open Custody is an Order of the Youth Justice Court and a young person sentenced to Open Custody will normally spend the first two thirds of the term in an Open Custody facility, and the final third in the community under supervision. If there is any serious breach of conditions

Table 6.12 Most common court orders (March 31, 2013)[39]

Orders	n	%
Probation (supervised)	281	68.2
Community service order (not a condition of probation)	32	7.8
Conditional discharge (without a reporting requirement)	17	4.1
Unsupervised probation	14	3.4
Community/personal service order	12	2.9
Pre-sentence report (awaiting sentence)	8	1.9
Secure custody portion (of custody and supervision order)	6	1.5
Deferred custody and supervision	3	0.7

during that period of time the young person may be returned to custody by the court (Open Custody, 2013).

The Open Custody program is delivered through community-based and non-institutional group homes. These homes are positioned in residential areas and have access to community services and activities under strict conditions. There are currently two group homes, the Home for Youth in St. John's and the Loretta Bartlett Home for Youth in Corner Brook. These are used exclusively for open custody and are administered by the John Howard Society. The Society is responsible for financial and personnel management of the facility, the coordination of policy and program development, property maintenance, advocacy, and community public relations. These group homes provide a supportive, non-institutional environment, along with educational programs, psychological and medical services, counselling, and coordination with other services in the community.

There are also two group homes in the communities of Naini and Sheshatshiu, which are "dual designation" meaning they can accept both Community Youth Corrections and Child, Youth and Family Services (CYFS) placements in specific circumstances. Recent numbers show that they are being used almost exclusively for youth who need child protection intervention. All group homes operate on a rotating shift model. Staffing consists of a coordinator, a senior counsellor, and up to seven group home counsellor positions. CYFS is responsible for overall case management of young persons placed within group homes.[40] The number of youth sentenced to open custody and the number of group homes operating have steadily declined since the implementation of the YCJA, as illustrated in Table 6.13. Open custody is still a popular option over secure custody, and has been used recently for youth convicted of some violent offences.

Table 6.13 Comparison of open custody utilization, pre- and post-YCJA (selected years)[41]

Fiscal year	Number of group homes[a]	Capacity	Average daily count
1996–1997	11	55	53.7
1997–1998	11	55	41.2
1998–1999	11	55	36.9
1999–2000	11	55	33.6
2000–2001	11	55	31.0
2001–2002	11	55	31.5
2002–2003	11	55	34.2
2003–2004	11	55	17.2
2004–2005	9[b]	43	18.0
2005–2006	9	43	16.0
2006–2007	9	43	16.7
2007–2008	9	43	12.0
2008–2009	9	43	10.2
2009–2010	9	43	12.3
2010–2011	4[c]	23	5.8
2011–2012	4	23	4.7
2012–2013	4	23	6.8

a Capacity includes two Aboriginal group homes in Labrador that are dual designated, meaning placements can be made from both Community Corrections and the Child Welfare program.
b Group homes in Whitbourne and Gander closed during this year.
c Group homes in St. John's, (Pegasus), Marystown-Burin, Grand Falls-Windsor, Stephenville, and Happy Valley-Goose Bay transferred to Protective Intervention Program. Current capacity composed on two John Howard Society group homes (St. John's, Corner Brook) and two dual-designated group homes (Naini, Sheshatshiu). We used Naini in the text. This item is not numbered.

Youth Corrections Remand and Secure Custody

This division of Youth Corrections is operated by the Department of Justice. The mandate of Youth Secure Custody is to operate an effective system of residential secure custody and remand services, and to deliver a Pre-trial Services Program as an alternative to having accused youth remanded into custody.

Remand is a type of court-ordered detention for youth awaiting trial or sentencing. The judge has to consider several provisions set out in the YCJA. Remand may not be used as a substitute for child protection, mental health services, or other social measures. Also, a youth cannot be detained if he or she could not be sentenced to custody for the offence, and the judge must enquire if there is a responsible adult to take over the care and control of the youth until trial.[42] Canada-wide statistics

(2010–2011) show that youth in remand outnumber those in sentenced custody for the fourth year in a row. In 2010–2011, on any given day, 54% of youths in custody were in remand and 44% in sentenced custody. The continued large numbers of youth in remand in Canada has come under considerable criticism. In NL, the situation is different since the numbers of youth in remand have been steadily declining along with the number of youth in secure custody, as shown in the table below.

The Newfoundland and Labrador Youth Centre (NLYC) is the provincial secure custody and remand facility for the province and is located in Whitbourne, approximately 90 kilometres outside St. John's. The Department of Child, Youth and Family Services also runs the St. John's Youth Detention Centre, which is available to temporarily hold youth until they can be transferred to the NLYC in Whitbourne. This facility also houses the pretrial detention program and can be used for counselling services for youth and families, family visits, professional appointments, and for when youth have their court appearances.

The NLYC is a modern facility built approximately 20 years ago. Staff at the facility deliver a range of programs to youth to help them successfully reintegrate into the community after release from custody. The core programs include an academic program, psychiatric services, psychological services, social work services, recreational programs, nursing services, a trades workshop, pastoral care services, and medical services.[43] Until recently this facility also offered farming and outdoor adventure programs, which were seen as very beneficial to youth. Cutbacks to staff and programming have taken place over the last 10 years as the number of youth in secure custody continued to decline.

Under the YCJA a youth can be sentenced to custody under certain circumstances, including the commission of a violent offence, failure to comply with conditions of a community sentence, commission of an offence for which an adult would be liable to imprisonment for more than two years, and having a history that indicates a pattern of guilty findings. A youth can also be sentenced to custody in an exceptional case where the young person has committed an indictable offence with aggravating circumstances. This provision is rarely used. Interestingly, according to Statistics Canada, crimes committed by youth admitted to custody tend to be non-violent. In 2010/2011, 61% were for property offences and other *Criminal Code* offences (including administrative offences), and 39% for violent offences. Youth in custody also tended to be disproportionately Aboriginal.[44] This is not the case in NL, where a very small percentage of the inmate population is Aboriginal.

Table 6.14 Whitbourne Youth Centre: Average # of residents/day; average length of stay/days; admissions/year, remand and secure/male and female[45]

Year	Secure #/day	Remand #/day	Secure/ length of stay	Remand/ length of stay	Secure/ male	Secure/ female	Remand/ male	Remand/ female	Total admissions secure/ remand/ overnight
2000/ 2001			203.65	16.36					
2003/ 2004	26.81	8.17	100.32						
2004/ 2005	20.14	8.39	113.52	13.37	61	10 (71 total)	215	56 (271 total)	507
2005/ 2006	17.02	6.16	114.67	25.97	62	5 (67 total)	90	24 (114 total)	346
2006/ 2007	16.92	6.92	155.43	18.28	46	3 (49 total)	99	15 (114 total)	346
2007/ 2008	10.4	7.77	119.60	20.10	37	3 (41 total)	106	38 (144 total)	388
2008/ 2009	10.34	5.97	125.41	21.76	35	7 (42 total)	77	21 (98 total)	301
2009/ 2010	7.65	4.48	91.7						
2010/ 2011	6.26	3.93	112.13						
2011/ 2012	10.47	4.63	110.14						
2012/ 2013	5.46	3.22	79.71		20 total		62 total		222

Note: Detailed statistics for some years not available.

Table 6.14 shows a steady decline of the number of youth going into secure custody and remand since shortly after the introduction of the YCJA. The average daily count of residents and the average length of stay have decreased as well.

Over the last five years youth incarceration rates have dropped in most provinces and territories, and the largest drop, 58% between 2005/2006 and 2010/2011,[46] was in Newfoundland and Labrador. The staff at NLYC state that the biggest change they have witnessed since the implementation of the YCJA is the decrease in numbers. One of the individuals interviewed stressed that they used to see a much higher number of youth charged with minor offences: "Under the YOA we certainly saw a lot more minor offences. We would get people here for breaching probation, for not going to school. It was very far on the other side of the spectrum, but now we are certainly seeing the highest risk kids of the province come in with more serious violent offences."

Interdisciplinary treatment teams are on staff to focus on the youth's needs. Youth who are sentenced to secure custody usually have multiple problems. The most common diagnoses are conduct disorder, substance dependence, and ADHD. Other problems identified are antisocial personality disorder and borderline personality disorder. An individual case plan is put in place for each youth, and there are well-trained staff and multiple resources at the NLYC to help youth. As an interviewee stated, "The youth are not coming in with only behaviour issues; they are coming in with serious substance abuse and mental health issues or diagnoses. So therefore the treatment is now a lot more complex."

Discussions with staff at the NLYC suggest that youth custody has become more treatment oriented, using a holistic approach. Funding for programs has increased to allow new positions such as a clinical therapist, who can focus on a family-based therapy in addition to individual treatment. Because custodial sentences are often short, there is a stronger focus on reintegration into the community right from the beginning so that youth may be able to go back to their family units with support, instead of being supervised in the community-based centres. Follow-up services are set up so psychologists and counsellors at the NLYC can continue to help youth when they are released, but availability can depend on which part of the province the youth lives in. There is better access to services in urban areas.

It seems that while the general attitude towards the YCJA is positive, there are also some concerns. Social workers and staff from both community-based programs and correctional programs all expressed frustration with seeing the same youth coming into the system for short stays multiple times, instead of receiving longer term intensive care. Furthermore, there were suggestions that the multiple sentences of probation and community-based sentences were not always the best answer for repeat youth offenders with complex issues. "It is the same thing, they are bringing in the same kids and the crimes are getting progressively worse in many cases. No one would want to return to the high numbers of the late '90s and the early 2000s when the facility was bursting at the seams," but many feel that there are more youth who could benefit from the services and expertise of individuals at the NLYC, and some who should stay for longer periods of time.

Community Programs

Newfoundland and Labrador has several community-based programs providing services to youth in trouble with the law and youth at risk. A small sample of these programs will be discussed here. Information was provided by individuals who run and work in these programs. The Thrive program website, www.thrivecyn.ca/who-are-we/about-us/, contains information about virtually every service for youth available in the community.

Thrive was established in 2001 and is part of the Province of Newfoundland and Labrador's Community Youth Networks (CYNs). CYNs were established to provide services and support to vulnerable youth 12 to 18 years old who live in poverty and have limited access to mainstream programs. It is an umbrella organization that works with the community to address gaps in service, to build community partnerships, to increase awareness of existing programs and services, and to conduct outreach to the most marginalized youth. Some of the many programs it runs include support services for service providers like a monthly lunch and learn session, monthly newsletters, and an email distribution to share information. It also offers trained facilitators to aid in community development and capacity building.

Thrive operates several educational initiatives for youth who have dropped out or at risk of dropping out of school. It coordinates Street Reach, a street-based outreach service for individuals needing help on their own terms. Thrive is the sponsoring agency for CASEY, which works on issues related to the sexual exploitation of youth. It also runs Velocity, a five-year project funded by the National Crime Prevention Centre, which uses adventure pursuits, team-building processes and individualized support to help kids who are at high risk for criminal involvement (see www.thrivecyn.ca/who-are-we/about-us/).

Choices for Youth is a community-based, not-for-profit organization that has been operating in St. John's for over 20 years to help youth who face a variety of barriers. These range from mental health and addiction issues to criminal involvement and prostitution to homelessness. It offers a variety of programs to help youth who are at risk and those who have been in trouble with the law. These programs include Shelter for Young Men, a transitional housing program, and the Lilly Building, which all help young people with various types of housing needs. The renovations on the Lilly Building were completed in part by young people in the Train for Trades program, which was started by Choices to put trainees alongside tradespersons to retrofit low-income housing units for energy efficiency.

Choices for Youth operates through partnerships and offers a number of programs for youth with a variety of needs, including the Moving Forward program for youth aged 16 to 21 who have complex mental health needs, and the Youth at Promise Challenge, which is a basic literacy skills program for youth who have limited employment and educational opportunities. It operates a Momma Moments, a support group for young pregnant and parenting women, a healthy baby club, and a postnatal support program. It is co-located with many of its community partners including Child, Youth and Family Services; Health and Community Services, St. John's Region; Community Youth Network – St. John's; and Daybreak Parent/Child Centre. (www.choicesforyouth.ca)

Waypoints, originally named the St. Francis Foundation, was founded in 1978 as a group home for young males. It has grown to a multi-service agency that offers a number of programs to young people, families, and the community. Waypoints used to operate an Open Custody group home, but with some major restructuring at Child, Youth and Family Services in 2010, and with declining numbers of youth going into custody, several Open Custody group homes closed.

Waypoints is a not-for-profit agency, run by a volunteer board and funded primarily by the provincial government. It helps young people between the ages of 8 and 18 by providing an environment that is creative, respectful, and strength based. All intervention focuses on promoting emotional, social, cognitive, and behavioural change through the use of daily life events. It offers a variety of services including a long-term group home and unique specialized living arrangements for youth in the care of the director of Child, Youth and Family Services, emergency placement units for young people in crisis, parent support and education groups, a family support program, and youth outreach and employment services. It also runs the Youth are Working program, which is a Skills Link project funded by Service Canada, providing exposure to life and employment-related skills. Waypoints offers a therapeutic and recreational program intended for youth who have been involved in criminal behaviour. Its philosophy is "there is no such thing as a bad kid. The behaviours are a direct result of the circumstances that a youth is in, and given the proper resources, a young person can overcome adversity" (www.waypointsnl.ca).

The *John Howard Society* operates a number of programs that are beneficial to youth who are in trouble with the law. In St. John's it operates Home for Youth, an Open Custody facility, a Community Support

Program, and the Youth Services Program. In Corner Brook, it operates the Loretta Bartlett Home for Youth.

Both Homes for Youth accept referrals from the Department of Child, Youth and Family Services for youth who have been sentenced to a period of Open Custody by the Youth Justice Court. The dedicated and well-trained staff provide a supportive, home-like environment to young people. The program stresses responsibility, life skills, and fosters independence. There are many weekly activities that focus on study, recreation, job search, self-awareness, and conflict resolution. Assistance is also provided to access educational, medical, and psychological services in the community. The Homes maintain close relationships with several community partners (http://johnhowardnl.ca/services/).

Shortly after the YCJA was introduced, funding was provided in 2004 through the federal government's Youth Justice Renewal Fund, the provincial government's Department of Health and Community Services and Eastern Health to develop a community support program for youth returning to the community after a period of time in custody. This program operates directly from the John Howard Society's Home for Youth (Open Custody facility). It expands on the level of support that is already being offered to youth upon release from custody. Referrals are made through Child, Youth and Family Services on a prioritized basis for youth on community supervision, youth on deferred custody orders, youth on supervised probation, and youth identified as being at risk of entering the custody system or as requiring supportive intervention. The staff provide enhanced after-hours supervision and support to youth and their families. The program also provides supportive counselling to improve youth's educational and vocational opportunities and involvement in pro-social extra-curricular activities. This program, held in high regard by those working with youth, has been successful in helping youth reintegrate into the community, but is now in danger of losing funding.

The Department of Child, Youth and Family Services' Youth Services Program provides supportive counselling and assistance to at-risk youth (offenders and ex-offenders) who are between 18 and 25 and need support with career-planning and employment opportunities. This support begins at the pre-release stage, and helps with comprehensive community planning when youth are released.

All these community groups provide much needed services to troubled youth. Many of these programs are funded on a short-term basis, which makes it difficult for ongoing program development and long-term retention of staff. Staffing levels are not always optimal in some organizations. At times, staff feel that having only one staff member on duty becomes a safety issue, resulting in some youth not being accepted to stay in their housing program. Many organizations are seeing staff cutbacks, possibly due, as staff suggest, to doing their jobs so success-fully that the numbers of youth in trouble decreased. But cutbacks can lead to staff being overworked or doing less than they did in the past.

Concerns were raised about a greater need for housing for youth transitioning out of custody, and at-risk youth in general. Education for at-risk youth is also seen as an issue. Many of the youth who get into trouble are not attending school on a regular basis, and there are only a small number of spaces available at alternative schools. It is clear from discussions with counsellors that many of the youths have very com-plex needs often involving behavioural and/or mental health issues. The waiting list for the Janeway Family Centre in St. John's is about 18 months. Although a comprehensive service is available, the needs of the youth are immediate and considerable damage can be done waiting for help. A further concern was expressed that youth are getting into trouble for what are really child protection issues and problems related to neglect. There is a need for more support for families and more ap-propriate alternative living arrangements for youth than are currently available. Many youth are not going into safe, affordable housing, and are getting into trouble because of this. There is a basic consensus that more effort needs to be put into prevention and keeping at-risk youth and youth in general out of trouble.

Conclusion

From all indications the implementation of the *Youth Criminal Justice Act* in Newfoundland and Labrador was "no problem." Those working in the youth justice system were prepared for the changes, and they took place without too much difficulty. The YCJA seems to have had a posi-tive impact on the number of youth being charged by police, going to youth court, and spending time in remand and in custody. The numbers have decreased by more than 50% in the past ten years. The steady de-cline in the youth population of the province over the last twenty years, and the economic changes in NL could also be contributing factors.

The provincial government put considerable effort into educating staff about the YCJA before it was implemented, and has provided ongoing education since. Some programs like Pre-Trial Services were put in place in anticipation of the YCJA, other programs like the John Howard Society community support program were introduced shortly after. An Alternative Measures program was already in place and evolved into extrajudicial measures under the YCJA. The success of these programs (as reflected by statistics in annual reports) has affected custody rates.

Funding was also increased for community organizations that work with youth. Many were able to expand and provide multiple services to both youth at risk and to youth who had offended. These programs are well used and highly regarded. However, many of these services are dependent on contract funding, and cutbacks to staffing have occurred in recent years. This has influenced service provision and entire programs may be in jeopardy in some cases.

The police generally have not seen a decrease in the numbers of youth they come into contact with, but much of the contact may be for non-criminal situations involving family disputes, child protection issues, and running away from group homes. Many youth who would previously have been charged are now being dealt with informally through warnings, mediation, and referrals. Those who are charged usually commit more serious offences, which may contribute to the police view that youth crime seems more serious. Police, and others involved in youth corrections and community groups, also report seeing more female youth involved in crime. There is work that needs to be done to develop a consistent system for the recording and sharing of police warnings.

It seems under the YCJA, the police role of gatekeepers for the CJS has expanded. The direction to police under section 6 (1) of the YCJA to consider alternatives before considering any judicial proceedings, certainly contributes to the lower number of young people being charged with offences. Police discretion is an important factor in how to proceed with a young person who gets in trouble with the law. This highlights the importance of the police being well educated in legislation, ethics, the use of discretion, the "root causes" of youth crime, and being familiar with the types of services available for youth in the community. It also points to the importance of the police developing positive relationships with youth through interaction, support, and programming. Both police services in NL appear committed to this goal.

Many of the cases that come to youth court are diverted to extrajudicial sanctions programs. About 75% of the youth who participate in these programs do not breach conditions of their program. The most serious cases, repeat offenders and multiple breaches, are appearing in court. The decreased numbers of youth being kept in remand is likely due to the success of the Pre-trial Services Program. When they do appear in court for trial and sentencing, their success in the Pre-trial program likely influences the type of sentence the youth receives.

Most youth are sentenced to probation and other community sentences. The numbers sentenced to open custody have decreased and the numbers going to secure custody are very low. Those youth who do go into secure custody have very complex, multiple problems often involving mental health and addictions issues. The NLYC is a multi-service facility with well-trained staff and intensive programming to help the most needy youth. For those who do receive custodial sentences, the average length of time is very low. This can raise concerns about short-term programming and availability of follow-up for some youth when they return to the community. There are two new community-based facilities being built in the province to help youth with complex needs around mental health and addictions. These youth are now being sent outside the province for help.

Then are several multi-service agencies in the community that work with youth who have been in trouble with the law and at-risk youth. They coordinate with Youth Corrections and Child, Youth and Family Services to help the young people. Some of the therapeutic services (Janeway Child Family Centre) have long waiting lists, which is a problem. Many of these organizations are dependent on project funding and have experienced reductions in funding and staff cutbacks in recent years. They are also not available in all areas of the province.

All those we spoke to who work in the youth justice system agreed that too many youth were going into custody for minor offences under the *Young Offenders Act*. They like the flexibility to not criminalize youth that comes with the YCJA. But there are concerns that youth are not being held responsible until they commit several offences or escalate to a more serious offence.

The guidelines in the YCJA that provide direction to police, the Crown, and judges have had a tremendous impact on the number of youth being brought into the youth justice system and receiving custodial sentences. It has truly become a last resort. That being said, it seems youth who do come into the system have a multitude of complex problems. More effort needs to go into prevention of youth crime by providing adequate support and help to youth, their families, those in the youth justice system, and community groups.

We would like to thank the people who work with youth, in the youth justice system and in the community for taking the time to talk to us and share their opinions and experiences. This piece of work is descriptive and anecdotal.[47] It was done in a short time frame with input from a small, but very interested, group of people. We hope it is reflective of the situation in NL since the implementation of the YCJA, and the opinions of the people we spoke to. It provides an overview, not an in-depth critical analysis, and points to the need for comprehensive research about the youth justice system in Newfoundland and Labrador.

NOTES

1 Winterdyk, J., & Smandych, R. Youth at risk and youth justice. Don Mills, Ontario: Oxford University Press, 2012.
2 All figures from the Canada 2011 Census.
3 Newfoundland and Labrador Provincial Economic Review, 2013: http://www.fin.gov.nl.ca/fin/publications/the_economic_review_2013.pdf.
4 News release: Heather May. Director of Communications, Department of Education, NL: http://www.releases.gov.nl.ca/releases/2013/edu/1018n06.htm.
5 Economics and Statistics Branch, Newfoundland and Labrador Statistics Agency, January 2014: http://www.stats.gov.nl.ca/statistics/Labour/PDF/LFC_NL_Youth.pdf.
6 Newfoundland Statistics Agency, January 2014.
7 Youth population Newfoundland and Labrador: http://www.stats.gov.nl.ca/statistics/population/PDF/PopAgeSex_BS.PDF.
8 http://www.statcan.gc.ca/pub/85-002-x/2013001/article/11854-eng.htm#a7.
9 http://www.statcan.gc.ca/pub/85-005-x/2012001/article/11749/c-g/desc/desc-01-eng.htm.
10 http://www.statcan.gc.ca/pub/11-402-x/2012000/chap/crime/crime-eng.htm.
11 Ibid.
12 http://www.canlii.org/en/ca/laws/stat/sc-2002-c-1/latest/sc-2002-c-1.html.
13 Department of Child, Youth and Family Services, November, 2013.
14 RCMP Youth Chargeable Offences Statistics B Division, 2013.
15 Statistics Canada, Youth Court Statistics in Canada. 2010/11, pp. 1–7.
16 Ibid.
17 Newfoundland and Labrador Provincial Court, Annual Report 2012–13.
18 Newfoundland and Labrador Provincial Court, Annual Report, 2012.
19 Newfoundland and Labrador Provincial Court, Annual Report 2012/2013.

20 Youth cases by decision, Newfoundland and Labrador Provincial Court, 2011–2012.

21 Historically, the presence of Aboriginal youth in the Newfoundland and Labrador youth justice system has been quite low, as reported here by Latimer (2004, p. 4): "The largest difference between the incarceration rates of Aboriginal and non-Aboriginal youth was in Saskatchewan where Aboriginal youth were 30 times more likely to be incarcerated compared to non-Aboriginal youth. In the Yukon, Aboriginal youth were 18 times more likely to be incarcerated compared to non-Aboriginal youth and in Manitoba, Aboriginal youth were 16 times more likely to be incarcerated compared to non-Aboriginal youth. The smallest differences were found in New Brunswick and Newfoundland and Labrador where Aboriginal youth were only 1.2 and 1.6 times respectively more likely to be incarcerated compared to non-Aboriginal youth."

22 Provincial Court of Newfoundland, *Annual Report 2012/2013*: http://www .court.nl.ca/provincial/publications/ProvCourtAnnReport_2012_2013 .pdf.

23 Department of Child Youth and Family Services, Government of Newfoundland, November, 2013.

24 Government of Newfoundland, last updated June 21, 2013: www.justice .gov.nl.ca/just/corrections/pre_trial_services.html.

25 *Ibid.*

26 Pre-trial Services, Newfoundland and Labrador Department of Justice 2014: http:www.justice.gov.nl.ca/just/corrections/pre_trial_services.html.

27 Program Statistics, Community Youth Corrections: http://www.gov.nl.ca/ cyfs/pdf/youthcorrections_statistics.pdf.

28 *Ibid.*

29 *Ibid.*

30 Department of Child Youth and Family Services, Government of Newfoundland, November 2013.

31 *Ibid.*

32 *Ibid.* Note: Although the table does not provide information on all fiscal years it does illustrate that the decline in the number of referrals being made to extrajudicial sanctions programs began prior to the implementation of the *Youth Criminal Justice Act*.

33 *Ibid.*

34 EJS program annual reports, 2011, 2012, 2013.

35 *Ibid.*

36 Department of Child, Youth and Family Services, Government of Newfoundland, 2013.

37 Department of Child, Youth and Family Services, Government of Newfoundland, 2013.
38 Youth Corrections, Statistics Canada, 2010/11.
39 Department of Child, Youth and Family Services, Government of Newfoundland, 2014. Note: According to Statistics Canada 2012, the average length of time for a youth to be on probation in Newfoundland and Labrador is approximately 365 days, similar to the Canadian average.
40 Department of Child, Youth and Family Services, Government of Newfoundland, 2014.
41 Department of Child, Youth and Family Services, Government of Newfoundland, 2014.
42 S. Bell, *Young offenders and youth justice a century after the fact*. Toronto, ON: Nelson Canada, 2012.
43 NL Youth Secure Custody–Thrive: http://www.thrivecyn.ca/directory-of-services/justice/nl-youth-secure-custody/.
44 Youth Correctional statistics in Canada, 2010-2011: http://www.statcan.gc.ca/pub/85-002-x/2012001/article/11716-eng.htm.
45 Newfoundland and Labrador Youth Centre, 2013.
46 *Ibid.*
47 See sample of key youth community groups in Newfoundland and Labrador listed below.

John Howard Home for Youth	Young people participating in the program have been sentenced to a period of Open Custody by the Youth Justice Court. Referrals are made by provincial Dept. of Health and Community Services	It provides a supportive, home-like environment to five male or female young people. The program stresses responsibility, life skills, and fosters independence. Activities include weekly recreation, daily study time, involvement with various community resources; and group sessions, covering topics such as job search, résumé writing, self-awareness, conflict resolution, and interpersonal skills. A young person residing at the Home for Youth will also be assisted in accessing educational, medical, and psychological services within the community.
Waypoints	Waypoints is a recognized leader in the field of child and youth care. Waypoints provides a variety of residential and support services to children, youth, and families. The vision of Waypoints is safe and healthy children, youth and families learning, growing, and participating to their full potential in supportive communities.	Philosophy: There is no such thing as a bad kid. The behaviours we see are a direct result of the circumstances that a youth is in; and given the proper resources, a young person can overcome adversity. 18-month residential program for adolescent offenders.
Choices for Youth	A not-for-profit community-based agency, which was established in 1990 after the closure of Mount Cashel Orphanage. Its mission is to provide youth with a range of supportive housing options, access to a variety of services that promote healthy personal development, and a sense of belonging within an environment of respect, tolerance, peace, and equity.	Shelter for young men between ages of 16 and 29. Supportive housing program for youth between ages of 16 and 21. Youth at Promise – basic literacy skills program for youth who have limited employment/educational opportunities. Life skills development.Drop-in recreational, etc.

John Howard Community Support Program	Funded under the YCJA in 2004 through the federal government's Youth Justice Renewal Fund, the provincial department of Health and Community Services, and Eastern Health.	It operates directly from the Home for Youth and expands on the current level of supervision and support being offered to youth returning from custody to the community. This program begins after 4 p.m. and provides after-hour supervision and support to families. It works to provide supportive counselling to improve youth's educational and vocational opportunities, as well as supportive involvement in pro-social extra-curricular activities.	Referrals are made through Eastern Health on a prioritized basis: (a) youth on community supervision, (b) youth on deferred custody orders, (c) youth on probation, (d) youth identified as being at risk of entering the custody system or identified as requiring supportive intervention.
John Howard Youth Services Program	Provides supportive counselling and assistance to at-risk youth (offenders and ex-offenders) who are between the ages of 18 and 25, and need assistance with their career plans including educational, training, and employment opportunities.	Referrals come from NL Youth Centre, Community Youth Corrections, HMP, Correctional Services of Canada, Corrections and Community Services, Eastern Health, John Howard Society program, various community agencies, and self-referrals.	Supportive counselling services starting at the pre-release stage, but focusing on comprehensive community planning once they are released from open or secure custodial facilities, or are serving a term on probation or parole.
Pre-trial Services program	Mandate – to reduce the amount of time a youth is detained in custody pending trial by providing verified information to the Youth Justice Court at each stage of the bail hearing, combined with community supervision and programming while under the jurisdiction of an interim release order.	By referral from the Crown prosecutor or the youth's defence council. Targets all male and female youth who are held in custody and between the ages of 12 and 18 appearing for a bail hearing or requesting a bail review.	Program components: Verification – eligibility of youth by verifying information that has been provided to the court. Supervision – provided following the release of the youth on bail to ensure the youth's compliance with conditions. Review – should a youth be denied bail, to assist and facilitate a judicial circumstance change and mandatory review dates.

Eastern Health	Central intake for Child and Adolescent Mental Health and Addictions.	To improve accessibility, standardize, and processing of referrals, monitor wait lists, and improve efficiency among the Community Mental Health and Addictions Eastern Health Services.	The Janeway Family Centre, Janeway Child and Adolescent Psychiatry, Family Services counsellors, Bridges program (mental health services), community mental health counselors. Addictions – Adolescent Outpatient Services and the Rowan Centre (day treatment for substance and/or gambling issues.
RNC Community Policing Programs for Youth	Junior Police Academy,STRIVE (Students Taking Responsibility in Violence Education,DARE Drug Abuse Resistance Education.	Partnership with St. John's Boys and Girls Club – Students taking responsibility for violent.	To build healthy relationships with youth.
RMCP Community Policing Programs for Youth	Youth Crime Prevention website aims to provide evidence-based and age-appropriate crime prevention messages, information, and tools to prevent youth crime and victimization.	Working with youth is one of the RCMP's strategic priorities. This website builds on over 15 years of success of its previous youth website, and includes many new features.	Ask and expert – allows Web users to ask questions to experts on various issues related to youth crime and victimization. What's trending – invites Web users to let us know what is going on in their communities via social media. Interactive learning tools, which include useful fact sheets and lesson plans on a variety of youth-related issues including substance abuse, bullying, cyber- bullying, dating, and family violence.

REFERENCES

Bell, S. (2012). *Young offenders and youth justice a century after the fact*. Toronto, ON: Nelson Canada.

Brennan, S. Youth court statistics in Canada, 2010/2011. Retrieved from www .statscan.gc.ca/pub/85-002-x/2012001/article/11645-eng.htm.

Choices for Youth. *Annual Report* 2010–2011.

Choices for Youth (2011). Backgrounder/pamphlet.

Choices for Youth. Retrieved from www.choicesforyouth.ca..Date accessed 30/09/2013.

Community Corrections Services (2013). Child, youth and family services, Government of Newfoundland and Labrador. Retrieved from www.gov.nl.ca/ cyfs/youthcorrections/community corrections/html. Date accessed 2/09/13.

Dauvergne, M. Youth court statistics in Canada, 2011/2012. Retrieved from www.statscan.gc.ca/pub/85-002-x/2013001/ article/11803-eng.htm.

Economics and Statistics Branch, Newfoundland Statistics Agency, January 2014.

Guidelines for police officers under the *Youth Criminal Justice Act*. Section 6 (1–3). Retrieved from http://www.canlii.org/en/ca/laws/stat/sc-2002-c-1/latest/sc-2002-c-1.html.

John Howard Society of Newfoundland and Labrador. Community Support Program. Retrieved from www.johnhowardnl.services/community.html. Date accessed 30/09/13.

John Howard Society of Newfoundland and Labrador. Home for Youth. Retrieved from www.johnhowardnl.services/hfy.html. Date accessed 30/09/2013.

John Howard Society of Newfoundland and Labrador. Loretta Bartlett Home for Youth. Retrieved from www.johnhowardnl.services/loretta.html. Date accessed 30/09/2013.

John Howard Society of Newfoundland and Labrador. Youth Services Program. Retrieved from www.johnhowardnl.services/youth.html. Date accessed 30/09/2013.

Key points related to the implementation of the *Youth Criminal Justice Act* in Newfoundland and Labrador. (2013). Government of Newfoundland, Department of Child Youth and Family Services.

Munch, C. Youth correctional statistics in Canada, 2010/2011. Retrieved from www.statscan.gc.ca/pub/85-002-x/2012001/article/11716-eng.htm.

May, H. News Release, Director of Communications, Department of Education, NL, 2013. Retrieved from www.ed.gov.nl.ca/edu/k12/evaluation /exams.html.

Newfoundland and Labrador Provincial Economic Review, 2013. Retrieved from www.fin.gov.nl.ca/fin/publications/the_economic_review_2013.pdf.

Open Custody. (2013). Child, Youth and Family Services, Government of
    Newfoundland and Labrador. Retrieved from www.gov.nl.ca/cyfs/
    youthcorrections/opencustody.html. Date accessed 23/09/2013.
Pre-Trial Services Program. www.justice.gov.nl.ca/just/corrections/pre_trial_
    services.html. Date accessed 25/02/2014.
Police-reported youth crime severity indexes, by province and territory, 2012
    Statistics Canada, Canadian Centre for Justice Statistics, Uniform Crime
    Reporting Survey.
Provincial Court Newfoundland and Labrador *Annual Report 2012–
    13.* Retrieved from www.court.nl.ca/provincial/publications/
    ProvCourtAnnReport_2012_2013.pdf. Questions and Answers on Youth
    Justice. Public Legal Information Association of NL. Retrieved from www
    .publiclegalinfo.com/yjustice_QAs.html.
RCMP Districts in Newfoundland and Labrador. http://www.rcmp-grc.gc.ca
    /detach/en/find/NL.
RNC Districts in Newfoundland and Labrador. http://www.rcmp-grc.gc/nl/
    images/map800.jpg.
Statistics Canada. CANSIM table 051-0001. Economics and Statistics Branch,
    Newfoundland and Labrador Statistics Agency. Retrieved from
http://www.stats.gov.nl.ca/statistics/population/PDF/PopAgeSex_BS.PDF.
Statistics Canada. (2012). Canadian Centre for Justice Statistics, Uniform
    Crime Reporting Survey.
Thrive Community Youth Network. Retrieved from http://www.thrivecyn
    .ca/. Date accessed 04/03/2014.
Thrive – Directory of Services – Justice. Retrieved from www.thrivecyn.ca/
    directory-of-services/justice/. Date accessed 30/09/2013.
Waypoints. Retrieved from www.waypoints.nl.ca. Date accessed 30/09/2013.
Youth accused of police-reported crime, Canada, 2002 to 2012. Statistics Canada,
    Canadian Centre for Justice Statistics, Uniform Crime Reporting Survey.
Youth accused of police reported crime, by selected offences and by province
    and territory, 2012 Statistics Canada, Canadian Centre for Justice Statistics,
    Uniform Crime Reporting Survey.
Youth Corrections, Department of Child, Youth and Family Services,
    Government of Newfoundland. Retrieved from http://www.gov.nl.ca/
    cyfs/youthcorrections/index.html.
Youth Court. Provincial Court of Newfoundland and Labrador. Retrieved
    from www.court.nl.ca/provincial/courts/youthcourt.html. Date accessed
    23/09/2013.
Youth justice process in Newfoundland and Labrador at a glance. Provided by
    Department. of Child, Youth and Family Services, November 2013.

7 Commission of Inquiry and Judicial Reform in Nova Scotia

SANDRA BELL

Introduction

In Canada, youth criminal justice is both a federal and a provincial matter in that while the law is federal, its implementation is for the most part left to the provinces. Of interest to both scholars and practitioners in the youth justice field is the extent to which federal legislation impacts youth behaviour and responses at the provincial level as well as the reverse, and how incidents and activities at the provincial level may affect legislative and judicial reforms. Through a reporting and analysis of a provincial commission of inquiry, government responses, newspaper articles, and informal conversations with people working in the field, this chapter chronicles events in Nova Scotia that began in 2004 with a stolen car driven by a 16-year-old youth, and culminates eight years later in 2012 with revisions to the *Youth Criminal Justice Act* and changes to the administration of youth justice in Nova Scotia.

The Incident

On October 14, 2004, in Halifax, Nova Scotia, Theresa McEvoy was fatally injured in a car crash as a result of her vehicle being broad-sided by a 16-year-old youth. According to subsequent news reports, the youth had been driving a stolen vehicle and was involved in a high speed chase with the police at the time of the accident. As the details of the case unfolded in newspapers over the following months, it became apparent that this youth had a history of criminal charges, mostly relating to car theft and "joyriding" that included theft over $5,000, fleeing police, possession of a stolen vehicle, and breaching a court order. Furthermore, the incident that resulted in Theresa McEvoy's death occurred only two days after the youth had been released from the Windsor, Nova Scotia court on charges related to a 55-km high-speed police chase. At the time that he was released from the Windsor court, an arrest warrant, issued by a Halifax court, already existed for the youth in relation to a number of charges for similar offences through April, May, and June of the same year (Stewart, December 15, 2005; Hayes, February 15, 2006; Nunn Commission of Inquiry, 2006, pp. 88–95; Bell, 2012, pp. 6–10, 103). Not surprisingly, the details of this case raised a number of questions about why the youth was released when there was an arrest warrant and seemingly sufficient evidence that he was at risk of reoffending. These questions were asked among professionals in the field, the public, and in particular, the McEvoy family.

On November 4, 2004, the McEvoy family asked for a public inquiry, and on November 10, 2004, the then Nova Scotia Justice Minister, Michael Baker, announced that he would hold a "full, independent and public inquiry" (Hayes, January 12, 2006). In June, retired Supreme Court Justice Merlin Nunn was appointed to head the inquiry (Bell, 2012, p. 8). While the larger questions for the inquiry concerned the *Youth Criminal Justice Act* (YCJA) and the administration of youth justice in the province of Nova Scotia, the McEvoy family had three questions: (a) what were the systematic and individual failures that lead to the release of the youth prior to Theresa McEvoy's death; (b) the extent to which the YCJA itself contributed to the youth's release; and, (c) the role of service providers in responding to at-risk youth both before and after criminal activity (Jeffrey, January 14, 2006; Bell, 2012, p. 7).

Incident Details from the Inquiry Report: "The Story"

The Nunn Commission of Inquiry began its work of looking into the "chain of events" that led to the death of Teresa McEvoy and the "actions of all involved as the events occurred" in October 2005. and continued until June 2006. Justice Nunn heard testimony of 47 sworn witnesses, 23 people at an open public forum, and reviewed close to 12,000 pages of documents entered as exhibits (Nunn, 2006, p. 1).

From Nunn's report we learn that the youth's formal involvement with the youth justice system began with an arrest after stealing a car with a friend in Halifax, in January 2004 when he was 15 years of age. By his 16th birthday that summer, the youth had accumulated 30 charges, mostly for car theft, and was known to Halifax police as one of the city's top car thieves and to the youth court as a "frequent flyer." In spite of this, the youth had no criminal record, no findings of guilt, had never been to trial, and had no sentences. Nonetheless, by the spring of 2004, the youth was on the "hit list" of the Halifax police auto theft investigation (Nunn, 2006, pp. 83, 89).

This January arrest led to a February 2004 referral (pre-charge) to a restorative justice program on the basis of a charge of possessing stolen property (a car) and a break- in instrument. He attended an intake information session in March and a mediation session in May. From this mediation, he agreed to attend anger management sessions and perform 60 hours of community service. On June 25th, the youth's file was referred back to the police because he had failed to complete the terms of his Restorative Justice agreement. This resulted in laying three charges from the initial January car theft offence (pp. 87–88).

Meanwhile, the youth had accumulated other new charges and was scheduled for a court appearance in Halifax (his first) on June 10th. He had been arrested on June 9th and faced a total of eight charges alleged to have occurred April 23rd, May 25th, May 30th, and June 9th, all car theft-related offences. At this first court appearance, the case was adjourned for a plea hearing scheduled for July 8th, and the Crown did not seek to hold the youth in custody since he had no criminal record. Instead the youth was released on an undertaking (house arrest) with fairly standard and some individually specific conditions. He was required to: keep the peace and be of good behaviour, to live at his mother's home, keep out of vehicles without the registered owner present, not have contact with specified individuals, stay away from two group homes (where he had recently lived), and, stay at home at all times. The following day, June 11th, the youth's mother reported that he had breached his conditions and was "missing from home." This began another spree of stolen cars and high speed chases with the police. On June 24th, two weeks after his first court appearance, the youth was apprehended and returned to court with 14 new charges. This time, with police recommendations, the youth was held in pretrial detention at the Nova Scotia Youth Centre in Waterville. A bail hearing was scheduled for June 28th where the Crown asked the judge to revoke the June 10th release conditions and undertakings and to add those initial eight charges to the current 14, all of which would be considered at a July 6th bail hearing where the Crown intended to argue that bail be denied (pp. 92–93).

Pretrial Detention and the YCJA

It is at this point that the *Youth Criminal Justice Act* and its pretrial release provisions are seen to have had a profound effect on the direction that this case took, and ultimately in the tragic death of Teresa McEvoy. More specifically, as Justice Nunn explains, these release provisions refer to "Judicial Interim Release," a process then controlled by Part XIV of the *Criminal Code* (section 515(10) and sections 28–31 and 33 of the *Youth Criminal Justice Act*. Section 515(10) of the *Criminal Code* required that a youth be brought before a youth court judge or justice of the peace within 24 hours of arrest and, at this hearing, the Crown must show why the accused should be held in custody. There are two reasons provided by the *Criminal Code* for pretrial detention that apply to both youth and adults: primary and secondary. Primary grounds are invoked when the court is convinced that custody is necessary to ensure that the youth will appear in court. Secondary grounds are invoked when the court believes that custody is necessary for public protection (Bala et al., 1994, p. 88; Doob, Marinos, & Varma, 1995, p. 101). This section of the *Criminal Code* also allows for tertiary grounds, that is, a youth may be held in detention if a judge considers that "detention is necessary in order to maintain confidence in the administration of justice," but case law under the YCJA has indicated that the tertiary ground should rarely be used. Where section 28 of the YCJA specifies the relevance of Part XIV of the *Criminal Code* to the YCJA, and section 30 and 33 of the YCJA speak to appropriate places of detention for youth and release from detention, respectively, it is section 29, prohibitions to detention, and section 31, provisions for a "responsible person," that had the greatest impact on the outcome of this youth's July 6th, and later, youth court appearances.

Section 29(1) specifies that the court cannot hold a youth in pretrial detention "as a substitute for appropriate child protection, mental health or other social measures" and section 29(2) specifies that a youth court judge or justice in considering if detention is necessary for the protection or safety of the public (secondary grounds), "shall presume that detention is not necessary ... if the young person could not, on being found guilty, be committed to custody on the grounds set out in paragraphs 39(1)(a) to (c)" (restrictions on committal to custody). This means that youth do not generally receive a custody sentence unless one of four conditions apply: that they have been convicted of a violent offence (section 39(1)(a)); or, have failed to comply with two or more non-custodial sentences (section 39(1)(b)); or have been found guilty of an offence (indictable) where an adult would be liable to a custody sentence of more than two years (section 39(1)(c)); or, have a history of a "pattern of findings of guilt" (section 39(1)(d)). The Nunn Commission interpreted section 29(2) in combination with section 39(1) (a through d) as a prohibition against detention if a youth has not committed a violent offence, but the courts have not been unanimous on this view. While some have interpreted these sections as an absolute proscription against detention, others have argued that the prohibition is implied and can be challenged (is rebuttable) (Bell, 2012, p. 265; Federal Department of Justice, 2008, pp. 31–32). In Nova Scotia, for example, almost a year before Theresa McEvoy's death, the court *R. v. M.T.S.*) accepted the Crown's argument that a youth's motor vehicle theft, in the context of his "out of control behaviour" constituted a danger to public safety. In January 2007, Crown prosecutors in Nova Scotia were notified that "the decision in M.T.S. accepted the Crown's argument that a youth's motor vehicle theft, in the context of his 'out of control behaviour' constituted a danger to public safety." The same month, Crown prosecutors in Nova Scotia were notified that "the decision in M.T.S. exemplifies the approach being taken by the courts in Nova Scotia" (Federal Department of Justice, 2008, pp. 31–32).

Even if a court has determined that there are grounds, either primary or secondary, to deny bail and hold a youth in pretrial detention, section 31(1) allows the court or justice to place a youth who has been arrested "in the care of a responsible person instead of being detained in custody," and section 31(2) specifies that the youth court or justice "shall inquire as to the availability of a responsible person and whether the young person is willing to be placed in that person's care." According to Nunn, this consideration of an available "responsible person," or at least an alternative to custody, is a requirement for the court or justice (2006, p. 99).

The Bail Hearing: Applying the YCJA

Meanwhile, back in Nova Scotia, the accused youth appeared in Halifax court for a bail hearing on July 6th, and the Crown's position was that the youth should be held in custody to await trial on the accumulated 22 charges. He argued that primary grounds did not apply since the youth had given no indication that he would not appear in court. A reason for denying bail might be found in secondary grounds. The first three conditions of section 39(1) did not apply to the youth, since his offences were not violent as then defined by the YCJA; the youth had not failed to comply with his sentences (since at that time he had none) and; it might have been possible that if found guilty and sentenced, because some of the youth's charges were indictable offences, that the youth would receive a custody sentence. However, because the youth did not, at that time, have a pattern of findings of guilt, detention was presumed not necessary for the safety or protection of society. The Crown argued that the number of offences the youth was facing was "an aggravating circumstance," and that even though this was not specifically covered in the legislation, the judge should look at all the factors of the youth's charges. The judge agreed and denied bail saying that the allegations against the youth were "extremely aggravating" and "give the court some considerable concern about the safety of the public," and ruled that he was "satisfied that detention could be ordered under section 515 and under section 29 of the YCJA." (Nunn, 2006, pp. 100–102). The youth's legal aid lawyer argued against both primary and secondary grounds for detention.

While the judge ruled that detention could be ordered, he still had to consider if a "responsible person" was available as an alternative to custody (sections 31(1) and 39(2)). Here, the youth's legal aid lawyer presented the youth's mother as a "responsible person," and argued that both the mother and stepfather were willing to have the youth return home. His mother maintained that she hoped he had learned a lesson from already being in custody in Waterville for two weeks and said, "I am praying to God that he had learned and he is home, should be home, where he belongs, with us." (Nunn, 2006, p. 101). The lawyer also pointed out that the youth had just turned 16, that he intended to find summer work and return to school in September, and was willing to follow conditions of his release. The youth stated: "Well, I kind of learned from my mistakes now ... I found out how good I had it at home and house arrest is a lot better than jail." He also stated his intention to spend the summer with his father in Newfoundland (Nunn, 2006, pp. 101–102).

The judge released the youth on a "responsible person undertaking" with the same conditions he had on his June 10th court appearance with the addition of a 10 p.m. to 6 a.m. curfew and permission to live with his father in Newfoundland. He left that day to live with his father who returned him to Dartmouth and his mother sometime in August, and his behaviour was reportedly improved. He appeared in court September 14th, with his mother, to plead guilty to nine of his outstanding charges and trial dates were set for the others. The court granted requests for a pre-sentence report and adjourned findings of guilt until the November

17th sentencing date. Trials on the outstanding charges were set for January and February 2005 (Nunn, 2006, p. 103).

Two weeks later, the youth's mother appeared in court to request release from her responsible person undertaking saying that she was "losing control" of her son and felt intimidated by him. She maintained that he was "doing his own thing," was defiant, was stealing from her and her husband, that he was no longer at home and was "running from the police" since she had called them and reported him as having broken into their home. The release was granted and a Warrant of Arrest was issued for the youth that would require all police officers in Nova Scotia, on his arrest, to bring the youth to Halifax for an immediate new bail hearing.

In the early morning of the following day, September 29th, the youth, along with three others, was involved in a 55-km high speed car chase (180 km/hr) with the Lower Sackville RCMP that ended in Windsor, Nova Scotia, where police had placed a spike belt across the highway. The four youths escaped into the surrounding woods and were eventually flushed out by a police canine unit. This was under the jurisdiction of the Windsor Rural RCMP, who made arrests and processed the paperwork for eight new charges against the youth in question: two charges of theft over $5,000, two charges of possession of stolen property, break and enter (of a cottage), evading police, theft under $5,000, and breach of an undertaking. The Windsor Rural RCMP then applied to the Justice of the Peace for remand and arraignment on these eight charges. While both the RCMP and the Justice of the Peace knew about the Halifax arrest warrant and charges, the warrant was set aside to address only the Windsor charges at that time. The youth was held in remand until a bail hearing the following day in Windsor Family Court. The Justice of the Peace assumed both the Halifax and Windsor charges would be addressed at this bail hearing (pp. 105–116).

While the circumstances leading to Teresa McEvoy's death were set in motion by the interim release and custody provisions of the YCJA, it was the administration of the law that propelled events from September 29th to the fateful crash on October 14th. This period, as documented by the Nunn Commission report, reads as a string of administrative and communication foul-ups that culminated in the failure of the Windsor court to address the youth's behaviour leading up to the Halifax charges, caused the expiry of his arrest warrant, led to the youth not being escorted back to Halifax police, and culminated in the youth's release from the Windsor court.

Administrating the YCJA

The administrative centre for the provincial and supreme courts in the Windsor, Nova Scotia region is the Kentville Justice Centre (KJC), located approximately 40 km from Windsor. In the afternoon of September 29th, Windsor Rural RCMP notified an on-duty Crown prosecutor of the Windsor court that they would be seeking a remand for the youth the following day, and that evening a 32-page document (application for a remand) was faxed to the Justice of the Peace Centre (JPC). It included the eight informations for the Windsor charges, as well as the arrest warrant with a schedule of the youth's 29 Halifax charges associated with the warrant. This centre is located in Dartmouth, Nova Scotia, and serves the entire province through a 24-hour, seven-day-a-week service, mostly accomplished through electronic means (phone, fax, and computer). The hearing was conducted by telephone that evening (lasting 9 minutes) and the Justice of the Peace approved remand, assumed the youth had been arrested on the Halifax warrant, and that the Halifax charges as well as the Windsor charges would be addressed by the Windsor court the following day. The staff of the JPC entered all this information into the province-wide court computer database (JOIS – Justice Oriented Information System), and the Halifax charges were removed from the Halifax court and transferred to the control of the Kentville court, which administrates the Windsor court. Also that evening, the original documents were prepared for courier to the Kentville Justice Centre, and were also faxed to the centre as well as to the Windsor RCMP. The fax intended for the KJC was unsuccessful, and a note was left for the morning staff to resend the document prior to the youth's scheduled 10 a.m. court appearance (pp. 120–124).

The following morning the failed fax attempt was noticed and the JPC staff were contacted by the KJC. The KJC informed the JPC that the documents should be sent to the Kentville Family Court (KFC) because the Windsor court was administrated through the KFC rather than the KJC. Nunn reports that the fax was received by the KFC at 8:19 a.m. but never went any further because, incredible as it might seem, the fax machine in the Windsor court was not working and had not been operative "for some time" (p. 124). At that point, there was no time before court to courier the material to the Windsor court so instead, the papers were faxed to the Crown's office, but he had already left for court by the time the fax arrived. As a result, the judge presiding that morning did not have all the information on the youth, only the paperwork on the eight Windsor charges. Nunn reports that there had been discussions prior to court between the arresting officer, the Crown and the defence lawyer that indicated they all knew about the Halifax charges and arrest warrant, but because of the missing fax, they all misunderstood the purpose of that morning's court appearance. None were aware that the Justice of the Peace had, on the previous day, adjourned all Windsor and Halifax charges to be addressed in the Windsor court that day. Nunn quotes the defence lawyer as saying, when questioned by the judge about the Halifax arrest warrant:

> My friend and I had some discussions to the effect of ... that maybe there is something we can't deal with here, that it's something that has to be dealt with in Halifax because that's in addition to his being picked up on the charges that are before the court this morning [the Windsor RCMP charges]. (p. 133)

The youth's hearing lasted 5 minutes, the court addressed only the Windsor charges and held the youth in custody until October 4th when these charges would be heard.

Meanwhile, the Halifax charges were on the JOIS system but staff at the KJC in recording the court decisions from September 30th and preparing court dockets for October 4th, deleted the Justice of the Peace's decision and the Halifax charges (pp. 136–138). The confusion over the status of the Halifax arrest warrant and charges continued on October 4th,and the hearing was postponed until October 5th so the Crown could examine the issue. On the 5th, the confusion continued. The Crown and the defence lawyer discussed what would happen with the Windsor charges and whether the youth wanted the Halifax charges transferred to Windsor. No one seemed to understand that the Justice of the Peace's decision on the 29th of September had already addressed this. The case was again adjourned for a bail hearing, now scheduled for October 12th (pp. 138–141). The Crown also phoned and left a voicemail message for the Crown in the Halifax Youth Justice Court on October 5th informing them of the youth's situation in Windsor. He never received a return call. A Halifax Crown did speak informally with a few police officers, as well as the police youth liaison officer associated with the Halifax youth court, about how to "deal with a warrant issue for a person in a different jurisdiction." This liaison officer was instructed to "make sure that something gets done to bring him to Halifax." (p. 143). The officer then contacted the Windsor Rural RCMP for details about the youth's case and informed the Halifax Crown later of the details and suggested that the Crown "simply do a pick-up order – an order of a court directing the transport of the youth to Halifax to face the Halifax charges" (p. 143). The pick-up order for the youth was never made (pp. 141–146).

On October 12th, the eight Windsor charges were the only ones before the judge in the Windsor court. The youth plead guilty to three of the charges; two counts of theft of a motor vehicle (CC section 334) and to operating a motor vehicle in a manner that is dangerous to the police (CC section 249.1). All other charges were put over to sentencing, scheduled for December 10, 2004. The Crown and defence lawyer agreed that the youth should be released from custody. In addressing the court on the question of release, the Crown stated:

> Yes, Your Honour, ... [the youth] has no record. He has trouble in the city. His surety has withdrawn the surety, but Metro Police aren't showing much interest in dealing with ... [the youth]. He's been in custody over a week now on our matters. They haven't arranged to transfer him to deal with the matters so I'm just going to deal with him strictly on ours. He has no prior convictions, Your Honour, and the Crown is not seeking to hold him, where he's a young offender. (p. 148)

On the basis of the information in this statement and before the judge, there were no grounds to detain the youth in custody and the court released him with a promise to attend court on December 10th and "to keep the peace and be of good order."

Two days later, October 14, 2004, Teresa McEvoy died.

6. Nunn Commission Recommendations and Arguments for Change

The Commission released its report and recommendations, *Spiralling Out of Control: Lessons learned from a boy in trouble* in December 2006. The report contains a total of 34 recommendations to address problems identified through the inquiry. In his report, Justice Nunn emphasized his support for the principles of the YCJA and insisted that the law is a vast improvement over its predecessor, the *Young Offenders Act*, and as such, is something we should strive to keep. Nonetheless, he was equally adamant that there are sections of the YCJA that need revision if we are to have the tools needed to address issues created by persistent offenders and youth who are "spiralling out of control," as was the youth who was the focus of his inquiry. At the end of his inquiry report, Justice Nunn states:

Along my way through the facts, I have made subjective comments on certain aspects of the evidence. Some of the facts are frankly troubling. As I have identified, the reasons for ... [the youth's] release from court are many and include oversight, miscommunication of key information, mechanical breakdown, well-intentioned but misguided actions or decisions, lack of clear procedures, and over all, the limiting provisions of the *Youth Criminal Justice Act.* (p. 150)

While 18 of Nunn's recommendations address changes to the administration of youth justice in Nova Scotia, in most cases he is unwilling to place responsibility for the death of Teresa McEvoy in the actions and decisions of the individuals who handled the case's morass of administrative stages and processes. He does, though, clearly state that the tragedy would not have happened without particular sections of the YCJA – more specifically, those relating to the definition of a violent offence, the provisions for pre-trial detention and responsible person undertakings, as well as provisions relating to custody requirements. "The real culprit," he states, "... was the *Youth Criminal Justice Act.*" (p. 227).

Further to Nunn's position is what happened when the youth finally appeared before court on December 20, 2004, for sentencing on all his Windsor and Halifax charges up to September 29th. Once again, referring to sections 38 and 39 of the YCJA, both the Crown and defence lawyer were of the view that the YCJA did not allow for a custody sentence. The defence took the position that the court did not have the authority to impose a custody sentence for any of the offences, and the Crown was of the view that the court should order custody given the charges and information available, but was concerned that the law would not allow custody and, therefore, recommended a lengthy period of probation. The presiding judge agreed that section 39(1) (a through c) did not allow for custody in that none of the offences were "violent" as defined, there were no previous sentences and therefore no instances of non-compliance, nor had there been any previous findings of guilt. Nonetheless, the judge did order a custody sentence and was able to do so under subsection (d) of section 39(1). He argued that one of the Windsor charges, theft over $5,000, was an indictable offence, and combined with its circumstances and those of the youth, that this constituted "exceptional circumstances" and a custody sentence was allowable (pp. 239–240). The youth remained in custody until he was eventually convicted for the offences connected to the death of Teresa McEvoy, criminal negligence causing death and dangerous driving, and in January

2006 was sentenced as an adult to five-and-a-half years in custody. As a 16 years old youth, a portion of this sentence (until he reached age 18) was served at the Nova Scotia Youth Centre in Waterville (p. 297).

YCJA Recommendations

Seven of Justice Nunn's recommendations are for the province of Nova Scotia to advocate to the federal government for the following changes to the YCJA:

1 Add protection of the public as a primary goal of the Act (Recommendation 20, pp. 235–236);
2 To amend the definition of violent offence in section 39(1) to "include conduct that endangers or is likely to endanger the life or safety of another person" (Recommendation 21, pp. 241–243);
3 To amend section 39(1) (c) "so that the requirement for a demonstrated 'pattern of findings of guilt' is changed to 'a pattern of offences' or similar wording" (Recommendation 22). Nunn argued that such a change would allow both prior findings of guilt as well as pending charges to be considered when making decisions and arguments regarding holding a youth in pretrial detention (pp. 242–243).
4 To amend section 29 so that it is not tied to section 39 and is able to stand on its own "without interaction with other statutes or other provisions of the *Youth Criminal Justice Act.*" Nunn argues that it was these interconnections that created the problems preventing an effective response to the youth in this case (Recommendation 23) (pp. 244–245).
5 Section 31(5)(a) should be amended so that if a responsible person's undertaking changes, the young person's undertaking and conditions remain (Recommendation 24). Here Nunn points out that this case would have been addressed more effectively if the law had not required the removal of the youth's conditions when the responsible person undertaking was revoked thereby necessitating a new bail hearing. He maintains that because a responsible person undertaking only occurs after it has been determined that pretrial detention is appropriate, a new bail hearing is not required and the youth's violations of the conditions of his release would have been sufficient to apprehend the youth and hold him in pretrial detention (pp. 246–248). He therefore recommends that:

6 Section 31(6) should be amended to remove the requirement for a new bail hearing before placing a youth in pretrial custody in those instances when a person designated as a "responsible person" has been relieved of his or her undertaking obligations (Recommendation 25).

7 Section 42(2)(m) should be amended to remove the time limits on court orders (currently 240 hours) to attend non-residential programs, such as an attendance centre (Recommendation 11). In making this recommendation, Justice Nunn cites testimony from Alan Markwart, assistant deputy minister of Children and Family Services in British Columbia who describes the time limit on non-residential programs as "madness." Markwart maintains that it is impossible to have any meaningful impact on a troubled youth in such a short time period, and Nunn points out that courts are reluctant to use these orders for just this reason and tend to use probation orders instead (pp. 206–208).

Administration of Justice Recommendations

Eighteen of the remaining 27 recommendations address the administrative issues uncovered through the inquiry. These include:

1 Delays in the Administration of Justice (Recommendations 1 and 2). Youth should appear in court within one week of arrest and the Province needs to reduce overall delay in youth criminal justice processing (pp. 283–284).

2 Court Administrative Procedures and Training (Recommendations 3 through 5). More training is required for police in the areas of court administration and procedures. The Justice of the Peace Centre needs to refine its administrative processes and procedures and ensure prompt communication to all affected parties, particularly with regard to court hearing outcomes. Training, monitoring, and auditing of court staff is required (p. 284).

3 Court Facilities, Communication, and Technology (Recommendations 6 through 8). Courthouses require adequate communication technology, particularly the Windsor court as well as all satellite or adjunct court facilities. The Department of Justice needs to coordinate and enhance its communication systems including electronic versions of informations. Separate facilities should be provided for Youth Justice Courts and adult courts (p. 285).

4 Dedicated Youth Court Police Liaison and Crown Attorneys (Recommendations 9 and 10). The Department of Justice and police
agencies should appoint youth court liaison police officers in all
judicial regions in the province. The Public Prosecution Service
should appoint dedicated youth court Crown attorneys throughout
the province (p. 286).
5 Attendance Centre and Bail Supervision (Recommendation 12
through 14). The Province should establish a fully funded attendance
centre and bail supervision program in and outside Halifax, and advocate for the federal government to change YCJA provisions for time
limits on attendance centres (Recommendation 11) (pp. 286–287).
6 Common Proceedings for Youth (Recommendations 15 through 19).
The Public Prosecution Service should provide training on law
and proceedings for Crown prosecutors especially on "responsible
person" requirements, pretrial detention, and encourage a common
approach across the province. Also required is a common protocol
on arrest warrants and timing of "findings of guilt" so that the latter
occurs at plea and not at sentencing (pp. 287–288).

The remaining nine recommendations were derived from the inquiry's investigation into the circumstances of the youth in his home,
community, school, and contact with community and social services
prior to his involvement with the youth justice system. Nunn's recommendations were:

1 Develop a Strategy for Children and Youth at Risk (Recommendations 26 through 30). The Province should implement an interdepartmental strategy to coordinate its programs. Community
Services, Justice, Health, and Education should appoint a senior
official as a "Director of Youth Strategy and Services." Community
Services should establish a separate division for family services. The
Department of Justice needs to systematically analyse and publicly
report a "service gap analysis" (pp. 290–292).
2 Education Initiatives (Recommendations 31 through 34). The Department of Education should develop, fund, and sustain programs
to support "school attachments," enforce school attendance as well
as, in conjunction with the Province, develop and staff in-school
alternatives to out-of-school suspensions, and address the needs
of students with attention deficit disorder and learning disabilities
(pp. 292–293).

Government Responses

Provincial

The Nova Scotia government through the Department of Justice and the Public Prosecution Service began responding to the incident even before the inquiry and the release of its report and recommendations were released. As early as December 2005, the Nova Scotia justice minister met with his federal counterpart to discuss toughening the YCJA with regard to car theft. The argument was that car theft and joyriding should be considered violent offences because they both pose a potential threat to public safety. The director of prosecutions in Nova Scotia also changed the procedures for cases where youth plead guilty, such that the Crown would now be required to request an immediate bail hearing to decide on detaining youth in custody prior to the sentencing court date (Hayes, January 22, 26, 2006). One month after the Nunn Commission report was released, the Nova Scotia government released its own report, *Helping kids – Protecting Communities: Response to the Nunn Commission* (January 2007), where it agreed with all of Nunn's recommendations and identified three components to the recommendations that it agreed to act upon: to implement measures to prevent youth crime, to lobby the federal government for changes to the YCJA, and to work to improve accountability and streamline the administration of justice (p. 6). By the time of this report, most of the recommendations had already been addressed either through budgeting funds for more personnel, through implementing changes, or in setting up committees to examine the issues further.

On Accountability and Streamlining the Administration of Justice

The Nova Scotia government supported all of Nunn's recommendations for changes to the YCJA, continued to lobby for change, and committed "more than $3 million from the 2007–08 budget" to "kick-start" its response to the Nunn report (p. 9). More specifically, $300,000 was budgeted to hire two new Crown attorneys who specialized in youth crime (R10), $461,000 to hire mental health professionals for court-ordered assessments (R2), $1.3 million was committed "to support the new attendance centre and youth bail supervision program in the Halifax Regional Municipality" (R12–13), $200,000 of this was allocated to a bail supervision program in Halifax and the hiring of two new probation officers (p. 28), $1 million was allocated to "hire a new senior official, the development of the child and youth strategy and the creation of the new Family and Youth Services division within the Department of Community Services" (R26–29) (p. 10). In addition to these funds, the province committed $65 million over four years for hiring 250 new police officers with an annual cost of $25 million (p. 25). While the placement of 109 of these new officers had already been determined, a "strategic deployment committee, representing both government and law enforcement" was established to determine where the remaining new officers would be "needed" (p. 25). While this police funding information was included in the government report, no mention was made of Nunn's recommendation (R9) for police youth court liaison officers in jurisdictions outside Halifax. Rather, the report simply states, in reference to this recommendation, that the Department of Justice "will consult with police, develop recommendations" (p. 51).

By February 2005, the province had implemented a new information system – the Justice Enterprise Information Network (JEIN) – at a cost of $1.9 million (cost shared with the federal government). All provincial courts will have access to this information system through high-speed Internet (except Sheet Harbour, which only has dial-up access), and the system has "significantly [improved] the effectiveness and information sharing among all provincial and satellite courts" (R6 and 7) (p. 21–22).

Key problems identified by the inquiry and Nunn's recommendations were delays in court processing times (R1 and 2), problematic court procedures and administration (R3 through 7), lack of youth court and specialized professionals and programs (R8 through 14), lack of knowledge and training (R15 through 19). On case processing time, the Nova Scotia government in its response to Nunn pointed out that in 2003–2004, it took an average of 144 days to process a youth from first court appearance to acquittal or sentencing. The national average that year was 141 days. By 2005–2006, average case processing time had reduced to 110 days due in great part to moving youth court matters from the Family Division of the Supreme Court to the provincial courts across the province and the appointment of three new Provincial Court judges. There are, on average, 2.5 adjournments before a youth's case gets to trial, and some of this delay is created for a youth to attain legal counsel. To address this, $700,000 was allocated to Nova Scotia Legal Aid to provide duty counsel for youth at their first court visit. Another major source of delay is the time required for court-ordered mental health assessments. The government reported that court-ordered assessments had tripled between 2004 and 2007, and extensions were requested of the courts in 80% of the cases. Hence, $461,000 was budgeted in 2007–2008 to hire additional professionals to conduct these assessments at the IWK Health Centre in Halifax through its Mental Health Forensic Service (pp. 15–18). In addition, a working group of justice partners was formed to continue working towards a more efficient court process.

Lack of knowledge and problematic court procedures were addressed in a number of ways. To improve understanding of the role of the Justice of the Peace, a stakeholder group made up of the RCMP, Legal Aid, provincial court judges, the Chiefs of Police Association, justice officials, federal and provincial prosecutors, and the Supreme Court was created to refine procedures and develop training plans for police and other justice professionals. Similarly, the Justice Learning Centre, operated through the Department of Justice and the Nova Scotia Community College partnership was committed to work with justice partners to develop and deliver training.

The JEIN system permits efficient information sharing among all justice partners across the province, and has been expanded to include a monitoring program and an internal audit division to monitor computer and telecommunications equipment and compliance with policy. All court users province-wide were trained in using JEIN, and electronic forms of court documents were being considered (pp. 20–22).

The Public Prosecution Service developed a "practice memorandum" outlining a standard approach to pretrial detention and is committed to annual training for Crown attorneys. In addition to a directive to all Crown attorneys to seek a finding and recording of guilt when a guilty plea is entered, they have also been directed to ask judges to hear evidence to verify that responsible persons actually have the ability to exercise control over the youth to be released (pp. 29–30). A common protocol for arrest warrants is to be developed through a consultative process involving the RCMP, police chiefs, and other justice partners.

The Nova Scotia government also agreed to establish an attendance centre in Halifax, to be opened in February 2007. The purpose of the centre was to provide programming to youth ordered by the court into community programming. Programming would be provided on a 24/7 basis in educational courses, employment counselling, parenting, substance abuse, and anger management by a team of professionals. A bail supervision program committed to look into how to implement such a program outside the metro area will be operated through the attendance centre and the government (pp. 27–28).

Five Years Later

The Nova Scotia government's implementation of the Nunn Commission of Inquiry's recommendations was examined by the Auditor General of Nova Scotia and a report – *Auditor General Report to the House of Assembly* – was submitted to the House of Assembly on October 28, 2011. The general conclusion of this report is that the province has "completed" 31 of the 34 recommendations. Those pertaining to court staff training and the bail supervision program both in Metro and outside Halifax (R5, R13 and R14) were not seen to have been sufficiently addressed (Auditor General Report, 2011, p.65). Implementation of many other recommendations for administrative change, while viewed by the auditor's report as sufficient, have altered considerably from the specifics recommended by Justice Nunn.

Recommendations Not Addressed

The Nova Scotia Department of Justice did establish, as we saw earlier, through it's Court Services, an "Organizational Effectiveness Unit" mandated to develop policies and procedures designed to improve "business processes," but it did not develop anything that would ensure staff training is always current. The Auditor General recommended that the Department of Justice "should monitor training of court staff." The Department of Justice subsequently reported that a "training needs assessment" has been conducted, and that the newly established Court Services Unit will continue to assess needs on a regular basis. Training content will be derived from these ongoing staff surveys and a monitoring process of training effectiveness will be developed (pp. 68, 70, 89).

    As we saw earlier, a bail supervision program for Halifax was funded in 2007–2008 and two probation officers were hired. The program became operational in March 2007, was attached to the Attendance Centre and operated within the structure of Community Corrections. The program was cancelled as of April 1, 2011. The decision to cancel was based on budget constraints and the result of an internal evaluation that indicated the program was not "effective" and that there was limited use of the program by the courts (pp. 74, 89). No information is provided by the Department of Justice as to the criteria used to assess effectiveness. The Auditor General's report expresses concern that the cancellation of this program leaves a gap between unsupervised bail release and pretrial detention, the very type of concern raised by Nunn, and recommends that the Department of Justice take appropriate action to address this gap (pp. 68, 90). In response, the Department of Justice reports that it will have a discussion with the Public Prosecution Service, the police, and the Judiciary to find ways of ensuring that bail release conditions will "provide a mechanism for monitoring compliance" (p. 90). There is no mention in the report or the Nova Scotia government's response as to whether these discussions or "mechanisms" will extend beyond Halifax. Bail supervision needs for other regions in the province, Nunn's recommendation 14, seem to have been ignored.

Changes Not Complying with Nunn's Recommendations

Many changes were made by the Department of Justice relevant to Nunn's recommendations relating to accountability and justice administration, but not all the changes have matched the recommendations. Justice Nunn's first and second recommendations were about reducing delays in court processing times, more specifically, that the time youth wait for a first court appearance on a serious or additional charge should be seven days and that targets should be set to reduce processing time from first appearance to final disposition. The Department of Justice agreed to a seven-day target for first appearance, and through its committee of justice stakeholders, formed in 2007, set a case-processing target of 98 days (excluding restorative justice cases that can exceed 200 days and bench warrants since the courts have no control over time for these cases) (pp. 68–69).

The newly established JEIN system of computerized records now provides regular data from justice centres for the entire province and the latest Department of Justice audit of case processing times indicates that neither targets have been met on a province-wide basis (Nova Scotia Department of Justice, *Case Processing in Nova Scotia Youth Court, 2007–08 to 2011–12*, June 2012). The Auditor General's report shows that in 2010–2011 it took 10 days on average for a youth to appear in court (p. 69). The Department of Justice report for 2011–2012, shows that first appearance times have dropped to nine days. These front-end times vary considerably across the province and are clearly, as averages, affected by Halifax where 68% of the serious cases are processed. Interestingly though, Halifax was the only area in 2011–2012 to meet and better the target with an average of four days for a serious charge to appear in court, while Yarmouth took 45 days. This wide range is attributed to variances in youth court sittings across the province, and efforts are underway to add additional youth court days in some court locations (2012, pp. 2, 7, 8).

Similar provincial variations are reported for average case processing times from first appearance to final disposition and Halifax and other areas have met and bettered the 98-day target. Since 2007–2008, when it took an average of 112 days to process a case, the province experienced an increase to 121 and then to 125 through 2008–2009 to 2010–2011, with a drop to 101 days in 2011–2012. Antigonish was well below the provincial average in 2011–2012 (at 65 days) as was Kentville, Pictou, Amherst, and Halifax (at 77, 79, 81, 96 days, respectively). The remaining justice centres report processing times above average and above target that range from 105 days in Bridgewater to 145 days in Digby (2012, pp. 4, 5).

Other administrative recommendations put forth by Nunn that have not been addressed in the manner intended by the recommendations are separate courtrooms and facilities for youth (R8), youth court liaison police officers outside Halifax (R9), and the creation of an Attendance Centre (R12). According to the Auditor General's report, the Nova Scotia Department of Justice maintains that the volume of youth matters before the courts simply does not warrant separate courts. The province will continue to schedule specific days and times for youth court cases so they are kept separate from adults. Halifax has holding cells for youth in an area away from adult cells as well as a separate waiting room for youth, while new justice centres throughout the province provide separate cells for male and female youth that "also separate youth from adults, both visually and audibly" (2011, p. 72). Similarly, the province argues that youth crime volumes do not warrant police court liaison officers outside Halifax (R9). Instead, it maintains that police serving as school resource officers can also serve a court liaison role, and in 2008 conducted a youth resource officer forum for police who are working primarily with youth (2011, p. 72). Finally, the Attendance Centre (R12) was funded and made operational in 2007 but was "modified" as of April 1, 2011, because of "budget restraints." According to the Auditor General's report, "the objectives of the centre have not changed." Yet, a key modification, as we have seen, is the cancellation of the bail supervision program that was operated through the Attendance Centre (2011, pp. 73, 74).

All of Nunn's nine recommendations pertaining to crime prevention in the community have been met or are ongoing with one exception. Nunn had recommended (R28) the appointment of a senior official (preferably a deputy minister) to develop and implement a family and youth strategy designed to meet the needs of youth and their families.

In 2007, the province, through the Department of Community Services, established the position of executive director of Child and Youth Strategy, but the position became vacant in 2010 and the responsibility for the strategy was then transferred to the executive director of Family and Community Supports. It is not clear with this change whether a Child and Youth Strategy will maintain the same priority within government without its own senior official or deputy minister.

Federal

On October 23, 2012, amendments to the YCJA came into effect and many of these changes, while not precipitated by Nunn's report and efforts of the Nova Scotia government, were certainly supported by them, and the federal government does in fact credit Justice Nunn in a preamble to the amendments. The courts also played an important role in stimulating these reforms, particularly regarding the lack of definition of violent offence in the YCJA. A Supreme Court decision in 2005 *R. v. C. D.*) made an issue of the meaning of "violent offence" relative to that of the definition of "serious violent offence" in the YCJA (section 2). The court argued that violence has a "spectrum of meanings" that can include property or crimes against the person. In that particular case, the court pointed out that the youth "did not cause, attempt to cause or threaten to cause bodily harm," therefore "their actions are not violent offences." The court further argued that a "narrow definition of violence is preferred" because a violent offence is grounds for a custody sentence. The Supreme Court maintained that viewing a young person's behaviour as violent would contradict the preamble statement in the YCJA – that the justice system reserves its most serious interventions for the most serious crimes, and in this case a custody sentence could not be imposed (Tustin & Lutes, 2009, p. 19).

Amendments to the YCJA were a long time in the making – six years from conception to implementation. Changes started as a promise by the Progressive Conservatives in the 2006 federal election campaign and were then introduced as Bill C-25 in November 2007 as part of a larger package of crime bills referred to as a "Safer Community Strategy." The Bill did not pass the house before the 2008 federal election and was reintroduced as Bill C-4 in March 2010. Then it was titled "Protecting the Public from Violent Young Offenders" and in discussions became known as "Sebastian's Law." Again though, even though the Bill got as far as second reading in the House and was under discussion by the Standing Committee on Justice and Human Rights, a new election was called and it was again tabled. Since the Progressive Conservatives were once again successful, but this time with a majority government, the Bill was re-introduced in September 2011 as part of the *"Safe Streets and Communities Act,"* now Bill C-10. This time it was successful and received Royal Assent on March 13, 2012, and YCJA amendments came into effect in October 2012. In relation to Nunn's recommendations for amendments, only R 20 to 23 were adopted. Those relating to withdrawal of a responsible person and requirements for a new bail hearing were not addressed in the Act (R24 and 25, section 31(5), 31(3)(b) and 31(6)) nor was there any change to time limits on non-residential court orders, which remain at a maximum of 240 hours (R11, section 42(2)(m)).

YCJA Amendments Relevant to the Nunn Inquiry

First, the Declaration of Principle in the YCJA has changed so that where section 3 (1) stated:

(a) The youth criminal justice system is intended to
 i. prevent crime by addressing the circumstances underlying a young person's offending behaviour,
 ii. rehabilitate young persons who commit offences and reintegrate them into society,
and
 iii. ensure that a young person is subject to meaningful consequences for his or her offence in order to promote the long-term protection of the public.

This is now changed to one that clearly places public safety as first priority, though, according to Bala (2015), this order might have no real significance:[1]

(a) The *Youth Criminal Justice Act* is intended to protect the public by
 i. holding young persons accountable through measures that are proportionate to the seriousness of the offence and the degree of responsibility of the young person,
 ii. promoting the rehabilitation and reintegration of young persons who have committed offences,
and
 iii. supporting the prevention of crime by referring young persons to programs or agencies in the community to address the circumstances underlying their offending behaviour.

Second, pretrial detention issues were addressed. The general rule for pretrial detention included reference to the *Criminal Code* as well as restrictions on the use of custody in the YCJA:

> 29(2) In considering whether the detention of a young person is necessary for the protection or safety of the public under paragraph 515(10)(b) [substantial likelihood – commit an offence or interfere with the administration of justice] of the Criminal Code, a youth justice court or a justice shall presume that detention is not necessary under that paragraph if the young person could not, on being found guilty, be committed to custody on the grounds set out in paragraphs 39(1)(a) to (c) [restrictions on committal to custody].

This subsection has been changed considerably and closely follows Nunn's recommendations. Justice Nunn had recommended (R22) that the federal government amend section 39(1) (c) of the YCJA so that the requirement for a demonstrated "pattern of findings of guilt" would be changed to "a pattern of offences," thereby enabling both a young person's prior findings of guilt and pending charges to be considered when determining the appropriateness of pretrial detention. In the amendment, the federal government actually added this notion to section 29 rather than section 39. Revisions also followed Nunn's recommendation (R23) for the statutory provisions relating to pretrial detention of young persons to stand on their own without interaction with other statutes or other provisions of the YCJA. Hence, section 29, subsection(2) is now far more complex:

> 29.(2) A youth justice court judge or a justice may order that a young person be detained in custody only if
> (a) The young person has been charged with
>> i. a serious offence,
>> or
>> ii. an offence other than a serious offence, if they have a history that indicates a pattern of either outstanding charges or findings of guilt;
> (b) the judge or justice is satisfied, on a balance of probabilities,
>> i. that there is a substantial likelihood that, before being dealt with according to law, the young person will not appear in court when required by law to do so,
>> ii. that detention is necessary for the protection or safety of the public, including any victim of or witness to the offence, having regard to all the

circumstances, including a substantial likelihood that the young person will, if released from custody, commit a serious offence,

> or

iii. in the case where the young person has been charged with a serious offence and detention is not justified under subparagraph (i) or (ii), that there are exceptional circumstances that warrant detention and that detention is necessary to maintain confidence in the administration of justice, having regard to the principles set out in section 3 and to all the circumstances, including

> (A) the apparent strength of the prosecution's case,
>
> (B) the gravity of the offence,
>
> (C) the circumstances surrounding the commission of the

offence, including whether a firearm was used,

> and
>
> (D) the fact that the young person is liable, on being found

guilty, for a potentially lengthy custodial sentence;

> and

(c) The judge or justice is satisfied, on a balance of probabilities, that no condition or combination of conditions of release would, depending on the justification on which the judge or justice relies under paragraph (b),

i. reduce, to a level below substantial, the likelihood that the young person would not appear in court when required by law to do so,

ii. offer adequate protection to the public from the risk that the young person might otherwise present,

> or

iii. maintain confidence in the administration of justice.

(3) The onus is on the Attorney General to satisfy the youth justice court judge or the justice as to the matters referred to in subsection (2).

Finally, section 39(1)(c) was changed to allow for not only a pattern of offences but also for extrajudicial sanctions records to be included in determining that pattern. Where this section did read:

39(1) A youth justice court shall not commit a young person to custody under section 42 (youth sentences) unless

(a) The young person has committed a violent offence;

(b) The young person has failed to comply with non-custodial sentences;

(c) The young person has committed an indictable offence for which an adult would be liable to imprisonment for a term of more than two years and has a history that indicates a pattern of findings of guilt under this Act or the Young Offenders Act chapter Y-1 of the Revised Statutes of Canada, 1985; or

Section 39(1) (c) has now been changed to:

> the young person has committed an indictable offence for which an adult would be liable to imprisonment for a term of more than two years and has a history that indicates a pattern of either extrajudicial sanctions or of findings of guilt or of both under this Act or the Young Offenders Act, chapter Y-1 of the Revised Statutes of Canada, 1985; or

The inclusion of extrajudicial measures and sanctions, made possible because changes to section 115(1.1) require police to keep records of any extrajudicial measures that they use with a youth, will allow warnings, cautions, and referrals to community programs to be used to establish a "pattern of offending." While Nunn recommended (R22) that a pattern of offending should be able to be used in court decision-making, it is not evident that he would have wanted to include extrajudicial measures.

Discussion

The fundamental issues of jurisprudence arising from the evidence of the Nunn Commission of Inquiry are those pertaining to pretrial detention and definitions of violence. The question that arises after learning all the circumstances of the youth's criminal actions and experience in the youth justice system is whether the October 2012 changes in pretrial detention as well as to violence definitions in the YCJA would have made a difference back in 2004. At first glance, the answer seems to be a resounding, "yes" and Nunn would agree. He states:

> I am confident that if there had been slightly more flexibility in the YCJA [as Nunn recommends] on ... [July 6th and October 12th] ... the Crown would have succeeded ... [in convincing the judges that the nature of the youth's offences warranted custody] ... and [the youth] would not have been released to offend again ... and cause the collision that killed Ms. McEvoy. (Nunn, 2006, pp. 242–243)

It is clear that changes to requirements for pretrial detention (section 29) should make it easier to hold youth in custody before trial, but sorting through the YCJA provisions may be just as difficult as before. The only real change with the new provision is that the section is now self-contained (does not require reference to the *Criminal Code* or section 39 of the YCJA) but, the new section 29 is equally complex as addressing all three sections were, and is still vague in some parts that are likely to invite new higher court challenges. So, for example, subsection 29(2)(b)(iii)(D) begs the question, what constitutes a "potentially lengthy custodial sentence"? The likelihood of a different outcome now where the Windsor hearing would have resulted in the youth being held in detention by the Windsor court is more apparent with the current clear definition of violent offence. The omission and lack of clarity of violence definitions allowed considerable latitude around detention and custodial decisions for the courts as evidenced in case law and Supreme Court decisions. The new definition of "violent offence" is now one that would cover car theft and joyriding, since both could be seen to have a potential for causing bodily harm.

The new question this thought raises is whether joyriding and car theft is truly what we mean by violence? The youth who was the focus of the inquiry and his offences are typical for youth auto theft in Canada. It is an offence most often engaged in by male youth aged 15 to 18, and the rate of overall auto theft is highest for this age group with a charge rate of 127/100,000 youth. It is also an offence that diminishes with age (Dauvergne, 2008, p. 7; Dhami, 2008, p. 188). Dhami's survey of youth from British Columbia in Grades 9 through 12 found that 14% reported riding in a stolen car, 7.7% that they had actually stolen a car, and 5.5% that they had been caught. She also found that youthful car thieves are often repeat offenders and their offences are not planned in advance, only a small number come to the attention of police, and they are not often deterred when they are caught or even when they have been in an accident. They are primarily motivated by boredom and a desire to "have fun," and in a majority of youth car thefts, the vehicle is recovered (Dauvergne, 2008, pp. 192, 196, 203). At issue is whether this type of behaviour should be addressed in the same manner as behaviour that is more traditionally thought of as violent, such as assault, which always results in some level of physical harm to a person.

It is also important to bear in mind, when considering these questions, that the incident leading to the Nunn inquiry was not typical of car theft or of joyriding in its outcome. In this sense, the government has been criticized for using one, atypical case outcome to justify changes to the legislation (Tustin & Lutes, 2009, p. 9). Of particular concern is that changes to provisions for pretrial detention in combination with the new definition for violent offences may actually increase the use of detention. While some might see this as a positive direction, caution is warranted when the actual use of detention since the YCJA was implemented in 2003 is considered. The implication that is easily drawn from the details of the Nunn inquiry and the Conservative government's changes to the YCJA is that pretrial was an option that was difficult for courts to implement and, consequently, that few youth were ever held in detention. Neither are true. Bala, Carrington, and Roberts (2009) point out that while it is difficult to assess the use of pretrial detention by the courts prior to 2003–2004 because Ontario and Nunavut are excluded from the statistics, it is the case that rates of youth in remand detention decreased in the latter years of the YOA, levelled somewhat when the YCJA was first implemented, and showed "substantial increases" beginning in 2006–2007. These trends were true across the country with the exception of Quebec where rates have always been relatively low and decreased when all other regions in the country were increasing. It is interesting to note that the highest rates of increases in rates of pretrial detention occurred in the Atlantic and Prairie regions (2009, pp. 142–43). In 2008–2009, 15,582 youth were held in remand and this accounted for 80% of the admissions to custody. It is also not true that only youth with violent offence charges are held in remand. Twenty-five per cent of admissions involved property offences and violence charges accounted for 35% of admissions. On any given day there were 981 youth in remand and they always outnumbered those serving a sentence of custody (Bell, 2012, pp. 260, 304–305). Toughening remand provisions are also problematic in that admission rates for Aboriginal youth are considerably higher than non-Aboriginal youth, especially girls. In 2008–2009, when Aboriginal youth accounted for 6% of the youth population in Canada, they accounted for 27% of admissions to remand overall, 25% of boys' admissions and 34% of girls' admissions. A total of 4,275 Aboriginal youth were held in pretrial detention in 2008–2009 (2012, pp. 303–304).

On the other hand, the answer to the question of whether changes in the YCJA would have made a difference back in 2004 is not such a straightforward "yes" when we reflect on the fact that the Act only set the stage for the youth's release, and remember that the majority of recommendations coming out of the inquiry were for changes to how the Act is administrated. The fact is that the Windsor court released the youth because the judge did not have the information that would have allowed pretrial detention. While Nunn says the YCJA is to blame, he also says that "The system, as it existed at the time, did fail." (2006, p. 28) and that reasons for the youth's release "are many." The details of the inquiry make it almost painfully clear that law is only as good as its administration. Or, the other way of framing the argument is to answer the question by pointing out that, even without changes to the YCJA, with the proposed and actual changes in the administration of the law that have occurred, a different outcome would likely have transpired. With the administrative changes, it is likely that the youth would have been held in detention because the Windsor court would have had all the information before it that should have been available from the Justice of the Peace hearing, or equally likely, the youth would have been transported back to Halifax after the Windsor hearing.

There is no question that the Nova Scotia government acted responsibly in setting up the Nunn Commission of Inquiry and also that through the Department of Justice, the Public Prosecution Service and the departments of Education and Social Services have acted responsibly and efficiently in responding to the Nunn Commission recommendations. Nonetheless, any optimism towards the future should be tinged with caution. Given that some of the Nova Scotia government's own processes and programs put into place as a result of Nunn's recommendations have already been cancelled or altered, to a great extent because of "budget constraints," it is reasonable to assume that new administrative processes, for this and any government, are likely to continue to erode over time.

NOTE

1 "The 2012 amendment also re-ordered the provisions, making accountability the first purpose listed: previously, rehabilitation had been listed first. However, legally, the order of the three purposes is not significant, since no principle is stated to be 'primary,' and this change was directed at public perception rather than legal change. The change in order of the provisions allowed the Conservative government to claim that accountability is now given greater prominence: this is true visually but not legally. Although many reported cases decided since the 2012 amendments came into effect, in particular regarding youth sentencing, have cited s.3(1)(a) of the *YCJA*, none have suggested that the change in order of the objectives or deletion of the modifier 'long term' for protection of the public has any legal significance. Rehabilitation, preventing crime, and accountability were and remain equally important principles for police, prosecutors, probation

officers, and judges to consider and balance in applying the Act, with the ultimate objective of protecting society" (Bala, 2015, p. 7).

REFERENCES

Bell, S. J. (2012). *Young offenders and youth justice: A century after the fact.* Toronto, ON: Nelson.

Bala, N., Hornick, J., McCall, M. L., & Clarke, M. E. (1994). *State responses to youth crime: A consideration of principles.* Ottawa, ON: Department of Justice Canada.

Bala, N., Carrington, P. J., & Roberts, J. V. (2009). Evaluating the youth criminal justice act after five years: A qualified success. *Canadian Journal of Criminology and Criminal Justice, 51*(2), 131–167.

Brooks, P. (2008, September 30). Former judge slams Tories' youth crime plan. *The Chronicle Herald* [Halifax], A1.

Canada, Department of Justice. (2008). *Pre-trial detention under the Youth Criminal Justice Act: A consultation paper.* Ottawa, ON: Department of Justice.

Dauvergne, M. (2008). Motor vehicle theft in Canada, 2007. *Juristat, 28*(10). Ottawa, ON: Statistics Canada, Canadian Centre for Justice Statistics.

Dhami, M. K. (2008). Youth auto theft: A Survey of a General population of Canadian youth. *Canadian Journal of Criminology and Criminal Justice, 50*(2), 187–209.

Doob, A., Marinos, V., & Varma, K. (1995). *Youth crime and the youth justice system in Canada: A research perspective.* Toronto, ON: University of Toronto, Centre of Criminology.

Hayes, B. (2006, January 12). Teen jailed in McEvoy death: Joyrider gets 4 1/2 years for fatal crash. *The Chronicle Herald* [Halifax], A1.

Hayes, B. (2006, January 22). Nunn ruling to have broad impact. *The Chronicle Herald* [Halifax], A5.

Hayes, B. (2006, January 26). Fax foul-up preceded teen's release, fatal crash. *The Chronicle Herald* [Halifax], A1.

Hayes, B. (2006, February 15). Lax laws failed son, McEvoy, says mom. *The Chronicle Herald* [Halifax], A1.

Jeffrey, D. (2006, January 14). McEvoy inquiry set to start Monday. *The Chronicle Herald* [Halifax], A1.

Nova Scotia, Auditor General Report to the House of Assembly. (2011, October 28). *Justice: Implementation of Nunn Commission of Inquiry Recommendations,* 65–90.

Nova Scotia. Department of Justice. (2007, January). *Helping kids, protecting communities: Response to the Nunn Commission.* Halifax, NS: Nova Scotia Department of Justice.

Nova Scotia. Department of Justice, Policy Planning and Research. (2012, June). *Case processing in Nova Scotia Youth Court, 2007–08 to 2011–12.* Halifax, NS: Nova Scotia Department of Justice.

Nunn, D. M. (2006, December). *Spiralling out of control: Lessons learned from a boy in trouble.* Halifax, NS: Province of Nova Scotia.

Stewart, J. (2005, December 15). Teen killer unrepentant hearing told. *The Chronicle Herald*, [Halifax], B3.

Tustin, L., & Lutes, R. E. (2009). *A guide to the Youth Criminal Justice Act.* Ontario, ON: Lexis Nexis Canada Inc.

8 Youth Justice in Nunavut

KATHRYN M. CAMPBELL AND TIM STUEMPEL

Introduction

The purpose of this chapter is to provide an overview of how youth criminal justice law is implemented in the territory of Nunavut. While cultures and peoples have existed in Nunavut for millennia, it has only existed as its own Canadian territory since 1999. Thus, its recent post-colonial history provides an interesting study of the evolution of youth justice and, in particular, the impact of culture in a territory where Inuit people make up 85% of the approximately 34,000 people who live there. In comparison to the rest of the country, rates of youth crime and youth victimization in this territory are inordinately high. This may be in part due to the rapid social and cultural changes that have taken place since the 1950s in this territory as a result of the effects of colonization and the forced assimilation of Inuit into sedentarized, Western lifestyles. However, despite difficult social conditions, the administration of youth justice in Nunavut does involve some attempts to integrate culturally appropriate programs for youth, while employing elders and others in the community in their implementation.

Nunavut Territory: Historical and Contemporary Perspectives

Nunavut is Canada's youngest official territory, emerging on April 1, 1999, through the division of the Northwest Territories into two distinct territorial jurisdictions and officially acknowledging the Inuit, who make up 85% of the population, of Canada's eastern Arctic and northern archipelago after more than 30 years of land claim negotiations. Nunavut also developed in response to four distinct problems, including:

a series of court decisions beginning in the 1950s that ruled Canada was responsible for the welfare of its aboriginal peoples; a long-standing policy of assimilating aboriginal people into mainstream culture; a burgeoning desire to open the North to mining; and the need to solidify Canada's international claims to Arctic sovereignty.[1]

A territory essentially made by, for, and of Inuit (Nunavummiut), Nunavut is unique not only in its relative newness, but also in its culture, demographics, political structure, and logistical barriers. Geographically, it is the largest political territory in Canada: its more than 1.9 million square kilometres, spanning three time zones, make up nearly one fifth of the country's total land mass, and, as Canada's northernmost territory, it experiences extreme weather conditions, logistical challenges, and an extremely high cost of living. Nunavut's population of approximately 34,000 reside for the most part in some 25 communities spread across this vast expanse, primarily accessible year-round only by air and, in the summer months, by sea. Of these communities, 14 maintain populations of between 300 and 1,000 inhabitants, while eight have between 1,000 and 2,000 people (three other identified communities maintain permanent populations of less than 10 people). The communities of Rankin Inlet and Arviat maintain populations between 2,000 and 2,500, while Iqaluit, the capital, has by far the largest population at roughly 7,000 (Census, 2011). Large-scale overland travel between communities is not practical, and roads between communities are essentially non-existent.

Inuit have resided in Nunavut for over 4,000 years. They have a rich and vibrant culture and many communities continue to practice traditional Inuit entertainment, including drum dancing and throat singing. Inuit history has been passed down orally and storytelling remains a significant means of sharing; storytelling is often about powerful spirits inhabiting the land and sea, which has inspired Inuit artists who create highly prized soapstone sculptures and prints.[2] However, their recent history of colonization has left an indelible impact on the people of Nunavut, and maintaining the influence of their traditions and culture on modern day living is difficult:

Canada "discovered" Nunavut and other far northern regions and their peoples in the early 1950s (Robertson 2000), but through the Cold War "two solitudes" existed. One was a Northern or Arctic policy centred on future technology (especially the extraction and transport of natural resources), economics, international law, military systems and strategies, and utopian fantasies. The other was the daily North of inadequate housing, alcohol problems, social welfare, racial discrimination, and, later, indigenous self-government and land/sea rights movements – a North of angry and semi-literate Inuit youths in torn T-shirts. The end of the Cold War was a spring thaw in virtually all aspects of Arctic life.[3]

Historically, unlike Canada's various other frontier regions, Nunavut's Arctic was left virtually untouched for centuries after the first European contact, and Inuit traditions were allowed to carry on essentially unchanged right up until the 20th century.[4] Since then, however, massive and rapid colonialist expansion has occurred, including "formal and informal methods (attitudes, behaviors, institutions, policies and economies) of subjugating and exploiting Indigenous Peoples, lands and resources in order to further the social, political, and economic power of the colonizer" (Wilson & Yellow Bird, 2005, p. 2). Inuit were a nomadic people and colonization forced them into a sedentary lifestyle in settlements that imposed living conditions and systems of governance that ran counter to Inuit values.

While Nunavut became a territory in 1999, the latter half of the 20th century was a time of great change in the North. During that time, for many Inuit the traditional lifestyle of hunting and trapping had given way to settlements in permanent communities and reliance on government welfare; at the same time there was growing concern over the proliferation of a whole host of social problems, including substance abuse, suicide, and violence. In part due to dissatisfaction with these conditions and a desire to have more involvement in resource development, the Inuit began to pressure the government to allow them to have greater control over their own affairs.[5] In 1971, the Inuit Tapirisat of Canada[6] (the national Inuit organization, now called the Inuit Tapirisat Kanatami) was formed and was able to demonstrate the extent of Inuit title in the Arctic, which ultimately formed the geographic basis of the Nunavut Territory. At the same time, a number of land claims decisions at the Supreme Court of Canada had also supported the existence of aboriginal title that gave impetus to the Inuit claims. In 1982, the population of the Northwest Territories voted to divide and create Nunavut; 10 years later the boundaries were established. Two acts of Parliament in 1993 settled the question of Inuit land claims: the first was the Nunavut Land Claims Agreement, which gave the Inuit control over their territory and a cash settlement; the second was the *Nunavut Act* that established the territory of Nunavut, which came into being in 1999. The last 60 years has seen upheaval on a scale never before encountered by Inuit culture, significantly altering the traditional way of life and re-quiring Inuit to adjust and adapt to new modes of thinking and foreign concepts, in particular foreign systems of justice and dispute resolution (cf. Eber, 2008). On the one hand both welcome and necessary, these rapid adaptations are also accompanied by a myriad of social problems.

Given that Nunavut contains the only jurisdiction in Canada with a majority Aboriginal population, the difficulties inherent to minority in-digenous populations in other parts of Canada, such as social and eco-nomic inequities, are spread throughout the territory. The sad statistics are revealing: Inuit are more likely to die by suicide, abuse substances, and commit and experience violent crime and sexual assault than Canadians as a whole; they are more likely to leave high school before graduat-ing, live in crowded houses in need of major repairs, die from smoking-induced lung cancer and heart disease, and experience shorter lifespans than non-Aboriginal Canadians (Nunavut Tunngavik Incorporation, 2010–2011, p. 5).

Colonialism and Social Concerns

This relatively recent history of colonial intervention has resulted in significant intergenerational distress among Inuit peoples. Canada's well-documented residential school system contributed a great deal to the trauma that many of Nunavut's Inuit continue to struggle with.[7] Moreover, the effects of colonialism for the Inuit, such as forced reloca-tions to settlements, dog slaughter, lack of recognition of land claims agreements, and no right to vote until 1960 continue to be felt today.[8] While Nunavut has been a territory since 1999, the promise that a gov-ernment of Inuit people for Inuit people would be in a better position to meet the needs[9] of the growing territory, however, has yet to be real-ized. The *Nunavut Land Claims Agreement*,[10] which provided the legal framework for the development of the territory and its subsequent gov-ernance states in article 32: "Inuit have the right as set out in this Article to participate in the development of social and cultural policies, and in the design of social and cultural programs and services, including their method of delivery, within the Nunavut Settlement Area." The latest *Annual Report on the State of Inuit Culture and Society* (2010–2011) indicates that both the governments of Nunavut and of Canada have not met their legal obligations in this regard.[11] In particular the report points out that the future health and well-being of the children and youth of Nunavut depend on the willingness of both governments to work with Inuit organizations and communities as equal partners in the development of policies and programs that affect them.

More than one-third of the population of Nunavut is under 15 years of age; this has been described as "both its promise and its problem."[12] While there are great economic opportunities in the North for working in the exploration and construction industries, there is also great apathy among many youth in Nunavut, where high rates of unemployment and violent crime are endemic. Moreover, low rates of high school completion for Nunavut youth (about 25%) mean that the available labour force is unskilled.[13] Unemployment rates of greater than 20% in 2011 and chronic overcrowding due to an inadequate supply of safe and affordable housing do little to ease these stressors. The resulting social confusion manifests itself in inordinately high rates of crime, substance abuse, suicide, and physical and sexual abuse. Remarkably, Inuit still maintain a distinct, recognizable, and thriving cultural identity (Lynge, 1999, p. 46).

Substance abuse (primarily of alcohol and marijuana, but also solvents and drugs such as cocaine and opiates) remains a considerable problem among Nunavut's population. Illicit drug use in the territory is approximately 4 times that of Canada as a whole, and includes both Inuit and non-Inuit users (National Crime Prevention Centre, 2012). Alcohol consumption by both youth and adults contributes to the majority of Nunavut's criminal activity, despite the fact that many of the territory's communities are considered "dry," either requiring a permit to import alcohol or prohibiting it altogether. Nunavut's suicide rate is especially alarming, at approximately 12 times that of Canada as a whole. If Nunavut were a country, its suicide rate would be the highest in the world, and the rate for Inuit youth is even higher (Nunavut Tunngavik Incorporation, 2010–2011). For Inuit youth aged 15 to 19 years, the suicide rate jumps astonishingly to almost 40 times the national average (Suicide Prevention Strategy Working Group, 2010, p. 43). Indeed, one would be hard-pressed to find a resident of Nunavut who has not been personally touched by suicide. Again, alcohol and substance abuse are often associated with Nunavut suicides. Moreover, this high suicide rate has been described as symptomatic

> ... of several interrelated factors negatively impacting on the health and well-being of our society, and youth are struggling under the weight of that burden. The combined effects of poverty, inadequate and overcrowded

housing, colonization, substance abuse, sexual assault and the consequences of inadequate mental health, and child, youth, and family services place enormous stress on our entire society. This stress is magnified within a framework of Euro-Colonization, and the political, social, cultural and economic disempowerment that Inuit are experiencing as a result. (Suicide Prevention Strategy Working Group, 2010, p. 43)

Nunavut Today

Prior to 1999, the communities and regions of the eastern Arctic that make up the territory of Nunavut were part of the Northwest Territories (NWT). This situation was less than ideal for several reasons. Canada's eastern Arctic is both demographically and culturally very different from the western Arctic. Hence when government legislation and policy was applied uniformly across the territory, it often neglected to take into account the disparities that existed across the land. A "one size fits all" approach was hardly appropriate to distinct populations with disparate needs.

Since 1999, however, the new territory of Nunavut has struggled to maintain the idealistic image of its birth. Crime rates have increased; Nunavut's per capita homicide rate is more than 12 times higher than the rest of Canada.[14] Some go so far as to argue that the nation-building "experiment" of Nunavut has failed, creating Canada's own Third World disaster (Marchilden, 2009).[15] Others, however, counter with optimism. They argue that Nunavut is in control of its own destiny, and essential services remain available despite the issues.[16] Regardless of the accuracy of either argument, Nunavut currently grapples with significant social issues, and youth criminality is but one. There are few jurisdictions where the *Youth Criminal Justice Act*[17] can have more impact; its interpretation and application are key to addressing the reality facing young people and communities in Nunavut today.

Youth Demographics and Crime in Nunavut

Youth make up a significant portion of Nunavut's population, especially compared to the rest of Canada. In 2011, approximately one sixth of Canada's population was under the age of 15, while the rate for Nunavut was double that, approximately one third. Indeed, more than 40% of Nunavut's population is under 20 years of age. This young population is not only the most vulnerable in society, as youth are

Table 8.1 Nunavut population by age groups, July 2011

Age group	Number
0–4	3,730
5–9	3,302
10–14	3,450
15–19	3,170
20–24	3,099
25–29	2,801
30–34	2,582
35–39	2,177
40–44	2,296
45–49	1,931
50–54	1,691
55–59	1,231
60–64	799
65 +	1,063
Total	33,322

Source: Statistics Canada, 2011

dependent on adults for food, shelter, support, and nurturing, but due to the myriad social problems in Nunavut, these youth also experience a concomitantly high rate of recorded youth crime.

Given its relative population demographics and the accompanying social challenges, how the YCJA is interpreted and implemented in Nunavut has a significant impact on the people who live there. While the reported rates of youth charged with crimes overall in Canada have been decreasing in the last decade (with an overall 11% decrease in 10 years), that is not the case with respect to the severity of youth crime. The most recent statistics from 2011 indicate a 5% increase in youth crime severity in comparison with 2000 statistics, and, with the highest ranking on the Canadian youth Crime Severity Index,[18] Nunavut deals with more young offenders per capita than any other province or territory (Brennan & Dauvergne, 2011).

The *Youth Court Survey*, from the Canadian Centre of Justice Statistics (Statistics Canada, 2005), revealed that the statistics from the territory of Nunavut reflected an increase in youth court cases from the period of 1999/2000 and 2003/2004 of 93%, whereas for the rest of Canada for the same period, the change was a reduction of 22%. While reasons proffered for this increase include increased reporting and more effective operations of the Nunavut Youth Court, it is also indicative of a growing youth population committing an increasingly higher rate of youth crime (Clark, 2011, p. 348).

In terms of overall crime, statistics reflect the scale of the issue. In 2010, Nunavut had an overall reported crime rate roughly 6 times that of the nation as a whole. Of greater concern is the violent crime rate in Nunavut; Nunavut residents experience 8 times the violence of Canadians as a whole. Remarkably high rates of assault (almost 10 times the national average) and sexual assault (over 9 times the national average) combine to produce high overall rates of violent offences in Nunavut. Only the Northwest Territories, which grapples with similar social issues as Nunavut, has a higher overall reported crime rate, a fact that underlines the seriousness of the issue in Canada's North (Brennan & Dauvergne, 2011). As for actual numbers of people charged with crimes in Nunavut, statistics continue to reflect the serious nature of recorded criminality in the territory. The rate of criminal charges per 100,000 people in Nunavut is almost 5 times the national rate, and the rate for youth charged is 3 times the national rate.

Nunavut also has one of the highest concentrations of police officers per capita in the country. In 2011, that rate was almost twice the national average (Statistics Canada, 2011). This is related not only to Nunavut's large land mass and the logistical difficulties associated with policing it, but also to its inordinately high crime rates.

Available corrections data echo these statistics. Nunavut incarcerates offenders at a rate approximately 5 times the national average. Nunavut's correctional system must continue to handle enormous demands while dealing with a mostly Inuit population. Indeed, Nunavut's Baffin Correctional Centre, for adult offenders regularly operates well over capacity, and the Isumaqsunngittukkuvik Young Offenders Facility, the territory's secure and open custody facility for young offenders, is designed to house only 15 offenders at a time in a jurisdiction with an increasing youth population and a growing crime rate.

Inuit Qaujimajatuqangit and the YCJA

Reflecting its Inuit base, criminal justice processes in Nunavut attempt to apply culturally appropriate methods when dealing with both adult and young offenders. Perhaps the most important concept relating Inuit tradition to the principles of the YCJA is that of *Inuit Qaujimajatuqangit* (IQ). IQ refers to the traditional wisdom of Canada's Inuit. More than simply traditional knowledge, it encompasses Inuit culture, values, world view, language, social organization, life skills, perceptions, and expectations.

Government of Nunavut IQ Statement of Policy
The Government of Nunavut shall incorporate *Inuit Qaujimajatuqangit* as a guiding principle for governance and operation. These guiding principles shall include all areas of Inuit values, customs, language, management practices, sustainable and self-reliant communities, perception, natural environment and all its entities.

The Government of Nunavut shall incorporate *Inuit Qaujimajatuqangit* as the foundation of its legislation, policies, programs and services for the betterment of Nunavummiut [the people of Nunavut] and future generations.

Inuit Qaujimajatuqangit is defined by: customs, beliefs and values based on past traditions, present context and future adaptations.

– *The First Annual Report of the Inuit Qaujimajatuqangit Task Force* (2002)

Nunavut is exceptional in that it officially mandates its various government departments to incorporate IQ into policies and programs. The Nunavut Department of Justice attempts to do so through the use of community and restorative justice committees that accept youth cases, diverting youth both pre- and post-charge from police and the courts.

These committees, made up primarily of volunteer community members and Inuit elders, review the cases and, through mediation, community justice forums, and elder panels, attempt to reach an agreement focused on restoring dignity, worthiness, and accountability to both the offender and the victim. Given that the concept of healing relationships between victims and offenders is rooted in Inuit community life, it is easy to see how such committees might succeed where mainstream adversarial processes might not. Furthermore, the principles of *Inuit Qaujimajatuqangit* are applied in a way that is impossible in other processes.

The principles of *Inuit Qaujimajatuqangit* are reflected in many of the programs and practices that take place at the Isumaqsunngittukkuvik Young Offenders Facility, situated in Iqaluit the capital of Nunavut and the regional centre for Qikiqtaaluk Region, which serves youth primarily in the North Baffin, South Baffin, Kitikmeot, and Kivalliq regions. Given the size of the territory and the great geographical distances between communities, there is only one institutional facility for young offenders in Nunavut.[19] With 15 beds for both male and female youth it has a threefold mandate: it is an open and secure custody facility that also provides beds for youth who are on temporary detention or remand.[20] While there are on average five or six young persons in the facility at a given time, most have committed some form of violent offence.[21] It offers a number of diverse programs, with the objective of providing meaningful opportunities to youth, aimed towards reintegrating them within their home communities.

The centre uses the Youth Level of Service/Case Management Information System[22] to assess youth once they are admitted, measuring criminal attitudes, peers, social achievement, and substance abuse – a mental health assessment is also done. The case management plan consists of an intake summary, case-planning goals, and a case summary. The intake summary assesses the youth's situation at time of admission, including information on his or her history and any predisposition, medical or psychiatric reports, as well as information on their educational level. Case-planning goals include all programs and services that the youth will participate in while in custody, and the case summary takes place on release and is passed on to the community social worker on discharge.[23] Case conferences occur every 30 days, whereby the youth's treatment goals and progress are assessed; reintegration planning meetings occur first at 60 days and then 15 days prior to discharge. The centre may release a youth temporarily just prior to discharge; however, the youth is still considered to be in custody.[24]

Programs offered to youth at the facility include standard educational and counselling programs as well as culturally relevant recreational and leisure programs. Counselling programs include informal and formal counselling, and provide assistance, guidance and information.[25] Educational programs include academic (comprising literacy, basic math, and language arts) and vocational training, and are flexible in nature given the varying educational levels of the students in the facility. Vocational programming includes life management units that offer training in first aid, career planning, life skills, drug and alcohol awareness, sex education, suicide prevention, carving arts and crafts, assets/behaviour skills programming, and gun safety.[26] The land program reinforces IQ and traditional Inuit values.[27] It constitutes an outdoor education program that emphasizes learning traditional skills both inside and outside the City of Iqaluit. It involves instructing youth in proper land-based skills such as sewing, food gathering, iglu and kayak building, survival off the land, safety on the land, snowmobile maintenance and repair, and skills such as skinning and storage of carcasses, and reading and remembering landmarks and orientation. No youth are allowed access to firearms while participating in this program. The land program is particularly significant as not only does it reinforce the importance of traditional values, but it also teaches youth important hunting skills, and accomplished hunters are highly regarded in Nunavut (Nunavut Tunngavik Incorporated, 2010–2011). There are also library, shopping, chaplaincy, and canteen programs, all of which allow the youth access to the community.

While the centre is a triple-designate facility (open/closed/remand) there is some overlap in the programming offered to youth with varying sentencing designations. Youth in open custody are on a privilege system that allows for increased privileges based on rule compliance. Moreover, the youth centre administers a system of behaviour management to all youth, incorporating what is described as "progressive discipline."[28] This system is aimed at encouraging responsible behaviour on the part of youth by using measures of increasing severity, from punishment, administering consequences, signal interference, object removal, specific privilege loss, redirections, prompting, restitution, and time out to obtain compliance.

There are a number of support programs that exist in the community to which youth in the facility and community youth under supervision orders may access. Related to the land program, Outpost Camps are available to youth sentenced to open custody as they function as transitional homes for youth in which to serve the community portion of their sentence.[29] Where available, youth tend to stay in these camps for a month where they learn hunting and survival skills. The camps are located in or near communities and operate privately through government contracts. Given the size of the territory and the distances between the many villages and settlements, as well as a scarcity of resources, communities must be creative in finding support services and elders are often engaged in helping youth reintegrate back into the community. A number of other key individuals also involved in program delivery to young offenders, whether they are resident at the Isumaqsunngittukkuvik facility or on community supervision, include key workers, parents (if possible or guardians), probation officers/social workers from the community, a clinician (MA in psychology), teachers, RCMP officer(s), role models, Resolution Health Workers, and guidance counsellors.

Given concerns over the high reported crime rates in Nunavut, the federal government, through the National Crime Prevention Centre, has recently funded four projects, valued at over a half million dollars directed towards youth crime prevention.[30] The first, Iqaluit District Education

Authority – *Students First/Sivuliit Illisaqtut Program for At-Risk Students* (Iqaluit, Nunavut) is aimed at encouraging youth who are at risk to drop out, to remain in school. The second, Municipality of Cape Dorset-Recreation Department – *Cape Dorset Youth Crime Prevention Strategy* (Cape Dorset, Nunavut), offers healthier lifestyle choices for at-risk youth through the youth centre. The third project, Arviat Community Justice Committee – *Arviat Community Justice Committee* (Arviat, Nunavut), provides after-school activities for youth by pairing them with peer partners. The final project, Inuksuk High School – *Piruvik ("to grow here")* (Iqaluit, Nunavut), is aimed at 15- to 18-year-old young offenders or those with a less than 50% school attendance record and provides career and life-planning support.

As noted, addiction rates to drugs and alcohol in Nunavut are high in comparison to the rest of the country. However, while there are five outpatient facilities in the territory, there is no residential facility for detoxification or treatment, thus individuals must fly south in order to receive treatment. It has been noted that, as seen in the other territories, Nunavut has adopted a fairly minimalist approach to its citizens' drug and alcohol addiction.[31] However, recently the federal government has attempted to address the problem of substance abuse among Inuit youth through two projects offered in Whale Cove, Kugluktuk, Rankin Inlet, and Clyde River via the National Anti-Drug Strategy. One project, *Substance Use Youth Outreach/Counsellors in Three Communities in Nunavut*[32] is aimed at at-risk[33] youth aged 12 to 24 years and involves training youth outreach workers to address addiction problems among this population, including the development of pamphlets and strategies for interested communities. The second project, *Whale Cove Youth Engagement Program*,[34] is aimed at educating youth about the health and social effects of illicit drug use, as well as emphasizing healthy lifestyle choices. This program is meant to integrate traditional Inuit teachings into the project's anti-drug messaging, through presentations by elders.

Concerns for the Future

The much criticized omnibus crime legislation Bill C-10, aimed at amending the *Criminal Code* and the *Youth Criminal Justice Act*, is now law and may pose great challenges to the administration of justice in Nunavut, both for adult and young offenders. It has been noted that the harsher penalties contained within Bill C-10 conflict with Nunavut's policy to incorporate Inuit society values into its justice system as well as its greater emphasis on community-based justice.[35] The Minister of Justice for Nunavut, Dan Shewchuk, has asked that Nunavut judges be granted discretion in sentencing Aboriginal offenders[36] and wants more funding to help pay the extra costs imposed by Bill C-10, as well as extra time to do so. It would appear that the changes wrought by Bill C-10, however, will have a greater effect on adult rather than on youth offenders (Bala, 2015).

A further looming difficulty relates to the demographics of Nunavut. As noted earlier, youth make up one-third of the population and estimates are that the youth population will continue to grow. The median age for the population of Nunavut territory in 2009 was 24.2 years, whereas for the rest of Canada it was 38.5 years, reflecting a very young population for the territory (McMahon, 2010). A burgeoning youth population in a depressed economy does not bode well for the future. There are simply too few employment opportunities for the numbers of available youth, amit a labour force that is often undereducated and unskilled for jobs available in the growing mining and other resource industries. Moreover, the decline in traditional subsistence activities of Inuit (fishing, hunting, and trapping) has contributed to a cultural disconnect among Inuit youth. No longer exposed to the teachings of elders in the same way as in the past, young people are also drawn towards the attractions of more Westernized lifestyles, with all of the concomitant corruptions of drugs, alcohol, and risk-taking behaviours. Within this context, high rates of self-destructive behaviour among Inuit youth are not surprising. Clearly, what is needed is a plan of action that engages youth in decisions that affect their future, draws from the benefits of IQ and Inuit traditions, and embraces the advantages that accompany modernization. Importantly, preventive efforts such as these must occur *before* youth enter the criminal justice system in order to have any sustainable long-term effects.

Conclusion

The territory of Nunavut has faced, and continues to face, a number of growing pains that are reflected in high rates of overall violent crime, youth crime, and endemic problems of serious substance abuse among large numbers of its population. The criminal justice system for young people has attempted to institute aspects of IQ through some of its programs, and as such provide a mixture of more traditional approaches incorporating Inuit values and practices alongside mainstream justice initiatives. Given that there are no outcome measures or studies of these approaches, it is difficult at this time to ascertain the extent to which they are effective and capable of addressing the complex and diverse needs of Inuit youth. Questions arise regarding the practical application of these initiatives, as there is the very real danger that such measures can be co-opted and result in an illusory "indigenization" of justice. Further, and perhaps more importantly, necessary supports must be in place in order for these initiatives to succeed. Each must be carefully refined to match the context and capabilities of particular northern communities. One further concern regarding a youth criminal justice system embracing alternative measures and *Inuit Qaujimajatuqangit* is that individual and societal protections might be compromised. The concerns of victims of abuse, especially women, cannot be overemphasized. When alternative justice measures are implemented in small, remote communities, for ex-ample, it is essential that consideration be directed towards victims and also that community and offender supports and protections are in place, especially given the often violent nature of youth crime in Nunavut.

The romanticization of the past is another danger that must be ad-dressed when implementing such initiatives, and any youth criminal justice system must recognize that glorified visions of history have little to do with either IQ or justice. While life in the North prior to Western settlement was simpler it was also considerably harsher, and although life expectancy has now increased, modern day Nunavut society poses many difficult challenges as well. Moreover, it has been argued that a culture of silence exists in the North, where "problems are denied or reflexively answered with an appeal to traditions of the elders."[37] While there is much to be gained from seeking the wisdom of elders, what is required now is a more concerted effort towards addressing the prob-lems faced by Nunavut youth through the construction of an approach that acknowledges and benefits from the advantages of both the Old and New Worlds.

NOTES

1 P. White. (2011, April 1). The trials of Nunavut: Lament for an Arctic na-tion. *The Globe and Mail.* Retrieved from http://www.theglobeandmail .com/news/national/nunavut/the-trials-of-nunavut-lament-for-an-arctic-nation/article547265/.

2 Retrieved online at: http://www.arcticinuksuk.com/index.php?option=com_content&view=article &id=4&Itemid=4. Please change to Retrieved from http://www.arcticinuksuk.com/.

3 P. Jull. (2001). Nunavut: The Still Small Voice of Indigenous Governance. *Indigenous Affairs*, *30*(1), 42–51.

4 Permanent settlement in Nunavut, known before 1999 as the Northwest Territories, started in the early 1960s. Though contacts between the no-madic Inuits and whalers from New England dated back from the 19th century, the Canadian governments started to take interest at this remote part of Canada in the early 1950s, without true consideration for its origi-nal inhabitants (Tester & Irniq, 2007).

5 K. J. Rea. Nunavut. Encyclopedia Britannica. Retrieved from http://www.britannica.com/place/Nunavut.

6 Retrieved from https://www.itk.ca.

7 Approximately 2,000–3,000 Nunavummiut resided at federal residential schools. Retrieved from http://residentialschools.tunngavik.com/.

8 NTI rebukes Prime Minister Harper on colonialism. October 1, 2009. Nunavut Tunngavik Incorporated. Retrieved from http://www.tunngavik.com/blog/news/nti-rebukes-prime-minster-harper-on-colonialism/.

9 These needs have been defined as adequate housing, food security, reliable social services, childcare, and access to equitable, Inuit-specific education de-veloped in equal partnership with Inuit communities (Nunavut Tunngavik Incorporated, 2010–2011, p. 53).

10 *Nunavut Land Claims Agreement*, S.C., ch.32, s. 1.1 (1993).

11 The report also castigates these governments for failing to live up to their obligations under the United Nations Declaration on the Rights of Indigenous Peoples (UNDRIP), particularly article 23: "indigenous peo-ples have the right to be actively involved in developing and determining health, housing and other economic and social programs affecting them and, as far as possible to administer such programs through their own in-stitutions" (2010–2011, p. 3).

12 J. Friesen. (2012, August 23). The youthful face of Nunavut expresses hope, despair. *The Globe and Mail*.

13 *Ibid.*

14 The actual homicide rate is measured through a statistical standard as per 100,000 members of the population. The Canadian rate is 1.73 per 100,000, while the Nunavut rate 21.01 per 100,000 population; the actual numbers reveal a different picture as for 2011 there were 598 homicides in Canada, but only 7 in Nunavut. *Nunatsiaq News*, Nunavut leads Canada in per

capita homicide rate: Stats Can. Retrieved from http://www.nunatsiaqon-line.ca/stories/
article/65674nunavut_leads_canada_in_homicides_statscan/.

15 While Marchildon is referring specifically to access to health services, oth-er analogies to the Third World have been made with respect to Inuit ac-cess to nutritious and reasonably priced food, adequate housing, and education services.

16 See for example the recently signed Memorandum of Understanding (MOU) on the Nunavut Roundtable for Poverty Reduction and the devel-opment of a Nunavut Food Security Strategy between the Government of Nunavut and the Nunavut Tunngavik Incorporated. Retrieved from http://www.tunngavik.com/blog/news/government-of-nunavut-and-nunavut-tunngavik-inc-commit-to-moving-forward-on-poverty-reduction/.

17 *Youth Criminal Justice Act* (S.C. 2002, c. 1) YCJA.

18 For Statistics Canada, the youth Crime Severity Index includes rates for homicide, motor vehicle theft, serious assault, break-ins, and robbery. Data from 2013 indicate that the overall rates for the country in youth crime se-verity have evinced a further drop of 16% from 2012, indicative of a fourth year of decline. No separate statistics for Nunavut were available. Retrieved from http://www.statcan.gc.ca/daily-quotidien/140723/dq140723b-eng.htm.

19 Given that there is only one residential facility for young offenders in Nunavut, some youth must travel far from their homes to serve their sen-tence. While not ideal, this has replaced earlier practices whereby such youth were removed from their communities and sent thousands of kilo-metres away to youth detention facilities in the south, usually in Montreal, Toronto, or Edmonton. In the past, not only were these youth isolated from their families, communities, and cultures, but some would also struggle to communicate in the English language. Many of these problems have been alleviated since the opening of the Isumaqsunngittukkuvik facility.

20 Youth tend to wait in remand inordinately long periods of time, some-times up to 18 months for serious offences.

21 Young offenders who commit serious crimes in Nunavut never, or rarely, receive adult sentences. In those rare cases of murder, a youth would like-ly receive an Intensive Rehabilitative Custody and Supervision (IRCS) order (sections 42(2)(r) and 42(7) of the *Youth Criminal Justice Act*), which allows youth who commit serious offences and who have mental health issues to receive the necessary specialized assessment and treatment. Additionally, there is no programming for youth in the adult facility, the Baffin Correctional Centre, where the staff ratio is 12 staff to 95 prisoners; the youth facility has 10 staff for approximately 6 youth.

22 The Youth Level of Service/Case Management Inventory, or the YLS/ CMI, is a risk/needs assessment and case management tool used to manage youth in custody, developed by Andrews and Hoge and adapted from the adult version of the Level of Service Inventory–Revised (Bechtel, Lowenkamp, & Latessa, 2007). The tool is aimed at identifying and measuring youth needs, strengths, barriers, and incentives based on identified "criminogenic" risk factors, from which a case management plan is developed. It appears to be used extensively in youth facilities across Canada, outside of Quebec. The extent to which the YLS/CMI has been adapted to the unique needs of Aboriginal youth is unknown.

23 Isumaqsunngittukkuvik Youth Centre, Standing Order, Chapter 11 – Case Management Process (1104.07) March 03, 2002.

24 Isumaqsunngittukkuvik Young Centre, Standing Order, Chapter 13 – Programs: Temporary Release (1304.01). March 3, 2002.

25 Isumaqsunngittukkuvik Youth Centre, Standing Order, Chapter 13. Programs: Counselling Program (1305.01). March 3, 2002.

26 Isumaqsunngittukkuvik Youth Centre, Standing Order, Chapter 13. Programs: Education Programs (1305.01). March 3, 2002.

27 Isumaqsunngittukkuvik Youth Centre, Standing Order, Chapter 13. Programs: Land Program (1312.01).

28 Isumaqsunngittukkuvik Youth Centre, Standing Order, Chapter 11 – Case Management – Principles of Progressive Discipline (1104.07) March 3, 2002.

29 The *Youth Criminal Justice Act* allows that when serving a custody and supervision order, a young person must serve two-thirds of the sentence in custody with the remaining one-third on supervision in the community (section 42(2)(n).

30 Retrieved from http://www.nunatsiaqonline.ca/stories/article/ We_are_determined_to_help_families_at_risk/.

31 Retrieved from http://www.canadarehab.ca/drug_rehab_nunavut.html.

32 Government of Canada works with Nunavut to help prevent young people from taking illicit drugs – Health Canada Release (2011, March 16). Retrieved from http://news.gc.ca/web/article-en.do?nid=599109.

33 At-risk youth are designated as youth in foster care, pregnant youth, and youth who have dropped out of school.

34 Government of Canada works with nunavut to help prevent young people from taking illicit drugs – Health Canada Release. (2011, March 16). Retrieved from http://news.gc.ca/web/article-en.do?nid=599109.

35 Moreover, Inuit society values sharing and humility above individual wealth and personal achievement (Nunavut Tunngavik Incorporated, 2010–2011).

36 Changes to the *Criminal Code* (section 718.2(e)) in 1998 and subsequent case law (*R. v. Gladue* and *R. v. Ipeelee*) have underscored the importance of

judicial discretion and flexibility when sentencing Aboriginal offenders. However, the reality is that few Aboriginal offenders are given such considerations in sentencing (Roach, 2009).

37 White, *supra* note 1.

REFERENCES

Bala, N. (2015). Reducing use of courts and custody for youth offenders despite "get tough" on crime talk: The *Youth Criminal Justice Act* and Bill C-10. *Saskatchewan Law Review*, 78 (1).

Brennan, S., & Dauvergne, M. (2011). Police-reported crime statistics in Canada, 2011. *Juristat*, 85-002-X.

Clark, S. (2011). The Nunavut Court of Justice: An example of challenges and alternatives for communities and for the administration of justice. *Canadian Journal of Criminology and Criminal Justice*, 53(3), 343–370.

Criminal Code, R.S.C., 1985, c. C-46.

Eber, D. H. (2008). *Images of justice*. Montreal, QC; Kingston, ON: McGill-Queen's University Press.

First Annual Report of the IQ Task Force. (2002). Retrieved from http://www .inukshukmanagement.ca/IQ%20Task%20Force%20Report1.pdf.

Lynge, A. (1999). *Remarks at the National Forum on the Future of Alaska Natives*. Retrieved from http://www.eci.ox.ac.uk/publications/downloads/ thornton01-subsistence.pdf.

Marchildon, G. (2009). Health Services in Nunavut: First World or Third World? Retrieved from http://www.uregina.ca/gspp/marchildon/WRTCfiles/ Marchildon%20seminar %20nunavut2.pdf.

McMahon, C. (2010). *Nunavut community population projections: 2010–2036*. Nunavut Bureau of Statistics.

National Crime Prevention Centre. (2012). *A statistical snapshot of youth at risk and youth offending*. Public Safety Canada. Retrieved from http://publications. gc.ca/collections/collection_2012/sp-ps/PS4-126-2012-eng.pdf.

Nunavut Land Claims Agreement, S.C., ch.32, s. 1.1 (1993).

Nunavut Tunngavik Incorporated. (2010–2011). *Annual report on the state of Inuit culture and society: The status of Inuit children and youth in Nunavut*. Retrieved from http://www.tunngavik.com/files/2012/11/2010–11-SICS-Annual-Report-Eng.pdf.

Roach, K. (2009). One step forward, two steps back: Gladue at ten and in the courts of appeal. *Criminal Law Quarterly, 54*, 70–505.

Statistics Canada. (2005). Youth Court Statistics 2003-2004. *Juristat 25*(4). Retrieved from http://www.statcan.gc.ca/pub/85-002-x/85-002-x2008005-eng.pdf.

Statistics Canada. (2011). *Justice system spending: Police officers, by province and territory*. Retrieved from http://www40.statcan.gc.ca/l01/cst01/legal05c-eng.htm.

Suicide Prevention Strategy Working Group. (2010). *Nunavut suicide prevention strategy*. Retrieved from http://www.naho.ca/documents/it/2010-10-26-Nunavut-Suicide-Prevention-Strategy-English.pdf.

Tester, F. J., & Irniq, P. (2007). *Inuit Qaujimajatuqangit: Social history, politics and the practice of resistance. Arctic, 610*(1), 48–61.

White, P. (2011, April 1). *The trials of Nunavut: Lament for an Arctic nation. The Globe and Mail*. Retrieved from http://www.theglobeandmail.com/news/national/nunavut/the-trials-of-nunavut-lament-for-an-arctic-nation/article547265/.

Wilson, W. A., & Yellow Bird, M. (2005). *For Indigenous eyes only: A decolonizing handbook*. Santa Fe, NM: School of American Research Press.

Youth Criminal Justice Act, S.C. 2002, c. 1.

9 The Youth Criminal Justice System in Ontario

KATHRYN M. CAMPBELL

Introduction

The province of Ontario has the largest population in Canada; recent census numbers indicated that there were 13.5 million people living in Ontario as of July 2012.[1] That number includes 1,821,000 young persons, aged 15 to 24 years, and while early projections indicate a slight decline in these numbers during the 2010s, youth population numbers for Ontario are then expected to grow, and are projected to reach over 2 million by 2036.[2] These very large numbers of young persons, and the concomitant relatively larger numbers of youth who become involved in the criminal justice system when compared to other provinces, pose unique challenges for the administration of youth justice for Ontario. The focus of this chapter will be to examine these challenges, as well as to provide an overview of the practice of youth criminal justice in Ontario. Beginning with an overview of the historical role of the province of Ontario in the development of legal responses to youth crime, this chapter then focuses on the demographics of youth offending and jurisdictional responsibilities related to youth offending in this province. This is followed by an overview of the administration of youth justice in terms of practice and programming, focusing on some youth justice implementation issues exceptional to Ontario, as well as how the province has attempted to address the unique needs presented by some young offenders.

Historical Perspectives

The status of children and youth during the colonial era bears little resemblance to the rights and responsibilities afforded them today. It is

worthwhile to situate contemporary youth criminal justice law historically as developments in the province of Ontario played a significant
role in the evolution of youth justice in Canada. As one of the first colonies of Canada, Ontario during the early 19th century (known then
as Upper Canada) had very little evidence of youth crime, and what
did occur was relatively petty in nature. Early records revealed incidents of vandalism, petty theft, brawling, swearing, violations of local ordinances, and the abandonment of indentured service contracts
(Carrigan, 1991, p. 203–205). Given the influx of immigrants during the
Victorian era, youth became far more visible and youth crime was often
blamed on poverty and on increased immigration to settle the colonies
(Bell, 2007). While serious crimes of violence committed by children and
youth were rare, those who committed the crimes had very few rights
and were often treated in the same manner as adults. Reports indicate
that children and youth convicted of serious crimes not only received
similar sentences as adults, including hanging, but also served their sentence in adult facilities. The only protection provided to children and
youth was the defence of *doli incapax* (effectively meaning the "incapacity to do wrong"), and children under the age of seven were considered
incapable of committing criminal acts. Immunity from prosecution was
available to children aged 7 to 13, but it could be rebutted by establishing that a child had sufficient intelligence to know the difference between right and wrong and could understand the consequences of their
actions (Department of Justice Canada, 2004).

It was during the late 19th century, in the new settlement of Canada,
that widespread poverty, lack of employment, and increased immigration became a concern for social reformers and urban relief agencies.
During that era the Brown Commission Report of 1848–1849 examined
the conditions in Kingston Penitentiary and found incarcerated youth
as young as age seven serving sentences for relatively minor offences
(Bell, 2007). Consequently, one of the recommendations from the report
was for a separate system of justice for youth, and in 1857 *An Act for
the Establishing Prisons for Young Offenders* was passed, followed by the
opening of two facilities, named "reformatories" in Quebec (1858) and
Ontario (1859). The Quebec facility opened first at Ile aux Noix, while
the Ontario facility opened the next year in Penetanguishene, which
initially housed 40 boys, growing to a population of 193 by 1872 (Hagan
& Leon, 1977). The aim of many of the reformers, or "child-savers"
(Platt, 1969) was to address what they interpreted was the problem of
immorality of the working class poor. In part, this approach reflected

a changing attitude towards children, who were now viewed as being different than adults, and thus separated in their own right. This more humane attitude was also evident in how wayward children were to be treated, and the reformers began to address their efforts towards the children's education and rehabilitation.

Given that during this era prisons came to be viewed as "schools of crime," reformatories were initially proposed as a more proficient means of rehabilitating young persons. What became evident early on, however, was that these two new reformatories were plagued with difficulties: they admitted adults as well as children, there were discipline problems, and there was little in the way of training, education, or reform (Department of Justice Canada, 2004). In fact, they differed little from penitentiaries and were primarily focused on work and punishment, not rehabilitation. As reformatories came to be viewed as failures, provinces sought other means of rescuing children and youth, and this led to the development of industrial schools for neglected and problem children. Industrial schools were often built along a cottage model and differed from reformatories as their focus was on vocational training, education, and physical exercise. The first industrial school in Ontario, the Victoria Industrial School for Boys, opened in 1887 outside Toronto. Its statutory authority was found in the *Industrial School Act* of 1874. However, it was only in 1894 that the first federal legislation was passed pertaining directly to "juvenile delinquents," which was *An Act respecting Arrest, Trial and Imprisonment of Youthful Offenders*. This law was particularly significant as it provided for the separation of youth from older offenders and habitual criminals in custody, and for unpublicized separate trials for youth under 16 years (Department of Justice, 2004). At the same time in the province of Ontario, this legislation allowed for children who were neglected or destitute to be placed in the charge of the Children's Aid Society, rather than imprisoned. Investigations by social workers in those cases where younger children were charged with offences, could result in them being placed in foster care, fined, given a suspended sentence, or sent to a reformatory or to an industrial school. Essentially this law reflected what social reformers had been lobbying for: delinquent youth would no longer be treated as criminals in need of punishment, but as children in need of help and understanding, where sentencing would be based on a consideration of background factors as well as the offence. The development of this law was also influenced by the changing social and economic climate of the last half of the 19th century and the gradual rise of the welfare state in many countries (Smandych, 2012).

The *Juvenile Delinquents Act*[3] (JDA) was passed during this era in 1908, effectively implicating juvenile delinquency as a legal status (Bell, 2007). W.L. Scott and J.J. Kelso, two prominent social reformers in Ontario, were instrumental in its development, as well as in the establishment of the Children's Aid Society. What became evident early on is that the JDA reflected the intention of the reformers, it was clearly social welfare legislation, and its philosophy was *parens patriae* where the state (or King) would act as a parent in those instances where families could not provide for the child. As Canada's first youth justice legislation, the *Juvenile Delinquents Act* remained relatively unchanged for almost 75 years. Since the 1980s legislation for young offenders in Canada has become more like criminal law in nature, moving far from the welfare philosophy of the 19th-century reformers, evident in the JDA. Both the *Young Offenders Act*[4] (YOA) of 1984, and the *Youth Criminal Justice Act*[5] (YCJA) of 2003 reflected a movement towards more crime control and due process provisions as a philosophy of youth justice, where proportionate sentencing was seen to be the norm.

Youth Crime in Ontario

Since the enactment of the YCJA in 2003 there have been drastic changes to the number of youth who are dealt with by the formal youth criminal justice system, as well as changes in the manner in which youth are dealt with once they enter the system. In fact, the youth crime rate in Ontario continues to be below the national average and has been declining since 2007; it is now 22% lower than in 2001. Similarly the youth violent crime rate has also been in decline.

Data from youth court and youth correctional statistics reveal some interesting trends. Youth court statistics for the country reveal an overall decline in the number of youth cases completed in youth court, and 2011/2012 was the third-consecutive year of decline at 10% nationally, while Ontario showed a 14% reduction in the number of cases from the previous year. Reasons for the decline in the number of cases coming before the courts can be attributed to several factors, including an increase in the use of extrajudicial measures and sanctions. As shown in Figure 9.1, with the implementation of the YCJA in 2003, the rates of youth charged in Ontario decreased while the rates of youth receiving diversion sentences increased.

In the province of Ontario for 2011/2012, the proportion of youth court cases resulting in a guilty outcome was among the lowest in Canada at

Figure 9.1 Police charging in Ontario 2001–2012, Rates per 100,000 population age 12 to 17

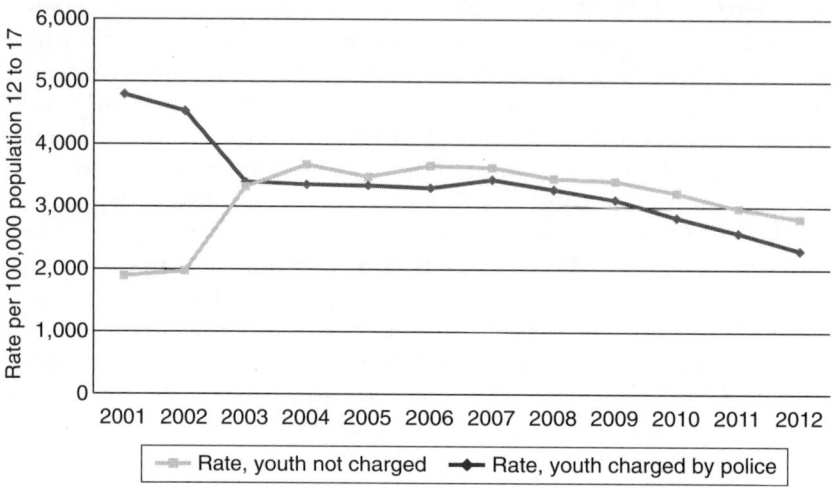

Source: Incident-based crime statistics, by detailed violations, CANSIM Table 252-0051

50% (compared with 79% in New Brunswick and a Canadian average of 57%) (Dauvergne, 2013). With respect to youth custody, there has been a downward trend in the use of custodial sentences since the proclamation of the YCJA in 2003, as shown in Figure 9.2 below. However, with respect to the proportion of guilty cases leading to a custodial sentence, Ontario stands at 21%, which is double the proportion of cases in Manitoba and higher than the national average (Dauvergne, 2013). However, when one considers the per capita rate of youth sentenced to custody, Ontario ranks much lower (5.39 per 10,000 youth population) than Manitoba (30.31 per 10,000 youth population) (Statistics Canada, CANSIM Table 251-008).

Dauvergne (2013) reports that nationally, custody was most often imposed for attempted murder (75%), being unlawfully at large (67%), and homicide cases (53%). Looking at data specifically for Ontario, the most common offences leading to a custodial sentence in 2011–2012 were: YCJA offences (20%), robbery (13%), failure to comply with an order (10%), major assault (10%), break and enter (9%), theft (7%), possession of stolen property (4%), mischief (4%), administration of justice (3%) and common assault (3%) (Bala, 2014). When considering the

Figure 9.2 Custodial sentences in Ontario, 2001–2012

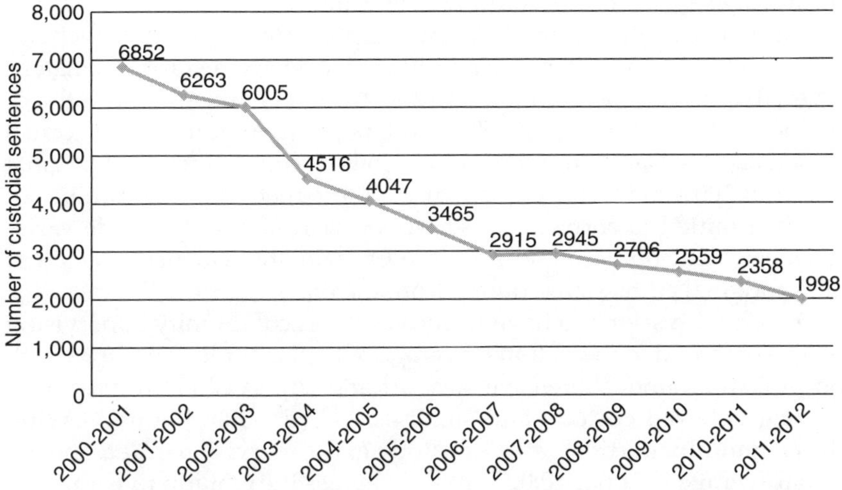

Source: Youth courts, guilty cases by most serious sentence. CANSIM Table 252-0068

principle of the YCJA to reserve custody for the most serious offences, these 10 most common offences appear to run contrary to the intent of the legislation.

In terms of correctional admissions, recent statistics from the Ontario Ministry of Children and Youth Services (MCYS) indicate that of the approximately 11,461 youth aged 12 to 17 years admitted into some form of correctional placement in 2012, 50% were under community supervision (33% on probation) while only 7% were in custody. Comparing data for Ontario from 2005 with 2012, there has been a 47% reduction in the number of youth held in pretrial detention and custody. Pretrial detention, however, was responsible for 42% of all admissions in Ontario in 2012 (MCYS, 2014).

As with most other provinces since the enactment of the YJCA in 2003, the numbers of youth receiving custodial sentences in Ontario has drastically dropped, with a concomitant increased use of community-based interventions and diversion from formal court proceedings. Statistics for 2011/2012 indicate that the average daily population in the ministry's youth justice system was 9,229 youth: 8,643 in the community on probation, 889 youth in diversion from formal court proceedings, 216 in open custody/detention, and 370 in secure custody/detention.[6]

Female youth represented only 21% of all youth justice admissions and the average age of all the youth was 16 years.

Aboriginal youth are generally over-represented in youth justice statistics and in Ontario they are admitted to custody disproportionately, given that Aboriginal youth aged 12 to 17 years make up only 2.8% of the population but comprise 7% of the population admitted to correctional services. Data comparing admissions by self-identified Aboriginal youth in 2001 and 2011 has shown a 50% reduction in the number of youth admitted to correctional services (MCYS, 2014), but wide variations between southern and northern Ontario are evident with 65% of all Aboriginal admissions coming from the north.

Ontario also seems to have fewer youth on community supervision when compared to the national average, which includes rates for youth on probation, under intensive support and supervision orders, youth serving deferred custody and supervision orders, and youth serving the community portion of their custody and supervision order. The national average is 71 per 10,000 youth, whereas the Ontario rate is 67 per 10,000 youth, and the average number of days for youth in Ontario to serve on a probation order was approximately 360.

Youth Justice in Ontario: Jurisdiction

Currently youth justice in the province of Ontario is administered through the Ministry of Children and Youth Services; however, the ministry was not established until 2004. Under the *Juvenile Delinquents Act*, all youth correctional services were the responsibility of the Ministry of Correctional Services, and were later transferred to the Ministry of Community and Social Services (MCSS) for all youth under the age of 16. In keeping with the welfare philosophy of the JDA, the MCSS's mandate was suitable to deal with children who were neglected or otherwise in need of protection. Sixteen- and 17-year-old offenders were under the purview of the Ministry of Correctional Services. Under the *Young Offenders Act* jurisdiction for establishing a system of custody, detention and community supervision for young offenders was split and shared by two ministries: Phase I youth aged 12 to 15 years were handled by the Ministry of Community and Social Services, while Phase II youth, aged 16 to 17 years, were dealt with by the Ministry of Community Safety and Correctional Services, which had the responsibility for adult offenders, fewer resources, and the reputation for placing less emphasis on treatment and rehabilitation than its counterpart (Bala & Anand, 2009, p. 177).

In 2001, the provincial Conservative government ended this split jurisdiction and placed all services for young offenders, aged 12 to 17 years within the Ministry of Community Safety and Correctional Services. While publicly this move was touted as a means of improving the efficiency of youth justice services, in reality it was consistent with the provincial government's "tough on crime" approach (Bala & Anand, 2009, p. 177). Following the implementation of the *Youth Criminal Justice Act* in 2003 and the election of a provincial Liberal government in 2004, all youth justice services became the purview of the newly created Ministry of Children and Youth Services (MCYS). This ministry has the responsibility for child welfare services, youth justice, community support, and children's mental health services. The model for youth justice in Ontario is separate from adult services and provides a continuum of evidence-informed community and custodial programs aligned with the YCJA. Youth justice service delivery is based on crime prevention, reducing recidivism, and contributing to community safety; at the same time youth are held accountable for their actions and service delivery includes a comprehensive risk assessment, effective case management, reintegration, and community-based planning (Youth Justice Services Division, n.d.).

Within this ministry, the Youth Justice Services Division (YJSD) was developed and was given the mandate to transform youth justice services following three key elements. The first was to create a dedicated, integrated youth justice system for youth aged 12 to 17 years based on their needs, rather than the offence; the second involved restructuring the youth justice system from one that was predominantly custody-focused to one that offers a continuum of services; and finally to integrate youth justice services into the broader framework of children and youth at risk. A number of strategies to meet these goals have been implemented by the YJSD. They include:

- the development of a dedicated probation system that is now separate from the adult system serviced by youth justice probation officers;
- a single case manager assigned to each youth in recognition of the importance of continuity of care for youth throughout their involvement in the system;
- a Youth Services Officer classification for those working in secure youth custody facilities accompanied by specific training;
- the development of an Alternatives to Custody Strategy that will guide a number of programs and services, including prevention, diversion, alternative sentencing, and reintegration, and respond to

the needs of specific youth populations (including Aboriginal youth and youth with mental health issues).

Given that a number of particular facilities in the province have been underused, specifically open custody, the ministry has reinvested those resources into other community-based programs, such as creating new Attendance Centres,[7] Intensive Support and Supervision Programs (ISSPs),[8] restorative justice demonstration sites, new Aboriginal programs, and extrajudicial measures. In terms of custodial facilities, this new strategy is aimed at transforming the system to be completely separate from the adult system, and youths who may be residing in such facilities will be removed. The strategy included establishing five purpose-built facilities with the aim of reducing violence and enhancing programming. In 2006, the MCYS reinvested $28.7 million from the closure of open custody beds and created the Alternatives to Custody and Community Interventions Strategy (ATCCIS). Its approach is holistic and integrated while developing a number of programs and services. It applies to youth involved in both minor and more serious offences, and includes the development of school-based prevention and diversion pilot projects, which offer peer mediation and other school-based services to assist young people (Mazaheri, 2006).

The Youth Criminal Justice System in Ontario: Practice

Programs for young offenders offered by the Ministry of Children and Youth Services in the province of Ontario function on a continuum of community-based and custodial programs, which are separate from those available to adult offenders. The programs include: prevention programs, diversion from formal court proceedings, alternatives to custody and community interventions, services/supports to targeted populations (Aboriginal youth, youth with mental health problems, girls), and open and secure detention and custody. There are four regional offices that manage the programs and service delivery. The province has 70 facilities, including 45 open custody and detention residences operating by contract through transfer payments[9] from the ministry. Similarly, it oversees 20 secure youth custody facilities, 6 of which are operated directly by the government while the remainder are operated by transfer payment agencies. These facilities are located throughout the province, with differing mandates, and range in capacity from 8 to 192 beds. Moreover, there are 198 transfer payment agencies that provide over 400 community-based programs and services, as well as 64 ministry-operated probation offices and two Aboriginal offices.

The largest custodial facility for young offenders in Ontario, the Roy McMurtry Youth Centre with 192 beds in Brampton, has been plagued with difficulties since it opened in 2009. Less than a year later, the Provincial Advocate for Children and Youth's office had received over 250 complaints from more than 160 youth; these complaints included beatings and denial of access to food and medical care.[10] The Advocate's office undertook a study and released a report in 2013 based on interviews with over one hundred youth and found that many commented on excessive use of force by staff, violence between youth, extended lockdown times in cells, and more than 40% had been physically restrained (Advocate, 2013). As a result of this report 19 recommendations emerged that addressed: partnering with youth and community stakeholders, improving communication, examining the "Relationship Custody" approach further to better its implementation, developing a plan to engage youth in more meaningful ways, decreasing all forms of violence, providing additional training to staff, better monitoring the use of intrusive procedures, improving investigative procedures around incidents, improving and facilitating youth contact with families and with professionals, ensuring basic care needs of youth are met, improving education, vocational, recreational programs and activities for all youth, and supporting gang-involved youth (Advocate, 2013). Given that one of the areas of concern within the institution was related to gang violence, 51 staff received training on working with youth involved in gangs, and the ministry adopted an assessment tool (Gang Risk Assessment Instrument) for use in clinical assessment. The Road to Redemption program was also adopted as a strength-based program assisting youth through a series of modules to seek out more positive alternatives. Furthermore, research has now indicated that a wrap-around approach to addressing gang-involved youth has been successful, thus youth with multiple risk factors are better served through a multidisciplinary service group of partners (Wortley, 2014). However, this is difficult to achieve in a large institution such as the Roy McMurtry centre.

When the federal government amended the YCJA through the controversial Bill C-10, the *Safe Streets and Communities Act* in October 2012, it did not alter the fundamental principles of the law but provided additional opportunities to locate a pattern of youth criminality and possibly detain youth. Specifically, while discretionary in the past, police forces are now *required* to keep a record of any extrajudicial measures taken. At the same time, the YCJA now makes it easier for courts to detain youth pretrial, it expands the definition of crimes of serious violence to include property crimes, and introduces considerations of denunciation and deterrence into youth sentencing principles.

Provincial child welfare legislation also affects how youth justice services are administered in the province of Ontario. The *Child and Family Services Act*,[11] is the enabling provincial legislation in Ontario for the YCJA. Part IV of the Act focuses on youth justice and provides direction around: the rights of children and youth in care (sections 103–108), use of physical restraints, levels of detention (section 94), responsibilities of probation officers and provincial directors (sections 89–90), use of secure isolation in residential settings (section 126), licensing requirements for children's residences (including open and secure custody/ detention facilities, section 192) and duties of professionals to report suspicions of child abuse or maltreatment (section 72). This legislation does not focus on the adjudication process, per se, but on the designations and management for custody, detention, and supervision programs resulting from the laying of charges and sentencing by a youth court (Youth Justice Services Division, n.d.).

Institutional and Community-Based Programming for Young Offenders

In attempting to address the needs of young offenders in custody and on community supervision, the Ministry of Child and Family Services adheres to what are described as "evidence-informed" programs and services, linked to "what works" in the literature on effective correctional intervention and in the reduction of recidivism. This appears to be a response to a long-standing debate in the academic literature regarding the efficacy of intervention with incarcerated populations. The death of the rehabilitative ideal in corrections can be traced to the 1970s, in part as a response to an increasing social reform movement that advocated for the rights of the incarcerated, and in part a response to Robert Martinson's seminal meta-analysis of treatment programs for offenders, which found that "nothing works." Martinson (1974) examined 231 studies of prison rehabilitative programs and concluded that "with few and isolated exceptions, the rehabilitative efforts that have been reported so far have had no appreciable effect on recidivism" (p. 25). This thinking was embraced at that time as it was consistent with the dominant conservative politics of the late 1970s and 1980s, a "just deserts" philosophy that served to justify harsher punishments and more severe penalties.

More recent research points to the importance of addressing needs associated with recidivism for change and matching the type and level of intervention to the offender's level of risk (Andrews et al., 1990; Bonta & Andrews, 2007). This appears to be the basis for the Ontario ministry's emphasis on "evidence-informed" programs, as they stress the importance of addressing youth needs associated with recidivism, matching the type and level of intervention to the youth's risk level, where higher risk cases receive more intensive services. Moreover, they foster a strength-based approach that recognizes the greater dependency and reduced maturity of youth as well as the importance of increasing youths' opportunities for academic and/or vocational achievements. In addition, enhancing community alternatives over custody is consistent with this approach, and is also in line with the changes that have resulted as a consequence of the movement away from custodial sentencing through the YCJA implementation.

Programs and services offered to youth in custody and in the community thus focus on specific youth needs and the risks they may represent; they are aimed towards teaching new skills, educating youth, and helping them learn conflict resolution skills. Programming occurs over the full day for youth in custodial institutions, and they are engaged through routines, activities, recreation, education, and structured rehabilitation programs. Risk assessments and treatment planning evaluate areas of education, employment, treatment, overall behaviour, family/peer relationships, and motivation to participate in programs. Structured programming can include education, addictions counselling, anger management, life skills, and recreation and cultural programs. All intervention programs will have rehabilitative and reintegrative aspects to them, taking into account the youths' needs, as well as cultural and familial background and supports. The province of Ontario applies the Collaborative Case Management approach to any youth sentenced to custody. This single case management model was adopted in 2004, and from the time the youth enters the system, he/she is assigned a probation officer who stays with him/her throughout to provide a continuity of care.

Addressing Unique Needs

The Ministry of Child and Youth Services has acknowledged the unique needs of many of its youth by developing a number of specialized services. In fact, while Aboriginal youth make up only 2.8% of the total youth population aged 12 to 17 in Ontario, self-identified Aboriginal youth represent 9% of all admissions to ministry youth justice services. Thus, in order to address this over-representation, the ministry opened Ge-Da-Gi-Binez Youth Centre in Fort Frances, northwestern Ontario in 2009. The name of the facility means "spotted eagle" in the Ojibwa language, and is meant to represent youth and learning. This facility is the first of its kind and, as a secure custody facility, it has 12 beds for Aboriginal youth who are on detention or sentenced custody. The building itself incorporates many unique Aboriginal design features. It offers a number of evidence-based rehabilitative programs that are consistent with Aboriginal culture. At the same time, the ministry has developed 41 community-based programs for Aboriginal youth who are at risk of, or in conflict with the law.

For gang-involved youth,[12] the ministry has piloted a multi-year strategy in four secure and open facilities. Specialized programming includes training in pro-social life skills and education around how to exit from gangs, as well as training for staff to identify, manage, and support gang-involved youth. On the federal level, since 2007, the National Crime Prevention Centre (NCPC) through the Canadian Department of Public Safety has been providing funding through the Youth Gang Prevention Fund to reduce the number of gang-involved youth in communities with a known or emerging gang problem.

A troubling aspect of Canada's youth gang membership is the disproportionately high representation of visible minority youth – particularly African Canadian – and Aboriginal youth in gangs. Efforts to address gang violence in the Toronto area include the African Canadian Youth Justice Program and Youth Opportunities Strategy (Caputo & Vallée, 2007). At the same time, the Violence Intervention Project (VIP) offers a number of workshops to youth run by the East Metro Youth Services in Toronto, which addresses issues such as bullying, gang violence, diversity, anger management, conflict resolution, etc. (Violence Intervention Project, 2005).

Media commentators focus on economic disadvantage and social marginalization suffered by minority youth, and particularly Black youth, as a key cause of gang membership. Khenti (2013) argues that the high rate of homicide among African Canadians is really an "unrecognized major public health crisis" and more a consequence of income inequality, poverty, poor quality of life, mental health risks, and sustained racism. In his recommendations regarding addressing the problem of gangs, Wortley (2014) underscores the importance of developing anti-racism, anti-poverty, and mental health strategies.

The province of Ontario has established some innovative programming to address issues resulting from youth suffering from mental health problems who also engage in criminal activity. The YCJA provides that youths who suffer from a mental illness and have committed a serious violent offence may receive a sentence of Intensive Rehabilitative Custody and Supervision (IRCS) (YCJA, sections 42(2)(r), 42(7)). At the same time specialized services must be available for these youth and they must also consent to attend. Youth who receive an IRCS sentence most likely serve part of their sentence in some form of secure custody. At the same time, a number of other programs exist in Ontario to support youth with mental health issues in the criminal justice system: they include diversion from formal court proceedings, community supervision, specialized clinical supports, crisis intervention, Telemental Health Program,[13] and the establishment of Youth Mental Health Courts. Furthermore, access to mental health services has been enhanced within the justice sector by expanding the current Youth Mental Health Court Worker program from 13 to 45 sites. These workers establish links between youth with mental health problems and community mental health and youth justice services, as well as diverting them from the criminal justice system where appropriate. Four "Service Collaboratives" to support local service planning have been assigned to the justice sector to strengthen the links between the community and hospital-based mental health services for individuals involved in the justice system.

In May 2008, a Youth Mental Health Court opened in Ottawa, the first of its kind in Canada.[14] Essentially, this court was an attempt to bring together the supports and resources from two different systems (criminal justice and mental health) in order to meet the needs of youth who commit criminal acts but are also suffering from mental illness. The goals of the court are to intervene early, expedite processing times, divert youth where possible, and provide individualized and appropriate treatment and intervention. Youth under court supervision in the program are closely monitored and referred to community-based rehabilitative programs. Referrals to this court can come from the judge, Crown attorneys, defence counsel, police, and probation officers. However, in order to be referred to this court youth must be aged 12 to 17 years and be either at risk of being charged by the police, have been charged by the police, or have been found unfit to stand trial, not criminally responsible, or on an Ontario Review Board disposition. The youth's offence must be considered low risk and manageable through community services, thus youth who receive an IRCS sentence are by definition not dealt with in the Youth Mental Health Court. A pre-screening form is completed and the Crown attorney assigned to the court screens for youth in crisis determines suitability and assesses the youth's needs with support from clinicians and/or community mental health staff. Approximately one week prior to the court date a Counsel pretrial meeting is held with the Crown, the court worker, defence counsel, a youth team case manager, probation officers, addiction workers, and other committed community partners. The youth mental health court worker then meets with the psychiatrist, reviews clinical assessments and reports, and then develops a tentative treatment plan. The psychiatrist will conduct a brief screening/evaluation of the youth, will meet with parents (or caregivers), implement or modify a tentative plan, and make recommendations to the court. When the youth appears in the court, submissions are heard by Crown and defence counsel, the psychiatrist's recommendations are heard, and the court makes a ruling.

In sentencing the judge must ensure that the treatment plan is proportionate to the offence and is consistent with the YJCA; in some cases he or she may order further assessments under section 34 of the YCJA or section 21 of the Ontario *Mental Health Act*.[15] Following the hearing, the youth's progress is monitored by the Crown. Youth involved in this court must take responsibility for their crime, as no contested trials are held. Moreover, at times youth are also subjected to other sanctions, such as diversion, extrajudicial sanctions, or stays of proceeding, depending on the circumstances of each case. This court's focus is clearly rehabilitative, however, it will also hear charges brought under the *Controlled Drugs and Substances Act*[16] as on many occasions youth abuse substances while committing crimes. While the court only sits one day per month, early anecdotal evidence indicates that recidivism rates are lower for these youth, they appear to be processed more quickly, and are more likely to be given a community-based diversion sentence.[17] The importance of this court cannot be overstated, given that 20% of all young offenders suffer from serious diagnosable mental illnesses (Taylor, 2008).

The province of Ontario considers female young offenders to be a special population and as a result the Youth Justice Services Division has attempted to incorporate gender considerations into policy development, programming, facility planning, and staff training since 2003. In terms of custody/detention, gender-dedicated services are ideal, however, the numbers are not sufficient to provide completely separate facilities in some cases. Thus co-located facilities have separate programming and accommodation for male and female youth, whereas co-ed facilities have separate accommodation but resident youth participate in shared programming and activities.

Issues Related to Youth Criminal Justice Law Implementation in Ontario

While the federal government has the mandate for criminal law and criminal procedure under section 91 of the *Constitution Act*, the provinces have been given the task of the administration of justice (section 92). As a consequence, there is a great deal of variation in how the YCJA has been implemented across the country, based in part on regional differences, culture, politics, and geography. An example of this variation is evident in how the province of Ontario has delivered alternative measures. Alternative measures, which involve providing youth with community-based programs for minor infractions, rather than involving formal court processes, have a long history in Canada. While under the *Juvenile Delinquents Act* police and Crown attorneys engaged in this practice informally for youth involved in less serious crimes, whereas it was only under the *Young Offenders Act* that statutory authority for alternative measures emerged.

What is interesting about alternative measures in Ontario is that following the implementation of the YOA, the provincial government at that time resisted implementing these programs and only did so after being forced to by the courts. In particular, in the case of *R. v. S. (S)*[18] the Ontario Court of Appeal held that failing to establish such programs constituted "a denial of equal benefit and protection of the law" under section 15 of the *Canadian Charter of Rights and Freedoms*. The reluctance on the part of the province has meant that restrictive policies for admission into the program were the norm for the mainly post-charge referrals, thus resulting in low annual rates (Bala & Anand, 2009, p. 336).

Since the enactment of the YCJA, however, the province has implemented a number of diversion programs including extrajudicial measures[19] (EJM) and extrajudicial sanctions[20] (EJS) programs. Since 2005, 27 EJM pre-charge pilot projects and six EJS post-charge pilot projects were implemented to identify best practices, and contrary to earlier policy were now directed at both minor and more serious types of offences (Caputo & Vallée, 2007). At the same time, a number of Restorative Justice pilot projects have also been developed in the province (Ontario: MCYS, 2006). These include family-group conferencing, facilitated conferencing, school-based conferencing, and victim-offender mediation, where referrals can be either pre- or post-charge. In addition, other community-based programs include attendance centre programs, reintegration and support services, youth outreach worker programs, and Aboriginal Alternatives to Custody programs (Caputo & Vallée, 2007).

Prior to the implementation of the YCJA, questions were raised regarding the constitutionality of some of its provisions and decisions in Ontario courts aided in clarifying these issues. In 2003, the Quebec government initiated a reference to its Court of Appeal, asking for the court's position on the constitutionality of the Act's presumptive adult sentences.[21] In *Reference Re. Bill C-7*,[22] the court found that presumptive sentences violated section 7 of the Charter, and that while adult sentences could still be handed down by youth court, the onus is on the Crown to justify why it is required. Before the federal government had time to amend the Act to provide clarity, in 2006 the Ontario Court of Appeal released a controversial decision affirming the Quebec Court of Appeal decision in *R. v. D. B.*[23] In that case a 17-year-old youth pled guilty to manslaughter and the Crown sought to impose the automatic or presumptive adult sentence. D.B. challenged this provision based on the notion that the burden should not be on the youth to persuade the court that he or she should not lose the benefit of the youth sentencing provisions. The trial judge allowed the Charter challenge and sentenced D.B. as a youth. The Ontario Court of Appeal upheld the decision, which was later affirmed by the Supreme Court of Canada in *R. v. D. B.*[24] The UN Convention on the Rights of the Child was cited and discussed in this case pointing out that because of their age, young people have increased vulnerability, less maturity, and a lower capacity for moral judgement. Furthermore, the court found that the presumption of diminished moral culpability is a principle of fundamental justice and that placing the onus on the young person constitutes a violation of section 7 of the Charter. According to Bala (2014) the decision in *R. v. D. B.* "constitutionalized" the requirement for different treatment for those under age 18 who are facing criminal charges. It was finally through the 2012 amendments to the YCJA in Bill C-10 that the presumptive adult sentence provision was once and for all removed from the written law.

Conclusion

Historically, the administration of youth justice in the province of Ontario has dealt with older youth (16–17 years old) through the adult correctional system. This was evident in both policy and practice; many

Phase II youth under the old system served their sentences in adult correctional facilities. Likewise, much of Ministry of Children and Youth Services' written policy emphasizes its separateness from the adult system. Moreover, it has been a very recent development for these youth to have moved from being under the direction of correctional staff responsible for adults to being administered through the Ministry of Children and Youth Services. As Caputo and Vallée (2007) note, the impact of this more "corrections based philosophy" likely still resonates today: it may be evident in the types of pre-sentence recommendations made to youth court, in Ontario's historically conservative stance towards the implementation of alternative measures, and its relatively recent development of extensive extrajudicial measures programs.

Moreover, section 35 of the YCJA allows a youth justice court judge to refer troubled youth to a child welfare agency for assessment in order to determine whether they are in need of child welfare services. At the same time, it is the agency, not the court, that decides if a child in fact needs such services and if they will be forthcoming. Consistent with a more "correctionally"-oriented approach to youth offending, the province of Ontario has statutory restrictions on child welfare agency involvement with youth 16 and older (Bala & Anand, 2009, p. 373). While clearly part of this decision is based on resource availability, if older youth are in need of such help, it is inaccessible to them in some cases. It would seem that the province's evolution or transformation from a youth justice system that was indeed linked to the adult correctional system and towards one that is more oriented to rehabilitation and reintegration of young offenders and community-based interventions, is still a work in progress.

The Ministry of Children and Youth Services has focused on two key principles of the YCJA in its approach to youth justice: reducing an overreliance on incarceration for non-violent offenders by providing more community-based alternatives to custody, and reserving the most serious interventions for the most serious crimes (Caputo & Vallée, 2007). It would appear that the statistics bear out this new approach; there have been substantial reductions in the use of custodial sentences and increases in community-based interventions, while custody is reserved for those youth who commit the most violent offences. At the same time there is indeed room for improvement as Ontario continues to rely on the most onerous of sanctions available to young persons. This appears inconsistent with the philosophy of the YCJA, with Ontario's commitment to transform its system of youth justice, and with developments in other parts of the country. However, it is hoped that continued efforts at improving the nature and extent of community-based and specialized programming, increased attention to staff training on relationship custody, and gang involvement with concomitant monitoring of outcomes may serve to realize the goals of youth justice in Ontario in coming years.

NOTES

1 Census Highlights Fact Sheet. Retrieved from http://www.fin.gov.on.ca/ en/economy/demographics/quarterly/dhiq2.html.
2 Ontario Population Projections Updated. Retrieved from http://www.fin .gov.on.ca/en/economy/demographics/projections/.
3 S.C. 1908, c-40.
4 R.S.C., 1985, C. Y-1.
5 S.C. 2002, c.1
6 Since 2003, the number of youth in secure custody has dropped from 1,017 to 370. Retrieved from http://news.ontario.ca/mcys/en/2012/03/ ontario-streamlining-youth-justice-facilities.html.
7 Mandated through section 42(2)(m) of the YCJA, this order requires the young person to attend a non-residential program in the community at specified times and on conditions set by the judge for up to 240 hours, over a period of six months. The program is closely supervised and may include contact with the family and community resources to engage and support the youth in the community.
8 Also mandated through section 42(2)(l) of the YCJA, ISSPs provide intensive clinical and community supports, supervision, and crisis management for youth in conflict with the law with diagnosed mental health or special needs whose offence might have resulted in a custodial sentence.
9 While transfer payment agencies are responsible to deliver provincially funded services and are accountable to the funding ministry, this arrangement raises questions as to the lack of accountability that may occur when government privatizes service delivery.
10 P. Winsa. (2013, August 7). Roy McMurty Youth Centre not living up to its promise, says advocate. *The Star*. Retrieved from http://www.thestar. com/news/crime/2013/08/07/roy_mcmurtry_youth_centre_not_living_ up_to_its_promise_says_advocate.html
11 R.S.O. 1990, Chapter C.11.
12 According to Totten (2012) there are approximately 180 gangs in Ontario, with about 80 in the Greater Toronto Area and 95 in York and other major

cities in Ontario and on Northern First Nations reserves. Moreover, only a handful are criminally sophisticated, highly organized, and linked to other groups in parts of Canada.

13 The Telemental Health Program is funded by the Ministry of Children and Youth Services and delivered by the Hospital for Sick Children, the Children's Hospital of Eastern Ontario, and the Child and Parent Resource Institute. Through these providers, clinical consultations occur via videoconferencing to children and youth in rural, remote, and underserved areas of the province. This service is also provided to youth in a number of secure custody and detention facilities as well (Youth Justice Services Division, n.d.).

14 Information on the Ottawa Youth Mental Health Court was obtained from a presentation by the Honourable Madam Justice H. Perkins-McVey, "Ottawa Youth Mental Health Court: Finding hope in a Courtroom" (2009). Retrieved from http://www.lfcc.on.ca/youth_mental_health_court_service.html. There is another Youth Mental Health Court in London, Ontario, however, this court is only open to youth 16 years and older, charged with an offence under the YCJA, and with a diagnosed or suspected serious mental illness, traumatic brain injury, or developmental disability.

15 Section 21: "Where a judge has reason to believe that a person who appears before him or her charged with or convicted of an offence suffers from mental disorder, the judge may order the person to attend a psychiatric facility for examination."

16 S.C. 1996, c. 19.

17 "Mental Health Court proves a huge success," *Ottawa Citizen*, November 13, 2008. Retrieved from http://www.canada.com/ottawacitizen/news/story.html?id=d343a2d3-a48f-4836-8298-0c149767ae05.

18 [1990] 2 S.C.R. 254.

19 These programs provide community-based pre-charge measures where a youth is held accountable for his/her actions, through a partnership model, promoting harm reparation; they are operated through police services (Youth Justice Services Division, n.d.).

20 Post-charge extrajudicial sanctions are referred by the Crown when a police caution or warning is considered insufficient. They are community based and can include an apology to the victim, community service work, restitution, cognitive/behavior skills, anger management, life skills, and substance abuse counselling/treatment (Youth Justice Services Division, n.d.).

21 The YCJA contained special sentences for "presumptive offences" and when committed by a 16- to 17- year-old youth (which include murder, attempted murder, manslaughter, aggravated sexual assault, and a third "serious violent offence") there was a presumption that an adult sentence would be imposed (Bala & Anand, 2009, p. 597).

22 [2003] Q.J. 2850.
23 [2006] O.J. N° 1112 (C.A.).
24 2008 SCC 25.

REFERENCES

Advocate. (2013). "It depends who's working": The reality of the Roy
     McMurtry Youth Centre. Toronto, ON: Report of the Provincial Advocate
     for Children and Youth.
*An Act for the Establishing Prisons for Young Offenders, For Better Government
     of Public Asylums, Hospitals and Prisons, and for the Better Construction of
     Common Goals*, N° 222, 3rd Session, 5th.
An Act respecting Arrest, Trial and Imprisonment of Youthful Offenders, Statutes
     of Canada, 1894, volume 1, chapter 58.
An Act respecting Industrial Schools, Statutes of the Province of Ontario, 1874,
     chapter 29. Parliament, 20 Victoria, 1857.
Andrews, D. A., Zinger, I., Hoge, R. D., Bonta, J., Gendreau, P., & Cullen, F. T.
     (1990). Does correctional treatment work? A clinically relevant and psycho-
     logically informed meta-analysis. *Criminology, 28*, 369–404.
Bala, N. (2014). Responding more effectively to youth crime: The legal context.
     Presentation to Canadian Youth Justice Conference, June 25, 2014, Toronto.
Bala, N., & Anand, S. (2009). *Youth criminal justice law* (2nd Edition). Toronto,
     ON: Irwin Law.
Bell, S. (2007). *Young offenders and youth justice: A century after the fact,* (3rd Ed.).
     Toronto, ON: Thomson/Nelson.
Bonta, J., & Andrews, D. A. (2007). *Risk-need-responsivity model for offender as-
     sessment and rehabilitation.* (User Report 2007–06). Ottawa, ON. Public Safety
     Canada.
Brennan, S. (2012). Youth court statistics in Canada, 2010/2011, *Juristat*
     (85–002-X), 1–27. Canadian Centre for Justice Statistics.
Canadian Charter of Rights and Freedoms, Part I of the Constitution Act, 1982,
     being Schedule B to the Canada Act 1982 (UK), 1982, c. 11.
Caputo. T., & Vallée, M. (2007). *Review of the Roots of Youth Violence: Research
     papers* (vol. 4). A Report prepared for the Review of the Roots of Youth
     Violence. Retrieved from http://www.children.gov.on.ca/htdocs/English/
     topics/youthandthelaw/ roots/volume4/comparative_analysis.aspx.
Carrigan, P. J. (1991). *Crime and punishment in Canada: A history.* Toronto, ON:
     McClelland & Stewart.

Child and Family Services Act, R.S.O. 1990, Chapter C.11.

Constitution Act, 1982, being Schedule B to the *Canada Act 1982* (UK), 1982, c 11.

Juvenile Delinquents Act S.C. 1908, c. 40.

Controlled Drugs and Substances Act, S.C. 1996, c. 19.

Dauvergne, M. (2013). Youth court statistics in Canada, 2011/2012. *Juristat, 3*, 85–002.

Department of Justice Canada. (2004). *The evolution of juvenile justice in Canada.* Retrieved from http://www.justice.gc.ca/eng/abt-apd/icg-gci/jj2-jm2/jj2-jm2.pdf.

Hagan, J., & Leon, J. (1977). Rediscovering delinquency: Social history, political ideology and the sociology of law. *American Sociological Review, 42*, 587–598.

Juvenile Delinquents Act, S.C. 1908, c. 40.

Khenti, A. A. (2013). Homicide among young black men in Toronto: An unrecognized public health crisis? *Canadian Journal of Public Health, 104*(1).

Martinson, R. (1974). What works? – Questions and answers about prison reform. *The Public Interest, 35*, 22–54.

Mazaheri, N. (2006). *A preliminary framework for the monitoring and outcome evaluation of the Alternatives to Custody and Community Interventions Strategy.* Ontario: Ministry Of Children and Youth Services, Research and Outcome Measurement Branch.

Mental Health Act, R.S.O. 1990, Chapter M.7.

Ministry of Child and Youth Services. (2014). Impact of the Youth Criminal Justice Act over the past decade in Ontario. Panel presentation to Canadian Youth Justice Conference, Toronto, June 25, 2014.

Ontario Ministry of Children and Youth Services, Youth Justice Services Division. (2006, April). *Restorative justice demonstration pilots: Program description (version 6).* Community Development and Partnerships Branch. Alternatives to Custody.

Platt, A. (1969). *The child savers: The invention of delinquency.* Chicago, IL: University of Chicago Press.

Reference Re Bill C-7, [2003] Q.J. 2850.

R. v. D. B. [2006] O.J. No. 1112 (C.A.).

R. v. D. B. [2008] SCC 25.

R. v. S. (S) (1988), 63 C.R. (3d) 64 (Ont. C.A.).

Safe Streets and Communities Act, S.C. 2012, c. 1.

Smandych, R. (2012). From "misguided children" to "criminal youth": Exploring historical and contemporary trends in Canadian youth justice. In J. Winterdyk & R. Smandych (Eds), *Youth at risk and youth justice: A Canadian overview*, pp. 3–25. Don Mills, ON: Oxford University Press.

Statistics Canada (2013) Youth correctional services, average counts of young persons by province and territory (CANSIM table 251-008). Canadian Centre for Justice Statistics, Corrections Key Indicators Report.

Taylor, P. S. (2008). A new court for mentally ill youth. *Maclean's*. Retrieved from http://www.macleans.ca/canada/national/article.jsp?content=20080611_19799_19799.

Totten, M. (2012). An overview of gang-involved youth in Canada. In J. Winterdyk & R. Smandych (Eds), *Youth at risk and youth justice: A Canadian overview* (pp. 253–278). Don Mills, ON: Oxford University Press.

Wortley, S. (2014). Social problem or moral panic? Understanding youth gangs and gang violence in the Canadian context. Presentation to Canadian Youth Justice conference. Toronto, June 26, 2014.

Young Offenders Act R.S.C., 1985, c. Y-1.

Youth Criminal Justice Act, S.C. 2002, c. 1.

10 Youth Justice in Prince Edward Island

FRANK T. LAVANDIER

It is said that no one truly knows a nation until one has been inside its jails. A nation should not be judged by how it treats its highest citizens, but its lowest ones.

Introduction

This memorable quote, typically attributed to Nelson Mandela, constitutes the foundational underpinning for the discussion topic explored in this text. Long before the *Youth Criminal Justice Act* (YCJA) was enacted on April 1, 2003, youth justice-related intervention methodologies varied considerably across the Canadian landscape, both in scope and design. As Canadians approached and have now surpassed the first decade of the YCJA's yet to be determined total lifespan, rehabilitation and the best interests of the child sometime seem to be not much more than mere vestiges of a demonstrably more enlightened era, long since spent. Notwithstanding, optimism still reigns supreme in those of us who are consistently encouraged, if not categorically inspired, by our youth, as they continue to look towards the distant horizon, to a place where most of us older folk will never see!

A Brief History of Youth Justice in Prince Edward Island

Whereas, Prince Edward Island (PEI) is the smallest province or territory in the nation, in terms of both geographical area (5,660 square kilometres) and population density (estimated at 145,273 as of July 1, 2013), its staunch Island inhabitants hold steadfast to the knowledge that almost 150 years ago, in 1864, Canada and the great country it has since become, had its humble beginnings in our capital city, Charlottetown, in a province that has long since been recognized as the proverbial "cradle of confederation." PEI, not unlike many other agrarian or commercial fishery-based economies, has always prided itself in having both an independent spirit and the capacity to take care of its own, in good and troubled times alike. However, for many years, in actual fact up until the mid to late 1980s, this was not the case, particularly when it came to young persons who found themselves in conflict with the law.

Youth Custody in Prince Edward Island

Prior to 1984, the year the *Young Offenders Act* (YOA) was granted royal assent, a young person in the province, between seven and 16 years of age, inclusive, as was the case in Nova Scotia, New Brunswick, Ontario, and Saskatchewan, appeared before the presiding judge/justice (Provincial Supreme Court Justice in PEI) and if found to be *delinquent*, could be sent to a youth facility for an indefinite period of time. For those children who found themselves in this unfortunate set of circumstances, being placed in custody not only meant they would be compelled to leave their parental home and transported to far-flung places like the Shelburne Youth Centre (formerly the Nova Scotia School for Boys), over 500 kilometres away and located along Nova Scotia's south shore, but were also committed to serve indefinite periods of custodial time, "the length of which depended on how their conduct at the school was perceived by staff" (Kaufman, 2002, p. 91). This unseemly practice, of sending our so-called *juvenile delinquents* to custodial institutions located in either Shelburne, or, alternatively, Kingsclear, New Brunswick, actually did not end until the late1980s, when the first of eventually three custodial facilities opened in Georgetown, a town of 693 (2011) inhabitants, located in the eastern PEI. The Kings County Youth Centre, an interim youth custody facility, located at the rear of the century-old Georgetown Court House, opened in 1987 and housed young persons who had been remanded and/or were actually serving secure custody sentences outside the province, and were returning to PEI in order to complete their sentences.

Approximately two years later, in 1989, the newly constructed Georgetown Youth Centre (GYC) opened its doors. The GYC was designated an *open custody* facility and had the capacity to house up to a maximum of eight *residents* at any one time. The GYC, which closed its doors in the spring 2005, offered a broad array of programs, including employment preparation, anger management, family awareness, community service, and an in-house academic program.

The Tyne Valley Youth Centre (TVYC) officially opened April 3, 1989, and is situated in the western part of the province, in the rural community of Tyne Valley. The TVYC was also designated an open custody facility, housed a similar number of residents, and offered comparable programs as those found in the GYC. The TVYC officially closed slightly more than 14 years later, in June 2003.

The Prince Edward Island Youth Centre (PEIYC) opened in 1988 with a total capacity of 32 residents, in four separate living units, or pods, and initially served as the only designated *secure custody* facility in the province. The PEIYC includes two residential buildings, a main complex, and large courtyard. Prior to the construction of this new facility, young persons serving remand and/or secure custody sentences were housed in an interim centre located adjacent to the courthouse in Summerside. Following the closure of the two aforementioned open custody facilities, and up until the present day, the PEIYC constitutes a dual designated (open and secure custody) youth facility and has the capacity of housing a total of eight residents in each of its two separate living units, which, in turn, are both situated in one of the two residential buildings. In this province, not unlike a number of other jurisdictions, interaction between young persons serving open and secure custody-related sentences is strictly prohibited. In 2012, the PEIYC designated one of the residential buildings to house adult offenders, up to a maximum of 16 at any one time, who, by law, are kept separate from the open and secure custody residents, and primarily includes, for the most part, those persons who have been convicted and sentenced to serve intermittent weekend sentences.

The PEIYC has a self-contained, fully equipped gymnasium, in-house academic program; and a total staff complement of 34.1 full-time employees who are responsible to provide intake, assessment, case management, security, rehabilitative programming, and discharge planning for its residents, who are serving both open and secure custodial sentences, as well as police lock-ups, remands, etc.

The youth workers work, in tandem, with their professional counterparts (youth justice workers) in the community setting, in order to initially identify the presenting issues, discuss appropriate case planning, and utilize individualized intervention strategies, which help to augment the young person's probability of success, especially during the important reintegration stage of the service continuum. Pursuant to section 90. (1) YCJA, when a youth sentence, involving custody, has been imposed, the provincial director in the province is required to designate what has come to be known as a reintegration worker (RW). The RW is, in turn, responsible to devise, enhance, and implement a *reintegration plan*, which clearly sets out the most effective initiatives/ programs for individual young persons, "in order to maximize his or her chances for reintegration into the community." Choosing who was going to occupy the RW role constituted a rather lengthy, reasoned, and deliberative process, with the ultimate decision being made to have the youth justice worker be the *primary worker*, who currently takes the proverbial lead when it comes to case planning and the overall case-management process. This collaborative approach, specifically in the areas of meaningful problem-solving and seeking creative solutions, has since proven to work nicely, particularly when the young person is transitioning between the custodial and community settings, as part of the standard two-thirds/one-third Custody and Supervision Order sentencing provision.

When reviewing the annual total number of resident days spent in lock-up, the greatest number (89) was attained in 2006–2007; the smallest number (12) in 2011–2012. Lock-up days were served in the secure custody unit at the PEIYC, and in the vast majority of cases were based upon provincial statute *Liquor Control Act* (LCA) violations. The young person was released from custody within 24 hours, unless additional charges were pending. The greatest total number of days spent on re-mand were based upon either pretrial detention, or, alternatively, breach of probation-related charges, and ranged from an annual low (150) in 2004–2005, to a high (597) in 2008–2009. In terms of open custody, the lowest number (580) of resident bed days was attained in 2004–2005; the highest (2,781) in 2012–2013. The number of secure custody resident days fluctuated from a low (572) in 2004–2005, to a high (1,593) in 2007–2008.

These data reveal at least two findings that require additional clarification: first, the total number of resident days increased every year, with the exception of 2007 to 2009; and fluctuated from a low (1,365) in 2004–2005, to a high (4,208) in 2012–2013, constituting an overall increase in the total annual number of resident days slightly exceeding 300%. This would appear, at first glance, to fly directly in the face of the overall purpose and intent of the YCJA, which is to demonstrably limit the use of custody as a means of dealing with young persons who come in conflict with the law. Second, the utilization of open custody, compared to secure custody committals, has gradually increased during the same time period, particularly over the course of the last three consecutive years. To understand these two anomalies, it is important to keep in mind, for instance, that one young person spending a year in either open or secure custody (365 bed days) can statistically skew the overall data distribution and mistakenly infer an entirely different reality. The truth of the matter is the province has mercifully not witnessed a young person being charged with either murder or manslaughter in recent memory, and when a serious violent offence (e.g., armed robbery, impaired driving causing death) does actually occur, it still constitutes a shock to the collective psyche of Islanders, province-wide.

In order to denote the average time spent, in days, at the PEIYC under an array of different formal sanctions available under the extensive YCJA sentencing regime, Table 10.1 depicts the average length of custodial sentences used in the province over the course of the last decade, particularly as it relates to remand, as well as open and secure custody.

Community Supervision for Young Persons in Prince Edward Island

Historically, community supervision, rather than its custodial counterpart, has been the legal remedy of choice in Canada, particularly when dealing with young persons (Ramcharan, de Lint, & Fleming, 2000). Interestingly, as a legitimate sentencing alternative in Canada, probation did not come into existence until the early 1950s (Coughlan, 1963, p. 199). In PEI, the decision to adopt probation, as the preferred means by which to provide community supervision, was made in 1972, specifically for those persons 16 years of age and older, who, in turn, fell under the administrative umbrella of the Department of Justice. Whereas, for those children who were between seven and 15 years of age, the Department of Health and Social Services would continue to maintain primary care and control, at least until the proclamation of the YOA in 1984. With the advent of the YOA, up until the allegoric threshold of its legislative equivalent on April 1, 2003, the province dealt with young offenders serving time in custody by means of a holistic, family-centred, and rehabilitative youth justice approach. However, throughout the vast majority of this same time period, those young offenders who received a community-based disposition ended up on probation with their adult counterparts, and were subjected to a distinctly different, law-and-order-based philosophical framework. Probation officers in the province, at least historically, had exhibited a more legalistic work orientation, particularly when compared to some of their professional

Table 10.1 PEI Youth Centre average length of custodial sentence

		Number of dispositions	Total length of disposition (days)	Average length of disposition
Apr–Dec 2003	Remand	9	353	39.22
	Open	17	1,200	70.59
	Secure	9	455	50.56
2004	Remand	10	172	17.20
	Open	10	176	17.60
	Secure	14	1,001	71.50
2005	Remand	19	232	12.21
	Open	19	887	49.28
	Secure	11	840	76.36
2006	Remand	19	232	12.21
	Open	26	1,447	55.65
	Secure	9	910	101.11
2007	Remand	16	361	22.56
	Open	21	1,073	51.10
	Secure	12	190	165.00
2008	Remand	17	251	14.76
	Open	15	197	13.13
	Secure	16	944	59.00
2009	Remand	36	625	17.36
	Open	20	977	48.85
	Secure	25	1,542	61.68
2010	Remand	16	262	16.38
	Open	31	1,554	50.13
	Secure	14	1,138	81.29
2011	Remand	26	216	8.31
	Open	37	1,564	42.27
	Secure	16	710	44.38
2012	Remand	19	348	18.32
	Open	23	804	34.96
	Secure	15	731	48.73
2013	Remand	23	219	9.52
	Open	20	1,075	53.75
	Secure	12	679	56.58

Source: PEI Community and Correctional Services Division.

colleagues across Canada (Lavandier, 1982); although, dealing effectively with young persons has consistently proven it requires a demonstrably different approach.

When the YCJA was proclaimed in the spring of 2003, the clear expectation was that individual provinces/territories should strive to meet national standards, yet simultaneously be solely responsible for administering a wide assortment of community-based sentences. In the case of PEI, this necessitated not only the reallocation of human resources from custodial to community programs, but more significantly, the broad-scale restructuring of the Community and Correctional Services Division, the sector of the provincial government apparatus principally responsible for the Act's overall administration. By the following November, the TVYC had already officially closed its doors on June 4, 2003, and divisional reorganization began in earnest, involving, in part, the creation of 14.5 new FTE Youth Justice Services team positions in five strategically located communities across the province (Souris, Montague, Charlottetown, Summerside, and O'Leary). The restructuring process not only brought the province into full compliance with the reorganizational and service delivery objectives spoken to in the YCJA, but more meaningfully, unequivocally transformed the overall complexion of youth justice in PEI, to the point where most practitioners in the field found the transformation irrefutably better.

This all-encompassing shift in work orientation, particularly within the community setting, has since proven to be an incremental, yet rather profound, organizational shift, whereby the entire case management function has been assumed by youth justice workers. An additional consideration was when this shift actually transpired, youth justice workers found themselves in the enviable position of dealing with caseloads less than half the size (25–35) of their adult (probation officer) counterparts, which, in turn, permitted them to spend additional time with individual young persons and their families, and develop custom-made case plans, which were both highly individualized and more likely to result in positive outcomes. It was established rather quickly that these helping professionals were not merely specialized in dealing effectively with this particular age group, but arguably and more noteworthy, were genuinely passionate about working with young persons and their families, in an attempt to have them reach their full potential in life and not become engaged in any further illegal activity.

In addition to the newly procured members of the Youth Justice Services team, the province had established the Alternative Residential

Placement (ARP) and Community Youth Worker (CYW) programs a number of years prior to the proclamation of the YCJA. Both the ARP and CYW programs constitute province-wide, community-based initiatives, with the overarching purpose of preventing youth crime and, in turn, reducing recidivism. These two programs dovetail rather nicely with the overall thrust of the YCJA, with its emphasis squarely upon reintegration and the identified target group of high-risk young persons who are, have been, or potentially could be, experiencing difficulty with the law.

The ARP Program comprises a network of specialized homes, located across the province, which provide a structured, safe, and nurturing home environment for high-risk youth and constitutes an effective alternative to custody. One of the fundamental eligibility requirements is for the young person to have a residency provision in his or her corresponding community-based supervision order, whether it be in the form of a probation order, custody and supervision order, etc. The average placement period is three to six months, and potential host families interested in providing this service are evaluated on their ability to provide a well-disciplined, structured, and caring home environment. Professional development, training opportunities, as well as ongoing support, are all offered to those who meet these specific criteria. With the introduction of the YCJA, utilization of the ARP Program has discernibly diminished; attributable, at least in part, to the increase in age of potential candidates and the corresponding lack of contractibility of these young persons to, in effect, enter into a substitute family setting.

The CYW Program provides one-to-one counselling and support services to high-risk young persons and their families. One of the program's primary objectives is to afford ongoing guidance and support to the ARPs, through regular contact, consultation, and networking with other helping agencies and community organizations. Community youth workers (CYWs) regularly help design and facilitate preventative programs, including groups involving anger management, a peer helper, roots of empathy, effective parenting of teens, and gender-specific programs. Group programming is offered based on the identified needs of individual communities, and CYWs carry out regular home visits in order to assess and strengthen family and community functioning.

Youth Justice Services also has been instrumental in developing a number of innovative school-based programming initiatives/programs in the province, which are strength-centred in design and preventative in composition, including, albeit, not limited to, the following:

Girls Circle and Boys Council Groups. Youth Justice Services staff have been certified in these two evidence-based, gender-specific programs, which are offered at both the junior high and high school levels. Both programs were initially designed to imaginatively address risk, as well as build upon protective factors, and have already given rise to demonstrably favourable outcomes, particularly in the area of crime prevention.

Multi-Agency Support Teams (MAST). Youth Justice Services staff are engaged in MAST at six different schools across the province. MAST comprises a collaborative intervention model, involving young persons with risk factors associated with a broad assortment of presenting issues, ranging from drug and/or alcohol addiction and dropping out of school, to peripheral involvement in the youth justice system. The various partners who help to comprise MAST work together in an effort to support young persons in making positive lifestyle changes.

Prevent Alcohol and Risk-Related Trauma in Youth (PARTY) Program. This program is typically delivered in high schools across the province, at approximately the same time these same young persons are graduating and/or immediately preceding their attending "prom night." The overarching message conveyed, via the PARTY Program, is students have a tremendous amount to lose if they ultimately become involved in a driving-while-impaired-related offence.

Youth Justice Services also offer at least two programs/initiatives, which are specifically designed to support Aboriginal communities in the province, which are briefly highlighted, as follows:

Daughters/Mothers/Grandmothers Circle. A culturally based program, offered in Scotchfort, which is home to one of the three reserves located in the eastern end of the province, and affiliated with the Abegweit First Nation. The program provides an environment within which Aboriginal mothers and grandmothers can strengthen ancestral intergenerational bonds through a combination of shared listening, storytelling, creative expression, and skill-building.

Youth Group Programming/Information Sessions/Pro-social Activities. This initiative takes advantage of a close-knit partnership between Youth Justice Services and the Aboriginal community of Lennox Island, which is home to Lennox Island First Nation and the province's largest reserve, situated in Malpeque Bay, just off the Island's north-west coast. This initiative offers supportive, empowering, and culturally appropriate programs and activities to Aboriginal young persons who reside on or near the reserve.

The Youth Criminal Justice Act Implementation Process

In PEI, the leading edge of the implementation process began to make its presence known approximately 18 months prior to the Act coming into force on April 1, 2003. The Community and Correctional Services Division, specifically its Youth Justice Services branch, spearheaded the effort, commencing with the secondment of human resources from within the division, in order to complete this pivotally important undertaking, including the appointment of a provincial YCJA Implementation Coordinator. One of the initially assigned tasks was to carefully review all 200 provisions of the Act in order to determine how, if at all, each one impacted the province. Next, a YCJA-related *Pocket Guide*, adapted specifically for police, was distributed to all six RCMP "L" Division detachments in the province, as well as four Municipal Police Services departments in Charlottetown, Summerside, Kensington, and Borden-Carleton. The pocket guide was originally developed by the province of Nova Scotia, with funding from the Department of Justice (Canada), and has since proven to be an extremely useful tool, particularly for police.

The YCJA Interdepartmental Implementation Committee was struck approximately one year before the Act came into effect, and consisted of a number of different stakeholders in the generic field of youth justice, including representatives from the Crown Attorneys' Office, Health and Social Services, Department of Education, RCMP and Municipal Police Services, Youth Justice Services, etc. Committee members met regularly and assumed the lead role in reviewing different provisions in the Act, anticipating potential problem areas, and examining the best ways and means of resolving identified issues that may arise. In addition, the committee identified different ways the new Act could potentially impact individual organizations/agencies such as Health and Social Services or the Department of Education, and attempted to discover best practices in order to ameliorate these same areas of concern. The YCJA Provincial Forms Committee, with representatives from the Community and Correctional Services Division, RCMP and Municipal Police Services, and Judicial Clerk's Office, created a number of new forms, a wearisome, yet integral, component of the implementation process. Comprehensive policies and procedures were formulated by a number of the primary stakeholders, including the RCMP and Municipal Police Services, Crown Attorneys' Office, Public Defender's Office, Judicial Clerk's Office, Community and Correctional Services Division, etc.

An Interdepartmental Training Subcommittee was established, which, in turn, identified, designed, and presented specialized training modules, tailor-made to meet the unique needs of a broad cross-section of individual partners, including school counsellors; social workers, Community Mental Health and Addiction Services workers, judicial clerks, Provincial Youth Justice Court judges, Community and Correctional Services Division personnel, Municipal Police Services members, etc. The RCMP employed its own training team, consisting of two co-facilitators who, over the course of two weeks, offered one full day of training to every RCMP member in the province. In addition, an information package, colloquially referred to as "YCJA in a box," was developed and distributed to all 720 RCMP detachments across Canada.

The PEI chapter of the Community & Legal Information Association (CLIA) developed and presented subject material, specifically related to the YCJA, to a number of different community groups/agencies/organizations across the province. A Youth Justice Renewal Implementation Help Team was established, comprised of a significant number of highly skilled professionals from across Canada and employed in the area of youth justice. This team, which is still operational a decade later, has proven to be an invaluable resource, essentially combining its abundant resources and responding to a broad range of ongoing implementation-related issues.

A YCJA review round-table, co-hosted by then Federal Minister of Justice, Rob Nicholson, and his provincial counterpart, the Honourable Gerard Greenan, took place in Charlottetown on August 12, 2008. Similar round-table discussions had taken place across Canada commencing the previous May. The overall objective was to consult with the various youth justice partners, ascertain their respective opinions and/or areas of concern, as well as discuss proposed revisions by the federal government, specifically related to how best to deal with violent young persons. The general consensus was the Act appropriately engaged the parents and home community of the young person; however, corresponding services/programs were not always portable and/or available in all geographical areas of the province. Overall, round-table participants agreed the YCJA appeared to be, in effect, moving in the right direction, particularly its emphasis on prevention and early intervention, and the critically important concepts of collaboration and integration.

In retrospect, at the time of these round-table discussions, the key issues identified, with respect to the YCJA, then five years old, were not discernibly different from those already brought forward in other jurisdictions and still very much in vogue today. Some of these presenting issues include (a) the overall complexity of the Act; (b) lack of sufficient resources to properly implement the YCJA and, by extension, its innovative and rehabilitative provisions; and (c) the comparatively more subtle issue, whereby the Act was then, and still is, five years later, regarded as a form of *legislative compromise*, whereby, "it endeavours to satisfy and 'hold the line' (Roberts, 2003, p. 416) against penal forces by shifting responsibility for preventing crime and sanctioning minor offenders to society as a whole, while reserving custody for persistent, non-compliant and seriously violent youth offenders" (Kramar, 2011, p. 68). This notion of *bifurcation* has been debated rather vociferously for the last decade (Bell, 2007; Bereska, 2011; Kramar, 2011), and particularly since Prime Minister Stephen Harper's Conservative Party of Canada introduced and then enacted the *Safe Streets and Communities Act* on June 13, 2012, which, arguably, merely expands the metaphorical divide between so-called violent young offenders on one side of the chasm and first-time, non-violent young persons on the other. In speaking about the potential legislative muscle of the YCJA, Kramar (2011, p. 69) makes a fervent plea to seek a different path, and proffers the following:

> On the level of practice, the act's major and overriding purpose is to reduce over-reliance on the courts and custody, not simply through a cynical bifurcation of youths and offences into minor and serious categories, but through a series of graduated extrajudicial and judicial, noncustodial and custodial sanctioning options that are designed to address the needs of all youth.

If one was of the cynical ilk, bifurcation in the context of the YCJA and of more recent vintage amendments contained within the *Safe Streets and Communities Act*, are both disconcertingly analogous to a little-known quip by celebrated big screen actor, Will Rogers, when he reminded us all that "Diplomacy is the art of saying 'nice doggy' until you can find a rock."

Charging Practices in Prince Edward Island

Even though it could reasonably be argued the rate of youth crime was, in actual fact, already decreasing in Canada prior to the proclamation of the YCJA, as is evidenced in Figure 10.1, it is equally apparent there has

Figure 10.1. Canadian and PEI rates of youth charged per 100,000 population.

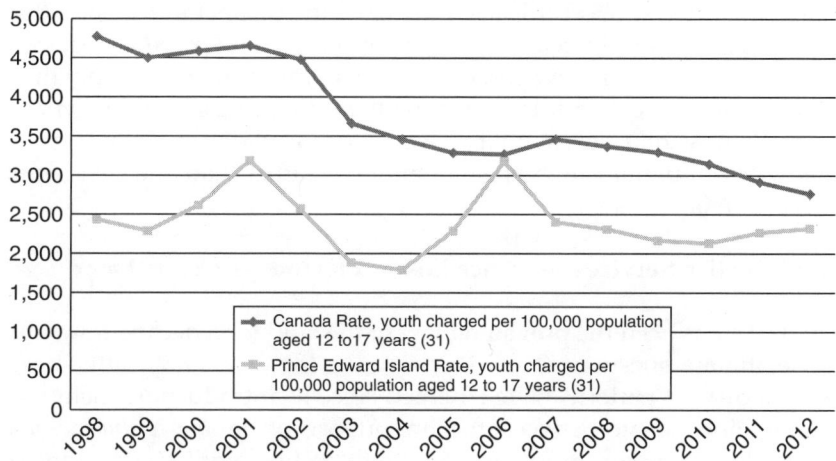

Source: CANSIM, Statistics Canada

been a well-defined and unmistakably enlightened shift in the manner in which young persons who break the law are ultimately dealt with, particularly as it relates to the so-called "front-end" of the youth justice system, which will be discussed further in a later section. Figure 10.1, for instance, using the rate per 100,000 youth/young persons aged 12 to 17 years, inclusive, and charged with all *Criminal Code* offences, indicates the national trend of high levels of police charging was already decreasing in the province, even prior to the enactment of the YCJA in 2003, commencing in the middle of 2001.

Figure 10.1 clearly illustrates the Canadian rate of decline was relatively more gradual and uniform than was the case in PEI, particularly when the two statistical relationship spikes, the first in mid-2001 and second in mid-2006, are taken into account. In an attempt to explain the well-defined incongruity in the data set, it was determined these two spikes could actually be explained, at least in part, by considering the fact that PEI has a total population slightly in excess of 145,000 inhabitants, and that a relatively small number of young persons would have to be simultaneously charged with multiple offences, as part of the same *transaction* (e.g., armed robbery into private homes and/or business establishments, or, alternatively, break and enters into private cottages during the off-season), in order to influence the data output. In addition, a common trend in most jurisdictions across the country is if youths engaged in armed robbery, for instance, have the distinct impression that there is a noticeable increase in police presence in one specific area, they more than likely will move to a different geographical area and ply their "trade" elsewhere. In addition, when attempting to analyse this type of data, the possibility exists that at least some of the charges have been brought, as it pertains to "repeat offenders," rather than one charge per young person.

Youth Justice Services in Prince Edward Island – 10 Years Later

The YCJA has been the prevailing law of the land for a decade now, and the legitimate question, "How is it working thus far?" naturally arises. Several distinct patterns have emerged since its introduction, including the ongoing debate between the importance of having a *child-welfare* versus *tough-on-crime* approach to youth justice, with the province's overall stance clearly more in line with the former. In striking contrast to the more politicized (Kramar, 2011; Bell, 2007; Schmalleger & Volk, 2014) and arguably more adversarial and crime-control, law-and-order-related approach (O'Grady, 2011) championed by the current governing Conservative Party of Canada, the province has adopted a manifestly different holistic approach to youth justice, whereby the ultimate objective is twofold. First, invest early in the life of individual young persons and do everything possible to prevent him or her from, in turn, *graduating* to the adult criminal justice system, thereby going deeper into the so-called "crime funnel." Second, it is imperative to develop and maintain individual programs that not only deter young persons from engaging in further illegal activity, but more importantly, expand their intellectual horizons and allow them to realistically look towards a brighter future.

Youth justice in PEI has evolved considerably over the course of the last decade, and like most things in life, determining "what works and what doesn't" depends, in large part, upon the person's perspective with whom you are speaking. Some of the strengths of PEI's model, arising from the YCJA, specifically in terms of its ongoing implementation, include the following:

1 The potential to invest more human and financial resources into the proverbial "front end" of the youth justice system, that is, the Youth Intervention Outreach Program, resulting in a marked reduction of a young person moving into the adult criminal justice system;

2 Using a graduated intervention approach and relying on a custodial sentence as the last resort, rather than taking a "one-size-fits-all" perspective and not tailoring the chosen intervention to meet the individual needs of the young person;

3 Having a professional, and highly motivated youth justice services staff within the Community and Correctional Services Division, who, in effect, specialize in dealing with young persons who find themselves in conflict with the law and are, in turn, more "in tune" with the multifaceted issues associated with this oftentimes challenging group dynamic, that is, Youth Intervention Outreach workers and youth justice workers in the community, combined with youth workers in the custodial setting;

4 Youth justice workers (community-based) and youth workers (custodial-based) have fewer cases, compared to their adult counterparts, thereby having more time to spend with individual young persons and their families; form partnerships with other helping agencies (i.e., schools, child and family services, community mental health and addiction services, etc.); and devise individualized case plans, which are designed with the best interests of the individual young person in mind;

5 Helping professionals in the area of youth justice, including police officers, having to strictly adhere to clear and unequivocal policies, procedures, and protocols, whereby the young person is best dealt with at the lowest possible stage or level of intervention;

6 Holding the young person accountable for becoming engaged in illegal activity by way of a number of meaningful intervention methodologies, rather than almost exclusively relying on the more crime-and-control, legalistically oriented remedies (e.g. custody, probation, monetary fines, etc.);

7 Strengthening familial and community relationships such that young persons who break the law have support systems to rely on when the need arises, whether it be in the area of mental health or addictions, education, employment, etc.

Some of the weaknesses of the YCJA, particularly as it relates to ongoing implementation process in the province, include the following:

1 In dealing with young persons who come in conflict with the law, the foundational underpinning of youth justice still appears to have a fundamentally unfair bifurcated, legalistic underpinning, and

strictly adheres to a somewhat rigid law-and-order approach in its overall practical application;

2 The YCJA has obviously become highly politicized over the last decade, particularly as it relates to the rather draconian "tough-on-crime" approach espoused by the current Conservative Party of Canada, which, according to Adler, Mueller, Laufer, and Grekul (2009, p. 7), in speaking specifically about the vast array of intervention and/or treatment methodologies involving youth justice and under the legislative umbrella sequentially of the *Juvenile Delinquents Act* (JDA) (1908), YOA (1984), and YCJA (2003), argued "Each is informed by a different philosophy that influences the manner in which youth are dealt with";

3 Restorative justice has not been sufficiently used in the province, as has been the case in a number of other jurisdictions; although, the guiding principles and substantive provisions of the YCJA clearly "endorse the use of restorative justice in youth crime and offer a statutory framework for its development" (Scott, 2011, p. 259);

4 The prevailing misguided misconception among some members of the general public appears to be that the vast majority of young persons who break the law are seasoned offenders who engage in serious criminal behaviour, rather than looking at these young people through a more measured, compassionate, and understanding lens, thereby perceiving them from a more favourable perspective;

5 The mentality of placing young persons who come in conflict with the law in custody as the most appropriate sentencing option, is unfortunately still very much alive and well; although, time and time again, it has proven itself to be disingenuous at best, and an unwarranted and indefensible indictment of our youth at its worst.

Youth Intervention Outreach Program (YIOP)

The veritable cornerstone upon which the YCJA was initially constructed, involved a deliberate and sustained effort to decrease the number of youth initially entering the formal justice system and, ultimately, spending time in custody. In anticipation of this primary and laudable objective, the Youth Intervention Outreach Program (YIOP) was established in the province in February 2002. The YIOP was not necessarily exceptional in its aspiration to reduce the number of young persons entering the formal justice system; though it was indeed the first program of its kind in the country in terms of how it intended to do so. It is a widely known fact that addressing the root causes of crime involves so much more than merely responding to the corresponding symptoms once evidenced, particularly when dealing with young persons who find themselves in conflict with the law. The YIOP was initially designed to appropriately address these root causes, and is now premised upon several key underlying program features, including an emphasis on prevention and early intervention, the significance of family and community-based solutions, voluntary participation of program participants, direct partnership with police, individualized support, resource brokerage, and advocacy.

Given that police officers are aptly referred to as either "first responders" or, alternatively, "gatekeepers," when it comes to the proverbial *front end* of the formal youth justice system, engendering a cohesive, tight-knit, and collaborative partnership between them and individual members of the YIOP team, not surprisingly, proved to be crucially important in the initial stages of implementation and subsequent ongoing success of the program. The YIOP functions according to two key operational dimensions: first, "the Youth Intervention Outreach Worker is physically co-located in the Police Department or Detachment" from where the referrals emanate, and second, using discretion, individual police officers comprise the one and "only entry point for referrals into the Program" (McQuaid & Smith, 2004, p. 3). In addition to reducing the overall number of young persons entering the formal youth justice system and correspondingly, striving to achieve a decrease in the crime rate among young persons in the province, the YIOP has simultaneously attempted to, with a noteworthy measure of success, mobilize "partners within government and the community to help support, enhance, and sustain the Program" (McQuaid & Smith, 2004, p. 5) and, by extension, strengthen the sometimes mercurial relationship between young persons and police officers in the community setting.

The YIOP, with a staff complement of four-and-a-half Youth Intervention Outreach (YIO) workers, is currently being offered at five different sites across the province, including the Kings District (Souris/ Montague), Queens District (Maypoint), and West Prince District (Elmsdale) Detachments of the RCMP, along with both Municipal Police Services departments in Charlottetown and Summerside. Admittedly, in the early developmental stage, a certain measure of trepidation on the part of some police officers existed, who were understandably somewhat reticent to fully engage in a collaborative partnership role with civilians who did not necessarily know a great deal about policing. However, as time passed, and the real strength of this innovative program began to make itself known, individual police officers and YIO workers gradually joined forces, culminating in a brand new and decidedly unique, innovative and progressive approach to community policing. In 2012, as an unequivocal and tangible sign of their overwhelming support for the program, the Queens District (Maypoint) Detachment of the RCMP hired a part-time YIO worker, who currently works out of the detachment; though is supervised by the manager of Youth Justice Services for the province, and is under the administrative umbrella of the Community and Correctional Services Division.

Police officers, particularly when dealing with young persons, have long appreciated the importance of abbreviating the elapsed period of time between the offence actually taking place and subsequently holding youth accountable for their actions. Police officers and YIO workers alike have similarly found the elapsed time between offence and intervention date has substantially decreased with the introduction of the YIOP, with individual Police officers now responding, by way of referrals, and contact with the YIO worker then taking place, within a matter of days, rather than, as previously was the case, over the course of weeks or, in some cases, months. Given that early intervention is currently the rule, rather than the exception, the likelihood of achieving positive outcomes is appreciably improved. Consistent with the axiom, "the more timely the intervention, the more meaningful it will ultimately be" coincides quite with the YIOP referral process, in that prior to taking any other action, and pursuant to section 6. (1) YCJA, a police officer shall, "with the consent of the young person, refer the young person to a program or agency in the community that may assist the young person not to commit offences."

It is important to note the investigating police officers, at the pre-charge stage of legal proceedings, may utilize their discretion and make a referral to the YIOP, as per the "community program" provision referenced in section 6. (1), and related specifically to so-called extrajudicial measures. Once the referral is made, participation in the designated community program by the young person is deemed voluntary and as a consequence, any further legal action at this stage by the police is legally prohibited. Referrals are made on the basis of offences related to a sweeping array of illegal behaviour, including damage to property, family conflict, common assault, public mischief and theft. Interventions aim to address underlying issues causing problematic behaviour, support familial ties, promote the reconnection of individual young persons with the community via pro-social activities, and reparation of harm, if and when deemed appropriate. Every effort is made by the YIO worker to choose an intervention strategy that is considered reasonable, achievable, and individually tailored to meet the identified needs of the young person.

YIO workers are acutely aware of the potential pitfalls associated with "intervention fatigue," including unduly extending the period of intervention without proper justification, and/or inadvertently creating a sense of dependency in the young person. The YIO workers also fully realize they cannot do the job themselves, and as a result work collaboratively with a number of different helping agencies and community organizations, including the Department of Education, Child and Family Services, Community Mental Health and Addiction Services, etc. When asked why the YIOP is so effective, one YIO worker responded by suggesting it is because of its individualized, strength-based approach; it diverts young persons from the formal justice system and makes them feel valued as individuals, and empowers the family unit and reconnects them to their local community.

Rather than resting upon its laurels, the YIOP has been the catalyst for a number of different innovative initiatives over the last decade, including the following:

Graffiti Wipe-Out. A program specifically designed to involve young persons, property owners, and members of the community in taking justifiable pride in eliminating graffiti in the city of Summerside, the province's second city, with a population approximating 15,000 residents (2011), by engaging the young persons who actually caused the damage. The program is offered during the summer and fall, and since its inception in 2012, Summerside Police Services have witnessed a 37% decrease in public mischief-related charges.

120 Program. A program offered in Montague, situated in the eastern end of the province, wherein young persons who have received a monetary fine as a result of an illegal possession of alcohol-related charge, are required to, in lieu of paying the fine, attend the 120 Program, which offers participants information sessions about the potential serious harm directly related to alcohol use, driving while impaired, etc.

School Presentations, in Conjunction with Police Officers. Regularly scheduled information-sharing sessions take place within the school setting, discussing age-appropriate topics that school-aged children are experiencing, often on a daily basis, including bullying, prescription drug use, vandalism, etc.

Active Parenting of Teens Program. A program offered to parents of young persons serviced through the YIOP, which designs strategies that help to address problematic behaviour and thereby strengthen the family unit.

Survival Techniques Program. A program that constitutes an adventure-based learning experience for high-risk young persons, whose primary objective is to promote positive choice-making and problem-solving, as well as offer skill-building, support, and a sense of empowerment.

Over the course of the last decade, the YIOP has proven to be an effective means by which illegal behaviour is perceived through a rehabilitative, supportive, and holistic lens. The program provides individual young persons with the opportunity to turn things around and proceed in the opposite direction, prior to finding themselves on a path that offers little else other than a lengthy criminal record and fewer bona fide opportunities to reach their full potential. Even though it is not a treatment program per se, Gendreau, Goggin, and Smith (1999, p. 180) remind us that "the effectiveness of any state-of-the-art assessment and treatment protocol is diminished, however, if careful attention is not paid as to how programs are implemented in the first place," with the YIOP being no exception. Virtually from its inception, the YIOP has been the recipient of what could only be characterized as rave reviews from both police officers who initially make the referrals, as well as the young persons and their families, the very people who benefit most from this truly life-changing youth justice initiative.

The Mi'kmaq Confederacy of Prince Edward Island (MCPEI) Mi'kmaq Prevention, Respect, Intervention, Development and Education (PRIDE) Program

In May 2005, the Mi'kmaq Confederacy of Prince Edward Island (MCPEI) Mi'kmaq Prevention, Respect, Intervention, Development and Education (PRIDE) Program, henceforth referred to as the PRIDE Program, in cooperation with the PEI Director of Child Welfare, and with the support, in principle, of the Provincial Treasury Board, submitted a proposal to the Child Welfare League of Canada, for the development of a MCPEI Mi'kmaq child and family support program. Not that long after, the PRIDE Program was established and is currently funded by Aboriginal Affairs and Northern Development Canada (AANDC), under the auspices of the Child and Family Services Program – Enhanced Prevention Funding Agreement. The PRIDE Program, with its vision, in part, to "provide a holistic and culturally sensitive approach to individual, family and community wellness," is a community-based prevention and protection support program for children and families living on reserve.

The First Nations of Prince Edward Island, Lennox Island First Nation, and Abegweit First Nation, form an integral part of the Mi'kmaq people, who have inhabited the Atlantic coast of Canada for thousands of years. The profound intergenerational impacts of the Indian Residential School System in Canada, the so-called "Sixties Scoop" and local child protection services have continued to cascade unabated throughout the collective psyche of First Nations peoples, along with feelings of deep-seated loss that have accompanied over 100 years of what has amounted to coerced assimilation, at best. With that in mind, the PRIDE Program was developed on the basis that children, families, and communities benefit most from services that are sensitive to and congruent with their own cultural beliefs and traditional value systems. One of the primary goals of the PRIDE Program is to promote the development and well-being of PEI's First Nations children, parents, and families.

The PRIDE Program employs six staff, two of whom are Community Child and Youth Care workers. The role of the Community Child and Youth Care worker is to engage children of all ages; albeit, primarily school-age children, and provide early intervention and support to assist children to develop into healthy adults. Key to the ultimate success of the PRIDE Program and its workers, as was similarly the case with the Youth Intervention Outreach Program, is the level of skill, commitment, and dedication of the staff. The Community Child and Youth Care Worker provides one-on-one services to First Nations children and youth, in order to assist them in the ongoing development of life skills, enhancement of the parent/child interaction process, and social and educational support. These helping professionals build relationships with internal and external service providers, and through these same relationships, assist in creating a viable support network for the young person. Partnerships with other programs are critically important in sustaining the PRIDE Program and have created windows of opportunities for staff to co-facilitate groups in schools, host after-school homework clubs, music programs, camps, and a broad spectrum of other special events. All these events are intended to essentially stimulate the creative juices in young persons, engage them in experiences in which they might not have otherwise had the opportunity to participate, reduce the risk of harm to themselves and/or others, and ideally help to ensure they are able to grow up in their own community and families healthy and intact.

The Mi'kmaq Confederacy of Prince Edward Island Aboriginal Justice Program

The Mi'kmaq Confederacy of Prince Edward Island (MCPEI) Aboriginal Justice Program (AJP) officially opened its doors in 2003, though had its genesis in the late 1990s. Over the course of the ensuing decade, the AJP began to spread its metaphoric wings and display its true worth, as it simultaneously underwent what could best be characterized as a lengthy developmental phase. Initially, the PEI Aboriginal Community Justice Committee, with funding from Justice Canada's Aboriginal Justice Strategy (AJS) and the Provincial Office of the Attorney General, established a program intended to increase the level of Aboriginal "citizen engagement" in the administration of justice in PEI. The original rationale for establishing the AJP, as is the case with most citizen engagement initiatives, aligned itself with providing Aboriginal peoples in the province an effective "voice," as well as the opportunity to occupy a seat at the proverbial "table." Even in its fledgling stage of development, the AJP proved to be adept in providing support, raising awareness, and developing capacity within the Aboriginal community in PEI and beyond. The AJP serves both young persons and adult offenders alike, estimated at a 50–50 split, and delivers a broad array of diverse services.

From its inception, the AJP has strictly adhered to and continues to champion four foundational guiding principles, which form the cornerstone of the AJS under the administrative egis of the Department of Justice Canada, and have been depicted as follows:

1 To contribute to decreasing rates of victimization, crime, and incarceration among Aboriginal people in Aboriginal communities operating AJS programs;
2 To assist Aboriginal people assume greater responsibility for the administration of justice in their communities;
3 To provide better and more timely information about community-based justice programs funded by the AJS; and,
4 To reflect and include Aboriginal values within the justice system.

The primary focus of the AJP has always been to heal the wound(s) inflicted by the young person or adult offender, and rehabilitate the same individual in an effort to avoid further harm, but also assist in the restoration of relationships, where and whenever possible. The AJP currently provides, at least in part, Aboriginal peoples across PEI with the milieu wherein they can rediscover their own form of "traditional justice," one that builds upon a time-honoured, consensus-building, holistic, and culturally appropriate dispute resolution tradition. It also allows Aboriginal peoples to seek restoration, harmony, and a sense of healthy balance, by looking forward, rather than back, and focusing their full and undivided attention on the needs of the individual, rather than the circumstances surrounding the commission of the offence, due process, and resultant sentencing stage of legal proceedings. Vachon (2002, p. 27) speaks to the oftentimes intransigent stance of some non-Aboriginals, when it comes to developing a parallel form of traditional justice, by expressing the following thought-provoking supposition:

> Why should it always be up to the Native people to come to city courts of justice to defend their rights and never up to the "civilized" to prove their titles in Native courts? Western man might then find it a little difficult to prove his rights in duty-community-cosmic-oral tradition-wampum-oriented-courts as Native people do in our courts based on civil law and written traditions.

One of the key components of the AJP is the "circle" process. Circles are varied in design, multidimensional in scope, and diverse in purpose. Granted, circles are by no means the only helping platform the AJP has at its disposal; however, they do undeniably constitute one avenue by which Aboriginal peoples can bridge their rich cultural legacy with a reconfigured non-Aboriginal justice system, which, candidly, has not always looked out for their best interests. The AJP, for instance, offers Conflict-Resolution Circles, which essentially provide willing participants the opportunity to actively take part in resolving their own conflicts, within an environment that robustly supports the healing process. This mode of circle enables Aboriginal peoples to mitigate conflict before it actually becomes illegal behaviour, or, alternatively, prevent conflict from arising in the first instance. The Conflict Resolution Circle and other proven efficacious adaptations of the Circle process, including Early Intervention, Sentencing, Healing, and Reintegration Circles, individually and collectively afford a seamless continuum of care for those Aboriginal peoples in the province who find themselves in conflict with the law and are, in essence, yearning for a relatively more inclusive, non-adversarial, and holistic approach to traditional justice.

In the case of Aboriginal young persons in the province, a sampling of spiritual activities, specifically designed for this particular age group, which may arise out of a circle, include the following:

- Traditional teaching, counselling, or treatment;
- Cultural awareness and sensitivity;
- Indian Residential School System awareness/counselling;
- Aboriginal singing, dancing, and/or drumming;
- Community Council Elders Sharing Circles;
- Support groups, Talking and/or Healing Circles;
- Elders teachings;
- Sweat Lodges;
- Forgiveness/Sacrifice Ceremonies;
- Arts/Regalia making;
- Offerings to the Sea;
- Community Service Work (e.g., participate at Powwows, assist elders, clean grounds, prepare and serve meals, fire keeper, etc.).

The AJP, in addition to circles, delivers a broad array of services, based upon the identified needs of individual participants, ranging from assisting him or her in securing steady employment; enrolling in some form of rehabilitative service; or attending educational workshops/presentations for young persons and/or adults on justice-related issues; as well as simply sitting down and meeting Aboriginal peoples at their "point of need." The program also promotes positive growth and mutual respect in Aboriginal and non-Aboriginal communities in the province, and strengthens the understanding of one another's uniqueness, through both training and cross-cultural sharing. The indispensable role of an elder is to pass down to future generations a veritable incalculable expanse of wisdom concerning the proud and august ancestral history, traditions, customs, values, and belief systems of First Nations peoples, and provides support to Aboriginal young persons before, during, and after a Justice Circle. Elders provide invaluable advice, assistance, and healing; are highly respected for their wealth of knowledge, as well as life experiences; and are individually selected by young persons or adult offenders, in order to offer much needed support while their kindred spirits are walking along life's sometimes rocky pathway.

One of the pivotal arguments for most, if not all, of the last decade, has focused upon how the AJP can most easily bridge/connect with the *mainstream justice system*, without simultaneously losing its substantive "self-determinate" objective, when it comes to administering justice in the Aboriginal community. One of the conflict-infused stumbling blocks, at least initially, for the Office of the Crown Attorney was its almost sacrosanct regard for "police discretion." The general consensus of members of the oversight committee was if an Aboriginal young person or adult offender broke the law and was willing to "accept responsibility" for his or her actions, the AJP would constitute a viable alternative to the mainstream justice system, particularly as it relates to the YCJA and pursuant to section 6(1). All parties concerned eventually agreed any and all mainstream criminal justice referrals to the AJP would have to go through the normal discretionary track beforehand, with individual police officers making one of two decisions: (a) make a direct referral to the AJP and have the matter dealt with under the purview of the YCJA, with most of these cases not having to proceed any further into the mainstream justice system; or, (b) recommend placement in the Alternative Measures Program, which operates under the administrative umbrella of the Community and Correctional Services Division in the province. In addition, it was agreed the AJP would have to work closely with either Probation (adult offenders) or Youth Justice (young persons) Services, in order to ensure strict adherence to proper legal procedures, particularly in the area of enforcement.

The initially envisioned goals and objectives of the AJP have not demonstrably changed since its humble beginnings a decade ago, in that, appreciable time, energy, and resources continue to be brought to bear in an attempt to educate Aboriginal peoples concerning the ways and means of the mainstream justice system. They also help bring those few Aboriginal persons who find themselves in conflict with the law, to what they themselves regard as a "better place." The Right Honourable Paul Martin, Canada's former prime minister between 2003 and 2006, and founder of the Martin Aboriginal Education Initiative, enunciated in a recent interview that "Aboriginal Canadians are the youngest and the fastest growing segment of our population, a great deal of our future depends upon them." Current sentencing trends in Canada, combined with a rapidly growing and youthful demographic among First Nations peoples across the country, does not necessarily bode well for future generations of Aboriginal children; however, "providing timely and effective alternatives to mainstream justice processes in appropriate circumstances" (Office of Strategic Planning and Performance Management, 2013, p. i), like the AJP, would seem like a promising way to begin the profoundly prized and transformational healing process.

In an effort to meet this seemingly Herculean task head-on, the AJP continues its proud tradition of dealing with Aboriginal young persons and adult offenders in a manner that is culturally sensitive, and as the AJP Mission Statement so aptly asserts, the Mi'kmaq Confederacy of Prince Edward Island Aboriginal Justice Program constitutes one more avenue by which "Aboriginal people in PEI can speak as one, with one history, as one voice for justice."

Summary Remarks

The YCJA, a decade later, has long since lost its original lustre, when its strongest proponents were still very much in the midst of espousing grandiose assertions, which have not necessarily all withstood the test of time. Due to its sheer size and complexity, it is understandable why even highly skilled helping professionals, who, for all practical purposes, work with this particular piece of federal legislation on a daily basis, are somewhat conflicted as to what actually constitutes its primary objectives. However, at some point, it would seem imperative to move beyond the nebulous inner machinations of the Act and consider proven best practices, some which have been highlighted here. The matter of determining the best means by which to deal effectively with young persons who have come in conflict with the law has been a source of considerable and sometimes acrimonious debate for well over a century in this country, and unless there is a monumental shift in the public discourse, competing divergent views will continue to be embraced, and the young person, yet again, will be left standing in the proverbial breach.

A disconcerting narrative, which appears to have taken on a life of its own and gained considerable momentum over the course of the last decade, is the ill-advised contention that violence among the youth demographic is rampant, and other than lengthy periods of incarceration, meaningful remedies are few and far between. The reality of youth justice in Canada does not necessarily support this assertion, with crime rates among the younger age group steadily declining and alternative, more holistic sentencing options repeatedly proving their worth. Bifurcated justice, often with a politicized bent, has similarly proven to be problematic and fallen short of the ideal. Intervention strategies, whether they be preventive or remedial in their intended purpose, are regrettably based principally upon past behaviour, rather than future potential, thereby making it practically impossible for a certain number of young persons to rid themselves of the immobilizing shackles of a troubled past. The opposing argument, as expressed by Kramar (2011, p. 71) proposes the YCJA's "bifurcated or graduated strategy is effectively capturing and targeting smaller numbers of persistent, noncompliant and seriously violent youth offenders for intensive interventions," which, in the view of some, unfortunately translates into lengthy periods of time spent in secure custody. Bell (2007, p. 59) argues from a relatively more balanced perspective, suggesting the end result of a bifurcated youth justice system is "one set of rules, rights and protections for minor offenders and another for those charged with more serious offences, the system will be a very different experience for youth depending on which 'half' she or he falls into." Finding the proper corrective blend of rehabilitation and punishment has always been a rather daunting challenge for practitioners in the field of youth justice and members of the general public alike, regardless of where they fall along the intervention continuum.

In conclusion, the Province of Prince Edward Island is well positioned to deal effectively, compassionately, and fairly with young persons who find themselves in conflict with law over the course of the ensuing decade and well beyond. With this objective in mind, the Honourable Minister of Environment, Labor, Justice and the Attorney General, Janice Sherry, in a speech delivered in the PEI legislature on November 14, 2013, declared, "The main goal of Youth Justice Services is to reduce the number of young people entering or re-entering the formal justice system. As a Department, we strongly believe that helping young people through prevention is much more preferable than having them enter the formal justice system." Minister Sherry went on to say, "By strategically locating programs and services throughout the Province, a system of community support increases the rate of our success." Or, as eminent 20th- century American cultural anthropologist Margaret Mead once enunciated: "The solution to adult problems tomorrow depends on large measure upon how our children grow up today."

REFERENCES

Adler, F., Mueller, G. O. W., Laufer, W. S., & Grekul, J. (2012). *Criminology* (2nd Ed.). Toronto, ON: McGraw-Hill Ryerson.
Bell, S. J. (2007). *Young offenders and youth justice: A century after the fact* (3rd Ed.). Toronto, ON: Nelson.
Canada. (2013). *Public law sector evaluation, final report*. Office of Strategic Planning and Performance Management.

Coughlan, D. W. F. (1963). The history and function of probation. *The Canadian Bar Journal, 16*, 198–213.

Gendreau, P., Goggin, C., & Smith, P. (1999). The forgotten issue in effective correctional treatment: Program implementation. *International Journal of Offender Therapy and Comparative Criminology, 43*, 180–187.

Kaufman, F. (2002). *The Stratton Report (Chapter V). Searching for justice: An independent review of Nova Scotia's response to response to reports of institutional abuse*. Vol. I. Province of Nova Scotia.

Kramar, K. (2011). *Criminology: Critical Canadian perspectives*. Toronto, ON: Pearson.

Lavandier, F. T. (1982). *A comparative study of work orientation in Saskatchewan and Prince Edward Island*. Unpublished master's thesis, University of Saskatchewan, Saskatoon, Saskatchewan.

McQuaid, S., & Smith, N. (2004). *Evaluation of the Youth Intervention Outreach Program*, Atlantic Evaluation Group Inc. Community and Correctional Services Division, Office of the Attorney General.

Ramcharan, S., de Lint, W., & Fleming, T. (2001). *The Canadian Criminal Justice System*. Toronto, ON: Prentice Hall.

Roberts, J. V. (2003). Sentencing juvenile offenders in Canada: An analysis of recent reform legislation. *Journal of Contemporary Criminal Justice, 4*, 413–434.

Scott, H. (2011). *Victimology: Canadians in context*. Don Mills, ON: Oxford University Press.

Vachon, R. (2002). Beyond the religion of human rights, the nation state, and the rule of law. *Inter Culture, 143*, 1–60.

11 The Situation in Quebec, "Vive la différence"?

MARC ALAIN AND SYLVIE HAMEL

Introduction

Most Quebeckers are firmly convinced that their situation, history, society, and culture, among other things, are unique and significantly different from what is referred to in Quebec as "the rest of Canada." But as we will explain in detail in this chapter, this commonplace Quebec perspective is more perception than reality regarding how this province has reacted historically to major changes in the federal laws regarding juvenile delinquency and young offenders including the *Youth Criminal Justice Act* (YCJA) and its recent reforms in Bill C-10. Perhaps, though, this general impression in Quebec of profound differences between itself and the other Canadian provinces, particularly by most people working in the youth justice system under the YCJA, is a reflection of how very little is known about youth justice practices and systems in the English-speaking provinces. Moreover, even within Quebec, as will also be evident later in this chapter, not much is known about the differences from one Quebec region to another, other than the most general aspects of the YCJA.

This chapter is divided into three parts. The first consists of a historical and sociological perspective on how the current juvenile justice system evolved in Quebec. Without such a historical context, it is extremely difficult to understand the unique and somewhat bewildering aspects of youth justice in the province. For example, only a single institution, the Youth Centre, is responsible for both the provincial child protection mandates and most of the administration of sentences under the federal YCJA. The second, more empirical part of this chapter involves a description of the results of a provincial survey regarding the reactions to and more general perspective of the YCJA by the key YCJA officials responsible for the implementation of this law. Two additional survey themes are described and discussed: how the YCJA was presented to these officials and how they made the transition from the former *Young Offenders Act* to the YCJA. As well, and more specifically, how did they adapt their routine practices in response to the new roles and options available to youth criminal justice officials in youth centres that are responsible for sentencing principles and objectives. The third part includes examples of potentially innovative intervention programs developed by two Quebec youth centres to fulfil the new YCJA mandates: the Montreal Youth Centre program regarding street gang intervention; and the Quebec City Youth Centre program to provide counsellors involved in probation supervision with better, uniform guidelines for their day-to-day practices with youths and their parents. Finally, in conclusion, we will present Quebec institutions' perspective on the most recent decisions of the federal authorities to reinforce some of the more punitive aspects of the YCJA.

Historical, Political and Sociological Evolution of Quebec's Approaches towards Troubled Youths

In Quebec, there has been a long history of a highly concentrated and formal institutional/bureaucratic response to children and adolescents "in trouble" associated with delinquent and criminal behaviours. The involvement of communities and community-based organizations in juvenile delinquency rehabilitation is both relatively new and not as widespread as in other provinces. It is only since the implementation of the new YCJA provisions that community-based organizations fulfil new roles. One outcome has been tensions that still exist between these organizations and the central and traditional youth justice public institution, the Quebec Youth Centres. While these tensions involve more recent history, it is important to briefly review the distinctive historical role the Roman Catholic Church has played in Quebec regarding children, youth, and families. This history, in part, explains why there is tension between non-governmental and government organizations in the contemporary period dating from the Quiet Revolution in the 1960s and the advent of the nationalist/separatist Parti Quebecois governments during much of the last 30 years. In other words, Quebec society underwent fundamental political, economic, and social changes during the last 60 years, unlike any parallel changes in the other provinces, which are reflected in youth justice laws and policies in this province.

Politically, a culture has evolved that emphasizes a predominant role for formal government institutions in providing extensive services to its residents, especially vulnerable families and youth.

From the French Regime to the Predominance of the Catholic Church in French Canada's Social Welfare

Needless to say, beginning in the 16th century, life in New France was harsh for French pioneers, who lived in geographical conditions that were quite different from those in Europe of that era. Children in all such colonies were expected to actively participate in survival tasks on almost equal terms with adults. Social and political conditions, however, were not very different from the home countries in continental Europe: political systems and institutions in the colonies were replicas in varying degrees of the predominant monarchical and aristocratic governments these pioneers often thought they had left behind.[1] For France, New France – as well as all its other colonies – was considered an economic reservoir of material goods where commercial trade primarily benefited the French royalty and its own government treasury. Very little consideration was accorded to the social problems that began to emerge in the small cities of New France. Soon, a significant number of vagrant youths were running in the streets of Quebec City and Montreal trying to survive (Justice Canada, 2012). According to available historical sources, youth criminality consisted essentially of minor offences, such as vandalism, simple thefts, immoral acts, blasphemy, and street fights (D'Amours, 1986). However, while youth crimes were overwhelmingly minor, punishments were severe:

> Penal practices and conditions in New France were harsh. On 19 January 1649 a young girl of 15 or 16 was hanged for theft in the town of Quebec. Punishments were freely handed out for every type of infraction. For swearing a person could be fined or put in detention. Repeat offenders could be put in an iron collar and subjected to public ridicule, while chronic recidivists could have their lower lip cut. Those put in jail were given a diet of bread and water. Jails were poorly ventilated, humid in the summer and cold in the winter. In 1686 Governor Denonville reported having to cut the feet off certain prisoners in Quebec for purely medical reasons: they had developed gangrene from the cold. Sentencing was given little uniformity by either principle or practice, and severe punishments were handed out for both major and minor crimes. (Carrigan, 2004, p. 9)

Even though judges in the colonial period tended to sentence youths to less severe conditions than those imposed on adults for a similar offence, jails made no real distinctions between adults and youths (Carrigan, 2004). For those very few institutions that were able to specifically take care of children, no distinctions were made between youths in need and young criminals. Most importantly, in France as well as in New France, these latter institutions were operated by the Roman Catholic Church.[2] The church was seen as having a primary role in the moral salvation of "wayward" families, and especially children, since the hegemonic theory of child and adult criminality was based on the theological assertion of the central role of the devil and evil.

By the latter part of the 18th century, France and other European countries gradually began to create public institutions responsible for families and individuals in need of public assistance for reasons such as poverty, health and mental health, and child abandonment. This was accelerated in France after the historic French Revolution of 1789 and in the subsequent Napoleonic period up to 1815. Both France and the newly formed German state developed large scale government ministries and agencies to provide citizens with a wide array of services by the second half of the 19th century. Nevertheless, these responsibilities remained completely under the control of the Church in New France, and in the colony of Lower Canada after the 1760 English conquest. When the British Parliament passed the *Quebec Act* of 1774, it reinforced the well-established control by the Roman Catholic Church not only over the social welfare system but also schools. Finally, when the British Parliament passed the *British North America Act* of 1867 to create the new dominion of Canada, this traditional role of the Catholic Church having near absolute control over social affairs in Quebec remained unchallenged until the beginning of the Quiet Revolution of the 1960s mentioned above. This crucial era is discussed in further detail later. Again, this very early predominance of the church over social affairs in Quebec, which continued into the second half of the 20th century, remains important in explaining why youth justice institutions in this province are still highly centralized today and why there is a reluctance to adopt decentralized options for community initiatives. However, another important theme involves how Quebec's provincial and municipal governments evolved from the British colonial period through to the 1960s.

For the entire 18th century and the first third of the 19th century, Quebec's economy was agrarian and the majority of its population, rural

(Hamelin & Provencher, 1990). Politically, the first independent municipal governments in both Quebec City and Montreal were established in
1842 (Lacoursière, 1995; D'Amours, 1986). The rise of municipal governments was directly related to a slow but steady movement of rural populations towards employment opportunities in the industries developed
in and around the cities. This industrial growth and related population
shift accelerated by the beginning of the 20th century.[3] It was primarily with the growth of cities that Quebec's legislature in 1869 passed its
first law regarding the control of juvenile delinquency. This law created
the "Reform schools" ("Écoles de réforme") and the "Industrial schools"
("Écoles d'industrie"), the former intended for delinquent youths and the
latter for youths needing protection and social support, mainly vagrants,
orphans, and victims of abuse. Most importantly, though, the 1869 Act effectively further formalized the control of religious institutions and their
congregations over "troubled" youth. The economic advantage of this
approach was that the provisions of these social services by the churches
and other religious organizations relied on their extensive networks of
volunteers rather than solely provincial taxes. Interestingly, this Quebec
approach, according to Ménard (2005) and Fecteau (1998), resulted in the
province being the innovative leader compared to other provinces concerning youth rehabilitation efforts. However, this trend was reversed at
the turn of the 20th century, when English-speaking provinces gradually
and, for the most part, adopted public measures that put most interventions, such as probation and foster families, back under the control of
communities (Ménard, 2005).

The importance of this distinctive Quebec history of the treatment
of children and adolescents in "trouble" by sending them to reform
schools for delinquencies and industrial schools for "social needs" is reflected in a similar rationale evident in the present discourses of Quebec
Youth Centre personnel. The latter maintain there are no fundamental
differences between such youth, therefore, they can be sent to the same
institutions (Strimelle, 1998). Strimelle and Ménard (2003) asserted that
the programmatic differences between reform schools and industrial
schools, historically, quickly became more theoretical than substantive:

> In fact, the creation of both industry and reform schools rested on the con-
> cept of offering the "residents" a better and more humane treatment. This
> concept, however, resulted in uniform treatments for both clienteles.
> (Ménard, 2005, p. 75)[4]

These researchers asserted the differences disappeared because youth in both types of institutions were treated rather equally based on their similar need for protection, mostly from themselves.

A related development occurred in Quebec regarding the evolution of specialized juvenile courts after the passage of the federal *Juvenile Delinquents Act* of 1908. In 1912, the Montreal Youth Court was established for both youths in need and those assessed for delinquency. At that time, Quebec was the first province in Canada to have deliberately chosen a global approach jurisdictionally by incorporating both "troubled" youths and youths in "trouble." Ménard (2005) and Trépanier and Tulkens (1995) asserted that the creation of this dedicated court further blurred the distinctions between the two types of youth, especially by imposing very similar types of measures directed at the youths and their families.[5] It was not until 1950 that the Youth Court was separated into two distinct jurisdictions, one for delinquent youth and one for youth who were victims of social problems.

Returning to Roman Catholic industrial and training schools in Quebec at the end of the 19th century, Montreal's Mont Saint-Antoine, founded in 1873, is one of the most important institutions in the history of juvenile corrections in Canada. Initially, Mont Saint-Antoine was consistent with other institutions elsewhere in North America and in Europe of that era that were dedicated to young delinquents. Intervention and physical conditions were less severe than those found in adult prisons, and the main objective was youth rehabilitation in their community of origin. For instance, youths slept in dormitories instead of individual cells like adult prisons, and the use of a reward system was favoured over punishment in motivating them. Since most youths going to this institution were from Montreal, the youth facility was quickly moved from Saint-Vincent-de-Paul, situated north of the Island of Montreal, to the new facility, directly in the city centre. It was proposed, at that time, that rehabilitation would be facilitated by this proximity. Nonetheless, Mont Saint-Antoine was still considered a prison, and very soon the routine program philosophy became increasingly similar to the predominant adult system; discipline became harsher and moral training took over the regular school program and professional skills training. A first inquiry in 1893 revealed the low level of skill and training of the youths from Mont Saint-Antoine who were hired by Montreal industries (Ménard, 2003). Public and ecclesiastic authorities quickly terminated this inquiry. Parents complained that their children had been subject to unjustified and arbitrary harsh physical punishment by the monks who were counsellors at the institution. This reaction from the authorities must be put in the context of the period, which immediately followed the Canadian Confederation:

> Monseigneur Bourget [the most important ecclesiastic authority in the province during this period] materialized his plan for the Catholic Church to gain almost total control over every social institution in the province of Quebec [schools, hospitals, asylums, etc.]. (Fecteau, Ménard, Strimelle & Trépanier, 1998; Pouliot, 1956)

While the English parts of Canada of this era gradually introduced more community-based approaches to rehabilitate their delinquents, Quebec completely abandoned such approaches in favour of institutional set-ups. The provinces, at that time, had limited taxation powers, and Catholic congregations could count on vast numbers of underpaid workers to take care of social institutions, an arrangement that was also quite beneficial for provincially elected authorities. Almost from its beginnings, Mont Saint-Antoine, originally intended for delinquents and as such labelled a "reform school," also took care of youngsters assigned to "industry schools," and treated both clientele indiscriminately (Ménard, 2003, p. 79).

According to specialized historians, the enactment of the first Canadian *Juvenile Delinquents Act* of 1908 did not change the established practices of institutionalizing young delinquents in Quebec. Directly following the provisions of the Act, Quebec opened its first youth delinquency court in 1912. Although the official objective of this court was to favour probation measures over institutionalization, not much changed in reality, and judges at that time still saw youth prisons as the best solution.[6] While both Quebec's conservative government headed by Maurice Duplessis (in power from 1936 to 1939 and from 1944 to 1959) and the Catholic Church of this period still hesitated to adopt non-institutional measures, things gradually started to change at Mont Saint-Antoine. The first social workers were hired as professionals in the early 1940s, while a psychological counselling bureau opened its doors in 1947. It was not until 1950, with the enactment of a new law intended to protect youths in need, that Quebec slowly started to understand the limitations of institutionalization for the treatment of young delinquents. It thus agreed for the first time to recognize the existence of a positive link between harsh social conditions and the appearance of delinquency and social problems.

The 1960s "Révolution tranquille" and the Gradual Empowerment of the Central State: The Creation of Youth Centres

Throughout most of the 1960s, Quebec went through major social and political reforms, a period known as the "Quiet Revolution." The election of a liberal government in 1960, after the long reign of the conservatives, was marked by an almost complete re-engineering of the province's state structure. Social institutions, such as schools, hospitals, and institutions devoted to youth, were among those mostly affected by the reform. The Catholic Church's rule over these institutions was replaced by state-controlled mechanisms within a very short time. In 1960, the Quebec legislature enacted the *Child Protection Act*, which replaced the 1950 law. The Act retained the important notion of the former law whereby, to receive services, youths or their representatives had to go to a special youth court for a judge to decide whether they needed protection and which type of services they would receive. Quebec replaced this mechanism only in January 1979, with the amendment to the *Child Protection Act*, which would instate the Child Protection Director. This was a non-judicial position, which would have complete authority over the receipt and processing of complaints regarding youths in need of protection.

From 1963 to 1970, the first completely state-financed secular network of social agencies began to take care of the elderly, as well as children in need of protection and delinquents. In 1971, the Quebec legislature adopted a new health and social services law, which resulted in the integration of some 60 agencies into 14 social services areas. Over the years, the number of areas gradually grew to 16 (recently to 18 with the integration of social care institutions for First Nations and Inuit). In cities like Quebec and Montreal, the older institutions, once ruled by religious congregations, are still being used by the youth centres as administrative and service-providing bases. Regional youth centres are set up in each of these 18 areas and are mandated to take care of youths in need of protection as well as youths convicted of a crime. Each regional youth centre has its own Child Protection Director, who also acts as the director for the application of YCJA sentences and measures. This double mandate appears to be unique in Canada, where one person is responsible for the application of a provincial and a federal law. However, in accordance with the general principle that a youth convicted of a crime is above all a youth who needs services and advice, it makes sense in Quebec to have one person acting for both mandates. In some ways, this phenomenon may be linked to the time when religious congregations took care of the two clienteles, most often under the same roof. As we will see later on in this chapter, however, this duality and the basic notion applied in Quebec that a troubled youngster is a youngster in need, is still at the base of numerous controversies between provincial and federal justice authorities.

But besides the fact that the two functions fulfilled by Quebec's provincial directors could be linked to some of the roles previously performed by religious authorities, it may also be linked to Canada's first *Juvenile Delinquents Act*. This law, as previously discussed in Chapter 1, revolved around the *parens patriae* principle, under which youths found guilty of a crime could not truly be held responsible for their actions. Within a positivist philosophy that clearly separated youth crime from adult crime (Trépanier, 1986, p. 198), the more protective role assumed by Quebec's youth centres and their respective provincial directors was in line with the objectives of the law. As we will soon see, however, with the major amendments introduced by the 1984 *Young Offenders Act* and, moreover, with the 2003 enactment of the YCJA, Quebec had reason to argue against these changes, since its own system was based on a philosophy of care rather than youth accountability and the protection of society. From a purely statistical standpoint, it seems that "Quebec's way" provided good results: the province had and still has the lowest youth crime rates among the Canadian provinces. However, to say that this system is the main reason for these rates remains to be undeniably proven, a task that, to our knowledge, has not yet been attempted.

Administering Youth Justice in Quebec: Youth Centres as the Hub of the Intervention Wheel

Whereas courts and judges remain at the base of the decisions made under the YCJA, youth centres throughout Quebec, with close to 11,000 employees, are responsible for the administrative follow-up of cases. However, the provisions of the law offer police officers numerous opportunities to divert youths from a judicial path. A police officer may decide to do nothing, or may give the youth an unofficial warning, in which case no file is open in Quebec's police information system. When an official warning is issued, a file is open and accessible to all police officers in the province. Still among the extrajudicial measures, officers can send youths directly to one of the many alternative justice organizations in Quebec. These organizations were given new, broader responsibilities with the enactment of the YJCA, and will be described in further detail later in this section. Finally, before submitting a file to a detective or a prosecutor, an officer may opt to send the youth directly to a local youth centre for the provincial director to take charge. This is the first instance where youth centres come into play.

As is the case in similar institutions elsewhere in Canada, the provincial director is the first person responsible for young offenders under his or her authority, whether through extrajudicial measures or after a sentence is imposed by the youth court. Directly under the director's authority are the youth delegates (YD). YDs are considered professionals in the institution and, as such, are all university graduates[7] and members of professional associations, such as the social workers association and its equivalents for psychoeducation,[8] psychology, and criminology. Since there are no probation officers (PO) for youths in Quebec, YDs assume most functions usually performed by POs: assessment and evaluation, pre-sentencing reports, youth case follow-ups, management, and recommendations (including follow-ups with alternative justice organizations and the court when required) and report writing. In most youth centres, the YDs form teams, along with inside (closed custody) and outside educators, headed by a chief of service. Some youth centres split the teams according to specific mandates, for example, YCJA cases or child protection cases, while others mix the two mandates. While most YDs work exclusively with YCJA files, some professionals have youths assigned to their caseload for criminal offences and/or a protection matters. This is sometimes the case where services are decentralized, in rural areas, for instance. It should be noted, however, that in both cases (YCJA-specific or dual YCJA and child protection mandates), the youth centres' professionals have complete access to electronic files on all youths under their employer's responsibility. While this element certainly has some positive impacts, it also raises important questions regarding permeability issues between two systems deployed for very different basic purposes. Most YDs in youth centres started their career as child protection agents and applied later on for a position on a YCJA team. One of the reasons for this professional path is that working mostly, or exclusively, with YCJA cases is considered somewhat easier (less crisis management, regular schedules, more office and paper work, and so on) and is therefore limited by union agreements. In other words, those who arrive as YDs are significantly older and more experienced than their counterparts acting as child protection agents.

From the YOA to the YCJA: The Actors' Perspective

After briefly describing Quebec's youth justice apparatus, we will now turn our attention to those who are at the heart of this apparatus. One of the most important objectives of this book is to reflect these professionals' perceptions of their role and the roles of those with whom they work. As we will see in the case of Quebec, opinions on the YCJA vary considerably from one intervention level and sector to another. Therefore, what emerges from interviews may be represented, at times, as nodes of opinions and, at other times, as nodes of collaboration. As we will also see, collaboration does not necessarily mean being of the same opinion. Before covering this topic, we will present the research methodology we used and explain who the respondents are, as well as how the interviews were conducted and in what context.

Elements of Research Methodology

The Social Science and Humanities Research Council of Canada (SSHRC) in 2007 funded the fieldwork for this research, which began in mid-2009. Given the controversies that historically have accompanied youth justice reforms in Quebec both internally and with the federal government, it was not surprising that 18 months of correspondence and research protocol negotiations were necessary to obtain official permission to access youth centre workers. As previously discussed, despite Quebec's highly centralized administrative structures governing its youth centres, permission from one youth centre's ethics committee did not necessarily guarantee us the right to conduct interviews in another youth centre. Of the five youth centres approached during this negotiation phase, four finally agreed to participate by allowing the researchers to organize interviews with groups of 8 to 10 participants. One objective of the initial research strategy was to conduct interviews in a geographic and socio-economic representative sample among the 16 youth centres in Quebec. In order to obtain as representative a sample as possible of the diverse socio-economic and geographical contexts, the sample, therefore, includes Quebec's two major urban centres, (Montreal and Quebec City), and two regional centres. The latter consisted of a semi-urban (suburban) region and a decentralized rural region.

For each of these four youth centres and regions – as well as a fifth region where the youth centre refused to participate – representatives

Table 11.1 Description of research participants

Organizations and functions (number of participating regions)	n
Youth centre counsellors, educators, and department heads (4)	34
Community-based alternative justice organizations (5)	9
Youth police officers (3)	8
Crown prosecutors (2)	3
Judge (1)	1
Total	55

of other organizations involved in youth trajectories through the YCJA were interviewed in order, first of all, to gather their opinions regarding the law and the roles they have to fulfil and, second, to better understand their own perspectives on the roles played by their counterparts. More precisely, the interview themes were:

• How did they handle the transition from the YOA to the YCJA;
• What is their overall opinion of the YCJA;
• What do they think of their own work and interventions with youth;
• What do they know and what do they think of the work and interventions done by their counterparts from other organizations (what is shared and why; what is not shared and why);
• Has the general profile of convicted youths changed significantly since 2003 and if so, in what way?

In all, 55 people were interviewed in Quebec over the course of seven months, distributed as illustrated in the table above.

The Dissemination of Information on YCJA in Quebec

In most other Canadian provinces, the YCJA was disseminated typically by the respective young offender correctional services across to the other professionals involved in youth justice-related roles including police officers, educators in custody centres, and people from community and foster-care organizations. In British Columbia, for example, the Ministry of Child and Family Development undertook the analysis and planning manuals that were distributed to other ministries and agencies including non-governmental ones. This did not occur in Quebec. Legal counsellors from Quebec's Ministry of Justice and Ministry of Social Affairs first translated the YCJA into French and undertook the analyses of its potential impacts on Quebec's model of youth justice. However, in addition, the largest police organizations in Montreal and Quebec City also had their own counsellors analyse the new YCJA provisions regarding police functions and roles. These police analyses remained within their respective organizations and focused on new procedure codes intended for patrolling officers and youth crime investigators. In contrast, the community organizations' representatives involved in the proposed new roles (primarily with judicial alternative sanctions options), who were interviewed for our research, were directly informed by representatives of the federal Ministry of Justice.[9]

The Quebec legal counsellors concluded that the YCJA was unnecessarily complicated and, more importantly, based on a youth justice model fundamentally different from Quebec's approach regarding serious and violent young offenders. For these youths, the sentencing philosophy was seen as shifting from the focus on their individual risk and protective factors, including complex family and neighbourhood factors, to reciprocity between the severity of the crime and the severity of sentence. In other words, the YCJA was seen in this Quebec analysis as too punitive and insufficiently rehabilitative. Very quickly most Quebec politicians and government officials argued that the YCJA represented yet another example of the federal government's enacting laws in response to public opinion in English-speaking provinces without consideration of Quebec's distinct history, traditions, and desires. As discussed above, there was a long history of a distinctive approach to youth justice in this province that continued into the contemporary period between the 1970s and the beginning of the 21st century. Quebec's de-emphasis of the stigmatizing of youth associated with judicial processing in favour of an administrative non-labelling process focused on assisting youth and their families effectively had become culturally valued. This negative view of the YCJA permeated the discourse engaged in by youth centre authorities, youth delegates, heads of services, and specialized educators. This perspective gradually spread to other organizations but at different rates and degrees depending on the type of organization and their geographic location. How this dissemination occurred was explored in the above interviews and is discussed in the next section.

Nodes of Opinions and Nodes of Collaborations: The Perspectives of Key Youth Justice Personnel a Decade after the Enactment of the YCJA

Police Officers, Crown Prosecutors and Judges

As in other provinces, the police are typically most routinely in contact with youth and young offenders in non-custodial settings such as in immediate neighbourhoods and other public spaces. Not surprisingly given their limited roles under the YOA, police officers interviewed in the three different regions were almost unanimous that, at first, the YCJA appeared to be a much more complicated law primarily because of the new discretionary powers involved with extrajudicial measures. These measures also further entailed more formal police contacts with representatives of other organizations (especially community-based ones). Applying the alternative measures and such contacts with other agencies was seen as leading to substantially increased paperwork. Yet, for police officers, this supplementary paperwork, especially concerning minor offending incidents, was viewed as wasted effort and time because the alternative measures were seen as not dissuading youth from continuing to engage in minor offending or delinquencies. However, the largest police organizations developed precise guidelines for patrol officers and specialized youth officers. These guidelines were gradually adopted by police forces in smaller cities, and now similar procedure codes, for example, regarding interventions with youth, are in place throughout Quebec. Nonetheless, most police officers continue to believe that extrajudicial measures and related recording requirements have not been effective, and, further, that these measures complicate their paperwork presentation of those cases reported on to the prosecutor:

> I have a file for a youngster who had been implicated in street fights eleven times. He had never been prosecuted! In some cases, the evidence was not strong enough, while in other instances, he simply was not accused. The last time I caught him, I had everything needed for the court, but since nothing had happened in the ten previous fights, the case was dropped for absence of antecedents.
>
> A patrol officer in Quebec City[10]

Again, the key theme is that the police processes involving the use of their discretionary powers under the YCJA are codified and frequently involve recording paper work without perceived positive outcomes for the youth. For the majority of officers and prosecutors interviewed, which included a small number of dedicated officers, detectives, and prosecutors, the more elaborate extrajudicial measures are a major reason why some youths engage in progressively more serious crimes. These officers asserted that these minor offenders typically do not face real consequences until they reach the end of adolescence. And, in addition, the extensive paperwork associated with cases going forward to prosecutors results in an unacceptable burden on the limited number of already over worked prosecutors:

> In our sector alone, we have two prosecutors, for youth as well as adult crimes. Me alone, I can process at least five to six cases per week. And everyone I know does the same! I don't know how the prosecutors can cope with that; personally, it would drive me insane!
>
> A youth detective in Montreal

Yet, in contrast to the above negative police perspective, there were police officers at two sites who expressed positive opinions on the YCJA as a result of their accumulated experiences with this law. For these officers, extrajudicial measures, as well as some other discretionary police actions, resulted in actual benefits for some youth:

> We also can be quite stubborn with some adolescents; I can give a youth three or four warnings, and he will stop there after that. For me, the YCJA gives me latitude I feel I did not really have with the previous law.
>
> A police officer from Longueuil

While this positive police perspective initially only occurred over time with a few officers, it will be evident in other chapters of this book that there appears to be a consensus among most actors working under the YCJA, not only in Quebec but also in other provinces, that the YCJA is seen as relatively efficient in diverting youths involved with minor or petty crimes. Nonetheless, the police remain among the most prevalent who assert that a gradualist approach in responding to minor multiple offending results in delayed or no deterrence effects. Accordingly, young offenders sentenced under the YCJA have been substantially older than those under the YOA (Bala, Carrington, & Roberts, 2009).

Still, despite this police concern about extrajudicial measures and sanctions, there appeared to be a positive perspective from the police concerning their working relationships with prosecutors for those cases that proceed to judicial proceedings when there was sufficient prosecutorial staff available. This staffing issue varies by type of region; not surprisingly, it is the large urban centres where the challenges have been most acute. Another factor that appeared to contribute to a positive working relationship between police and prosecutors was that police officers were trained by prosecutors and legal counsellors from the Ministry of Justice and the Ministry of Public Safety. Police were exposed to procedural intricacies that prosecutors must consider under the YCJA and, therefore, have a better appreciation of their mutual roles in the judicial process. In contrast, police more commonly expressed less understanding of their relationships with youth centre staff. For example, police officers shared the opinion that their own work is to return those who have "escaped" the institution to the youth centres, without knowing much about what youth centres actually and specifically do:

> I would say that the new law did not change much for us; what I would also say is that the flow of information from the youth centres seems to be even slower than before. If our own liaison officer at the youth court is not there when a probation sentence is pronounced, we have no clue whatsoever if the youth has ever cheated on his conditions. We have our own information system and the youth centres have theirs; and they don't communicate at all.... For me it's like sending the message to the youth that he can cheat as much as he'd like and nothing will happen to him.
>
> A police officer from Montreal

While police officers did not commonly express the view that the YCJA had resulted in fundamental changes in their relationships with youth and other agencies, excepting youth centres, there was considerable concern expressed by prosecutors about the new YCJA sentencing philosophy's perceived shift towards crime control as discussed above. A main issue was this law introduced tougher measures and sentences, while limiting latitude that judges and prosecutors somewhat had with the YOA. Equally, if not more important, Quebec prosecutors interviewed believe that this province's youth justice system in every aspect, including detention or custody, was not punitive but rather rehabilitative, unlike other provinces under the YOA:

> We thought at that time that closed custody [in the rest of Canada] was no different for youths than for adults; youths were "parked" in jails with no rehabilitation program whatsoever. In Quebec, youth custody was not at all a jail ... In the English-speaking provinces, youths who commit crimes

are considered as offenders, while in Quebec, they are considered as youths with special problems and needs for which the YOA gave us many more opportunities than the YCJA.

A prosecutor from Quebec City

However, and, at first glance, paradoxically, prosecutors, along with judges interviewed, considered the restrictions imposed on custody sentences under the YCJA as counterproductive to rehabilitation. Since custody has not been considered punitive but rather a controlled rehabilitative environment for multi-problem youth in need of structured context, restricting its use for only older and more serious and violent young offenders was seen as simply wrong. In Quebec youth justice, professional counsellors primarily considered what the youth's problems and needs were and custody, for a small number of youth, was viewed as the appropriate environment to provide structured services irrespective, for the most part, to the youth's age and offence.

For prosecutors and some youth centre employees as well, the new restrictions on custody would result in minor delinquent or criminal youths not receiving structured services they might need because these needs likely would stay undetected for long periods of time, and/or until they were finally caught for a serious offence punishable by custody. The related concern also is that this delay in diagnosing problems and providing services could result in a youth being too old for an appropriate rehabilitation program, which could have changed their criminal trajectory. From the prosecutorial and judicial perspectives, these concerns are expressed in the following successive statements:

> Nowadays, we witness the real impacts of this measure in the 2003 law. Youths are too old to change things significantly in their lives and this is a direct consequence of the restriction imposed on judges in terms of pronouncing custody sentences. We no longer make decisions from the perspective of the youth's needs, but solely on the criminal act he committed. You take articles 38 and 39, and they are a "cut and paste" of article 718 of the Criminal Code: the sentencing principles, the comparison between similar offences, the seriousness of the offence and so on. It's always around the offence and never around the person.
>
> A prosecutor from Montreal

The federal government wanted to introduce a much more rigid relationship between the seriousness of the offence and the sentence. It is now so rigid that we cannot pronounce a custody sentence even when we are deeply convinced that it would best serve the youth and his problems. The YCJA imposed considerable restrictions on our discretionary powers, only because of abuses in some provinces.

> A judge from Quebec City

This same judge explains further that, under the YCJA, there were cases where the conditions under which the youth were sentenced to probation could be considered more severe than the conditions genuinely wanted by the prosecutor, simply because a custody sentence could no longer be imposed. The probation conditions were so restrictive that the youth inevitably would not meet them and, therefore, the youth would be returned to youth court for the original custody option considered to be needed by both the prosecutor and judge:

It's a little like saying to the adolescent: "I cannot give you closed custody anymore, even if this is what you would really need. So I'll submit you to conditions that you will not be able to fulfil, you will fail, and then I'll be in a position to sentence you to the measure you really need."

Despite the shared mutual rehabilitative objective between youth counsellors and prosecutors, there appears to be little actual exchange of information as is the situation reported above for police officers and youth centre counsellors. In contrast, judges share and exchange certain information more or less regularly with counsellor teams in youth centres. These information exchanges, however, typically concern elements of legal interpretation rather than the specific risk and needs of certain youths. Nonetheless, informal conversations about these themes do occur because youth counsellors from the youth centres in Quebec are responsible for writing pre-sentencing reports requested by judges before sentencing certain youth. Yet only approximately one fifth (19%), of youth referred to Quebec youth courts[11] are evaluated by youth centre counsellors before a sentence is pronounced.

While prosecutors and judges in Quebec youth justice have the central roles in this system, it typically has been a more limited role than in other provinces because of the far more pervasive functions involving Quebec youth centre workers. Surprisingly, these workers appeared to have been the least informed about the YCJA implementation.

Youth Centre Workers and Community-based Organizations:
The Dynamics of Intervention Contingencies

Contrary to what occurred in most other Canadian provinces, the enactment of the YCJA in Quebec left youth justice institutional personnel rather unprepared.[12] Basically, as explained above, the anticipated changes imposed by the YCJA were not well understood and were feared by both Quebec politicians and youth justice personnel. There was considerable pride about the fact that rehabilitation rates in Quebec seemed to surpass those in English-speaking provinces, and youth crime rates in general had been below the Canadian average for quite some time.[13] In other words, the system in Quebec appeared to show convincing results, and youth justice personnel clearly did not understand why the Quebec model had to change. Ten years after the enactment of the YCJA, the general feeling expressed by youth delegates (YDs) and their supervisors is a sense of loss, and in some cases, the frustration is still very palpable:

> I think we have fallen into sentencing. Instead of carefully evaluating the adolescent I have in front of me, his needs, I now have to adjust to the law, I became more legalist. Before, I was a human relations specialist, now I feel a little like a lawyer ... We really lost all of what we had. It's a shame, we really fell into a penal world and it has significantly diminished our possibilities of re-educating the youth.
>
> A youth delegate from the Montreal Youth Centre

It appears that this decade-later perspective on the YCJA continues to reflect the original concerns about the negative impact of the YCJA in Quebec. Apparently, the initial information provided to youth justice practitioners from the youth centres focused on the widely negative perceptions of the crime control and justice procedural themes of the YCJA:

> Our main apprehension was that the new law would be much more repressive and punitive, that it would be a law which would not take into consideration the youth's needs.
>
> A youth delegate from Chaudières-Appalaches Youth Centre

We expected nothing but a cataclysm! That it would be impossible to apply this law and that we wouldn't be able to do our work anymore.

A youth delegate from Montérégie Youth Centre

However, despite the above negative perspective of the YCJA and the initial apprehensions, the same two delegates somewhat surprisingly express a more benign view after having worked under this law:

As a matter of fact, this is the least severe law that I have worked with, and I have known the three laws including this one.

A youth delegate from Chaudières-Appalaches Youth Centre

In the end, there were some adjustments and no cataclysm occurred; there was no drama of any sort, and everyone adapted their practices.

A youth delegate from Montérégie Youth Centre

More generally, therefore, the YCJA is still seen by youth centre practitioners as focusing on protecting society far more than on the youths' needs and problems, but some of these practitioners also recognize that the YCJA has been a major incentive for the development of new programs and practices (see below). Again, though, it is important to reiterate that there appears to be a near continued consensus among YDs about the YCJA restrictions imposed on the use of closed custody. Most interviewed youth delegates in Quebec persist in viewing closed custody as a beneficial clinical resource for certain multi-problem youth. Specifically, closed custody is seen primarily as a re-educating opportunity context:

It was a loss. A loss in the sense that a youth will engage in crime much more now than before when we always had the possibility of using custody before it was too late.

A youth delegate from Chaudières-Appalaches Youth Centre

One of the first things we feared about the new law was the restrictions imposed on the use of custody ... The youths for whom we would have recommended closed custody for their own rehabilitation are now in society, with all the risks this poses for them and for society.

A youth delegate from Montérégie Youth Centre

For me, one of the most important impacts [of the new law] lies in the fact that we cannot give them custody anymore! Before the new law, we could send them into custody while they were young enough to be re-educable. Now they come to us too old for anything to really change.

A youth delegate from Montreal Youth Centre

More generally, youth centre employees' opinions on the YCJA can be portrayed by four categories. First, there are YDs who felt somewhat betrayed by the new legislation, a significant loss in their clinical expertise, and forced into a punitive role regarding the YCJA. Second, there are the YDs for whom the new law seemed unnecessary and essentially guided by wrong political motives, yet they agreed to cooperate and tried to introduce innovative ways to cope with the restrictions imposed by the YCJA on custody and other perceived punitive measures. Third, there is a small minority who initially were afraid of the law but now realize 10 years later that their dramatic apprehensions were unfounded since very little had changed in most of their actual routine practices. Four, an even smaller number of YDs surprisingly assert that they are supportive of the YCJA step or sequence approach to youth, where the YD role is now more limited to the end of the youth justice system:

Personally, I sort of like the idea that we now have to work with older youth more involved in crime. After all, we're supposed to be one of the last steps in a long chain of actions, and the youths we now have in our caseloads are those that our work and institutions were made for.

A youth delegate from Chaudière-Appalaches Youth Centre

A consensus among the YDs emerged from youth centres that: (a) youth who come into contact with youth centre services under the YCJA are significantly older than under the YOA; and (b) the vast majority of youths who access YCJA services from youth centres have mental health problems. In this study there was an attempt to explore what kind of collaboration youth delegates request of outside resources and services regarding mental health service needs, especially from community-based organizations. Respondents throughout Quebec are almost unanimous that coordination mechanisms between youth centres and alternative justice community-based organizations exist in differing degrees, but most fully in urban centres. However, while there is coordination concerning responsibilities to provide services and the sending of youth to community resources, there are little subsequent official exchanges of information about specific files and individual cases. Yet, alternative justice staff do frequently express their unofficial opinions about cases to their YDs colleagues.[14] However, the former believe that youth centres' staff are using community resources the same way they did under the YOA; information exchanges are controlled by youth centre employees. The latter are seen as predominating because they ask questions about a youth's case progress without reciprocating information that could assist the community-based organizations in providing services that address more specific needs rather than more general needs. Another concern expressed by alternative community resources' staff is the loss of their credibility with youth clients, as well as the compromising of confidentiality and professional integrity when sensitive treatment information shared with youth centres can be seen as resulting in negative consequences to the youths in situations such as drug therapy services, which are generally provided by community-based organizations:

> Youths are sometimes very suspicious of our services and our organization, because those who are followed by youth centres openly discuss the fact that when they fill out a drug test questionnaire, the results may be used against them to increase their sentence or to draw up new charges. Yes, this has happened to some of the youths we had in treatment here.
>
> A drug therapist from a Quebec City community-based organization

Yet, historically, there was the opportunity shortly before the enactment of the YCJA to formalize the collaboration between alternative justice organizations (AJOs), organizations and the youth centres. These discussions, however, varied greatly by region and depended essentially on personal networking. An important step in this discussion process occurred in 2002 with a formal agreement among all the AJOs in Quebec to create a provincial association that consisted of more than 30 community-based organizations. This association also created an information database shared by all members in order to ensure that all AJOs' youth clients were followed to understand the outcomes of their services and further assist those youth that returned. The AJO network was anticipated to be integral to the YCJA because of its new opportunities for intervention services, particularly regarding the reinforced extrajudicial measures. In Quebec, the Ministry of Justice, based on its interpretation of the YCJA, decided to formally stipulate all the new services that would be granted exclusively to the new AJO network. Despite youth centre authorities being aware of this initiative, they were not formally consulted and included in the decision-making process even though these centres have daily relationships with the youth and the AJO network. Not surprisingly, this lack of consultation resulted in frustration among some YDs as explained by an AJO counsellor:

Personally, I felt real frustration from the youth delegates when the arrangement and the new law gave us much more latitude with interventions such as victim mediation and reconciliation. Before that, youth delegates hesitated a lot before initiating contact with the victims, or they would refuse to do so. It is a little like they felt that mediation between an offender and his or her victims would fall outside their duties and responsibilities. For them, it was a loss.

A counsellor from a Chaudières-Appalaches alternative justice organization

In effect, generally, this agreement under the YCJA resulted in AJOs having new and broader responsibilities mostly involving prerogatives formerly assumed by youth centre employees. Nonetheless, this expanded role for the AJOs is not necessarily viewed as a complete victory for its representatives because of the complexity of providing these services with limited resources and limited authority. For example, AJOs became responsible for the contracts with local organizations (e.g., schools and day-care centres) for community work sentences. Yet the YCJA, particularly article 39, restricts the types, and, therefore numbers, of young offenders judges can sentence to closed custody. Consequently, community work sentences and numbers of hours required to fulfil these sentences inevitably increased substantially. This increase resulted in a completely new set of problems for AJOs because serious young offenders were directly sent to them rather than minor young offenders who are seen by AJO staff as more amenable to their services:

Before, youths came to us after an assessment by a youth delegate with a recommendation for 5 or 10 hours of community work. But nowadays, I just don't see this anymore. They come directly to us from the court, with 120 to 160 hours of community work ordered! I'm asking myself, what does this mean: how will a youth understand more about the consequences of his actions with a 160-hour order? He'll just be more pissed off, and, a lot of them, they just don't care, they don't collaborate and after a while, they just don't come anymore! Personally, I think this doesn't make any sense: it is painful and difficult for us to supervise, and it is as difficult for local organizations to cope with the youth's bad mood or, worse, his repeated absences. There is nothing surprising, then, that it is becoming more and more difficult to find organizations that are willing to take in youths who have been sentenced to community work.

A counsellor from a Montérégie alternative justice organization

Despite AJO frustration with this particular challenge, the extent of frustration with the changes brought about by the YCJA varies by region and by type of organization within or related to youth justice. In most urban youth centres, especially Montreal, the levels of frustration expressed by YDs, educators, and heads of services from youth centres, as reported above, are very palpable even 10 years after the enactment of the YCJA. In contrast, AJO representatives from Montreal present a far more positive perspective. The AJOs interviewed state that they and their services are very well integrated in the communities and, therefore, they provide far more specifically targeted and needed services to both the youths and their communities compared to those traditionally provided by youth centres. Part of this AJO successful view of provincial YCJA policies is attributed to the above YCJA mandates established by Quebec's Ministry of Justice. To reiterate, youth centre representatives believe that the older youths sent to them under the YCJA are far less amenable to their rehabilitative services than the younger and, typically, less serious offending youth who were sent to them under the YOA. AJO representatives believe that their services are most suited to less serious young offenders who used to be sent to the formal and institutional youth centres. In other words, AJO representatives agree with the YCJA that diversion to less formal community resources is seen as less stigmatizing and the more appropriate rehabilitative options for less serious offenders.

Youth centre counsellors have been known for their reliance on office meetings and office-based interventions and operations. For example, in an ongoing study exploring data from a youth centre database,[15] we were able to calculate that in a given year, more than 98% of registered activities were conducted within the youth centres' facilities, mainly in the YDs' offices. In other words, on-site visits with the youths' families and in their communities remain quite rare YD activities. AJO counsellors, meanwhile, rely very intensively on this approach with their respective individual caseloads.

As was discussed in the context of the YOA, youth centre YDs relied extensively on their professional expertise when assessing youths for pre-sentencing recommendations based on the principle that the youth's personal problems as well as family and community problems had precedence over the nature and severity of the criminal offence. However, under the YCJA, YDs view that their expertise is underused, while AJOs have a clear advantage based on their new role and expertise. In metropolitan areas, particularly because of the geographic proximity of both the youths and their victims, AJOs are better able to organize and effect community-focused alternative measures and alternative sanctions sentencing involving reparative and reconciliatory themes. This advantage is not as evident in the rural regions where services, perpetrators, victims, and their families often are extremely decentralized:

> I try not to victimize the parents. But my territory is very large; from my office to, let's say, a small village along the US border, there is easily an hour and a half of driving. If I ask them to meet me here, at my office, what do I do with the parents? What are they going to do during a two-hour meeting with their youth? Plus the three hours of driving to get here and back to their home? So, instead of asking them to drive their youth here, I go there, even if it means that I will not be able to conduct a group session for youths living in villages closer to our town.
>
> A counsellor from a Chaudières-Appalaches
> alternative justice organization

As we clearly see from this example, resources in Quebec are not necessarily divided according to geographical contingencies related to intervening under the new provisions of the YCJA. In contrast, a YD whom we interviewed from the same rural geographical region (Chaudières-Appalaches) stated that despite the initial major concerns about the negative impact of the YCJA on their roles in youth justice, this law in practice did not confirm the original apprehensions.

Before concluding this chapter, it is important to briefly describe two programs that were implemented shortly after the YCJA in anticipation of either the new possibilities or new constraints imposed by this law.

The YCJA-based Innovative Intervention Programs

Based on the youth centre employees interviewed, most remain quite doubtful about the efficacy of the YCJA in Quebec given their initial criticisms of this law. Yet, at the same time, even these critics recognized that this law provided new opportunities for their service programming. The first involves the Montreal Youth Centre, which has been considered innovative in introducing prevention programs for youth most vulnerable to joining street-gang, criminal-related activities. The second example involves the Quebec City Youth Centre and the program needs resulting from the anticipated greater use of probation orders under the YCJA.

*The Montreal Youth Centre Youth Street Gangs
and Delinquency Initiative*

Undoubtedly, street-gang-related problems are now part of the urban
reality in several large neighbourhoods in Montreal (Hébert, Hamel, &
Savoie, 1997). Because the Montreal Youth Centre (MYC) was responsible
for both the YOA sentencing processes and the provision of main services for youth in need under Quebec's *Youth Protection Act* (YPA), it witnessed a significant increase in the number of street-gang-affiliated youth.
With the YCJA's new provisions regarding the increased service roles for
community organizations, the MYC initiated street gangs and youth delinquency programs in May 2006 that resulted in its becoming the central coordinating and expert agency for all related services (Fredette &
Laporte, 2005). This expertise centre includes youth centre representatives (in part because of its new role in crime prevention), Montreal police
officers, community-based organization leaders, and researchers from
Montreal's universities. The MYC expertise centre initiated this new role
by first, introducing representatives of these disparate agencies to each
other; second, acquiring a common vocabulary by training together; and,
third, establishing communication protocols and channels. The last stage
is now the central part of this gang initiative program since gang information routinely flows from the bottom (field personnel) to the top (senior
managers and administrators) as well as top to bottom quickly, and hori-
zontally across all supporting agencies. For example, when a youth delegate experiences problems in the probation supervision of a youth in his
or her caseload that he or she suspects are related to street-gang activities,
the youth delegate relays this concern to the supervisor who then requests
further information from the police. The police then can refer the case to a
community-based organization in the youth's neighbourhood to explore
the potential service reactions to the gang-suspected youth. Finally, once
feedback information is transmitted back to the youth delegate, prevention measures are initiated to assist this youth from participating in further gang-related crimes and activities. Since its inception, the MYC gang
expertise centre has made prevention its principal program objective by
focusing on gang recruitment, prostitution, sexual exploitation of young
girls, and neighbourhood gang awareness and education.

The Quebec City Youth Centre's Probation Program

The Quebec City Youth Centre (QCYC) policy challenge involved
the internal management of probation supervision and the support

services youth delegates had to provide to sentenced youths. As discussed above, most youth delegates typically sought these positions and were appointed to them, in large part, because of their accumulated experience as child protection agents. In the latter role, these highly skilled professionals routinely made important case decisions quickly, sometimes with very little information. In addition, they engaged in crisis interventions, for example, when both the parents and their children were very uncooperative despite the explicit needs and/or threats to the latter. When transferred to the YCJA team, the newly appointed youth delegates not surprisingly retained the child protection work routines. However, YCJA-related mandate decision-making is based on far more procedural and legalistic criminal justice criteria. This occurs because these agents act now more as representatives of the youth justice system than the social services system. More importantly, they have to rely on legally codified and organized information from the youth court and other judicial bodies. In effect, the youth delegates have less discretion in their case decision-making because the codified information gives them less latitude to figure out what key information is missing than they had in their previous child protection roles. Under the YCJA, the QCYC senior management discovered that youth delegates too often proposed probation recommendations for case monitoring that varied considerably from one delegate to another. This lack of consistency posed a potential problem of unjust treatment when, for example, the youth delegates' recommendations for youths sentenced for a similar crime advocated different probation lengths and/or restrictions.

For these reasons, the QCYC senior management decided to produce both a new practice guide for the new daily practices involving probation supervision and support, and an implementation program for youth delegates (Weaner & Alain, 2010). In order to mitigate the anticipated resistance from youth delegates to the practice guide, special efforts were devoted to integrate knowledge already shared by the YDs, to include them in discussions while the guide was being written, and to assure that this guide was not simply perceived as being imposed on the youth delegates.[16]

The practice guide is organized to facilitate differentiated diagnoses, whereby following the assessment, the intervention plan and proposed measures are related as closely as possible to the assessment findings regarding the youth, including their life course trajectory and history; the type of relationships youths maintains with their family and social network; the youth's criminal record; their history of potential drug abuses; and risk level for recidivism. The intervention plan then is based on both the risk and protective factors identified in the assessment and, as closely as possible, the court-ordered sentence.

The training implementation of the new guide included four days where YDs, heads of services, judicial counsellors, and educators participated in the guide's use regarding the coordinated integration of four assessment and service activities. The guide's theoretical training was always followed by case studies where the teams could challenge its prescriptions. Between the daily integration activities, the heads of services and the YDs they supervised had to match their respective caseloads to the practice guide prescriptive criteria. By the end of the four training sessions, the YDs assigned to YCJA cases adapted naturally to using the guide before establishing a follow-up plan. However, in actual subsequent practice, it took another year and a half before the YDs completely integrated the guide in their routine use for their follow-up plan, or to modify or modulate certain elements of the plan because of the youth's evolving situation. The Quebec Youth Centre senior management arranged for an external evaluation team to track and assess the entire guide integration program for the three years during which it took to completely implement the guide.

Conclusion

It is possible to argue that Quebec, historically, has always had a distinctive youth justice system compared to other provinces because of the dominant role the Roman Catholic Church has had institutionally. In recounting the church's role above, it was evident that it influenced both decision-making and the provision of services to children, adolescents, and their families deemed in need of assistance from the state for reasons (such as poverty, abandonment, and crime) right up to the Quiet Revolution of the 1960s. During this lengthy historical period, federal authorities in Ottawa appeared to accept the right of Quebec to pursue its distinctive approach to youth justice. However, once the movement to reform or replace the welfare model-based JDA with the more justice-and crime-control-oriented YOA, Quebec politicians, youth justice authorities, and practitioners, along with the majority of the public, have resisted most of these federal initiatives. The most recent clash occurred in 2011 and 2012 during federal and provincial meetings and exchanges concerning the reforms to the YCJA in Bill C-10 proposed by the Conservative government led by Prime Minister Harper. In Quebec, particularly, this bill's amendments to the YCJA are perceived as shifting the sentencing philosophy and pretrial detention philosophy too far towards the principle of more protection of society from dangerous young offenders and away from the rehabilitative philosophy so dominant in Quebec's youth justice history and culture. Now the YCJA included deterrence as a sentencing principle previously excluded in the original 2003 law. Bill C-10 did not mention the primacy of rehabilitation and resocialization as objectives to be considered for youths convicted of minor crimes and misdemeanours. Therefore, Bill C-10 was seen in Quebec as falsely reinforcing a negative and too hopeless view of serious and violent young offenders often intensified by media excessive representations of the actually few extremely violent young offenders.

One thing remains clear: in this matter, as well as in others before, no one in Quebec seems to have even attempted to learn more about opinions in other parts of Canada. In other words, there was a clear consensus in Quebec regarding Bill C-10 that, once again, the so-called "rest of Canada" was working unanimously against what has been the foundation of the province's way of dealing with its delinquent youth. Whether or not this was the case, the matter should have warranted an open inquiry, a process by which Quebec would probably have had better political leverage against some of the more controversial elements of the new law, which was finally enacted in the first months of 2012.

NOTES

1 So similar were these institutions and the harsh rules imposed on pioneers of lower social status that a significant number of young French men preferred to quit the colony to share the life of Aboriginal people of that time, even if it meant going through painful initiation rituals. These young men became known as "coureurs des bois" and later became fur traders, smugglers, and guides for the explorers of the Americas (Germain, 2003).

2 England of that time had already enacted the *Poor Law Act* of 1601, ruling that necessary care for the poor and needy people were a state responsibility.

3 In 1881, 73% of Quebec's population lived in rural areas; in 1911, this proportion dropped slightly below 52%, and by 1921, the majority (56%) lived in cities (Coates, 2000; Séguin, 1980).

4 Our translation.

5 During the same period, Ontario hesitated between a state-controlled institutionalized mechanism and a more community- and

foster-family-oriented approach for its youths in need of protection. It seems, according to Bennet (1986), that the latter option was favoured over the former one. However, by opening the youth prison in Penetanguishene at the end of the 19th century, Ontario chose what can be understood as a more punitive and institutionalized approach towards its young delinquents (see Chapter 9).

6 Ménard (2003) explains that the use of probation and other community measures for young delinquents was not really seen as the most favourable option by the Montreal judicial system, when he describes the evolution of the population of Mont Saint-Antoine between 1912 and 1919, which grew significantly during this period.

7 In some instances, youth centre employees with an undergraduate diploma work as YDs, essentially on the basis of accumulated experience.

8 Psychoeducation is a discipline known only in Quebec that could be considered as somewhere between psychology and social work. This discipline was created in the late 1950s in Boscoville, one of Montreal's largest institutions devoted to troubled youths and delinquents (see Leblanc, 2006; Gendreau 1990). Since its beginnings at the University of Montreal, psychoeducation has been listed in the programs of six other Quebec universities, offering undergraduate and postgraduate psychoeducation diplomas.

9 A Montreal police officer told us that he was first informed of the proposed changes through the information sessions given by federal representatives to community organizations, months before any information was provided by his own organization.

10 All interviews were conducted in French, and excerpts are translated by the authors.

11 In 2010–2011, a grand total of 7,396 adolescents were referred to youth courts; of these referrals, judges requested a pre-sentencing report on 1,406 occasions (Quebec Association of Youth Centres, 2011).

12 See, for instance, the introduction to Chapter 2 as an example of the level of preparedness British Columbia showed when the law was enacted in 2003.

13 However, it has yet to be demonstrated how the manner in which youth centres conduct their mandates can have any measurable influence on general youth crime rates.

14 Some alternative justice employees interviewed explained that they have regular telephone and personal exchanges with youth delegates from the youth centre of their region. Yet these exchanges depend almost exclusively on informal relationships between individuals developed usually over a long time period.

15 In this database, which relies on a standard format for all youth centres in Quebec, YDs and educators have to register all actions conducted under their authority in a youth file, whether the intervention is conducted under the *Youth Protection Act* or the YCJA.

16 Another youth centre tried to implement the Quebec City practice guide a year after its implementation in Quebec City. This guide failed completely because it was presented to the YDs by the senior management authorities at the second site as another top-down imposed accountability measure intended to ensure better practice standards.

REFERENCES

Bala, N., Carrington, P. J., & Roberts, J. (2009). Evaluating the Youth Criminal Justice Act after five years: A qualified success. *Canadian Journal of Criminology and Criminal Justice, 51*(1), 131–167.

Canada, Justice (2012). L'évolution de la justice des mineurs au Canada. Retrieved from http://www.justice.gc.ca/fra/apd-abt/gci-icg/jm2-jj2/sec01.html.

Carrington, D. O. (1991; re-edited in 2004). Crime and punishment in Canada: A history. Toronto, ON: McClelland and Stewart.

D'Amours, O. (1986). Survol historique de la protection de l'enfance au Québec, de 1608 à 1977. *Service social, 35*(3), 386–415.

Fecteau, J.-M. (1998). Note sur les enjeux de la prise en charge de l'enfance déliquante et en danger au XIXe siècle. *Lien social et Politiques* (40), 129–138.

Fecteau, J.-M., Ménard, S., Strimelle V., & Trépanier, J. (1998). Une politique de l'enfance délinquante et en danger: La mise en place des écoles de réforme et d'industrie au Québec (1840–1873). *Crime, Histoire et Sociétés, 2*(1), 75–110.

Fredette, C., & Laporte, C. (2005). Gangs et délinquance: Une pratique de pointe du CJM-IU. Centre jeunesse de Montréal, Institut Universitaire, Montréal.

Hamelin, J., & Provencher, J. (1990). *Brève histoire du Québec*. Montréal: Boréal.

Hébert, J., Hamel, S., & Savoie, G. J. (1997). Jeunesse et gangs de rue (Phase I): Revue de littérature. (Rapport No Rapport de recherche adressé au S.d p.d.l.C.u.d.M. (SPCUM), Montréal: IRDS.

Lacoursière, J. (1995). *Histoire populaire du Québec*. Montréal: Septentrion.

Ménard, S. (2003). *Des enfants sous-surveillance: La rééducation des jeunes délinquants au Québec*. Montréal: Études québécoises.

Ménard, S. (2005). L'Institut Saint-Antoine et la question de l'institutionnalisation des mineurs au Québec (1869–1950). *Globe. Revue internationale d'études québécoises, 8*(2), 73–90.

Pouliot, L., S.J. (1956). Monseigneur Bourget et son temps. *Tome II, l'évêque de Montréal, première partie: L'organisation du diocèse de Montréal (1840–1846)*. Montréal: Éditions Beauchemin.

Strimelle, V. (1998). *La gestion de la déviance des filles et les institutions du Bon Pasteur à Montréal (1869–1912)*. Montréal: Université de Montréal.

Trépanier, J. (1986). La justice des mineurs au Québec: 25 ans de transformation (1960–1985). *Criminologie, 19*(1), 189–213.

Trépanier, J., & Tulkens, F. (1995). *Délinquance et protection de la jeunesse: Aux sources des lois belge et canadienne sur l'enfance*. Ottawa: Presses de l'Université d'Ottawa.

Weaner, M., & Alain, M. (2010). Le programme sur la mesure probatoire auprès des adolescents contrevenants du Centre jeunesse de Québec – Institut universitaire *Pratiques innovantes auprès des jeunes en difficultés*. Montréal: Presses de l'Université de Montréal.

12 Moving Forward and Standing Still: Assessing Restorative-Based Justice in Saskatchewan after the *Youth Criminal Justice Act*

JOSEPHINE L. SAVARESE

Introduction

In April 2013, the *Youth Criminal Justice Act* (YCJA) marked its 10th anniversary as the governing statute for youth justice in Canada. This chapter analyses the influence of the YCJA on the courts, policing, and youth corrections in the province of Saskatchewan in the decade since its implementation.

For Saskatchewan, the revisions to youth justice policy were welcome due to the widely recognized need for change to a flawed system that failed to provide youth with necessary supports (Wardell, 1987). Views were divided, however, on the appropriate direction for reform. Some commentators called for heightened retribution to curb youth violence. Opinion polls conducted in Saskatchewan in 1998, for example, revealed the broader public critiqued the perceived leniency of the youth justice system and wanted tougher responses to youth offenders (Government of Saskatchewan, 1998). The majority (90%) wanted lengthier penalties for serious violent or chronic offenders and most (87%) wanted the names of convicted youth to be made public (Government of Saskatchewan, 1998). Seventy-six per cent of respondents stated that "public protection" should be the main goal of the youth justice law to achieve a better balance between safety and juvenile reform (Government of Saskatchewan, 1998).

For others, the over-incarceration of Saskatchewan youth in comparison to other jurisdictions demanded redress (Quigley, 1999). Advocates, including Hylton, promoted community-based programming to reduce the alarming number of Saskatchewan youth in custody during the time when legislative reform was under discussion (Hylton, 1994). Scholars and advocates prompted greater reliance on restorative measures to end Saskatchewan's pronounced prisonization of young people. Anand pressed the finding that the youth justice system under the *Young Offenders Act* (YOA) disproportionately involved indigenous and marginalized youth (2003). Researchers, like Endres, found Saskatchewan youth were sentenced to custody at a rate that exceeded the rate of custodial sentencing in Quebec by nearly 5 times (2004). The over-representation of young Aboriginal persons in the justice system and their corresponding over-representation in custodial facilities demonstrated the need for the more equitable system.

The implementation of the YJCA offered an opportunity for positive change. In its final report in 2004, The Commission on First Nations and Metis Peoples and Justice Reform expressed optimism the new law would make a difference. In their report, the commissioners described "the potential of the *Youth Criminal Justice Act* to be a mechanism for returning justice to communities" (Government of Saskatchewan, 2004, pp. 4–8). In her call for sweeping change, Judge Bria Huculak highlighted the potential for expanded use of conferencing and circles processes as well as rehabilitation and reintegration. She stated, "The Youth Criminal Justice Act is an acknowledgement of the restorative justice approach. The Act offers an opportunity and challenge to do justice differently" (Huculak, 2005, p. 296).

Given the emphasis on restorative-oriented reform, in this commentary I adopt community integration as the benchmark of the new law's success (Wilson et al., 2002; Anand, 2003). I evaluate whether community justice-based processes guided the YCJA's implementation. This is appropriate because concerns about reintegration, rehabilitation, and the over-representation of indigenous youth in custody were factors for legal reform. I show Saskatchewan's progress towards the less punitive system for youth that key aspects of the legislation envisioned. This has resulted in lower rates of custody through reliance on alternative measures and the use of community programming. Changes to policing to better serve indigenous communities and their youthful members were also made during this time period. Community-based organizations, including those with an arts focus, provided important programmatic options to serve youth. While the reforms are not wholly due to the YCJA, they gained momentum from the policy direction of the new law. These steps have supported the development of the policy framework and programming net that helped to ensure that the Act's restorative aims were achieved in practical terms.

While positive innovations were realized during the new law's first decade, I also present findings that the progress towards a restorative-based system envisioned by various professionals, advocates, and scholars has been incomplete. I make the case that Saskatchewan failed to heed the call by many, including youth court judges, for a more fulsome social and community justice response that might have provided struggling youth with avenues outside of the criminal justice system. As a result, the most marginalized youth continue to experience the brunt of the law's punitive force because they are seen through a racialized lens that portrays them as beyond rehabilitative potential and marked by criminality (Hogeveen, 2005).

In conclusion, I suggest that the implementation of a restorative justice framework gained momentum through the new law and realized important gains. Given the success, a shift towards greater programmatic options and stronger community interventions for the remaining youth may be possible. The time for a more complete transformation appears to have arrived as Saskatchewan moves into the next decade of youth justice governed by the *Youth Criminal Justice Act*.

Part 1: The Context for the Delivery of Youth Justice in Saskatchewan

The name Saskatchewan originates from the Plains Indian word, "kisiskatchewan" or "the river that flows swiftly," a reference to the main river system (Aboriginal Affairs and Northern Development Canada, 2001). Saskatchewan's provincial motto "From Many Peoples, Strength" refers to the ethnic diversity and vigorous spirit that characterizes the province (Government of Saskatchewan, n.d.).

The cooperative prairie spirit and strong egalitarian ethos may have been factors in the implementation of restorative-based youth justice, albeit uneven, that this paper tracks in the YCJA's first decade. In fact, Saskatchewan was already implementing restorative justice programming for youth prior to the implementation of the new law. In a 1999 study, for example, Statistics Canada found that the Prairie provinces had higher rates of participation in alternative measures than other regions (Kowalski, 1999). Saskatchewan had the fourth-highest youth participation rate in alternative measures with 179 youth reaching an agreement for alternative measures per 10,000 (Kowalski, 1999). Among the provinces, Saskatchewan had the largest proportion of Aboriginal youth participating in alternative measures. According to the Statistics Canada study, Aboriginal youth comprised 15% of the youth population, while comprising 36% of alternative measures cases (Kowalski, 1999).

The Commission on First Nations and Metis Peoples and Justice Reform also reported on the network of community-based resources for youth that predated the YCJA. The Commission took this as an indication the justice system could move towards a fairer and safer system (Commission on First Nations and Metis Peoples and Justice Reform, 2004.) In its brief to the Commission, Saskatchewan Justice and Saskatchewan Corrections and Public Safety outlined the implementation of community-based justice and listed a range of partnerships on the delivery of services (Government of Saskatchewan, Department of Justice and Saskatchewan Corrections and Public Safety, 2003, pp. 2–7). According to the brief, efforts to implement alternatives to the formal justice system intensified after 1993. The departments of Justice and Corrections and Public Safety emphasized that partnering with indigenous organizations also became a focus, and programs for youth operated throughout the province (Government of Saskatchewan, Department of Justice and Saskatchewan Corrections and Public Safety, 2003, pp. 2–7).

In 2005, Judge Mary Ellen Turpel-Lafond praised the Commission for its leadership in reform. She observed that Saskatchewan had almost two decades of justice system innovation that included the articulation of a clear community-based justice policy that encourages community participation (Turpel-Lafond, 2005). Turpel-Lafond commended the police, court service workers, and probation and correctional services who were working with grassroots community members to create solutions for youth. Some individuals were garnering national attention for their leadership on implementing alternatives to the mainstream justice system.

A restorative justice achievement in relation to youth crime was the implementation of the Help Eliminate Auto Theft program (HEAT) to reduce Regina's increasing number of auto thefts by young offenders. This initiative was a component of the Regina Auto Theft Strategy implemented in 2001–2002. The program adopted a restorative justice approach and provided classes to help youth develop better decision-making skills. The Regina Alternative Measures Program (RAMP) assumed responsibility for screening candidates. It focused on youth aged 12 to18 charged with first-time auto theft or joyriding. On the successful completion of the HEAT program, the auto theft charges were stayed. Youth, who reoffended with an auto-related offence, were removed from the program. Youth who did not complete the program returned to the formal court process. The youth were referred to the program after being charged and after their first court date (Pfeifer & Skakun, 2002).

In 2002, the program was evaluated positively by researchers from the University of Regina led by Dr. Jeff Pfeifer. Pfeifer and Skakun stressed that the strategy was "clearly developed through the collaborative efforts of a number of frontline workers" (Pfeifer & Skakun, 2002, p. 10). The resulting program "addresse[ed] the needs of young offenders" in practical ways and "reflect[ed] a high degree of ownership from frontline workers" (Pfeifer & Skakun, 2002). The HEAT program no longer operates. It was, however, a model for the successful reintegration of youthful offenders through community-based strategies. Its success was a hopeful indicator that the YCJA's reintegrative focus was achievable.

Economic Growth and Youth Justice

Other signs also suggested that positive change could be realized. In 2003, when the YCJA was implemented, the province was experiencing economic growth and was showing signs of increased prosperity. In 2012, the provincial population exceeded a million people for the first time in decades. The 2011 census data revealed that Saskatchewan had experienced a 6.7% increase in its population from 2006 (Government of Saskatchewan, Bureau of Statistics, n.d.). Saskatchewan's population was 1,122,588 on April 1, 2014, which is another increase.

Upward trends in the Saskatchewan economy have been accompanied by downward trends in youth crime. While simplistic causal relationships between low income and crime are rejected, researchers identify a correspondence between low income and involvement in the justice system (Mulvale & Englot, 2011). Saskatchewan crime figures are moving in the direction these researchers predicted. The Saskatchewan youth crime rate declined 4% in 2009/2010 to 17,657, which was a downturn that exceeded national declines by 2.9 times (Government of Saskatchewan, Ministry of Justice and Attorney General, 2010). For youth, the number of cases continues to decline, dropping to 5,022 in 2011 from 5,140 in 2009/2010, a decrease of 2.3%. Lesser criminal justice involvement and expanded life outcomes should become a reality for all youth if the vision of justice that significantly informed the new law is to be realized.

In the next sections, I outline specific reforms during the Act's first decade. I also comment on the persistence of social inequalities that result in the over involvement of marginalized youth in the justice system.

Part II: Advocating for Youth under the YCJA

Advocacy for Youth by Practitioner/ Scholars

While the high volume of youth cases processed under the *Young Offenders Act* troubled many, it also allowed for specializations in the busy youth court dockets. Some translated their direct observations into research for a reformed system. Practitioners with experience in the youth court demanded change through studies on restorative-based transformation. Ross Green and Kearny Healy, co-authors of *Tough on Kids: Rethinking Approaches to Youth Justice* (2003), winner of a Saskatchewan Book Award, are examples of the practitioner/schol-ars who critiqued Saskatchewan's "tough" approach to youth justice. *Tough on Kids* was a touchstone for the YCJA's implementation given its emphasis on crime prevention, social inclusion, and community-based alternatives as the foundations for youth justice policies. Green and Healy stressed the importance of listening to the voices of youthful, marginalized, and disproportionately Aboriginal youth. The stories the author's conveyed showed the considerable human costs of the system driven by the YOA and by retributive imperatives.

Judicial Responses to the Youth Criminal Justice Act

The advocacy for youth by Green and Healy was supported by other practitioners who called for a revised approach to youth justice. Certain judges of the Saskatchewan Provincial Court emphasized restorative justice principles in their rulings. Many recognized the clearer legisla-tive direction in the YCJA's stated principles was a platform for advoca-cy for restorative-based youth justice. Because provincial court judges provided leadership in ensuring that new approaches to justice were realized after 2003, I conducted a brief qualitative investigation to re-veal important information on the reception of the law. Watershed deci-sions that set out fresh directions for the youth system were discussed, without any attempt to summarize the large body of YCJA-related case law that emerged in Saskatchewan over the last decade.

In a string of cases, judges used the *Youth Criminal Justice Act* to re-quire a thorough investigation into the circumstances of the offence and the offender, rejecting the assembly-line justice that seemed to characterize the system that emerged under the *Young Offenders Act.*

R. v. M. (B.), 2003, is illustrative of the effort made to bring fresh energy to youth justice. The case was originally decided on May 30, 2003, and was later reviewed by the provincial court judge and then by the Saskatchewan Court of Appeal. Judge Turpel-Lafond urged the judiciary and other professionals to approach youth justice matters in a new light, "to strive for improved quality of justice in terms of process and substance" (*R. v. M. (B.)*, 2003, para. 4). She refused to accept a joint submission for a two-year custodial sentence for a 16-year-old Aboriginal youth convicted of charges of armed robbery and assault (*R. v. M. (B.)*, 2003, para. 2). He had a prior criminal record for robbery and was suspected to be involved with criminal gangs in Saskatoon. In her judgement, Turpel-Lafond made various comments on the fresh perspective mandated by the courts due to the YCJA. In keeping with the directives on comprehensive sentencing, Judge Turpel-Lafond worked to obtain an extensive profile of the youth to assess the appropriate sanction.

Rejecting the custodial term warranted under a retributive sentencing approach, Judge Turpel-Lafond imposed a term of probation. She found that the presence of gangs in secure custody institutions posed a barrier that would prohibit B.M. from accessing the needed programming towards gang desistance. She mandated that B.M. reside with his aunt and uncle in La Ronge to provide him with some protection from gang influence. When this living arrangement proved unworkable due to B.M.'s behaviour and family stressors, Judge Turpel-Lafond was required to review her sentence in a subsequent decision (*R. v M. (B.)*, 2003).

In altering the sentence, she was forced to concede that custody was unavoidable. Judge Turpel-Lafond stressed the lack of genuine alternatives to imprisonment for disadvantaged youth, particularly those impacted by parental alcohol consumption. She stated:

> In dealing with this youth with FASD it seems often that our expectation[s] are out of line with the practical consequences of the neurological deficits of this disability. It is somewhat akin to expecting the wheel chair bound youth to climb a set of stairs. We expect youth like M. (B.) to simply conform to a set of expectations or new behaviours without any structure, support, education or coaching. Even more regrettably, we resort to penal machinery, such as youth jails, graduating to adult facilities, to provide the "therapeutic" environment, which is often little more than a warehouse. Then we return them to society without any new skills or pro-social support systems (*R. v M. (B.)*, 2003, para. 21).

She reiterated her objection to "assembly line justice" where cases were processed with insignificant attention to the background and needs of the offender (*R. v M. (B.)*, 2003, para. 21).

The case ultimately went to the Saskatchewan Court of Appeal and the non-custodial sentence was reversed (*R. v. B. L. M.*, 2003). The appeal court concluded that the offender's serious crimes and gang initiation activities made the custodial sentence requested by the Crown and defence at the original sentencing hearing appropriate. Custody was further deemed warranted due to the breakdown in B. M.'s living arrangement with his aunt and uncle in La Ronge as well as the additional charges against him. The appellate court clarified that the new law restricted access to community reintegration in certain cases where the offender was believed to pose a risk to public safety. On behalf of the court, Judge Jackson concluded that the Court "regret[ed] the lack of more extensive programming" to support fetal alcohol spectrum disorder–designated youth in overcoming their challenges (*R. v. B. L. M.*, 2003, para. 67). However, she held that the imposition of a probation order without appropriate supports did not "[protect] the public" and was not a "fit sentence" (*R. v. B. L. M.*, 2003, para. 67). At the same time, the Saskatchewan Court of Appeal stated that it was not precluding sentencing judges from "looking for appropriate solutions in appropriate circumstances" (*R. v. B. L. M.*, 2003, para. 51). While it reconsidered the sanction, the appeal court affirmed the youth justice court judge's efforts to find an alternative to custody to foster B. M.'s rehabilitation. Ultimately, it concluded that no options existed outside of those found in closed custody, in this particular case. The appellate court's decision may be evidence of a willingness to return to custody as a common resort. The appellate court reactions, however, also demonstrate the strong need for early childhood interventions and concentrated efforts to address the social inequalities linked to criminal justice involvement that Judge Turpel-Lafond worked to expose.

Even though faced with further appeals, Judge Turpel-Lafond took a controversial stand on the results of a risk assessment tool used to assess a young person's general risk to reoffend. This information was included in a pre-sentence report prepared for the Youth Justice Court. Prior to the determination of a sanction, defence counsel challenged the admissibility and use of this risk assessment tool. A sentencing hearing commenced. Before it concluded, counsel agreed to a joint recommendation on penalty, which was accepted by the presiding judge. However, Judge Turpel-Lafond made findings in *R. v. D (B. H.)*, 2006, on the LSISK instrument used to prepare the risk assessment. She held that the risk assessment tool was applied through an interview process with the young person. Conclusions were reached on the basis of this interview along with the review of documents on the file and interviews with persons who knew the young person. She concluded that informed consent from the young person was required to conduct the interview. The file revealed that the young person's agreement was not provided based on full information of the consequences of participating (*R. v. D. (B. H.)*, 2006).

The issue was reviewed by the Saskatchewan Court of Appeal in Saskatchewan (Attorney General) v. Q.K., 2007 SKCA 120 (CanLII). The court concluded the judicial findings in *D. (B. H.)* were "unsupportable" and "wrong in law" (para. 7). According to the appeal court, there was no duty on justice officials to obtain the young person's informed consent before applying the risk assessment instrument, even though the results were incorporated in the pre-sentence report (para. 7). Other judges followed Turpel-Lafond's thinking in cases discussed in Saskatchewan (Attorney General) v. K.Q., 2006 SKQB 516 (CanLII), yet the findings were also overturned in the appellate ruling.

As the discussion has demonstrated, the restorative aspects of the new law stressed by Judge Turpel-Lafond were reversed by the Court of Appeal in several instances. Her quest for non-custodial options, while not always affirmed by the appeal court, was shared by other judges who also imposed non-custodial sanctions in situations where community sentences would not have been acceptable under the old law. Shortly after the YCJA's enactment, Judge Whelan voiced strong concern for reintegration in *R. v. G. (H. W.)*, 2003. Judge Whelan stated that exploring alternatives to custody was "mandatory" under the youth law (*R. v. G. (H. W.)*, 2003, para. 38). In other decisions, including *R. v. T. M.*, Judge Whelan emphasized the law's focus on custody as a last resort. She emphasized in her decision that Parliament mandated a substantially different approach in relation to sentencing under the YCJA. In her view, section 38 of the YCJA clearly stated the purpose of sentencing (para. 37). She refused the Crown's request for a term of probation that included confinement to the household. She concluded, "Accountability does not exist in a vacuum. Rather it may be achieved by imposing sanctions with meaningful consequences which promote rehabilitation and reintegration" (para. 37).

Recent case law suggests that sentencing judges are continuing to heed this call for a revitalized and thoughtful approach. In *R. v. J. C.*,

2010, Judge Gray stressed, for example, that the principle of deterrence, the need for retribution, or the expression of denunciation for the resulting harm, were not appropriate considerations when assessing a proper youth sanction (*R. v. J. C.*, 2010, para. 36). In *R. v. J. C.*, a male who was nearly 17 years of age with no previous criminal history was found guilty after trial of aggravated assault by wounding and disfiguring. The victim attempted to intervene in a fight and J. C. struck him with a broken beer bottle resulting in the loss of an eye. The victim could not return to work as a heavy equipment operator because of his limited vision. Due to the violent nature of the attack and the level of personal injury, the Crown sought an 18-month custody and supervision order with periods of secure and open custody along with 10 months of community supervision and probation. In contrast to the Crown's recommendation, the Court imposed 18 months of probation and 100 hours of community service. Judge Gray stated that a "noncustodial sentence would have meaningful consequences for J. C. and would best promote his rehabilitation and reintegration to society" (para. 37). According to the judge:

> A community-based sentence would see him return to a family who are nurturing and supportive. It cannot be said that a custodial sentence would be more conducive to his rehabilitation, maturation and eventual ability to be a productive, contributing member of the community (para. 35).

Judge Gray's comments illustrate that judicial interest in the Act's restorative potential continued well into the first decade of enactment. This is also clear in the 2010 decision, *R. v. R. C.* where Judge Kolenick of the Provincial Court of Saskatchewan refused the Crown's request for a sentence of open custody of six to nine months followed by a probation order for an 11-year-old who committed assaults against three other children in the same therapeutic foster home. Noting the presence of past trauma as well as evidence of fetal alcohol syndrome, the court found that the offender was a good candidate for community-based treatment due to the supportive plan that was developed for him.

In cases, including D. B., the Saskatchewan Court of Appeal demonstrated willingness to reverse non-custodial sentences. At the same time, it has also shown some commitment to restorative-based sentencing. In *R. v. J. C .N.*, 2005, the appeal court substituted the sentence imposed on conviction for break, enter and theft, as well as break and enter with intent to commit an indictable offence. The Crown and the defence made a joint submission for a sentence of five months of open custody, two and a half months of community supervision and four and a half months of probation. The trial judge imposed a harsher penalty of six-months custody and three-months community supervision. In allowing the appeal, the Saskatchewan Court of Appeal stated that the trial judge should have placed greater emphasis on the rehabilitation and reintegration of the offender into the community, and should have more thoroughly considered the reasons underlying his behaviour, including his difficult family background. (*R. v. J. C. N.*, 2009).

In a 2013 Saskatchewan decision under the YCJA, *R. v. R. H.*, Judge Whelan deliberated upon the need to balance the offender's interests with the protection of society for a youthful offender (R. H. (Re), 2007 SKQB 155 (CanLII). The Crown requested a custodial sentence for a youthful offender who was facing a variety of charges ranging from mischief to abduction to robbery. R. H. was exhibiting the potential to cause serious harm given the abduction of his infant niece as an act of revenge against his aunt and his involvement in the robbery while masked. He had limited reasoning capacity and demonstrated diminished capacity for self-reflection. Whelan gave careful consideration to the appropriate sanction, particularly given his young age of 13 and his family supports. In the end, she refused to impose further custody beyond the time that R. H. had spent in pretrial detention. Judge Whelan supported the Crown's call for the development of an "intensive plan" by the family and mental health specialists to address the underlying concerns and behaviours that influenced R. H.'s offending (para. 85). She encouraged the maintenance of his strong ties to his family, even though they were having troubling coping with his behavioural challenges. She expressed hope that the plan would be effective in allowing R. H. to "make a safe and productive transition back into the community" (*R. v. R. H.*, 2013, para. 85).

Cases like the ones cited in this selective overview demonstrate that the desire to implement restorative-based sentencing influenced some members of the bench and led to a range of cases where alternatives to custody were stressed. As *R. v. R. H.* (2013) demonstrates, reintegration remains a guide, notwithstanding the re-emergence of a "get tough" mindset by some lawmakers and a segment of the populace. The calls for change I have summarized resulted in the implementation of the youth justice statute. The need for reform was also reinforced by revelations about the delivery of policing services in Saskatchewan.

Justice and Policing

The need to revisit the delivery of policing services became a main focus of attention at the same time the new law was being implemented. The YCJA was often referenced as holding out promise for change and a brighter future for indigenous youth as Saskatchewan grappled with very difficult revelations about policing in the province. While the revisions to youth justice policy were not alone in motivating policing reform, they were a rallying point for change.

The calls for justice reform were reinforced by the reopening of the suspicious death in 1990 of a 17-year-old youth, Neil Stonechild. Public demands for an investigation into Neil Stonechild's unexplained demise became strong in the early 2000s when the case of Darrell Night, a man who survived abandonment in a Saskatoon field in freezing temperatures, became public.

Like many Saskatchewan Aboriginal youth, Stonechild had prior involvement in the youth justice system and had been detained in Saskatoon's main youth facility, Kilburn Hall, along with serving periods of community custody. Stonechild's prospects for positive change demonstrated by his age, congeniality, intelligence, and athletic prowess were factors that galvanized the public and brought home the seriousness of the justice system's reactions to indigenous people, including youth. At the time of his disappearance, Stonechild was unlawfully at-large from a group home in Saskatoon. The discovery of his frozen body on the edge of Saskatoon near the adult correctional facility was considered by many to be the result of the policing practice of abandoning indigenous men at the city's outskirts in the extreme cold known as the "Starlight Tour." The suggestion by police that Stonechild walked to the jail to turn himself in to officials, was given little credence by his family and supporters. Stonechild's death was ultimately linked to members of the Saskatoon police who were found to have detained him on the night of his disappearance (Wright, 2004).

The Stonechild Commission, spearheaded by Mr. Justice Wright, released its final report in 2005. The report included eight recommendations aimed at improving relationships between the police and the indigenous community (Chartrand, 2005). While the commission did not exclusively focus on the policing of youth, it argued for renewed and revitalized policing in Saskatchewan. Around the time provincial justice officials were mobilizing towards a new youth justice approach, Saskatchewan's justice minister, Eric Cline, established an inquiry into the death of Neil Stonechild in November 2001.

The Commission on First Nations and Metis Peoples and Justice Reform

The creation of the Commission was a response to the shocking revelations about the treatment of indigenous people at the hands of police in Saskatchewan. The Commission's mandate was identifying reforms to the justice system to reduce offending and victimization, leading to reduced incarceration and safer communities for First Nations and Metis peoples. Demands for significant reform to policing were also made by The Commission on First Nations and Metis Peoples and Justice Reform.

A Dialogue in Progress: Focus on Youth

In its deliberations, the Commission incorporated a focus on children and youth. The Commission's second Interim Report *A Dialogue in Progress: Focus on Youth* was released on January 15, 2003. It made a range of recommendations towards youth justice based on information from elders, youth, community members, and workers in the justice system. One important theme was keeping youth out of the formal justice system through family supports and community development. The report examined the YCJA that was scheduled to become law later that year and encouraged policymakers to embrace this opportunity for increased commitment to alternatives for youth. The report also reflected the Commission's interest in the courts and their role in serving communities. The operation of youth gangs in Saskatchewan was a preoccupation for the Commissioners, who encouraged positive strategies for engaging youth, including culturally appropriate education. The Commission's reports have been described as breaking ground towards the realization of justice and human rights for Saskatchewan indigenous peoples and youth (Mulvale, 2007).

Lessening Custodial Reliance under the YCJA

Owing to the efforts by youth justice advocates and professionals, a range of achievements were realized through the YCJA including reduced reliance on custodial institutions. Judge Bria Huculak of the Saskatchewan Provincial Court was one of the thinkers who argued that community reintegration was possible for the majority of youth in the system. The YCJA created a window to revisit restorative justice principles and processes (Huculak, 2005). Importantly, the "Preamble" included an emphasis on the role of society in addressing the challenges faced by young persons.

The YCJA stressed reserving the most serious interventions for the most serious offences, and promoted increased emphasis on extrajudicial measures and sanctions. Community-based solutions were emphasized as the best response to youthful offending, particularly for first-time offenders.

In keeping with Huculak's vision, one of the most important successes of the law's first decade is the reductions in youth custody. The decreases were partially realized from legal reforms. The depth of these changes has been newsworthy. In April 2013, Betty Ann Adam of the Saskatoon *Star Phoenix* reported that custodial facilities for youth were closing. According to Adam, the reduction in the number of incarcerated teens in Saskatchewan was so dramatic that it was necessary to close units at three youth detention centres. Another unit was being transformed into a centre for adult women on remand in Regina. Adam further stated that the number of youth in custody had decreased by 45% since 2000–2001 (Adam, 2013). According to figures from Saskatchewan Corrections and Policing cited by Adam, this placed the average daily count of youth in custody at 185 in 2012 compared to 342 in 2000. Nick Jones, an associate professor in the Department of Justice Studies, University of Regina, was interviewed for the article in regard to the changes to youth corrections. He commented that some measure of the success was due to the YCJA enacted in 2003. Certain features of the law were leading to non-custodial options. This included the greater discretion granted to police to issue warnings in response to wrongdoing rather than proceeding to a criminal charge. In addition, the Act promoted increased reliance on community-based interventions, including mediation and sentencing circles. These avenues were successful because they provided victims with the opportunity of meeting with the offenders to uncover their motivations. Offenders were granted the chance to apologize and to describe their future intentions. The expression of remorse and the likelihood of rehabilitation were factors that encouraged non-custodial sentences.

Jones pointed to Canadian and international research that found that harsher punishments, particularly custody, were not leading to greater change than community-based sanctions for youth. He further highlighted that the YCJA encourages rehabilitation and reintegration rather than punishment. Jones argued punishment and custody are occasionally necessary, and clarified that the YCJA presented these options as last, rather than first resorts. Under the former YOA, the impetus went in the opposite direction. This was changed because custody is costly.

According to Jones, societies are "better off" when youth are managed in the community. (Adam, 2013).

Jones's outlook is shared by many who applaud the reductions in institutional placements. Researchers query that youth at high risk due to racialization and marginalization continue to encounter the system's punitive force through sentences in closed custody and transfers to adult courts. With notable exceptions, the YCJA's restorative measures have largely been applied in situations where community sanctions were clearly warranted given the less serious nature of the charges and the presence of strong mitigating factors.

Saskatchewan continues to be among the top provinces in relation to youth incarceration rates, according to a Statistics Canada report in 2010/2011 (Munch, 2012). As Statistics Canada points out, the rate of youth in the correctional system varies significantly on any given day across Canada. The highest rates of youth in the correctional system were in the Northwest Territories at 254 per 10,000, followed by Manitoba at 205 per 10,000 with Saskatchewan ranking third at approximately 175 per 10,000. This is close to double the national average rate of 79 per 10,000. In contrast to the Prairie provinces, British Columbia experienced the lowest rate of youth in the correctional system at 33 per 10,000 youth.

Many provinces provided additional data on the number of youth in custody whether on remand or serving custodial sentences. The highest rates were reported in the Northwest Territories at 39 per 10,000 youth population, followed by Manitoba at 28 per 10,000 youth population. While Saskatchewan did not report in this category, it is possible that it held its high ranking given that the Northwest Territories and Manitoba remained front-runners. The overall decreases in youth crime and custody are hopeful indications of change. The recent data on youth incarceration, however, is disconcerting. The figures indicate that options beyond custody are out of reach for a segment of Saskatchewan youth who are typically the most marginalized.

Community-Based Arts Programming and Social Change

Community-based arts organizations, including Common Weal Community Arts, Inc., have played a leading and important role in offering supports to youth at risk in Saskatchewan. Common Weal has offered a range of programs for youth. While only some had a direct criminal justice mandate, all of the programs sought to engage at-risk youth and to promote pro-social lifestyles, as well as understanding for marginalized individuals from the community at large. In 2010, for example, Common Weal worked with the Regina Open Door Society to provide children of immigrants living in Regina with the opportunity to express themselves through photography. The results were exhibited in the city in a show titled *Through their Eyes: Photographs by Immigrant and Refugee Youth*. Common Weal has sponsored other arts-based projects with youth that promote social change and greater equity.

One project initiated shortly after the YCJA was introduced was titled *Up Against the Wall*. It involved a discussion about graffiti art in the cities of Regina, Saskatoon, and Prince Albert. This program encouraged discussions about graffiti art, in response to challenges that were surfacing between street artists engaged in graffiti, police services, and residents. The aim of the panel discussions coincided with community justice approaches because the most important goal was to promote dialogue and understanding between artists, justice professionals, and the broader public to work against prosecution. Those in attendance ranged from artists, representatives of youth organizations, police officers, and community members.

A Saskatchewan artist Mackasey Michèle, has worked for Common Weal and for the Young Women's Christian Association (YWCA). Michèle worked as the Artist in Residence at the YWCA Crisis Shelter and Residence. This placement involved offering a weekly art class for the youths residing in the Youth Program. The YWCA houses high-risk youth who are under the supervision of the Ministry of Social Services.

The links between the efforts of community-based arts organizations like Common Weal and others to reductions in youth custody are impossible to firmly establish. Their presence and work has, however, played an important role in the creation of stronger, vibrant Saskatchewan communities. These organizations and the artists they engaged have offered programmatic responses for youth that showcased their viability as contributing members of society, promoting a social and restorative justice-oriented perspective. The projects serve as models for positive adult-youth relationships. At the micro-level, arts-based programming for marginalized youth confers educational benefits to the participants through engaged and egalitarian processes. At the macro-level, the projects affirm the participant's ability to play a positive role in recreating culture. The ongoing efforts of organizations like Common Weal Community Arts, Inc. promote the new law's vision of restoration of youth.

Policing Reforms

In addition to reductions in youth custody and the creation of a pro-community arts culture, there is evidence that the delivery of policing services also changed as a result of the inquiries into justice and policing, which drew strength from the new law. According to government documents, the recruitment of indigenous police officers was made a priority following the investigations into the freezing death of men, including teenager Neil Stonechild. The RCMP Cadet program, which involved First Nations youth in programming that fostered leadership skills and promoted crime prevention, was identified as a feature of the revitalized youth strategy in a report to the United Nations (Government of Canada, 2006).

More recently, Saskatoon Police Chief Clive Weighill reported that the force had made progress after the Stonechild Commission's report was released in 2006. In a presentation to the Truth and Reconciliation Commission in 2012, Chief Weighill stated that the Saskatoon Police Service had introduced diversity training, improved the processing of complaints against police, and had recruited additional indigenous members evidenced by the 11% Aboriginal representation among the city's policing ranks. These reforms may have a positive effect on the delivery of youth justice over the long term. Chief Weighill was careful to note, however, that the efforts towards more equitable policing are ongoing (Canadian Press, 2012). Academic commentators, like Rick Linden, have also made this point, particularly in regard to the Prairie provinces (Linden, 2005). Elizabeth Comack states that productive interactions are possible between the police and the community, including youth at risk (Comack, 2008).

Community Mobilization Prince Albert

Youth justice advocates in Saskatchewan continue to promote community-based programs to move youth justice beyond a law enforcement focus (Chatterjee & Elliot, 2003). There is some evidence that these calls are being heard. The Community Mobilization Prince Albert (CMPA), a police-sponsored initiative from Prince Albert, Sask. has, for example, garnered national attention (Keely, 2012). This project brings government, human services, police, and community organizations together to reduce crime rates through preventive solutions including enhanced one-on-one interventions with youths and their families when problems surface in school, or in the wider community. The program announced significant achievements in crime reduction: police reports indicated that crime reports overall declined 8.2%, youth crime dropped 12.8%, and youth victimization dropped 7.5% from 2010 to 2011. The Centre of Responsibility (COR) is the mainstay of the program. It supervises the Prince Albert program along with similar programs in Yorkton, La Ronge, and North Battleford.

When the program was extended in 2012, Prince Albert's Chief of Police Troy Cooper stated that he saw its aim as more than "crime reduction." The mandate extended to "community strengthening" (Keely, 2012). Owing to its success, the CMPA model of service delivery is guiding a province-wide strategy – Building Partnerships to Reduce Crime – which will bring the community mobilization approach to other sites in Saskatchewan. It is also being replicated by the City of Toronto, an urban centre that is similarly working to create a safer city (Keely, 2012).

Arts-Based Successes Promoting Policing Reform

Advocates and researchers, including those located in the arts, have reminded policymakers about the ongoing need for programming beyond custody and control. In 2008, Saskatchewan-based filmmaker Sarah Abbott produced the half-hour drama, *Out in the Cold*. It's the story of a youth named Thomas, which is loosely based on Neil Stonechild. Thomas was picked up and then dumped by police on the outskirts of town in the dead of winter. He meets the spirits of two deceased men who had met similar fates. One named "Soft as Snow" encourages him to survive the abandonment to tell their stories (*Out in the Cold*, 2008).

In 2012, Sarah Abbott, was awarded the Lieutenant Governor's Arts Award partially due to her work on this film. One of the film's contributions was the discussions it provoked on the relationships and ongoing tensions between Aboriginal and Metis people and the Canadian justice system. Saskatchewan Aboriginal youth and their supporters emphasized the need for more positive interactions with indigenous communities. In their view, the progress made was insufficient, even though important gains were realized. Commentators urged police officers to become more culturally sensitive and to prioritize community building versus law enforcement.

The Dedication of Resources to a Children and Youth Agenda

The recommendation for ongoing dialogue signals to the continuing challenges that the youth justice system experiences in meeting the needs of marginalized youth. A recent Saskatchewan initiative attempts to address the service and equality gaps that remain, notwithstanding the last decade of reform and forward movement. The provincial budget in 2011–2012 included the first Saskatchewan Children and Youth Agenda budget. It invested over $34 million in an interdepartmental approach that involved seven government departments (Saskatchewan Children and Youth Agenda Budget, 2011). The drive for responsive, inclusive youth policies resulted from documented needs, including the pronounced over-representation of indigenous children in state care. The impetus for the focused agenda for children and youth came from an investigation into the child welfare system aimed at reducing the number of children in care and in providing better supports to the system. An earlier report investigating the delivery of child welfare services titled *For the Good of Our Children and Youth*, (2010), recommended the creation and implementation of a plan of action that would guarantee that children and youth were a provincial priority, and that they were provided with a good start in life. The budget was aimed at addressing "the complex issues facing Saskatchewan children, youth and families" (Saskatchewan Children and Youth Agenda Budget, 2011).

The budget dedicated funds to improvements in the child welfare system towards better case management, monies towards education and employment for First Nations and Metis residents, including high school completion programs, and resources for programming supports for autism and fetal alcohol syndrome (Narine, 2011). According to the budget documents, the government's aim was to provide "better coordinated, comprehensive and responsive strategies" to Saskatchewan people. It stated that the focus on children and youth would "result in better outcomes and brighter futures for some of the Province's most vulnerable people" (Narine, 2011). The budget also highlighted crime and violence reduction as priorities. Under this item, the government emphasized its investment in "police enforcement capacity" as well as the work of human service agencies in promoting effective practices to reduce crime and violence (Saskatchewan Children and Youth Agenda Budget, 2011). The plan is encouraging in its efforts to dedicate resources towards youth. The plan is disappointing, however, since it focuses

on policing as its central strategy for law enforcement rather than mobilization towards social and community justice.

Part III: Continuing Challenges

An ongoing challenge faced by the youth justice system is that many
Saskatchewan youth remain vulnerable to poverty, a strong precursor
to criminal justice involvement. In a 2011 report, University of Regina
social work professor, Dr. Garson Hunter, found that poverty rates decreased only slightly in some categories. For Hunter, the dips were disappointing in light of the "economic bubble" that was underway due
to "increasing revenue generated in the resource extraction areas of oil,
gas and potash" (Hunter, 2011). In his report, Hunter cautioned that
Saskatchewan's growth was unsustainable. He emphasized the uneven
distribution of prosperity where many remained impoverished.

Saskatchewan's overall poverty rate was 11.7% (112,000 people) in
2009, which was a decrease from the 2008 rate of 14.7% (139,000 people).
Saskatchewan's child poverty rate was 15.2% (33,000 children), a reduction from the previous year at 20.2% (43,000). Notably, Hunter found that
Saskatchewan children living in female lone-parent families experienced
an increase in their poverty rate. In 2008, this group had a poverty rate of
48.6% (15,000), which increased to 52.4% (18,000) in 2009 (Hunter, 2011).

Recent reports also document the continued socio-economic and
political challenges indigenous youth encounter in Saskatchewan as
well as other Canadian locations (Shantz, 2010). These problems were
canvassed in prior literature (Wotherspoon & Schissel, 2001). One concern that particularly deserves emphasis is the educational challenges
faced by indigenous youth. Researchers document the strong, and wor-
risome, correspondence between school involvement and pro-social
lifestyles (Friedel, 2010). While the need for school involvement is
clear, figures provided by Saskatchewan Education demonstrate that
Aboriginal youth face significant educational barriers. For Aboriginal
students who entered Grade 10 in 2001–2002, 51.6% completed Grade
12 by 2008–2009 (Saskatchewan Education, 2009). Slightly over 6%
were still working towards their high school completion. According
to the government, these figures are significantly below those of the
overall Grade 10–12 population. According to a study released in 2013,
First Nations peoples without a high school diploma stood at 55.8%,
which is twice the figure for the rest of the population (Maharaj, 2013).
The persistent challenges that indigenous youth face in the educational

system are linked to their chronic over-involvement in the youth justice system (Foss, 2004).

The over-representation of Aboriginal youth as early school leavers and as justice system "clients" is disappointing. The brief presented to the Justice Reform Commission by Saskatchewan Justice and Saskatchewan Corrections and Public Safety reported on increases in education levels of indigenous youth between 1986 and 1996, suggesting that the negative educational trends were reversing. The entrenched pockets of family and child poverty, as well as low school involvement among indigenous youth, may explain why Saskatchewan is ranked highly on numbers of youth in custody. Reported youth crime is moving downward and the overall numbers of youth in custody are decreasing. These signposts of change are laudable, yet more is needed to address struggling youth.

R. v. Slippery

The case of Jonathon Tyrone Slippery is illustrative (2007 S.J. 424) (QL). Slippery appealed the second-degree murder sentence imposed by his trial judge, who had determined that he was to serve an adult sentence. Slippery was 15 years old when he, along with two other males, approached a group of people to demand payment for a drug debt. The discussion became heated and the accused stabbed the victim once in the chest. The victim died shortly after. The trial judge subjected Slippery to an adult sentence of mandatory life imprisonment, with a minimum period of parole ineligibility of five years. The defence emphasized Slippery's age as well as the physical and mental cruelty he experienced from his parents. As a result, he had lived in as many as 16 foster homes and had attended 11 schools.

Slippery started to abuse drugs at the age of 10. The appeal court reviewed his circumstances, including tendencies towards violent behaviour. More positively, he was reported to have "good cognitive skills and intellectual functioning." He performed well in relation to "hands on" problem solving and was proficient at verbal expression. This quality made him a natural leader, which he had "used primarily for criminal purposes." In addition, Slippery accepted responsibility for the crimes. During the sentencing circle, he admitted that although he had changed, he required more custodial time for further rehabilitation.

Even while his attributes and young age were acknowledged, the appeal was dismissed. One reason was the accused's high risk to reoffend.

The documents before the court stressed the need for high intensity programming. It was confirmed that Slippery needed consistent contact with healthy adults and help fostering pro-social supports. He required a setting that would emphasize his strengths and help to generate a more positive self-image that would allow him to focus beyond his "Slips" identity. In the end, due to the lack of program options, the appeal court determined that a youth sentence was not suitable. Documents before the court indicated that "[a]n appropriate program to reduce Mr. Slippery's risk to reoffend [was] not available." As a result, Slippery was, for the appeal court, correctly subjected to an adult sanction. By the time Slippery's case concluded, he had already spent many years in prison and was 20 years old.

When his case was argued before the appeal court, Slippery was serving his sentence in the maximum-security unit at the Prince Albert Penitentiary. In that setting, he did not have access to programming or "a normative living environment "to acquire necessary life skills. The assistant director of the penitentiary indicated in documents filed with the court that he could not assure that Slippery would have access to treatment programs even after being sentenced. These findings suggest that opportunities for reform are very limited, even in the federal system where Slippery was sent, due to the absence of programming in other settings.

Based on cases like Slippery where youth with highly troubled backgrounds are subject to punitive measures, scholars continue to emphasize the deficient response to the systemic inequalities that often drive youth justice involvement (Lavallée & Poole, 2010). Many caution against the practicality of a fully restorative system for youth. Their concern is the lack of resources for high-risk persons, including the absence of culturally appropriate early childhood programming. Ongoing social justice challenges include poverty, educational achievement deficits, intergenerational trauma, inadequate pro-social supports that may precipitate gang involvement, and other psychophysical challenges such as fetal alcohol syndrome. These concerns continue to inform the delivery of youth justice. The insufficiency of supports for youthful offenders dealing with issues, like the ones Slippery confronted, has been consistently noted by professionals and researchers who have joined with the courts in calling for change.

While Slippery was not diagnosed with fetal alcohol syndrome, the research confirms its influence on youth in the justice system (Bracken, 2008). It was noted by the appeal court that Slippery was identified as taking part in gang activities, yet the full extent of his involvement was unknown. Gang participation has also been identified as a challenge to the youth justice system given that gang involvement entrenches youth into criminal lifestyles, making positive change more difficult (Criminal Intelligence Service Saskatchewan, 2005). In 2002, Saskatchewan reported the highest concentration of youth gang members among the Canadian provinces. Researchers with Criminal Intelligence Service Saskatchewan report that criminal gangs are experiencing growth in the province and that Aboriginal youth are particularly at risk for recruitment (Federation of Saskatchewan Indian Nations, 2003). Prairie-based researchers Raven Sinclair and Jana Grekul have encouraged a cautious approach to these figures and call for further study and greater statistical accuracy. However, they acknowledge the existence of Aboriginal youth gangs as well as the fact that they are "highly problematic" in some locations. As a result, investigations into best practices in holistic programming are required (Sinclair & Grekul, 2012).

Importantly, there is a lack of adequate resources flowing to community-based alternatives to custody and incarceration. The historic and contemporary traumas experienced by Aboriginal youth, their families, and their communities has been well documented in addition to the extensive research on the overuse of custody that has been linked to past and present inequality. Recent and ongoing legislative initiatives to implement "tougher" youth justice strategies recreate the need for proactive strategies to realize the law's restorative potential. The time to shift from restorative justice rhetoric to reality appears to have arrived as Saskatchewan moves into the next decade of youth justice governed by the *Youth Criminal Justice Act*. Saskatchewan has experienced a time of unprecedented prosperity and growth. Greater opportunities and expanded life outcomes should become a reality for all youth if the vision of justice that significantly informed the new law is to be realized.

Conclusions

In this chapter, I have discussed central developments in the first decade of the *Youth Criminal Justice Act*. The province of Saskatchewan underwent significant change in the decade following the implementation of the *Youth Criminal Justice Act* in 2003. Since the law's enactment, it has experienced economic growth and population expansion. For many youths, these developments have resulted in expanded opportunities in relation to their leisure activities, educational plans, and professional prospects. For others, the challenges that persisted prior to the implementation of the Act including social, economic, and political disparity continue to limit their life outcomes and seem to play a role in the over-representation of disadvantaged and Aboriginal youth in the justice system.

Critics of the *Young Offenders Act* recognized that socio-economic inequalities influenced the overuse of custody for youth in Saskatchewan. While some gains towards reducing inequalities have been realized, Saskatchewan continues to experience social, political, and racial divisions that reinforce social problems, such as gang involvement, that lead to the over-representation of indigenous youth under the control of the justice system. As a result, obstacles to the full integration of youth outside of criminal justice surveillance and oversight have proven persistent, and have even gathered strength over the last decade. These include the prevalence of fetal alcohol-affected youth who are particularly overrepresented in the youth justice system, and the expansion of criminal gangs in urban centres. Long-standing barriers to social inclusion have proven particularly difficult to overcome. Social inequalities predated the new law and were factors in the over-incarceration of Saskatchewan youth, particularly indigenous youth, under the *Young Offenders Act.*

In 2003, Saskatchewan Provincial Court Judge, Bria Huculak concluded her article on the new law by emphasizing its restorative potential and its capacity to return youth into communities from custodial facilities. She also noted that collaborative efforts were required to realize significant reform. She writes:

> The *Youth Criminal Justice Act*, which came into force April 1, 2003, offers a new opportunity to revisit restorative justice principles and processes. Moving restorative justice from the margins to the centre of how we do justice in Canada is the challenge. The *Youth Criminal Justice Act* offers hope and opportunity to change our response to crime. Whether this happens depends on a number of factors such as community involvement, resources and genuine will (Huculak, 2005, p. 301).

Judge Huculak's observations continue to drive the implementation of the Act. As she noted, its success in promoting crime prevention and social inclusion was dependent on a range of factors including commitment and the dedication of sufficient resources. While the desire for better outcomes for youth has been obvious in Saskatchewan in the YCJA's first decade, the need for concentrated efforts to strengthen community and social supports continues to be an urgent priority. The absence of a clear imperative that calculated risks are acceptable is another factor contributing to the diminished impact that the YCJA has had in Saskatchewan, even in the face of hopeful signs and positive change.

More importantly, inadequate resources are provided to community-based alternatives to custody and incarceration for high-risk youth. The historic and contemporary traumas experienced by Aboriginal youth, their families, and their communities has been well documented in addition to the extensive research on the overuse of custody that has been linked to past and present inequality. Recent and ongoing legislative initiatives to implement "tougher" youth justice strategies recreate the need for proactive strategies to realize the law's restorative potential. Saskatchewan has experienced a time of unprecedented prosperity and growth. Even in the face of economic prosperity, inequalities continue to drive the criminal justice involvement of youth. While these pitfalls have yet to be completely overcome, the new law has encouraged restorative justice thinking and has led to the establishment of crime prevention initiatives that have become central to the delivery of youth justice. This is the promise of the YCJA's first decade in Saskatchewan.

REFERENCES

Aboriginal Affairs and Northern Development Canada. (2001, July). *Aboriginal place names*. Retrieved from http://www.aadnc-aandc.gc.ca/eng/110010001 6346/1100100016350.

Adam, B. A. (2013). Decrease in young offenders closes units detention centres shrinking. *The Star Phoenix*. Retrieved from http://www.thestarphoenix .com/news/Decrease+young+offenders+closes+units/8186763/story.html #ixzz2R8b4kXyc

Anand, S. (2003). The Youth Criminal Justice Act: Crafting youth sentences: The roles of rehabilitation, proportionality, restraint, restorative justice, and race under the Youth Criminal Justice Act. *Alberta Law Review, 40*(9), 43.

Bracken, D. C. (2008). Canada's Aboriginal people, fetal alcohol syndrome and the criminal justice system. *British Journal of Community Justice, 6*(3), 21–33.

Canadian Press. (2012, June 25). Weighill emphasizes rebuilt relationship with Aboriginals. Retrieved from http://saskatoon.ctvnews.ca/ weighill-emphasizes-rebuilt-relationship-with-aboriginals-1.852110.

Chartrand, P. (2005). Aboriginal people and the criminal justice system in Saskatchewan: What next. *Saskatchewan Law Review, 68*, 253–275.

Chatterjee, J., & Elliott, L. (2003). Restorative policing in Canada: The Royal Canadian Mounted Police, community justice forums, and the Youth Criminal Justice Act. *Police Practice and Research, 4*(4), 347–359.

Comack, E. (2008). A Canadian exception to the punitive turn? Community responses to policing practices in Winnipeg's inner city. *Canadian Journal of Sociology, 33*(4), 815–844.

Commission on First Nations and Metis Peoples and Justice Reform. (2004, June 21). A dialogue in progress: Focus on youth. Retrieved from http://www.justice.gov.sk.ca/justicereform/docs/JRC_report.pdf.

Criminal Intelligence Service Saskatchewan. (2005). 2005 Intelligence trends: Aboriginal based bangs in Saskatchewan. *Criminal Intelligence Service Saskatchewan, 1*(1), 1–8.

Dakin, Keely. (2012, December 10). Community mobilization gets more funding. *Prince Albert Daily Herald.* Retrieved from http://www.paherald.sk.ca/News/2012-12-10/article-3137575/Community-Mobilization-gets-more-funding%0D%0A/1.

Endres, K. (2004). The Youth Criminal Justice Act: The new face of Canada's youth criminal justice system. *Family Court Review, 42,* 526–673.

Federation of Saskatchewan Indian Nations. (2003). *Alternatives to non-violence report: Aboriginal youth gangs exploration: A community development report.* Saskatoon, SK: Federation of Saskatchewan Indian Nations. Retrieved from http://www.fsin.com/fsindownloads/justice/downloads/violence3.pdf.

Foss, L. C. (2004). *A One-Day Snapshot of Aboriginal Youth in Custody Across Canada: Phase II.* Toronto, ON: MacMillan.

Friedel, T. (2010). The more things change, the more they stay the same: The challenge of identity for Native students in Canada. *Cultural and Pedagogical Inquiry, 2*(1), 543–556.

Government of Canada via The United Nations. (2006, February 3). *International Convention on the Elimination of All Forms of Racial Discrimination, Seventeenth and Eighteenth Reports of Canada.* Retrieved from http://www.pch.gc.ca/eng/1356366329336/1356366502426.

Government of Saskatchewan. (1998, February 4). *Saskatchewan calls for changes to the Young Offenders Act.* Retrieved from http://www.saskatchewan.ca/government/news-and-media/1998/february/04/saskatchewan-calls-for-changes-to-the-young-offenders-act.

Government of Saskatchewan. (2004). *Report of the Commission of Inquiry Into Matters Relating to the Death of Neil Stonechild [Stonechild Commission Report].* Regina, SK: Queen's Printer.

Government of Saskatchewan. (2009). Saskatchewan education indicators report. Retrieved from http://www.education.gov.sk.ca/IMS/Indicators-Program.

Government of Saskatchewan. (n.d.). *Emblems of Saskatchewan.* Retrieved
  from http://www.gov.sk.ca/Default.aspx?DN=47dfeff1-17ae-49b9-a024-
  9e76764fd153.
Government of Saskatchewan, Bureau of Statistics. (n.d.). *Saskatchewan
  Statistics.* Retrieved from http://www.stats.gov.sk.ca/.
Government of Saskatchewan, Department of Justice and Saskatchewan
  Corrections and Public Safety. (2003). *Section 2: Working together for safer
  communities.* Submission to the Commission on First Nations and Metis
  Justice Reform. Retrieved from http://www.justice.gov.sk.ca/WTFSC.pdf.
Government of Saskatchewan, Ministry of Justice and Attorney General.
  (2010). *Fact sheet on police-reported crime: Statistics in Canada.* Retrieved from
  http://www.justice.gov.sk.ca/crime-stats-factsheet2010.pdf.
Green, R. G., & Healy, K. F. (2003). *Tough on kids: Rethinking approaches to youth
  justice.* Saskatoon, SK: Purich Publishing Ltd.
Hogeveen, B. R. (2005). Toward "safer" and "better" communities?: Canada's
  Youth Criminal Justice Act, Aboriginal youth and the processes of exclusion. *Critical Criminology, 13*(3), 287–305.
Huculak, B. (2005). Restorative justice and the Youth Criminal Justice Act.
  In W. D. McCaslin (Ed.), *Justice as healing: Indigenous ways: Writings on
  community peacemaking and restorative justice from the Native Law Centre*
  (pp. 296–301). St. Paul, MN: Living Justice Press.
Hunter, G. (2011). Poverty in Canada and Saskatchewan in 2011: No closer to
  the truth. University of Regina, Social Policy Research Paper. *Poverty Papers,*
  4. Retrieved from http://www2.uregina.ca/spr2/recent-publications/
  poverty-papers/.
Hylton, J. H. (1994). Get tough or get smart options for Canada's youth justice
  system in the twenty first century. *Canadian Journal of Criminology, 36,* 229–243.
Kowalski, M. (1999). *Alternative measures for youth in Canada.* Ottawa, ON:
  Canadian Centre for Justice Statistics. Retrieved from http://www
  .publications.gc.ca/Collection-R/Statcan/85-002-XIE/0089985-002-XIE.pdf.
Lavallée, L. F., & Poole, J. M. (2010). Beyond recovery: Colonization, health
  and healing for Indigenous people in Canada. *International Journal of Mental
  Health and Addiction, 8*(2), 271–281.
Linden, R. (2005). Policing First Nations and Metis people: Progress and pros-
  pects. *Saskatchewan Law Review, 68,* 303.
Maharaj, S. (2013, January 21). Turmoil-filled future without strong First
  Nations workforce in Saskatchewan. *Global News.* Retrieved from http://
  globalnews.ca/news/381382/turmoil-filled-future-without-strong-first-
  nations-workforce-in-sask/.
Mulvale, J. P., & Englot, K. (2011). Shaping a poverty-free Saskatchewan:
  Thinking strategically, *Human Ecology of the Canadian Prairie Ecozone, 40*(11).

Mulvale, J. P. (2007). Justice and human rights for Aboriginal peoples in Saskatchewan: Mapping the road ahead. *Sociology of Crime Law and Deviance, 9*, 215–238.

Munch, C. (2012). *Youth correctional statistics in Canada, 2010/2011*. Retrieved from Statistics Canada, *Juristat* 85002X.

Narine, S. (2011, June). Child and youth agenda in budget is positive response by Government of Saskatchewan, *Sage, 15*(9), 5.

Quigley, T. (1999). Are we doing anything about the disproportionate jailing of Aboriginal people? *Criminal Law Quarterly, 42*, 129.

Pfeifer, J., & Skakun, K. (2002). *Regina auto theft strategy: Process evaluation*. Regina, SK: Canadian Institute for Peace, Justice and Security, University of Regina.

Saskatchewan Children and Youth Agenda Budget. (2011). Retrieved from http://www.finance.gov.sk.ca/budget2011-12/SSBackgrounder.pdf.

Shantz, J. (2010). The foundation of our community: Cultural restoration, reclaiming children and youth in an Indigenous community. *Journal of Social Welfare & Family Law, 32*(3), 229–236.

Sinclair, R., & Grekul, J. (2012). Aboriginal youth gangs in Canada: (De)constructing an epidemic. *First Peoples Child and Family Review, 7*(1), 828.

Turpel-Lafond, M. E. (2005). Some Thoughts on Inclusion and Innovation in the Saskatchewan Justice System. *Saskatchewan Law Review, 68*, 293–302.

Wardell, W. J. (1987). The Young Offenders Act: A report card, 1984–1986. *The Journal of Law and Social Policy, 2*, 39.

Wotherspoon, T., & Schissel, B. (2001). The business of placing Canadian children and youth "at risk." *Canadian Journal of Education, 20*(3), 321–339.

Wright, D. H. (2004). *Commission of Inquiry into Matters Relating to the Death of Neil Stonechild*. Regina, SK: Government of Saskatchewan.

CASE LAW REFERENCES

R. v. B. L. M., 2003 SKCA 135 (CanLII)

R. v. D. (B. H.), 2006 SKPC 32 (CanLII).

R. v. G. (H. W.), 2003 SKPC 122 (CanLII).

R. v. J. C., 2010 SKPC 113 (CanLII).

R. v. J. C. N., 2009 SKCA 126 (CanLII).

R. v. M. (B.), 2003 SKPC 133 (CanLII).

R v. R. C., 2011 SKPC 145 (CanLII).

R v. R. H., 2013 SKPC 8 (CanLII).

R v. Slippery, 2007, S.J. N° 424 (Quick Law).

R. v. T. M., 2003 SKPC 162 (CanLII).

Conclusion

MARC ALAIN

One key finding from this in-depth examination of how the provinces implemented the *Youth Criminal Justice Act* (YCJA) is the retained diversity of youth justice systems so evident under the previous *Youth Offenders Act* (YOA) and *Juvenile Delinquents Act* (JDA). This is somewhat surprising since the YCJA by far is the most comprehensive and detailed national youth justice legislation, which appeared, in part, designed to enhance the standardization of goals and processes across provinces and territories. Yet, commonalities are evident especially involving the reductions of the use of custody, the increase in extrajudicial measures and sanctions, and efforts to increase services for particularly vulnerable categories of young offenders such as Aboriginal youth, those with extensive health/mental health profiles, and gang-involved youth. Nonetheless, to facilitate a comparative understanding of how the YCJA has been implemented, it is important to summarize the diversity and complexity of youth justice systems along several key dimensions: centralization/decentralization of case management information; overwhelmingly formal government institutions and services/ extensive combination with non-government agencies' services; and, social services ministry control of youth justice/justice and correctional services control of youth justice. For example, Quebec, Manitoba, and Alberta have highly centralized systems compared to British Columbia, Newfoundland and Labrador, and New Brunswick. With regard to processing and services, Manitoba almost exclusively utilizes government institutions and agencies while Quebec and British Columbia rely far more on combinations of government and community-based organizations. Finally, in British Columbia, Quebec, and Ontario, youth justice is primarily the responsibility of social and family ministries while, in Alberta, Manitoba, Nova Scotia, and several other provinces, it is under the primary responsibility of correctional and justice ministries. These three conceptual dimensions or axes obviously are very complex given the extensive details of the wide- spread provincial differences in processing and services provided in the all the chapters. They, therefore, need to be conceptually elaborated to better comprehend their comparative utility.

Centralized and Decentralized Case Management Information Control

Youth justice needs to be viewed from the most basic perspective, that is, at the level of the individual including the youth justice official or service provider and the youth. The centralization/decentralization dimension focuses on how individual cases are processed. Case file data related to the sentenced youth are critical in the control and management of youth at every stage, but especially the sentencing and post-sentencing stages. In a largely decentralized provincial/territorial system such as British Columbia, youth files are allocated to the local geographic administrative entity where the youth resides. Key case management information and decision-making, typically, appear to be more easily shared among the local youth justice stakeholders for several reasons. Familiarity with each other professionally and the immediate shared concern, to different degrees, about the youth at the community level, whether its accessing resources or reintegration, arguably, is viewed as more efficient and effective. At the opposite end of this dimension, centralized information management data systems, however, have several advantages: (a) increased likelihood of more equitable or standardized services, especially treatment, within diverse regions in the province, and (b) case management information is more easily available for provincial administrative purposes, policy evaluation and, of course, for research projects.[1] Yet, based on primarily the in-depth interviews that took place with key stakeholders in each province, a much more nuanced perspective is evident concerning the advantages and disadvantages of either of the above polar tendencies.

Centralization traditionally has been associated with "silo" information control where there is an apparent reluctance to disseminate information quickly, or in a timely manner, because of inherent organizational information control dynamics. These include time-consuming application or processing resources often related to major concerns with confidentiality and with maintaining bureaucratic authority (Bowles &

Gintis, 2002). Decentralization, on the other hand, has been linked to the difficulty of implementing and maintaining equal treatment of youth within a province. The difficulty has been shown to increase because of *à outrance* intervention contingencies proposed for specific cases; ad hoc case management decisions can result in unequal distribution of limited resources for other similar cases depending on non-standardized criteria. Of course, given the general principle that everyone should be treated as equally as possible, this unequal availability of resources can be considered unfair and, possibly, even illegal in extreme cases. The dilemma with either extreme is that absence of efficient information processing and sharing can result not only in inequities or lack of innovative and timely interventions but also tragedies. Two examples discussed in the preceding chapters clearly illustrate this unfortunate policy challenge; the Ashley Smith case in New Brunswick, and the death of Theresa McEvoy in Nova Scotia. As discussed in several chapters, the latter event led to the Nunn Commission report urging the provincial authorities to mandate more efficient systems of information transfer between youth justice institutions responsible for pretrial detention decision-making.

Government Institutions Dominated Services versus Extensive Combination with Non-government Agencies' Services

It is evident that provinces had developed diverse juvenile justice cultures and systems in the near 75-year history of the JDA, and then diverse youth justice cultures and systems during the subsequent 20-year history of the YOA. Not surprisingly, depending on these prior histories, one distinguishing theme is whether the implementation of the YCJA involved mainly government agencies or a combination of these agencies and non-governmental agencies. Quebec, in particular, I explained, has had a historically unique approach, which I will discuss further below. But, the key theme here is the role of non-governmental agencies regarding extrajudicial measures and sanctions and other post-sentencing programs and services.

In British Columbis, for example, provincial correctional services have primary responsibility through their youth corrections and probation officers to case manage young offenders, but community-based non-government organizations such as DARE provide extensive services. Alberta extensively utilizes community-staffed youth justice committees. In addition, the administration of the YCJA is divided between the Ministry of Justice and Attorney General, and the Ministry of the

Solicitor General and Public Safety. Despite Quebec's highly central-ized information administration system (under the responsibility of its 16 youth centres), it shifted substantially to community-based organi-zations for young offenders' services. Also, in Quebec, while a Ministry of Health and Social Services institution conducts most of the case pro-cessing, this responsibility is still delegated by Quebec's Ministry of Justice.

As we discussed in Chapter 7 of this book, the perceptions of respon-sibilities being equally shared between the government-based agencies and the community-based organizations vary greatly from one region of the province to the other. Nonetheless, since 2003, a significant part of intervention programing has been provided by community-based or-ganizations, especially regarding the extrajudicial measures. In contrast, Manitoba has shifted to government agencies. Before the enactment of the YCJA in 2003, most of the intervention and prevention programs were delivered by more or less organized community-based organiza-tions and initiatives. In Manitoba, it seems, the enactment of the YCJA was accompanied by an increased government institutionalization of youth justice services and intervention processes. Sadly, for Manitoban young offenders in general but particularly Aboriginal youth, there ap-pears to have been a corollary increase of youth detention, which is in-consistent with the YCJA and the custody trends in most other provinces.

Social Services Ministry Control of Youth Justice versus Justice Ministry and Correctional Services Control of Youth Justice

Again, the Canadian federal political system is central to understanding how diverse the implementation of the YCJA has been across Canada. For several provinces such as British Columbia and Quebec, it appears that few major institutional changes occurred primarily because fun-damental changes had already taken place under the previous nation-al youth justice laws; the JDA for Quebec and the YOA for BC. A key theme throughout the history of all provinces and now territories has been whether crime- focused ministries such as justice, attorney gen-eral, or corrections versus social services or family/child services min-istries played the primary role in administering juvenile youth justice systems. The underlying assumption typically is that the former min-istries more likely favour a crime control perspective in processing and sentencing young offenders, especially the serious and violent, while the latter ministries favour rehabilitative approaches.

While this assumption is debatable,[2] there is some evidence to support it. For example, social services ministries have taken the primary role both in British Columbia and Quebec, which have had the lowest custody rates for a considerable period. In contrast, Ontario originally and Manitoba more recently have emphasized justice, solicitor general, or corrections ministries/agencies in the primary role for serious and violent young offenders. For several provinces, there is a more mixed approach. Newfoundland and Labrador is a good example of this approach by having the Department of Child, Youth and Family Services provide most of the services to sentenced young offenders; however, youth custody services remain under the responsibility of the provincial Department of Justice. Though, as Anne Morris and Malin Entröm report in their chapter, there were only 10 young offenders in custody at any given time in 2013 compared to 90 to 120 youth a decade ago. Similarly New Brunswick emphasizes a more mixed approach directly following the tragic Ashley Smith affair where, in response, provincial policymakers addressed the major communication gaps that existed between the social services and the correctional authorities.

Nonetheless, despite the continued fundamental differences for a few provinces concerning ministerial policy/services dominance profiles, it appears that the YCJA possibly has facilitated a more mixed approach, thereby, diminishing the conceptual utility of this third dimension. Arguably, the YCJA, unlike its predecessors, has provided provinces/ territories with comprehensive and detailed principles and processes that have contributed to lessening the variability in how youth and young offenders are dealt with in their respective youth justice systems. This is most evident in the widespread decline in youth custody in all jurisdictions and the corresponding increase in extrajudicial measures and sanctions as discussed in the introductory chapter.

Outstanding Common YCJA Policy Themes From Interviews

Throughout all the interviews with key policymakers and practitioners, I noted a common concern about "escalating" sentencing severity being perceived as more effective regarding recidivism for minor/moderate young offenders but not for serious and violent offenders. While there have not been any extensive or experimentally designed studies validating this perspective about the YCJA's impact on differences in recidivism for these two broad categories of offenders, it was evident also in all the chapters that extrajudicial measures and sanctions are strongly supported as effective, even where substantial administrative and resource needs issues occurred, such as in Alberta and Manitoba. In contrast, few policymakers and practitioners perceived or reported a similar positive program perspective concerning serious and violent young offenders, albeit they reduced in number. In fact, a major concern is that these offenders have either more extensive offending profiles and/or mental health needs profiles. Again, as discussed in the introductory chapter, several major policy themes, and even dilemmas, remain about how to respond with appropriate programming to reduce recidivism. Common concerns remain about disproportionate numbers of Aboriginal young offenders in the youth justice system receiving custodial sentences, along with how to provide services in custody that continue into the community for young offenders with extensive needs profiles.

To end on common optimistic themes, first, most policymakers and practitioners had generally positive views regarding their efforts to implement the YCJA in their jurisdictions. Second, and here again taken from the BC correctional services top officers interviewed in 2010 at the Justice Institute in Burnaby, several provinces such a British Columbia and Ontario had undertaken extensive research to better address the above policy challenges. Third, despite initial major criticisms and concerns about the YCJA expressed by certain scholars and policymakers, especially from Quebec, and more recent concerns about the potential negative impact of Bill C-10 (these impacts, as shown in multiple sections of this book, were very minor, and, as Bala, 2015, clearly stated, it had no real consequence on the founding principles of the YCJA across Canada), most interviewees retained confidence that they would continue adapting the YCJA to reduce the numbers of vulnerable youth entering their youth systems, assist young offenders from penetrating too far into them, and reduce the recidivism of serious and violent young offenders.

NOTES

1   For example, in Quebec, there are standardized data for files for all youth who have gone through its youth centres. As a result, I have been involved in a current research project looking at YCJA-sentenced young offenders whose sentences have been administered by the Quebec City's Youth Centre from 2003 to 2012. The study population consists of 5,400 adolescents and their individual data files each with approximately 2,000 variables.

2 It must be mentioned here that there is no necessary correlation between what entity is delivering the services and the degree of social control accompanied by such an "offer." For instance, even though Quebec has for decades now favoured a social services approach in the treatment of its adolescents found guilty of a criminal violation, it remains to be seen if all has been done to offer services as benevolent as possible for the "treated" juvenile. In other words, it may not necessarily depend on who delivers the services but more on how they are delivered that indicates the degree of control accompanied, willingly or not, by the mechanisms. For instance, and again taking the Quebec case as a clear demonstration of what is at stake here, the provincial *Youth Protection Act* states that a youth may be forced into protection measures for the motive of "behavioural problems" (*"troubles de comportement"* in French), and, therefore, be sent to a youth centre facility very close to what is referred to, in other provinces, as closed custody under the provisions of the YCJA. It was quite common, before the last reform of the Act, which took place in 2007, to find within the same facilities youths sentenced to closed custody by the virtue of the YOA, or later, the YCJA, and youths assigned to "social custody" for the sake of their own protection. Quite often, youths "under protection" had to reside in these institutions for significantly longer periods of time than their YOA/YCJA-convicted counterparts (Turcotte, 2010).

REFERENCES

Bowles, S., & Gintis, H. (2002). Social capital and community governance. *The Economic Journal*, 112 (November), F419-F436.
Turcotte, D. (2010). Évaluation des impacts de la nouvelle Lois sur la protection de la jeunesse et les conditions de vie des enfants. Québec, Centre de recherche sur l'adaptation des jeunes et des familles à risque. Programme Actions Concertées, Rapport synthèse, p. 142.